POPULISM AND
IMPERIALISM

POPULISM AND IMPERIALISM

POLITICS, CULTURE, AND FOREIGN POLICY IN THE AMERICAN WEST, 1890–1900

NATHAN JESSEN

UNIVERSITY PRESS OF KANSAS

Published by the University Press of Kansas (Lawrence, Kansas 66045), which was organized by
the Kansas Board of Regents and is operated and funded by Emporia State University, Fort Hays
State University, Kansas State University, Pittsburg State University, the University of Kansas, and
Wichita State University

Library of Congress Cataloging-in-Publication Data

Names: Jessen, Nathan, author.
Title: Populism and imperialism : politics, culture, and foreign policy in the American West,
1890-1900 / Nathan Jessen.
Description: Lawrence, Kansas : University Press of Kansas, 2017. | Includes bibliographical
references and index.
Identifiers: LCCN 2017020135
ISBN 9780700624645 (cloth : alkaline paper)
ISBN 9780700624652 (ebook)
Subjects: LCSH: West (U.S.)–Politics and government–19th century. | Populism–West (U.S.)–
History–19th century. | Politics and culture–West (U.S.)–History–19th century. | Anti-imperialist
movements–West (U.S.)–History–19th century. | United States–Territorial expansion–
History–19th century. | United States–Foreign relations–1865-1898. | United States–Foreign
relations–1897-1901. | BISAC: HISTORY / United States / 19th Century. | POLITICAL
SCIENCE / Political Process / Political Parties.
Classification: LCC F595 .J54 2017 | DDC 973.8–dc23
LC record available at https://lccn.loc.gov/2017020135.

British Library Cataloguing-in-Publication Data is available.

Printed in the United States of America

10 9 8 7 6 5 4 3 2 1

The paper used in this publication is recycled and contains 30 percent postconsumer waste.
It is acid free and meets the minimum requirements of the American National Standard for
Permanence of Paper for Printed Library Materials Z39.48-1992.

For my wife,
Jing Sun

CONTENTS

ACKNOWLEDGMENTS

No work such as this is the product of a single individual. It required resources from facilities in a number of states and the District of Columbia, including the knowledge of archivists from the Nebraska State Historical Society, Colorado State Archives, History Colorado Center, Denver Public Library, Washington State Archives, Pettigrew Home and Museum, and Library of Congress, who aided my research at every stop. The insights and enthusiasm of these individuals are a credit to all who preserve the historical record.

Just as vitally, this study is built on the writings of those who came before me, and it was influenced by the guidance and suggestions of more scholars than I could possibly mention here. Still, I must acknowledge some of those who helped me take this project from rough draft to published book. I relied heavily on others to help me navigate the disparate fields of nineteenth- and twentieth-century politics, society, belief systems, and international relations. Members of my doctoral committee were especially valuable in helping me pull this information together, and I owe a debt of gratitude to Jack Maddex, Glenn A. May, and Jane Kramer for all their assistance. In the later phases of preparation, David Berman and Robert Johnston took the time to carefully review the manuscript and provide feedback that shaped the final form of this book.

I would especially like to thank my doctoral adviser, Dr. Jeffrey Ostler. My own work has been greatly influenced by his contributions to the history of the US West, even though he is too modest to emphasize their significance. His thoughtful responses to my arguments made me work harder to substantiate my claims, yet he allowed me the freedom to research and write the book I wanted to create.

Finally, but most importantly, I must tell my wife, Jing Sun, how much

I appreciate her support as I struggled through the last years of graduate school—just as she was pursuing a doctorate of her own. Since then, she allowed me the time to turn a sprawling manuscript into a readable book. Also, she tolerates me when I am not writing. For that, I cannot thank her enough.

POPULISM AND
IMPERIALISM

INTRODUCTION

Historians of the United States have long been fascinated by the convergence of certain events in the 1890s. The first years of the decade witnessed the development of a large-scale political movement organized by farmers and laborers that advocated wholesale changes to the economic and governmental systems. In the final years of the nineteenth century, the United States engaged in an ostensibly anticolonial war against Spain and a colonial war of its own in the Philippines. Historians have attempted to explain how one such event was related to another, but thus far they have failed to correctly describe the nature of the activists' involvement in foreign policy debates and the influence of these wars on the prospects for domestic reform.

The use of an example may demonstrate what historians have missed up to this point. On January 26, 1899, California representative Curtis Castle delivered one of his last addresses in Congress. The Populist congressman was increasingly troubled by the aggressive rhetoric employed by his colleagues from across the aisle, and he decided he could not let it stand unchallenged. Hawaii had been annexed the previous summer, American soldiers occupied Cuba—and some suggested they would have to do so in perpetuity—and many were now focusing their attention across the Pacific at the Philippine archipelago. For Castle, this policy was utterly at variance with American principles. Like other anti-imperialists, he decried it as a violation of the principle of self-governance, a bedrock concept on which all other freedoms rested. But that was not the only reason he opposed the creation of an American empire. Conquest and colonies would distract from making necessary changes at home and serve as a boon for the wealthy few, he said. Only recently, Populists and their allies had "begun the glorious struggle," Castle stated, "and I call upon you, my countrymen, to let no paltry bauble divert your energies or turn you from these radical reforms—this

1

greatest work of all the ages." Common farmers and laborers in particular must resist the temptation of empire. Although "plutocracy beckons you to the feast," he warned, those who held America's wealth had "provided no seat for you at the banquet board. You are asked to furnish a great army to provide the feast, which will be used, after the banquet is over, to fasten upon your arms the gyves of industrial slavery." The growth of empire had been responsible for the concentration of wealth in ancient Rome, Castle said, and this trend continued until the Roman elite finally overthrew the Republic. If his bellicose colleagues won the day now, "The wealth of imperial America, drawn from conquered lands, will be distributed as Rome's wealth was. With colonial conquests America's imperial plutocrats will grow richer and more insolent. With one sucker in the Philippines, one in Cuba, one in Porto [sic] Rico, and the remaining five in the United States, the wealth-absorbing octopus will grow apace." Empire encouraged the agglomeration of wealth and power, which would lead inevitably to the death of American economic and political freedom.[1]

Castle was hardly alone in suggesting that America's foreign wars would impact inequality at home. Populists such as Jerry Simpson of Kansas, John C. Bell of Colorado, and William V. Allen of Nebraska, along with former Republicans Richard Pettigrew of South Dakota and Charles Towne of Minnesota and Democrats James Hamilton Lewis of Washington and William Jennings Bryan of Nebraska, were among many from the western states who echoed this sentiment. Many of these western reformers had followed Bryan in 1896 and would do so again in 1900, when opposition to empire was one of the cornerstones of his campaign, but that contest remains even more obscure than the figures who fought it. Given Bryan's popularity as a subject for historians, the mass of literature devoted to the study of Populism and the People's Party, and the considerable number of studies of turn-of-the-century American foreign policy, one would expect the opposite. There are, however, specific factors that can explain the oversights or misinterpretations of previous scholars. Some sought to use history to provide a commentary on the politics and society of their own eras, and in the process, they exaggerated certain facts and left other details out altogether. Some scholars were merely limited by the assumptions of those who came before them. Regardless of the methods they employed, the true nature of the relationship between Populism and American empire has remained beyond the reach of historians.

Richard Hofstadter was one of the first to associate US entry into the War of 1898 with the reform movement. The rural Populists and Democrats were some of the loudest jingoes, Hofstadter points out, so surely it was the people of the hinterland who were most desperate to pursue the unnecessary war with Spain. The United States was going through a "psychic crisis" in the 1890s; the Populists and associated rabble-rousers were simply a product of the frustrations unleashed during that decade. Although he certainly understood that only a small portion of the electorate ever joined the People's Party, Hofstadter claims that many others shared the views held by the dissenting farmers and laborers. Additionally, many in the middle and upper classes had frustrations and ambitions of their own that they thought could be resolved through a foreign war, and some already believed that such a conflict could quiet the discontent at home. As a consequence, when Middle Americans lashed out against Spain, there was no substantial group left to oppose them. The Philippine archipelago was ceded to the United States as a consequence of the war, and afterward it became impossible to prevent a war for humanity from evolving into a war of conquest. Although Hofstadter identifies Populist regions as the center of "opposition to the fruits of war" after the conflict of 1898 subsided, in his depiction, the Populists held an essential place in the great psychic convulsion that created an American overseas empire.[2]

Other historians have focused instead on the economic causes of American imperialism, but they too attribute the drive for empire to the reformers. They credit the impulse primarily to businessmen and conservative politicians (at least by 1898), but the works of Walter LaFeber and William Appleman Williams include statements from Populists and other nonconformists about the importance of overseas markets. Williams and LaFeber hoped to prove the existence of an American foreign policy consensus, and the most direct way to demonstrate uniformity was to use the words of the dissenters. Their works demonstrated that many of those who favored silver currency were also ardent advocates of trade with Asia, and they likewise showed that members of nearly every sector of society called for increased foreign trade to offset the effects of "overproduction." Williams in particular singled out agriculturalists and Populists and contended that they first spurred the "search for markets"—an initiative that would dominate the minds of America's foreign policy leaders in the last years of the nineteenth century. For both Williams and LaFeber, any anti-imperialist sentiment expressed after the war with Spain was essentially meaningless, and they presumed it was done merely for political effect. Imperialism was the inevitable consequence of a culture that embraced capitalism, and the Populists were as guilty as anyone.[3]

More recent works have shifted the focus in important ways, but they too cast the advocates of reform as the instigators of the war with Spain. According to Kristin Hoganson, Bryan's followers were especially keen to argue that greed had suppressed American manhood—a view they expressed on the campaign trail in 1896 and in the halls of Congress in 1898. She points out that invocations of manhood and critiques of wealth were deployed simultaneously to demand protection for the Cubans through an assertion of American power. In this way, the Populists and Democrats acted as warmongering jingoes, and in her depiction, that was the extent of their role in the drama. Paul T. McCartney, who focuses on the influence of American exceptionalist ideology on the nation's foreign policy discourse, also notes how the campaign rhetoric of 1896 crept into the debates that led up to war in 1898. Bryan's followers grew tired of an insensitive and business-oriented administration and vented their frustration in those prewar debates. McCartney also notes that some Populists and Democrats opposed the retention of the Philippines, but the movement for economic equality had no real place of its own in his narrative. McCartney's thorough emphasis on the diametrically opposed interpretations of exceptionalism left all anti-imperialists to be lumped together rather than dissected further. Neither Hoganson nor McCartney overtly blamed the Populists for the war, but their narratives certainly lent credence to the old arguments.[4]

Scholars have clearly stated that members of the reform movement played a vital part in the development of America's overseas empire, but their depiction of that role remains unclear and, in fact, may be misleading. The motives of the reform politicians are presented so differently in each study that it is impossible to see how the events unfolded through the eyes of Bryan or his allies. Worse yet, most works have ignored these individuals' anti-imperialism, so the reformers have been identified as warmongers and jingoes without any acknowledgment of the complexity of their views. In reality, the vast majority of Populist Party leaders and their closest associates in the Democratic Party and the breakaway Silver Republican Party expressed views like those espoused by Curtis Castle. Members of these three parties at work in the nation's capital openly opposed American possession of the Philippines, and together they made up one of the largest blocs in the Senate. Despite that fact, even historians of the anti-imperialist movement or US foreign policy have discounted their significance.

The history of the anti-imperialists is recorded in a literature of its own, but those who have researched the opposition to territorial expansion essentially ignore the Populists and Democrats altogether. Historians Robert Beisner, E. Berkeley Tompkins, Daniel B. Schirmer, and more recently Michael Cullinane have emphasized the Anti-Imperialist League, an organization led by members of the upper echelons of northeastern society, including prominent social critics, industrialists, and aging politicians.[5] Only a few of these works devote even a handful of paragraphs to the Populists, Bryanite Democrats, and radicals that some claim made up a substantial part of the movement. With a brief tip of the hat, each of these authors then shifts the attention back to the conservatives who headed the league.[6] All works on the subject have essentially followed in the footsteps of Beisner, the first to devote a book-length study to these opponents of expansion. He emphatically states that the heart of the movement rested with a small clique of classical liberal mugwumps and a few regular Republicans who broke ranks with William McKinley on this issue alone. As he put it in a later article, Democrats (and he says nothing of anyone else) were "basically anti-imperialist in 1898 and 1900, but largely out of ritualistic partisanship."[7] His thesis has remained largely unchallenged. As a consequence, the literature on American anti-imperialism has little to say about those who questioned the nation's economic order.

Recently, other scholars have shifted the focus from the domestic origins of imperialism to its impact on life in the United States. Several of these works suggest that American policies of conquest and colonialism significantly influenced culture, conceptions of race and citizenship, and even the scope of American governmentality.[8] Yet none of these works attempts to explain the political effects of war and expansion. The two most important studies that did attempt to do so are now quite dated, and both thoroughly discount the importance of imperialism in the election of 1900. Thomas A. Bailey, in a ten-page article published in 1937, states categorically that the questions that followed the acquisition of the Philippines had a negligible impact on the election of 1900. There were, he said, too many other issues at stake, all of which seemed more pressing to average voters.[9] Despite its age, his is still the most widely cited secondary source on the campaign. The second source is a book by Swedish historian Göran Rystad, who acknowledges that imperialism was a major component of the campaign but concludes that other factors decided the election. Both Bailey and Rystad claim that the truly decisive factors were "prosperity" and opposition to the moribund silver movement.[10]

Despite the dearth of alternative works on the subject, it is clear that Bailey and Rystad based their claims on several potentially flawed suppositions. First, they essentially accepted an economic determinist view of Gilded Age politics, despite the lack of a strong correlation between economic factors and electoral results over the course of the 1890s.[11] More vitally, they discussed the situation as though "the nation" consisted of a singular entity that was relatively homogeneous throughout. In fact, a look at the electoral map of 1896 reveals the tremendous regionalization of American politics at the end of the nineteenth century. Rystad devoted a substantial portion of his work to the state of Indiana, which he used as a stand-in for the whole of the United States. Bailey, too, rarely looked farther west than Chicago. Any study that focused on the Midwest or the East would have neglected the regions most opposed to the economic orthodoxy of McKinley and his conservative Republican followers. Such a study would detect the impact of McKinley's imperialist policies only if there were widespread opposition to them; support or tolerance of such policies would be essentially undetectable. Most important, any historian with such a focus would miss the biggest political change that took place over the last few years of the decade: the collapse of the Populist movement in the West.

For anyone interested in studying change over time, the trans-Missouri West is the best region to examine. There, Populists, Democrats, and Silver Republicans had united in 1896 to challenge the status quo, and they still held sway in much of the region by 1900. McKinley's supporters in the West had failed to defeat them through advocacy of the gold standard and business-as-usual politics in 1896, so the appeal of new issues might have been greatest among them. Finally, westerners such as William Jennings Bryan, Richard Pettigrew, Henry Teller, and others played pivotal roles in the debate over empire, but their contributions have thus far been neglected. The story of their fight and the ultimate collapse of the reform movement in its last stronghold has yet to be told.[12]

The purpose of this study, then, is to examine the precise relationship between the western reformers (the Populists, Democrats, and others in the region who sought to transform America's system of political economy) and American foreign policy at the end of the 1890s. The inclusion of these reformers in the narrative of intervention in 1898 and the debate over empire thereafter provides a unique perspective that allows new insights into both the movement for change and the interrelations between domestic politics and international affairs. For instance, the foreign policy views of the western reformers differed markedly from those of the commonly portrayed easterners—jingoes and anti-imperialists alike. Core elements of the westerners' worldview influenced their interpretation of the international situation in significant ways. Their analysis of global finance and capitalism strongly affected their views of colonialism, both in Cuba and in the Philippines. Their basic republican conceptions of America also shaped their critique of the domestic causes and consequences of imperialism. But while the Populists and their allies railed against wars of greed, the emergence of new foreign policy issues provided western conservatives with material that they could employ to their advantage. By labeling their opponents "unpatriotic," Republicans swept aside an economic debate they had been losing for most of the decade. What followed were considerable reverses for the western reformers. After notable losses in the 1898 off-year election, in 1900 the remaining Populists and Democrats were largely driven from power in the West.

Although the aim of this work is to describe the politics of the West broadly, it would be impossible to conduct a detailed study of such a large swath of the country. Generalizations always prove unfair to the exceptions, and any serious examination requires a close study of the issues, candidates, and contests in a local environment. In conducting this survey of the West, a small number of states were selected for close inspection. Several criteria were used to determine which states would best serve this purpose. First, the state should have experienced some sort of political change during the 1890s associated with the reform movement, of which the People's Party was the most significant component. Second, each state selected should be unlike the others chosen—for example, only one Plains state. Third, the state should have had a large and stable population, relatively speaking. The three states that best fit these criteria are Colorado, Nebraska, and Washington. Each represents a different subregion of the West, each was powerfully affected by the political movements of the 1890s, and each had a reasonably large population (in comparison to other western states) from the beginning of the decade.

The first two chapters of the book provide the necessary ideological background and political context. Chapter 1 focuses on the ideology and worldview of members of the Populist Party. Although the party and the movement were not one and the same, the People's Party best represents the movement of the 1890s. The chapter describes the basis of Populist thought, primarily by tracing the republican and liberal foundations of the Populist program. It also covers the oft-neglected "money power" conspiracy, as well as Populist conceptions of civic nationalism and proper manhood. These core concepts help explain Populist interpretations of both domestic politics and foreign affairs. Chapter 2 covers the political histories of Nebraska, Colorado, and Washington from roughly the beginning of the decade to 1897. Each state's unique geography and history of development played a significant role in determining how individuals and parties reacted to monopolistic capitalism and tight credit. Despite the different niches Populists filled in each state, throughout the West they succeeded in shifting the political discourse from a focus on cultural issues to an emphasis on political economy. In doing so, the Populists also altered the old parties in meaningful ways, eventually allowing for the creation of a coalition for reform. The preceding events provide the necessary context to better understand the impact of the War of 1898 and imperialism on local politics.

The next three chapters examine the contributions of western Populists and allied reformers in Congress in 1898 and the changes that occurred in the political situation in the West that year. Chapter 3 focuses on the beginning of the Fifty-Fifth Congress and westerners' contributions to the debate over entry into the War of 1898. I argue that both the plight of the Cubans and the administration's war-funding measure came to be seen through the reformers' economic lens. Their suspicions about McKinley's motives and policies foreshadowed the fight over empire that followed. Chapter 4 covers the debate over Hawaiian annexation and the development of a western reform critique of American imperialism. Populists especially viewed the acquisition and administration of distant territories and diverse peoples as a threat to the decentralized, self-governing republic they sought to restore. Chapter 5 focuses on the state elections of 1898. Republicans in many western states succeeded in shifting the political debate to the new issues arising out of the war, and in doing so, they were able to turn the tide against their rivals.

The last three chapters examine debates over empire and political economy as they played out between the reformers and conservatives in Congress and at the polls in 1899 and 1900. Chapter 6 discusses the situation in early 1899. War broke out between the Americans and Filipinos, western reformers in Congress voiced their opposition to colonialism, and even western state politics became tied up in the imperialism issue. Populists, Democrats, and apostate Republicans from the Great Plains to the Pacific coast united to stand against empire, and this was the moment when they voiced the most thorough expressions of their analysis. Political and economic freedom, they said, could not endure in an imperialistic nation. Chapter 7 covers some of the major issues that appeared in Congress and the media in 1900—a time when many national and global events were viewed in relation to America's new policy. The administration gave western Populists and Democrats even more material to add to their critique. A controversial bill that defined the colonial status of the newly acquired territories and a seemingly unrelated federal military intervention in the Coeur d'Alenes were portents of things to come, the reformers said. The last chapter deals with the election of 1900, the second consecutive presidential contest waged between William Jennings Bryan and William McKinley. As they had in 1898, Republicans in the West gained the upper hand, and they did so by emphasizing their support for the war in the Philippines and their opponents' supposed acts of treason.

The conclusion uses the example of the Populists to illuminate how patriotism and nationalism have consistently been used to silence dissent in the United States. Critics of wartime policies in the United States have often been suppressed, whether through labels such as "un-American" or through actions of the state. The Populist example provides an additional reminder that Americans may need to reconsider either their foreign policy positions or their definitions of patriotism to encourage broader, more open policy debates.

1. WESTERN POPULIST IDEOLOGY AND WORLDVIEW

Amidst the turmoil of the 1890s, increasing numbers of Americans demonstrated frustration with the growing economic inequality and sought new alternatives to the system of unrestrained accumulation that they perceived as a threat to their rights and their well-being. Calls for change took many incarnations over the course of the decade, but in the West, the movement for reform was best embodied by the People's (or Populist) Party. It would be impossible to comprehend the politics of the region during this period without an understanding of the core philosophies of the party, but historians have long struggled to make sense of the ideas that drove the movement.

In the last eighty years, the Populists have been identified as proto-progressives, backward-looking conservatives, quasi-Marxists, and radical republicans. The source of all this confusion is the Populists themselves, who frequently disagreed on policy specifics even as they concurred in their broader social analyses. A brief contrast will suffice to demonstrate the extent of their individual distinctiveness.

In April 1894, when confronted with the problem of high unemployment despite the great wealth of the few, one anonymous writer for the Populist *Advocate* of Topeka, Kansas, declared, "It is cruel, it is inhuman, to attribute these conditions to laziness, drunkenness, and incompetency. They are the natural product of a false and vicious system by which the few grow rich beyond all need, and the many are doomed to eternal poverty and want." The writer went on to propose that those who were willing should have a right to work and be justly compensated.[1]

John Rankin Rogers, onetime editor of the Union Labor Party's *Kansas Commoner* and a future governor of Washington State, disagreed entirely. An active writer throughout his career, he also maintained a correspondence with reformers nationally, even while in office. In a response to one such activist, he explained his views of the struggling urban laborers. "The destitute poor of the cities can only be helped by what is ordinarily termed 'charity.' They are for the most part incapable of helping themselves. As a matter of fact I do not believe that very much can be done for them. If they were transported to a good farming region and each given a farm it is probable that they would fail as farmers." American laborers' greatest opportunities had been in the era when land was cheap and readily available, he said. Only land reform and a return of workers to the countryside would improve the situation for those "who lacked the ability to take the initiative." He also called for structural changes in the American economic order, but he embraced Spencerian ideas regarding "survival of the fittest" and in most cases considered the urban poor to be the dregs and castoffs of American society.[2]

These two perspectives could not be more different. One identified urban laborers as producers who held the right to a vocation, while the other came close to blaming the poor for their own failures. Despite the obvious differences, Rogers was every bit the Populist that the writer in the *Advocate* was. Western Populists were necessarily a diverse bunch. Many had sided with the Union during the Civil War, a few others had supported the Confederacy, and at least as many had been either too young to participate or not yet residents of the United States. Longtime third-party organizers were often important in the development of the first state parties, but Republicans constituted the largest share of these parties' initial supporters; over the course of the 1890s, ex-Democrats would make up an increasing percentage of their voters and leaders. As a result, party members were ideologically diverse. Although few of their views were necessarily incompatible, the result was a constant struggle within many state parties over the limits and meaning of reform.[3]

Before advancing to a study of Populist foreign policy, it is important to understand the foundations of Populist thought. Rather than focusing on their programmatic demands, this chapter discusses the broadest elements of the worldview shared by Populists (and many of their contemporaries). Three primary arguments at the center of this chapter help explain both the uniqueness of the movement and the later expansion of the Populist ideology to include complex analyses of foreign affairs. First, the Populist conception of political and economic citizenship must be understood as rooted in both the liberal individualist and radical republican traditions. The strength of the latter in their critiques of capitalist power suggests that the Populist program could have been extended beyond the limited goals of later state and national reform advocates. Second, the Populists' views of politics were shaped by their perception of global finance. Ultimately, these views would contribute to their resistance of the foreign policy initiatives of the McKinley administration. Third, this chapter discusses Populist conceptions of proper patriotic manhood. By invoking traditional understandings of masculinity and employing civic-nationalist reform rhetoric, Populists attempted to funnel mainstream elements of postbellum identity into a movement for change.

POPULISM, LIBERALISM, AND REPUBLICANISM

The historians' debate over Populist ideology reaches back roughly sixty years. From the time of Richard Hofstadter's *Age of Reform* in the mid-1950s to Lawrence Goodwyn's contribution in the 1970s, the conflict was between those who considered the Populists to be "left of center" and those who viewed them as backward-looking conservatives.[4] That debate subsided when studies of high politics fell from their place of dominance in American history. A new debate is now taking place, although its origins are rooted in the remnants of the previous one. Scholarly disagreements are now between those who contend that the Populists were radical republicans and those who claim that they represented a form of "modern" individualist liberalism.[5] Though not as contentious as the earlier fight, each side has largely made the two bases of thought appear mutually exclusive.

The truth does not always lie in the middle, but in this case, it is difficult to believe one side to the exclusion of the other. Those who describe the Populists as "modern" have rightly pointed out that they accepted a great deal about the new world created by industrialization and global market connections.[6] The Populists were certainly not deluded followers of an agrarian myth; they largely believed in capitalism, industrialization, and individualism. However, these adherents of Populist modernism have not discredited the material presented by other historians. The republican thesis has not been disproved; instead, its detractors describe a viewpoint that seems out of place for old-fashioned radicals.

In fact, there is no reason to consider the two strains of thought to be diametrically opposed. Historians of early America in particular have demonstrated that liberalism and republicanism shared much in common and that most of the seminal liberal thinkers accepted much of the republican tradition.[7] James Kloppenberg has explained that the two concepts should not be seen as mutually exclusive, and he suggests that they continued to commingle well into the late nineteenth century and beyond. According to Kloppenberg, the two streams of thought invoked different values, so if the Populists employed both, they must have felt a need to argue for something that could not easily fit into a single ideological framework.[8]

A brief examination of Populist texts provides certain insights into the complex bases of their thought. Among those examined were William Peffer's *The Farmer's Side* (1891), James B. Weaver's *A Call to Action* (1892), and John Rankin Rogers's *Politics* (1894), supplemented with articles from selected Populist newspapers such as the *Farmers' Alliance* of Nebraska and Davis Waite's *Aspen (Colorado) Union Era*. Obviously, such an investigation cannot come close to covering the breadth of western Populist thought. Still, it makes two fundamental points clear: First, Populists did readily employ both liberal and republican arguments. Second, Populists were universally opposed to the "centralization" of power, whether in private hands or in the government. Both traditions would be deployed to justify the restoration of democratic control over the market.

Perhaps the strongest point that united all western Populists was their "antimonopoly" position. Large capital enterprises held tremendous power in the relatively new western states, and incumbent Republicans encouraged the expansion of that power by taking an unabashedly pro-growth stance.[9] To an extent, they believed that the great concentrations of wealth were a product of laws that created special privilege. In early 1890 a future Populist congressman from Nebraska, William McKeighan, wrote to the *Farmers' Alliance* stating his frustration with the rise of wealth inequality in the country. The cause could be "found in the special legislation of the country, extending aid and protection to capital."[10] Waite's newspaper likewise informed readers that in order to save freedom and attain a just distribution of wealth, "monopoly and special privilege, which are created by law, must be destroyed by the repeal of such laws."[11] The partnership of government and big business had to be stopped.

The Populist attack on corporate favoritism demonstrates their disdain for the emerging "class state."[12] Like many of the classical liberal critics of the day, Populists wanted to put an end to preferential laws that seemed to benefit only the few. For westerners, the most obvious beneficiary of friendly government policies was the railroad industry. Weaver pointed to one of the most obvious gifts given to the railroads—the enormous land grants in the western states. "In Dakota," he wrote, "the Northern Pacific gets as much land as there is in the two States of New Jersey and Connecticut," while in

"Washington Territory its grant equals in extent the size of the three states of New Jersey, New Hampshire, and Massachusetts." Weaver declared these subsidies to be unnecessary because almost "none of the aided roads . . . were built until a profit in construction could be seen without the aid of land grants."[13] These grants were not designed to promote progress; they were favors bestowed by friends in high places. A writer for the *Aspen Union Era* came to an even more serious conclusion: the huge gifts given to the railroads in 1862 and 1864 hinted at bribery on an even greater scale than that exposed in the Credit Mobilier scandal. For proof, the writer pointed to the congressional votes in 1864, in which nearly half the senators and almost the same proportion of congressmen had refused to vote at all. It was impossible to say "that a large part of the absent, or not voting senators and representatives were not bribe-takers." Whether it was favoritism or outright corruption mattered little in the final analysis.[14]

Another of the more obvious targets for critics was the system of protective tariffs implemented by Republicans in Congress for the support of "infant industries."[15] Populists declared that these business combinations were infants no longer. The *Aspen Union Era* stated that organizations such as the steel trust were able to become monopolies "by the assistance of the protective duty on steel rails," and they now "control the markets and fix the prices at which its products are to be sold."[16] Peffer, too, wrote that "there is a very strong disposition in certain quarters to pervert our tariff legislation from its original design into one for the benefit of a particular class of people, and that class represented by a very small number of persons."[17] Although the national Populist Party did not consider the tariff itself to be a major concern, its members were sure that protection was yet another example of congressional favoritism for those who needed little help.

Populists believed that legislative favoritism had spurred the growth of monopolies, but they were most upset that the great corporations now controlled state and federal governments. Weaver was making no great revelation when he informed readers that "monstrous combinations" controlled "the business of every city" and "thrust their paid lobbyists within the corridors and onto the floor of every legislative assembly." The national government was no better in his eyes. Even elitists like Alexander Hamilton had not contemplated that the Senate "should become the stronghold of monopoly."[18] In addition to their control of Congress, giant corporations had taken over the courts. Weaver was furious that courts had granted constitutional rights to "corporate persons," and he claimed that judges with ties to the business world had so perverted the Constitution that they had remade it into a tool of corporate power. Peffer claimed that there were "probably not less than one thousand lawyers" in the employ of the major rail lines, and anyone foolish enough to bring suit against them would find that "all important avenues to the courts are brought under control of the interested corporation."[19]

As the giant corporations held the government under their thumb, there was no entity to prevent them from cornering their respective markets. "Once they secure control of a given line of business," wrote Weaver, "they are masters of the situation and can dictate to the two great classes with which they deal—the producer of the raw material and the consumer of the finished product."[20] Weaver explained the abstract potential of monopolies, but much of western Populist literature focused on more tangible examples that were familiar to the people of the region. Peffer pointed to a combination by meat packers that reportedly controlled the sale prices of all livestock. "When cattle from the West reached Chicago there was no competition among buyers. The stock business there was controlled by commission merchants, railroad companies, and packing houses, who divided the profits among themselves."[21] This industrial cartel guaranteed that competition was kept to a minimum.

Many of the Populists' specific criticisms of trusts can be identified as concerns fueled by liberal self-interest, and their potential remedies sound little different from those promoted by their classical liberal mugwump contemporaries. Their grievances represented the frustrations of the producers and consumers of certain goods against those perceived to be abusing the system of exchange. The free market was collapsing, and they often stated that their platform merely called for a return of equitable competition. In reality, their critique went much farther.

In some of his most damning condemnations of American corporations, Weaver denied the legitimacy of their very existence. Corporations received legislative approval of their charters, which he claimed were the equivalent of letters of marque bestowed on the privateers who had targeted enemy shipping in earlier times. Such persons had been "little else than licensed pirates," but at least they had attacked the commerce of an enemy state. In his own time, "The corporation is always authorized by the Sovereign to make its reprisals upon an unoffending people."[22] A writer for the *Aspen Union Era* likewise flayed the wealthy for their crimes. "One-half the wealth of our nation is now owned by 31,000 people of an entire population of 62,000,000" due to the power of monopolies. This was no better than "legalized robbery," which was fundamentally "the parent and cause of all other forms of robbery." The author offered no suggestion that this wealth had been amassed through any type of criminal mischief. Instead, the collection of such a sum was innately a crime against the community.[23]

Populists responded to this system of economic exclusion with calls for cooperation or, as some put it, combination. According to historian Charles Postel, the Populists were living in an era of growing corporate combinations and trusts, and farmers' reactions followed the business model of the day. Cooperation was a tactic to allow individual entrepreneurs to compete in the modern market system.[24] Postel is largely correct when he demythologizes the history of farmer cooperation. Late-nineteenth-century farmer and labor cooperation was based less on traditional community instinct than on the desire of people in the same occupation to share in the benefits that pooled resources could provide. For many Populists, cooperation promised the possibility of leverage against the power of monopolistic industries and cartels of buyers. "The railroad companies and the cattle dealers united their forces years ago for the purpose of making money," wrote Peffer. "So it is with manufacturers. So it is with bankers. . . . Hence they form organizations." Peffer had his grievances against such associations, but they were not the only ones that could cooperate. "Now, let the farmers and their co-workers learn from the lessons which these things teach; let them organize, not only for social purposes . . . but for business."[25] Time and again, Populist writers informed the rank and file that cooperation was a way of business that they must adopt. It was in this tone that a writer for the *Advocate* told readers, "When farmer competes with farmer for a chance to sell his products, and when wage-worker competes with wage-worker for an opportunity to sell his labor, capital is king." Cooperative selling could reverse the equation, for "when capital competes with capital to secure the products of the soil or the services of the wage worker, labor will be king."[26] Cooperative buying and selling was the tactic of the business world, and it was time for farmers and laborers to experience the benefits it could provide.

Cooperation was ultimately described as a modern necessity if farmers and laborers were to maintain any semblance of economic independence. One newspaper writer used an allegorical tale to explain the simple value of cooperation. The author began with a description of his life ten years earlier, when he had resided in a town in Kansas where roughly a hundred men "were constantly employed dressing stone." One day a machine salesman showed up with an offer for the stoneworkers:

> If you gentlemen will chip in ten dollars apiece I'll put up a machine that will do the work you are doing better and faster; so fast that ten of you

with the machine will do as much work as all are doing. You will own the machine and can divide up into squads of ten, each squad work one month and lay off nine months and accomplish as much as you are all doing now and get the same pay for it.

The men refused, preferring to work in their own way. Soon, the story went, a capitalist met up with the salesman and purchased the machine the artisans had just rejected. In a short time, he had ten unskilled workers running the machine and producing at full capacity, while "the one hundred men cursed the machine, the inventor, and the capitalist, and struck out to swell the army of the unemployed."[27] The moral of the story was direct enough: cooperation, in conjunction with the acceptance of technology and modern methods, was necessary if individuals were to compete in the world of business.

Cooperation was a theme in the work of all Populist writers, even those who had difficulty reconciling it with their other beliefs. For example, one would not consider cooperation the most logical topic for a thoroughgoing individualist like John Rankin Rogers. He was far more likely to cite Herbert Spencer's social views or David Ricardo's iron law of wages—the latter of which he mentioned in *Politics*—than Laurence Gronlund's *Cooperative Commonwealth*.[28] His private letters demonstrate his tentative views about mutual aid. As the governor of Washington, he was in communication with a group working to establish a cooperative colony inside the state. Rogers told the group's secretary that the key to their success was respect for individual property rights. Each family must be "owners of their separate homes." Only then would "combining together for active assistance in industries" be possible, he said.[29] Private property and its accumulation remained too vital for him to reject. As he wrote in one of his later works, "Man lives to acquire. . . . Some small gain, in one direction or another, must be his."[30] Cooperation had its merits, but the individual's drive to improve his or her own situation was at the core of the market system the Populists embraced.

Individualism and independence were consistent themes in Populist literature, and their views of the subjects linked economic self-sufficiency with political autonomy. Nearly all of the movement's thinkers doubted that one could work for another and still maintain political autonomy. Even Peffer, perhaps the most "modern" of the western Populists, wrote extensively about the dehumanization faced by contemporary wage workers. He declared:

[They] are practically as much machines as the unconscious mechanical combinations to which they attend. By this process of absorption in large manufacturing establishments the individuality of the separate workers is virtually lost. The man who was once an individual citizen among the farmers is now a part of a great manufacturing establishment in the city, doing his work with the same precision, the same regularity, the same method that an inanimate implement does.[31]

Because of the imbalanced power relationship, workers had little ability to resist the demands of corporate masters, resulting in the loss of workers' political freedom.

Similar messages were sprinkled throughout Populist publications. Some were directed at laborers, telling them that economic independence must remain their ultimate goal. A writer for the Coming Crisis (a Populist journal from Pueblo, Colorado) asked, "You producers of wealth, you workman, do you think you were born to work for wages, and other men born to hire you and make a profit?" Responding to his own question, the writer answered in the negative. "When you study politics more, you will find nature never intended you as a beast of burden."[32] Rogers suggested that republican virtue could be attained only by those who were free from the psychological burden that came with subservience in the workplace. "Either [man] will be a producer of values or a mere dead weight upon the body politic," he wrote. Through the control of land and the individual's own labor, "liberty and independence can be maintained and the individual freed from that soul debasing dependence which is so destructive of manhood and character."[33] Independence—and with it, manliness—required access to property of one's own.

Their emphasis on autonomy caused many Populists to question one of the most fundamental rights in the Western world: individual property rights. In the case of Rogers, his extreme emphasis on an individual's right to property led him to question the entire concept of inheritable titles. He believed that all people had a God-given right to the resources of nature, and those who claimed sole possession of any naturally available resource denied its free use to all other individuals (or, as some would put it, the community). The theory that such substantial rights could belong to one person—"the principle upon which this deprivation of the masses is based"—necessarily violated the rights of all other individuals. It was in this way that monopolies "gain their power and exert their sway." Rogers's greatest fear was the development of "land monopolies" that would reduce all farmers of the future to the status of mere tenants. "Land and its natural products," he explained, "form the provision made by nature—of the Creator—for the use and suste-

John Rankin Rogers. Courtesy of the Washington State Archives

nance of men, of all men, during life. . . . His need is his warrant." In Rogers's view, every person should be guaranteed a grant of land that expired with his life; private ownership in perpetuity amounted to robbery, he said.[34]

Rogers's beliefs fit well within mainstream Populist thought. Weaver likewise feared the development of a land monopoly, which he considered a violation of natural rights to the soil. The right to "till it unmolested, as soon as he has the strength to do so and to live upon the fruits of his toil without paying tribute to any other creature" was "among the most sacred and essential" rights that all must share. Believing that nearly all suitable land had already been claimed, Weaver predicted that a "complete readjustment" of property would be required in the very near future.[35] Davis Waite's partner in the *Aspen Union Era*, G. C. Rohde, came even closer to Rogers's statements when he wrote that "private property in land is legalized robbery. . . . The sooner we recognize the fact that the earth belongs to all the people in usufruct, and not to those who have chanced to secure possession thereof, the sooner justice is done to labor." Like Rogers, he argued in favor of a universal right to use the land and against inheritable titles to property. The earth should be reserved for the benefit of all.[36]

Populists questioned the existing concept of property because of their belief that the interests of the many outweigh those of the few. In its most extreme form, this concept was the basis of their desire for the public take-over or government-led destruction of monopolies. Although Populists continued to push for local regulation of industries such as the railroads, these were stopgaps. Regulation was impossible in the long term.[37] As their 1892 presidential candidate stated, "We have experimented through the life-time of a whole generation and have demonstrated that avarice is an untrustworthy public servant, and that greed cannot be regulated or made to work in harmony with the public welfare." Populists had lost faith in the government's willingness or ability to rein in corporations. "Laws are made now-a-days to shield men of wealth—not poor men," claimed one writer for the *Advocate*. The "interstate commerce law is no exception to the rule," he continued, and "neither that or the so-called Sherman anti-trust law were ever designed to operate against the interests of organized capital. They were designed solely as covers for legislation by which organized capital should be enabled to make further conquests over labor." Private capital would never adequately value the rights of the people.[38]

Yet it was only with some hesitation that Populists advocated such an enlargement of the federal government's power. Some, including Peffer, did not even favor government ownership of the railroads.[39] Federal power was also at stake in the subtreasury plan. Originally developed by a southern Farmers' Alliance leader, the plan called for farmers to receive loans upon the deposit of agricultural goods at government-owned warehouses. The scheme was designed to eliminate the crop-lien system and minimize the power of merchants of the South, while also providing an outlet for the distribution of government greenbacks. Despite its potential benefits, the plan had virtually no support in the western states. Jay Burrows of the Nebraska Alliance called it "too hair-brained [sic] for even patient criticism," while a local Kansas Alliance considered it "detrimental to the farmers and industrial classes" and rather damningly identified it as "class legislation."[40]

Western Populists sought to employ the power of the federal government to reshape the national economy, but they also distrusted centralized control.

They demonstrated elements of this attitude when they attributed the rise of monopolies to the intrigues of congressmen. But as frustrated as Populists were with the regular abuse of power, they were especially alarmed by those conservatives who intended to turn the federal government into a tool for the maintenance of "law and order," especially in response to labor unrest. In the weeks after the Homestead strike, a writer for the *Advocate* reminded readers that a growing American aristocracy "is determined to control the policy of our government and debase the masses of our people." The author then cited an article from the "hireling press" that had recently declared, "we will welcome the rise of [a] centralized government whose arm is long enough to reach and strong enough to hold by the collar all rebels against the government near and far."[41] In a similar article for the *Aspen Union Era*, the author quoted another "leading plutocrat paper of the western coast" that contentedly looked forward to American "centralization." States would become mere federal districts, and governors would be appointed by the national administration. "Behind them will be arrayed the Federal government and the army of the United States—that pitiless machine. Bayonets do not think. . . . If they were ordered to shoot down the mass of Huns, Slavs, Croats, Irishmen and the few Americans who make up the mob at Homestead, they would do so without a moment's hesitation." According to that "plutocrat paper," the American economic elite was willing to support such a plan, and "it is the workingmen who are driving them."[42] In his summation of similar events in his tract *Politics*, Rogers argued that for every $10 created by producers, "monopoly has announced its decision to bring on the army and a 'stronger government' unless $9 out of each $10 be obsequiously handed over."[43]

Whatever their misgivings, the most pressing reform the Populists advocated did require the use of federal power. Financial and currency issues were the foremost concerns of most who joined the new party in the 1890s, and Populists predicted that these changes would have the widest effect in their efforts to restructure the national economy. The system in place was (to say the least) untidy. Gold, silver, and various paper currencies all circulated simultaneously, and different exchange rates developed for each. Silver had been demonetized in 1873, and only supplementary acts passed in 1875, 1878, and 1890 had allowed any of the white metal to remain in circulation at all. Greenbacks had been issued by the federal government since the Civil War, but as the only currency without an intrinsic value—combined with legal limitations on their use—they had the lowest exchange rate of all. Gold had become the de facto standard, but its rarity meant that hard currency remained in short supply. Privately issued bank notes filled in the gaps, but the whole system fostered incessant currency speculation. Additionally, the relative inflexibility of a structure based at its heart on specie had led to chronic deflation by the 1890s.[44]

Populists understood that limited gold currency had impacted the economy, and they demanded an increase in the money supply to benefit commodity producers. Farmers almost universally desired currency inflation, but before 1892, these calls had resulted in only useless platform planks by both major parties; most knew that neither Republican nor Democratic leaders intended to enact such proposals.[45] The new party's leaders developed more concrete proposals. Although the struggle of the 1890s has often been stereotyped as the "battle" over silver currency, the majority of Populist leaders and commentators were committed to greenback theories of money in which paper fiat currency would be printed and controlled solely by the federal government. And whether they favored silver or paper, all called for the abolition of the system of private "national" banks. They demanded instead that the nation's money serve the good of the people.[46]

Most Populist writers described the serious impact of the Treasury's engineered monetary contraction in their works. In his book *The Farmer's Side*, William Peffer described the results of these policies in pragmatic terms. As a result of deflation, "values of farm products have fallen 50 per cent since the great war, and farm values have depreciated 25 to 50 per cent during the last ten years." Just as the "population had increased 15 per cent and the volume of business 40 to 50 per cent," and just "when the business of the people required more money," Congress reduced the circulating currency by more than half. Producers were the core of the economy, but they could not succeed without currency. "Without money commerce would cease; without money, all movement of trade would stop; without money there would be no business; all exchange would be barter, and that would take us back to barbarism."[47] At the same time, Peffer suggested that the structures of transaction had been contrived for the benefit of the financial sector and with the intent of crippling farmers. The agriculturalist had been "shorn of his power to help himself in a thousand and one little ways," and he was now "at the mercy of combinations which are in effect conspiracies against the common rights of the people." Although he had argued that money was necessary for the transaction of business, Peffer eventually explained that the financial services sector acted in a way that harmed others *because* it was a business. At the heart of it was the commercial model: "the pecuniary interest of these useful agencies is to maintain the interest business." The only solution, wrote Peffer, was to "relieve the individual money lender of his present responsibility in that behalf and substitute a disinterested agency"—namely, a nationalized banking sector. Summing up his ideas in this regard, Peffer emphasized that "*the proper function of money is to serve a public use.*" Peffer contended that the public good required the expropriation of a part of the economy, and no claim of individual ownership could legitimately stand in opposition.[48]

The Populists' view of banks and financiers was necessarily complicated, but their analysis was not limited to sectors that directly affected them. There is another side to the Populists' worldview that cannot be accounted for in histories that depict them as orderly businessmen in the strictest sense. One whole strain of Populist thought on the subject has, in fact, been largely neglected by historians on both sides of the modern-versus-traditional debate, and it is tied intimately to their views on finance. Convenient as it is to say that Populists were rational—and they certainly were no less rational than their contemporaries—their conspiratorial beliefs must also be evaluated.

THE MONEY POWER CONSPIRACY AND THE GLOBAL FINANCIAL SYSTEM

Conspiratorial thought is a subject that has practically vanished from recent works on American Populism, despite both ample evidence of its importance and a current environment that strongly warrants its inclusion. For recent historians, it has been easier to avoid the subject than to exorcise the ghosts that still haunt the historiography of Populist thought. In this study, the money power conspiracy theory is evaluated as a reflection of Populist ideology and, in particular, as an example of the confrontational relationship that existed between Populists and those who managed the systems of government and finance.

The money power conspiracy theory was one of the most powerful and widespread ideas of the nineteenth century.[49] The growing strength of the banking sector fueled persistent fears of financial conspiracy, and the theory had been widely disseminated by the time of the Populist revolt. Certainly, nearly every leader in the new movement felt compelled to reference it. In 1890, the first year the Alliance or independent political tickets ran candidates in states such as Kansas and Nebraska, President Leonidas Polk of the National Farmers' Alliance and Industrial Union said that it was time to discard "all the rubbish of the negro question, bloody shirt, tariff and federal control of elections." The real issue "is the money power, the rule of plutocracy, that has been keeping people down."[50] A few years later, James R.

Sovereign, grand master workman of the Knights of Labor, warned, "Whenever the money power becomes stronger than the people, it will apply its arrogant lash with relentless fury, and liberty will be lost until through a reign of terror the oppressors have exhausted their forces in the gloom of another night."[51] In the best-known example, the eccentric novelist Ignatius Donnelly included language based on the money power in his preamble to the Populist Party platform in 1892. "A vast conspiracy against mankind has been organized on two continents," he said, "and it is rapidly taking possession of the world."[52] Furthermore, the money power conspiracy features prominently in all the Populist books, pamphlets, and newspapers analyzed earlier in this chapter. But if it was so common, why have historians written so little on the subject?

Richard Hofstadter is probably the individual most responsible for delegitimizing the academic investigation of the money power conspiracy. The influential author of *Age of Reform* cast the Populists as frustrated and delusional rural Americans, and he cited the money power conspiracy as one of the noteworthy examples of their irrationality. Their attacks on the money power were tied to anti-Semitism, he said, all the while attributing a new rise of prejudice in America to the movement for reform. Hofstadter's depiction of Populist hatred—just ten years after the end of World War II—only added to the controversy surrounding his book.[53] Many scholars were troubled by his general characterization of the Populists as backward looking or reactionary, and his portrayal was very different from the more positive images presented by the earlier Progressive historians. The responses in the academic literature of the 1960s in particular show a concerted effort by many researchers to disprove Hofstadter's analysis through a more thorough examination of Populist thought. However, Hofstadter's claims regarding prejudice against Jews and conspiratorial beliefs bordering on neuroses were dealt with dismissively.[54]

As historians refuted Hofstadter's contentions, discussion of anti-Semitism or conspiratorial language among Populists became taboo.[55] One of the few historians after Hofstadter who took the money power conspiracy seriously is Jeffrey Ostler. In his article "The Rhetoric of Conspiracy and the Formation of Kansas Populism," Ostler places the money power within the long history of American political conspiracies. He observes that works published since the late 1960s on the American Revolution and on the development of the Republican Party have noted the importance of conspiratorial language in the writings of some of the nation's political leaders. Just as it did in those cases, Ostler argues that the money power provided the ultimate

motivation to take extreme action: it justified the abandonment of the existing political framework and the transformation of the nonpartisan Farmers'
Alliance into a viable alternative.[56]

Where Ostler went—a full four decades after the publication of *Age of
Reform*—few have followed.[57] Still, the conspiracy represents one of the most
common themes in Populist literature, and surely it must have represented
some thing or things that were important to their view of the world. Although the story's origins are quite old, a modernized version of the money
power thesis was likely stimulated by the tumult associated with the Panic
of 1873. One of the earliest examples of the new money power literature
appeared in July 1878, in the official organ of the Amalgamated Association
of Iron and Steel Workers. The article, which the author identified as a
"Second Declaration of Independence," listed a series of congressional acts
that were responsible for currency contraction and served as special favors
to financiers, beginning with those designed to fund the Civil War. Silver
was demonetized, the author declared, due to "the lobbying influence of one
Ernest Seyd, of London, by the use of $500,000 furnished for that purpose"
to bribe American congressmen. Financial hardship was the result. "Farming and other real property has lost its normal value," the article stated, and
"the stock of monopolies have taken the front rank." It called on readers to
renounce these travesties, reject the two old parties that had supported these
policies, and join the Greenback-Labor Party. The article's content represented an almost fully formed version of one of the most common conspiracy stories circulating in the late nineteenth century, and it was through the
greenback tradition that it filtered into the Populist Party.[58]

The money power conspiracy was not confined to those outside the two
main parties. After all, as historian Mark Wahlgren Summers has suggested,
conspiratorial language was the norm during the Gilded Age, and groups like
the Populists should not be viewed as outliers.[59] In late 1877 (months before
the aforementioned newspaper article) members of Congress incorporated
portions of the conspiracy into their speeches—including details about the
involvement of Ernest Seyd. The accusations had become so pointed that
Senator Henry Dawes (Republican of Massachusetts) felt the need to openly
refute them and defend the character of a deceased colleague (Republican
Samuel Hooper). His efforts to quash the story proved fruitless.[60]

Clearly, some rather sophisticated people came to embrace the money
power theory. To appreciate its importance, it must be seen as more than the
product of small minds from small towns. To determine its significance and
meaning, it is useful to discuss a sample conspiracy tract in some detail. Prob-

ably the best known and most influential work on the subject in circulation in the 1890s was Sarah E. V. Emery's *Seven Financial Conspiracies Which Have Enslaved the American People*. Though published half a decade before the formation of the national People's Party, it was widely adopted by members of the new organization as a statement of the movement's sentiment regarding currency and finance.[61]

Emery's text opened similarly to Henry George's *Progress and Poverty*, by pointing to an inexplicable contradiction of the age—the existence of great wealth and progress alongside squalor and poverty.[62] This, she claimed, was the result of an eons-old system of parasitism that people had endured unnecessarily. Emery divided all people into two groups: "the one class who live by honest labor, the other who live off of honest labor." In old times, the parasites had been "roving bandits," some of whom might occasionally settle down to become kings. In modern times, contemporary "robber chiefs" did not resort to violence so openly. They replaced "spoils and plunders" with "interests, dividends, revenues, and rents." They became the monopolists and financiers.[63] Emery's basic division of society was based on greenback producerist interpretations of value, and it fit well with the ideology of contemporary reform movements that presaged the new party.[64]

Yet according to Emery, the "plunderers" were not given much of an opportunity to prey on their fellow citizens in early America. In fact, she tied economic fairness to national independence. "The system of American government as instituted by our fathers afforded little if any opportunity for robbery and oppression," she wrote. But all that was about to change, for "in an evil hour, the tempter came, the guardians were betrayed, and the very sanctuary of our liberties became the charnal-house [sic] of American freedom."[65] The evil hour that Emery referenced was the American Civil War. While many dreaded the coming conflict and others readied themselves to serve, some groups were thrilled by the opportunities the war would provide. For the "money kings of Wall Street" and certain of the "great political chieftains," their desire for wealth "had stifled the finer instincts of their nature, and they rejoiced because they saw in the preparation for the war their long-coveted opportunity for plunder." The national government soon found itself short of money to fight the war, hard currency became scarce, and the banks demanded outrageous interest on any loan. The Union was caught between an enemy—the Confederacy—and a supposed friend— "Shylock, clutching his gold and demanding therefor a rate of interest that would drain the life blood of the nation more effectually than the bullets of a Southern foe." Bankers were no less of a threat to the American union.[66]

Just as Emery depicted a nation plunged into war and at the mercy of greedy financiers, she presented a patriotic hero: Abraham Lincoln. The president, who "loved the people better than Shylock, and justice better than oppression," decided that Congress had the constitutional authority to make money. The federal government would print treasury notes (greenbacks), which would be as good as gold. For Emery, this should have been the great innovation of the war. "With an abundance of money," she observed, "not even the blight of war could check the prosperity of the country. . . . Commerce, industry, and education received a new impetus, and flourished as never before in the history of the country." The greenback was the ideal currency for an economically vital egalitarian republic.[67]

The bankers' setback would prove temporary, according to Emery. Those who controlled the hard currency would not be left out of the profits of war making. In early 1862 bankers from major eastern cities forced Congress to pass the Legal Tender Act. It required that import duties and interest on public debt be paid in coin (hard money), devaluing the greenbacks and increasing the market value of gold and silver. Further, because greenbacks could be used to purchase bonds, bankers could exchange their precious metals for cheap greenbacks and then buy government bonds. This guaranteed huge returns to the financiers and left the common people to pay the price. Emery believed that from this time on, Congress essentially handed over the reins of government to "Shylock."[68]

In the chapters that followed, Emery outlined case after case in which Congress provided special benefits to the financiers. The National Bank Act of 1863, the retirement of millions of greenbacks by the Treasury after the war, the Credit Strengthening Act of 1869 (which required that bonds be repaid in "coin"), and the "re-funding" of the debt (postponing final repayment until 1907) followed. These acts established a monetary system revolving around private bank notes (backed by government bonds), increasingly scarce government-issued notes, and specie. The entire system also rested on what Emery considered to be a menacing and perpetual national debt.[69]

Only in one of her last chapters did Emery deal with the Coinage Act of 1873 and the demonetization of silver—the so-called Crime of '73. This chapter may have attracted the most public attention. Throughout most of the pamphlet, Emery had cited a rather nonspecific scheme of "Shylock" for each of the conspiracies, for which American (especially New York) bankers were most likely to blame. This time, it was different. Emery claimed that, according to a story in *Banker's Magazine*, just as silver was being demonetized in Europe, "$500,000 was raised, and Ernest Seyd was sent to this country with this fund, as agent of the foreign bondholders and capitalists," to bribe American congressmen into following suit. In truth, Seyd was a real man, an employee of the Bank of England, and he was in Washington to advise Congress. In a statement in the *Congressional Globe*, Congressman Samuel Hooper noted, "Ernest Seyd of London . . . has given great attention to the subject of mint and coinage" and provided advice that helped shape the final version of the bill.[70] This evidence seemed conclusive to Emery, but she did not stop there.

Emery offered additional proof that this was merely part of a long-established plan by the British. She alleged that, as early as 1862, an agent of British financiers by the name of Hazzard had been disseminating a tract to American bankers that outlined a new plan to control global labor. It was Hazzard's job to encourage Americans to join the scheme. The *Hazzard Circular*, as it came to be called, noted with approval the likely destruction of chattel slavery, "for slavery is but the owning of labor, and carries with it care for the laborer." The European plan, in contrast, was designed to establish "capital control of labor, by controlling wages. This can be done by controlling the money." The circular also tied the cost of the war to this new system of control. "The great debt" the nation would have after the war "must be used as a measure to control the volume of money," it said. "To accomplish this the bonds must be used as a banking basis." The only threat to this plan was fiat money. "It will not do to allow the greenback, as it is called, to circulate as money any length of time, for we cannot control that."[71] Thus, the currency was limited and controlled by the few, and all the workers of the country now served them.

It would be impossible to suggest that *Seven Financial Conspiracies* sparked the movement that would become Populism. Although one contemporary publication claimed that 400,000 copies of *Seven Financial Conspiracies* had been printed by 1896, it was only one of many conspiratorial tracts in circulation.[72] As noted earlier, the money power theory was not new, but by the 1890s, there was a powerful demand for publications on the subject. Before, large numbers of those from the old parties had likely been familiar with the conspiracy, yet it never became an accepted part of either major party's dogma. But in the early 1890s, members of the new political party integrated it into their worldview.

Populists of all stripes took the conspiracy stories quite seriously. Weaver and Rogers both included references to Seyd and Hazzard, respectively, in their works.[73] Davis Waite's *Aspen Union Era* regularly advertised the *Hazzard Circular* on the front page, and one writer became furious upon hearing rumors that Emery's tract had been banned from circulation through the postal service."If it is true," the writer declared, "it is an act of tyranny that would shame the acts of the Russian Czar."[74] Thomas Patterson, a Denver newspaperman and Waite's chief rival for control of the Colorado Populists, worked to obtain a sworn confession from a former confidant of Seyd's to corroborate the conspiracy story.[75] The appeal of the conspiracy was not limited to the West. For example, *History of the Wheel and Alliance and the Impending Revolution*, a publication and recruiting tool of the Farmers' Alliance of Arkansas, was littered with references to the money power, the *Hazzard Circular*, and "Shylock."[76]

While the conspiracy theory was an important source of unity for the otherwise diverse group that made up the new party, portions of it also spoke to very real elements of the party's ideology. For those with republican inclinations, the conspiracies proved that financiers were consciously attempting to consolidate economic and political power by destroying independent farmers and small businessmen. James Weaver, for example, suggested that the financial elite had decided to destroy "the spirit of independence and self-reliance among the people," which had been "increasing in the same ratio with the accumulation of property among the masses."[77] Likewise, John Rankin Rogers saw evidence that the conspirators were hoping to break down traditional American society. He described the modern conflict as one in which "wealth, the power of money, or mammonism . . . is engaged in the effort and attempt to secure power over labor by deprivation."[78] William Peffer, too, wrote of the money power in *The Farmer's Side*, noting that "since our great war began what is commonly known as the 'money power' has had almost exclusive control of our financial legislation." Though not the greatest publicist of these theories, he agreed with most Populists when he declared that the "money power . . . impoverishes the people. It controls the business of the country, the markets and the values."[79] Like all the rest, he agreed that covetous financiers threatened American freedom.

To further analyze the utility of the conspiracy theory, it is useful to look beyond the story of conspiracy itself and examine the broad points in Emery's work that are integral to the theory and demonstrate its wider significance. First, the conspiracy was depicted as part of a sectional and global scheme. Much of Emery's pamphlet placed the blame on New York—or at least northeastern—bankers. However, she ultimately saw the flow of investment capital as a transatlantic phenomenon—as an attempt by the British to regain their position as overlords and an attempt by American bankers to share in the spoils. To whatever extent the basic facts were stretched, she was not wrong to see New York and London as centers of financial power that influenced the lives of ordinary Americans.

Other Populists put an even greater emphasis on this supposed connection between Wall Street and Lombard Street and, ultimately, the producer's subservience to them both. They understood that they lived in a raw material–producing region and that the profits from their production were siphoned off by a distant financial and industrial elite. In modern parlance, they developed a primitive world systems analysis of their situation. Today, the world systems interpretation centers on a pattern of unequal trade between "core" economic activities—those in which small numbers of sellers offer products with high profit margins—and "peripheral" economic activities—those involving competition among sellers and low profit margins. Globally, these activities tend to be divided by state, with quasi-monopolistic core industries located in strong states and peripheral industries in weaker ones, but these divisions are not necessarily based on national boundaries. Those on the periphery are often caught in a cycle of unequal trade with those who make up the core, resulting in uneven global economic development.[80]

Some scholars have suggested that the American West at this time was a peripheral region engaged in unequal trade with the core regions of the East and Europe. The core offered high-profit products (manufactured goods and financial services) in exchange for the low-profit commodities (foodstuffs, ore, and lumber) of the West. As a few have noted, Populists understood their unequal position as well.[81] Peffer was disgusted that "wealth is accumulating in the large cities, more especially those in the East, and those accumulations are continually fed by drains flowing away from the country people and working forces in the towns."[82] William V. Allen, a Nebraska Populist elected to the US Senate in 1893, expressed the same frustration. In a brief article for the *North American Review*, he described westerners' feeling that it "is the purpose of Eastern money loaners and capitalists to drain our industries of their profits by unfriendly legislation." Currency contraction gave financial interests leverage in their dealings with western producers, while the tariff forced westerners "to purchase their manufactured goods from the East, with low-priced products of farm and mine, and pay the freight both ways." Government and business had engineered a system that would perpetuate inequality.[83]

Obviously, farmers and laborers did not need conspiratorial language to make them aware that they were subject to the whims of global commodity and financial markets. Yet allusion to the money power suggested the nature

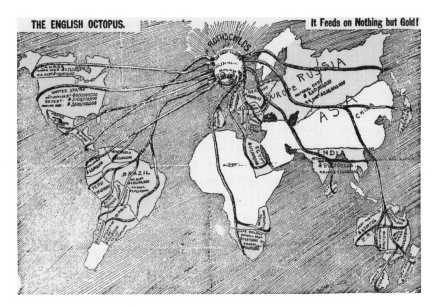

The English Octopus. From William H. Harvey, Coin's Financial School *[Chicago: Coin, 1894], 124*

of a power relationship that more tangible facts could not express. During the summer of 1893, for example, Senator Allen told audiences in Nebraska that "certain parties in Europe and America" were attempting to demonetize what remained of the circulating American silver, just as "the money power of Europe has forced Austria, Hungary, the Argentine, and a number of other countries." He warned, "The truth is that it is the determination of Europe to control the finances and industries of this country." Although "England failed during the dark days of the revolution and again in 1812," it "now seeks to secure control through the gold question."[84] In 1892 one of Weaver's supporters in Colorado put it similarly when he told all within earshot that "the moneyed power has controlled every national convention for sixteen years." As a result, "the money changers of Wall street, Thread-needle street, and Lombard street" had "so manipulate[d] the legislation of this country, as actually to defraud the producing classes of this state out of 34 per cent of its total products."[85] Use of the money power conspiracy did more than demonstrate frustration over uneven economic development. It blamed eastern and European economic interests for undermining American democracy and threatening national sovereignty. The Populists' enemies were utterly delegitimized.

Their perspective led some Populists to make overt comparisons between the situation of the United States and that of colonial or semicolonial states around the world. In 1894 a Populist paper in Chicago went so far as to suggest that a recent issuance of federal bonds was part of a plot by the money power to "place a financial agent of our European creditors over the affairs of this government," whose decrees would be enforced, "if necessary, by an appeal to arms of the united powers of Europe." In this regard, America was "simply following in the same path trod by Egypt, Greece, India, Turkey, and Peru."[86] In somewhat broader terms, one Kansas newspaperman bluntly stated: "Lombard street controls Wall street, and Wall street the money and produce markets of the United States. English syndicates buy up flouring mills and elevators all along the line at Minneapolis, Chicago, and New York. The farmers of this country are as surely under the heel of English tyranny as though we were an [sic] British province."[87]

The greatest appeal of the money power conspiracy was tied to its representation of the growing distrust of government. Emery and others resorted to conspiratorial rhetoric to explain how American politicians could support policies that, to them, seemed to benefit the few at the expense of the many. Whereas some contemporaries saw dysfunctional politics as the product of a failed democracy, the Populists denied that a true democracy had allowed these events to transpire.[88] Instead, they posited that some great power was at work subverting the political and economic systems established by the wise founders. Americans had not merely made poor choices. Many individuals and the bosses of both old parties had been corrupted. The talk of such massive corruption should be viewed in a sympathetic light when one considers the context. In *Age of Reform*, just before railing against the Populists as irrational and reckless, even Richard Hofstadter reminds readers that the Populists had "seen so much bribery and corruption, particularly on the part of railroads, that they had before them a convincing model of the management of affairs through conspiratorial behavior."[89] The stories seemed plausible, and for people who believed that democracy could still serve the masses, they were necessary.

The money power conspiracy should not be seen as the cornerstone of Populist thought or as demonstrative of defects in the Populist mind. The conspiratorial conception of American politics they embraced was not the sole or even the primary tool they used to analyze their situation, but it is reflective of so much more than historians have thus far suggested. It both illustrated and reinforced their skepticism of the overpowerful in both business and government. It also revealed how the Populists thought of their region and its place in the world. In a similar way, it would later play a part in shaping their view of colonialism. All these elements would reappear during the debates over empire at the end of the decade.

POLITICS, CULTURE, AND GENDER

At their core, Populists maintained a profound faith in American democracy. This faith was only reinforced by a civic nationalist vision of what America could become.[90] Populist speeches were loaded with patriotic and nationalistic rhetoric, especially references to the founders or to the martyred Lincoln. For reformers who hoped to overcome the corruption of the previous generation, identification with traditional American ideals held tremendous importance. Of course, Populists employed the language of patriotism and nationalistic pride to legitimize their agenda, and they did so at least partially out of necessity. At least since the outbreak of the Civil War, discussions of patriotism and of loyalty to a cause had become standard political discourse, and the two old parties had already deployed this language to solidify their control of identifiable voter groups. Republicans spoke of the "bloody shirt" and loyalty to the Union. Democrats emphasized white supremacy and noninterference in other cultural concerns, appealing to southern whites and new immigrants.[91] Both parties could then tell their typical constituencies that to deviate from their organization was to be a traitor to their identity and to the values they held most dear. They had each developed a certain vision of the nation and of loyalty, and anyone who hoped to make headway in this environment would have to challenge those visions directly.

Populists understood the difficulties that came with entering the fold in such an environment, and they were prepared to redefine patriotism to serve the needs of reform. One article in the *Advocate* asked how conservative appeals to patriotism were supposed to function when the national government refused to serve its citizens. "Can you deny a man the common rights of humanity, render him an outcast by laws and customs of his country, and can you *teach* such an [sic] one patriotism?"[92] Weaver observed that, after taking control of the reins of government, the economic elite now "prates about patriotism and places those who plead for redress, or complain of tyranny in the attitude of seditious and disobedient subjects."[93] Perhaps the most effective refutations of Republican claims came from those whose loyalty could not be questioned. In Kansas during the campaign of 1894, Populists used the speech of an old Union veteran in support of the reelection of former

Confederate William A. Harris to the House of Representatives. While the Union man admitted there had been a great deal of talk about "patriotism and loyalty" from the Republican side, and some had even told audiences to "vote as we shot," he believed there was more than one kind of patriotism. "One kind is to our homes, our families and our country." The other kind, the one being invoked by Republicans, was patriotic loyalty "for the great corporations, trusts, note shavers, combines and men who, when we were fighting to save this nation, were sitting behind bank counters scheming how they could rob our country." Harris, he said, was full of the former kind of patriotism and had none of the latter.[94]

The Populist definitions of patriotism were not merely rejections of those adopted by the old parties. The Populists had a special need to appeal to a patriotic foundation to justify their entrance onto the political stage. The new party did not exist only to be a less offensive alternative to the party in power. Instead, it planned to be the party that would restore American equality from its perilous position. It would be the party of new ideas and the party of national rejuvenation. As one Populist summed up the goal of their organization, "It seeks to teach the laborer his rights and impress him with the manhood and patriotism to demand them fully."[95] Populists' deployment of nationalistic language placed their calls for reform at the same level as those of Andrew Jackson's Democrats or Abraham Lincoln's Republicans. At the same time, it implied the disloyalty of the old parties—those that followed the money power.

In many Populist addresses, patriotic language went hand in hand with the language of manhood.[96] During the Gilded Age, the type of men who became Populists—just like their eastern middle-class counterparts—faced certain challenges to their manly identities, and their movement sought to address some of those challenges. Yet much of what has been written about the views of John Hay, Theodore Roosevelt, and others of their ilk does not directly apply to western farmers or laborers. For certain eastern professionals and members of the "old money" elite, the standard Victorian definitions of self-restraint and independence seemed inappropriate in an era of increasing orderliness dominated by giant monopolies. These members of the comfortable classes did not seek to disrupt the political or economic basis of society; instead, they sought to adjust or reimagine conceptions of manhood.[97] Precisely the opposite was true of the Populists. By attacking corporate dominance and the existing two-party system, Populists were reimagining what society could be rather than reconceptualizing their place within it.

The traditional version of "manhood" or "manliness" accepted by the

Populists was defined by economic and personal traits. Self-restraint and integrity were necessary for a man's personal character, but these and related characteristics were supposed to be demonstrated in the commercial realm as well. Labor organizations and the Farmers' Alliances had preached sobriety, the Protestant work ethic, and financial responsibility to their members in an attempt to both improve their productivity and inoculate themselves against charges of sloth and socialism. At the same time, they emphasized the manhood of members who were financially independent and served the role of breadwinner for their families.[98] This economic role secured their position in the family patriarchy and, these organizations claimed, allowed them to think for themselves. Because Populist writers continued to equate economic independence with political independence, they also linked manhood and freedom of action in the political field.

Just as they argued that political and economic freedoms were under threat, Populists contended that the principles of patriotism and manhood were being destroyed by the greed of others.[99] A writer for the *Coming Crisis* told readers that the American aristocracy was threatening their political and economic rights, but it had used the mainstream press to blind people to the danger. Consequently, the author asked readers: has "patriotism" been "lulled to sleep?" "Awake!" the writer commanded. "Trust no man, no men with your liberties."[100] Waite's paper suggested that American manhood had already been cowed by the "machine system of politics." The typical (non-Populist) man was now a coward who could only "take the lead in cringing servility and abject negation to all claims to independent manhood." The only solution was political education, for "knowledge begets independence."[101]

If manhood was endangered by the "money power," the exertion of manhood was characterized as the solution. The state chairman of the Colorado People's Party, Dr. Alexander Coleman, decried the "plundering of all that is sacred, the destruction of manhood and the sale of womanly virtue" brought about by political corruption and financial distress. "In this great struggle, gold stands against manhood," he said, but manhood could fight back. The chairman went on to call for self-sacrificing manhood to replace the office-seeking of the other parties and rejuvenate American freedom. "Men who fail in strength and cannot keep up with the advancing column must be dropped by the way; strong men who have liberty above personal gain and party must be crowded to the front; and the leader of today may be an almost forgotten follower of tomorrow." Individualism was a cause of the great troubles of the age, not a solution. In this hour, the "individual man is nothing, but the principles of American freedom, human rights and civil liberty . . . must be maintained."[102]

Other leaders of the new party often equated the abandonment of the old parties or the political status quo with manhood. A prominent member of the Knights of Labor in Leadville, Colorado, told his fellow Knights: "We have come to the parting of ways" with regard to the Republicans and Democrats. "We have waited long and waited patiently for the two old parties to reconstruct and regenerate themselves." To follow them any further "would be false to our individuality of manhood." Instead, it was time to join a new party "led by true and noble men whose watchword is patriotism and love of the people, and whose every effort is scored for the meek and lowly and humble of the earth."[103] Similarly, a writer for the Aspen Union Era stated in 1891 that there was "not one jot of evidence to prove that the government has not already passed from the control of the people to" the influence of "prejudices and hatreds and party bosses." He warned, "You can not prove your manhood" unless you have demonstrated "your ability to build up and tear down parties." Only then could a man claim to have "sloughed off the old sin of plutocracy and all the old ways of political sin."[104] To free oneself from the old parties and choose reform was to choose manhood and country over ignorant devotion and greed.

By embracing the traditional expectations of Victorian manhood, Populists were able to claim a place that might have been unavailable to them otherwise. Because of the radical economic message that many equated with socialism, they were frequently characterized as failures and malcontents. If they had rejected the principles of independence and self-restraint, they might very well have played into the hands of those who accused them of being no better than anarchists and thieves. In some cases, opponents tried to desex or feminize the Populists. Democrats in North Carolina derisively referred to Populist leader (and later senator) Marion Butler as "Mary Ann Butler."[105] Other Populists and third-party supporters were identified as "she-men" by their enemies.[106] The partisan epithets for outliers or potential radicals would only have gained greater potency if the Populists had dismissed traditional conceptions of manhood.

The Populist acceptance of restrained masculinity contrasts starkly with the Rooseveltian conception of rugged manliness. Theodore Roosevelt called for men to be aggressive, even violent at times, to demonstrate their worth as leaders. For Populists, it was more important to show individual responsibility. But because the Populist message was tied to a program of social reform, their emphasis on emulation of the middle class made sense. They would not be deemed worthy if they did not appear respectable. Roosevelt's target audience, in contrast, was already respectable. He wanted middle- and upper-class men to show their physical and mental power through triumph in conflicts. Of course, working farmers and laborers had no need to demonstrate their rugged power; nor did they need to seek out more conflicts than those they already confronted.[107]

Also unlike many of the eastern middle-class men who felt threatened by women's suffrage, the Populists demonstrated at least some willingness to give women a voice.[108] Before the new party was even formed, the Knights of Labor and the Farmers' Alliances had allowed women to become full voting members of their organizations, which was quite exceptional for the day. Notable members of the Alliances and the Knights also made statements in support of women's suffrage. Populists often struggled with this balancing act, for it was not their objective to overturn existing gender norms.[109] When the national party was formed in 1892, women's suffrage was left off the platform. Although this omission may have been for largely pragmatic reasons—namely, a fear of alienating any potentially sympathetic voters—other factors contributed to the new party's limited support for women's suffrage. Many of the agrarian reformers had actually conceptualized only a modification of a woman's place.[110]

Populists did support women's suffrage under the right circumstances. This was demonstrated in Colorado in 1893, when the issue appeared on the ballot statewide. Populists joined state and national women's suffrage leaders (including Carrie Chapman Catt) in promoting the measure, but they did so using explicitly economic arguments. The vote for women, they said, would add strength to the votes of farmers and laborers. Even Catt—by no means an economic radical—contended that women would vote for free silver and economic equality. As a result, Colorado became the first state to adopt women's suffrage through popular referendum.[111] Populist men believed that the women experiencing economic struggles by their sides—their wives—understood the situation as well as they did. In this case, Populists viewed suffrage through the lens of class, not gender. Their actions should not be mistaken for the abandonment of patriarchy but instead should be seen as a practical alteration of it.

The term *populist* has, in common usage, become almost synonymous with *parochial*, but the Populists of the 1890s were trapped by neither old ideas nor their surroundings. Those who formed the People's Party looked well

beyond their own communities when they formulated a response to the increasing power of economic interests. They feared the (further) development
of a centralized, militarized, unresponsive government, which they believed
would become the ultimate tool of concentrated wealth. They accepted a
conspiracy theory that both reflected these fears and demonstrated their
perspectives on global capitalism and exploitation. These features of their
worldview fueled their reform efforts over the whole span of the party's existence, but they also became more directly tied to foreign affairs as the decade
wore on. Although their views on international trade or imperialism could
be described as little more than embryonic by 1892, the basic premises used
by Populists to judge America's overseas policies were already well formed by
that time.

Though they were a diverse group, the Populists came together under the
banner of reform to launch the late nineteenth century's most serious challenge to the nation's political and economic systems. It was a movement of
self-identified outsiders who hoped to construct a new system that could em-
power a greater number of Americans and help them find their voice. They
distrusted those who held the reins of power, making them especially eager
to disrupt the existing political and economic arrangements in favor of more
broad-based alternatives. Despite any cynicism, they maintained a tremendous faith that the egalitarian ideals of the founders could and should be realized, no matter the means. It was this skepticism combined with this vision
that eventually led them to champion forms of direct democracy. In their
attempts to combat the power of entrenched interests, their demands were
not so much "statist" as they were based on a desire for a bottom-up form
of governance, something that was less important to the next generation of
reformers. The West of the early 1890s was ready for just such a message.

2. THE LOCAL CONTEXT
Nebraska, Colorado, and Washington, 1890-1897

When the Populists launched their first national campaign on July 4, 1892, they took the opportunity to declare their independence with a powerful statement of principles designed to comprehensively repudiate the old parties and the powers that controlled them. Ignatius Donnelly, a reform politician, Minnesota Alliance leader, and apocalyptic novelist, was the author of the statement, and it was agreed that his words fit the occasion perfectly. "We meet," it declared, "in the midst of a nation brought to the verge of moral, political and material ruin. Corruption dominates the ballot box, the legislatures, the congress, and touches even the ermine of the bench." It blamed both of the old parties for this state of affairs. They had struggled with each other "for power and plunder, while grievous wrongs have been inflicted upon the suffering people." Now Democrats and Republicans alike "propose to sacrifice our homes, lives and children on the altar of Mammon; to destroy the multitude in order to secure the corruption funds for the millionaires." The words of the preamble represented a decisive break from the old parties, which were as much the focus of attention as any aspect of the economy.[1]

Their rejection of the old parties seemed complete, but just four years later, the People's Party nominated William Jennings Bryan, a Democrat, for president. He was a Democrat unlike those who controlled the state parties in much of the West in 1892. Like the Populists, he announced his commitment to the needs of the common people over those of the interests, and he did so with no less passion than that contained in the Populists' declaration of independence. Like them, he claimed to speak for those without power and against those who abused power. If he was not one of them—and in many ways he was not—he at least shared much of their worldview. He saw many of the same problems they did, and he attributed blame to the same forces they did. Populists were aware of the differences when they nominated Bryan for president, but they considered him someone they could work with in 1896 and beyond.

Bryan's dramatic rise shows how the Populists' worldview came to take a dominant place in the public discourse of the 1890s West. The Populists were not the originators of most of the policies they advocated. Others in the West (and nationally) had favored reform of the currency and transportations systems for years, but obstacles had prevented the old parties from advocating change. The rise of the Populists altered the political landscape by creating a party that appeared to be a legitimate vehicle for reform. When the party sprang up from the various reform organizations assembled by farmers and laborers to defend their rights, it embraced ideas that were missing or suppressed in other parties of the day. Its entry into the field freed voters of their allegiances while simultaneously creating fractures in the old parties. By 1896, the political debate in the West placed matters of political economy foremost, and by the time of their national conventions, western Democratic and Republican delegates alike pushed their parties to take up policies to aid farmers and laborers. When western Republicans bolted from their national convention and Democrats adopted a core element of the Populist platform, the Populists no longer felt they had to act alone.

This chapter examines the many political transitions that took place in the West during the period from 1890 to 1897. These years cover the formation of the Populists as an independent political force and the course of events that eventually led them to develop an alternative strategy. Whereas historians have typically attributed the decline of the Populist movement to fusion, western Populists saw things quite differently. They believed that the changes that had occurred by 1896 would allow them to join a coalition of like-minded reformers, and in this way, their battle against concentrated capital would go on. For the Populists, 1896 was not the "first battle" (as Bryan would later dub it), but they also believed it was far from their last.[2]

REGIONAL CONTEXT AND POPULIST ORIGINS

Before the Civil War, political complications limited Anglo-American settlement of the trans-Missouri West. The sectional and party conflicts in Congress that held back the organization of new territorial governments and western development projects finally came to an end when the southern states seceded from the union. The departure of their congressional delega-

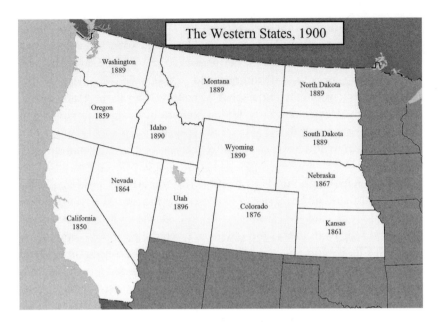

The Western States, 1900

Washington
1889

Montana
1889

North Dakota
1889

Oregon
1859

Idaho
1890

South Dakota
1889

Wyoming
1890

Nevada
1864

Nebraska
1867

Utah
1896

Colorado
1876

California
1850

Kansas
1861

Map of the western states. Courtesy of the US Geological Survey, with modifications by the author.

tions and the national supremacy of the party of Lincoln in the years that followed allowed Republicans to shape the West as they saw fit. The center-pieces of their economic program included the Homestead Act, national and local subsidies to promote the construction of railroads and the development of industries, and protective import tariffs for certain agricultural and industrial products. Whereas the Homestead Act theoretically provided an economic foundation for those willing to farm the West, subsidies and tariffs eventually promoted the growth of corporate entities to sizes previously unseen in American history. The Republican plan proved effective at repopulating the West—in the twenty years from 1870 to 1890, the region's population grew by approximately 400 percent—but it also laid the foundations for future conflict.[3]

Corporate power increasingly became a factor in the economic and political lives of westerners, but the Republican Party maintained its hegemony despite growing discontent. The power of the Republican narrative of "progress" should not be underestimated, but it was hardly the only tool at their disposal. Especially in those areas that spent considerable time as territories before achieving statehood, Republican control of the presidency (encompassing every term but one from 1869 to 1893) allowed the party to distribute patronage throughout the region. In addition, the party had a significant cultural card to play during election season. In the weeks leading up to a contest, stump speakers and editors would drag out the "bloody shirt," imploring voters never to forget the Civil War and placing all the blame for the conflict on the Democratic Party. Union veterans made up a substantial portion of the population of the West, and especially among the Plains states, the Grand Army of the Republic (GAR) had posts in every community of any size.[4]

Despite Republican efforts to unite a coalition around rapid economic growth and the shared experience of preserving the union, real opposition to the status quo emerged. Throughout the 1870s and 1880s, Greenbackers, Grangers, Knights of Labor, and others attacked the powerful corporate interests that had become a dominant force in many of the western states. Railroads (and the grain elevators operated by them) squeezed farmers as both consumers and producers, and worse yet, they became the strongest political actors in states such as Nebraska and Kansas. In Colorado and the other Rocky Mountain states, laborers fought against mining corporations (largely owned by out-of-state investors) for political influence and a voice in the workplace. In the more economically diverse states of the Pacific coast, the lobbyists of lumbermen and shipping companies joined with those of mine owners and railroad managers to compete for the ears of local politicians. In Washington State, too, farmer and labor organizations clamored for change. Everywhere, activists demanded an economy that was more responsive to democratic forces. Although these movements were still growing in the West at the dawn of the 1890s, up to that point, they had largely been unsuccessful at enacting change.

Frustration continued to build among western voters, in no small part because neither of the existing parties proved to be worthy vehicles for reform. Despite the obvious problems under their regimes, Republicans continued to pile up huge victories every November. Quite simply, the Grand Old Party felt no real threat from its Democratic rivals, so there appeared to be no immediate need to change. So why did disaffected voters refuse to join the Democrats? Aside from any disinclination to do so born of lingering memories of the war, the fact was that most state Democratic parties in the West were in no position to support new policies. Their national organization was still funded primarily by what is now referred to as the financial services industry, and farmers were not about to line up behind the party of bankers. Many state parties were also at least as ideologically conservative as their opponents. Often, old party leaders such as J. Sterling Morton of Nebraska and Charles S. Thomas of Colorado preferred laissez-faire policies to promote their states' development rather than the overt favoritism toward business shown by Republicans. Such an ideology also fit perfectly with the party's base of Catholics and immigrants, groups that felt threatened by prohibition legislation and other cultural initiatives pushed by old-stock Protestant Republicans. In other cases, such as in the new state of Washington, Democratic leaders like Thomas Burke favored federal spending and subsidies for development, essentially endorsing the Republican vision. Either way, the Democrats' fundamental conservatism made them less than ideal proponents of reform.[5]

With no outlet, tensions began to boil over in 1890. The Farmers' Alliance, a nonpartisan organization that originally focused on political education and cooperative purchasing and marketing efforts, led the way toward third-party politics. After one last attempt to secure railroad regulations failed and the governor's inability to rein in these powerful corporations became obvious, Jay Burrows, secretary of the Nebraska Farmers' Alliance, called for a local convention of reform organizations to be held that summer. In late July a joint convention of Alliance delegates and representatives from the Knights of Labor met and agreed on an independent ticket and platform for the upcoming campaign. Among their proposals were currency inflation (through both paper and silver), laws to hinder the creation of a "land monopoly," and government ownership of the railroads.[6] Stories of the events in Nebraska and similar happenings in Kansas soon spread westward. Even though the Farmers' Alliance in Colorado had barely been established—it claimed only 5,000 members in 1890—some leaders of the organization decided to test the political waters. On July 4, 1890, they met with representatives of the Knights of Labor and Grangers, and together they called for a convention to establish a new ticket the following month. The new party formed in August demanded government ownership of the railroads, state ownership and control of irrigation systems, free coinage of silver, and the end of the national bank system.[7]

The results produced by these early third parties were somewhat mixed. In Colorado, the challengers received just over 6 percent of the statewide vote in their first election. However, that first defeat laid the foundations for greater things to come. Just months later, Alliance membership had jumped from 5,000 to 15,000.[8] In Nebraska, the new Independent Party's gubernatorial nominee, Alliance president John Powers, received roughly 1,000 votes fewer than the winner in an election in which more than 200,000 votes were cast. The next legislature would have Independent majorities in both houses, and Independents also claimed two of the three US House seats (with William Jennings Bryan winning the other).[9]

The proof of success in Nebraska and Kansas (where Alliance tickets also won congressional and legislative seats) convinced others in the West of the viability of third-party initiatives. In Washington, the Farmers' Alliance had been unprepared to take the leap into independent politics in 1890. But following the veto of railroad regulations and an anti-Pinkerton bill by the acting governor in early 1891, Alliance and Knights of Labor leaders declared their intent to challenge the two old parties. The People's Party of Washington was formally declared at a meeting in Ellensburg in December. By early 1892, state parties had at least begun the process of organizing in every western state.[10]

CREATING THE POPULIST PARTY

Over the course of 1891 and into early 1892, the various independent state parties throughout the West and in portions of the South began to coalesce into a national body that could challenge the Republicans and Democrats for control of Congress and the presidency. When successful western organizations called for the creation of a third national party, a number of reform groups agreed to meet and discuss their options. Despite hesitancy among some of those present at the conventions held in Cincinnati and St. Louis in 1891 and early 1892, respectively, large numbers of attendees supported the establishment of an independent ticket. The 1891 gathering officially launched the People's Party, but the 1892 meeting was of greater significance. There, the Populists secured the support of the southern-based National Farmers' Alliance and Industrial Union (NFAIU) and laid out the platform that would be reused that July in Omaha.[11]

The Populists had planned to hold their convention after the Republican and Democratic conventions, hoping that those parties' disaffected and disappointed members would be open to alternatives. Two prominent Coloradans showed why they had reason to be optimistic. Just months earlier, Senator Henry Teller and several of his colleagues had attempted to push a silver currency bill through Congress. The Benjamin Harrison administration used its control of patronage to pressure members of Congress, converting the nominal pro-silver majority into supporters of "sound currency." Teller voiced his frustration after the bill's defeat and renounced both par-

Thomas M. Patterson. Courtesy of the Library of Congress

ties, which, he claimed, worked only to "secure the State of New York, controlled as it is by a little circle in and about Manhattan Island," and which were "exactly alike on this silver question."[12] Not yet ready to abandon his party, Teller worked assiduously to halt Harrison's renomination. Again he was outmaneuvered, and Harrison won the nomination on the first ballot at the Republicans' June convention. Though Teller still would not bolt from the GOP, many of the rank and file felt less need for loyalty.

Thomas M. Patterson, owner and editor of the *Rocky Mountain News*, went one step farther than Teller. As a delegate to the Democratic National Convention, Patterson tried to use his influence to steer the party toward reform, at least with regard to the currency question. He used the pages of the *News* to campaign for free silver in the months leading up to the convention and then fought to have a silver plank added to the platform at the event. Instead, his proposals were brushed aside, and the party nominated known gold standard proponent Grover Cleveland. Shortly after the convention, Patterson announced his support for the Populists.[13]

While the Democrats and Republicans continued to resist economic reform proposals, the People's Party adopted the whole suite of reforms advocated by the Alliance, Knights, and other farmer or labor organizations. The platform was broken into three parts that responded to dangers in three fundamental sectors of the economy: money, transportation, and land. The money plank demanded the abolition of the national bank system, the establishment of the "sub-treasury plan of the Alliance, or a better system," the free coinage of silver, an increase in the circulating currency to $50 per capita (in both coin and paper), a graduated income tax, and a federally run postal savings bank. The transportation section of the platform called for government ownership of the railroads, and the section devoted to land condemned speculation and demanded the abolition of alien landownership. With few other viable options (considering the untimely death of NFAIU president Leonidas Polk in June), the party then selected former Greenback presidential candidate James B. Weaver to head the ticket. Joining the aging Union general was former Confederate general James G. Field. It was a move designed to show that reform now took precedence over the bloody shirt.[14]

The emergence of the Populists had an immediate impact on the political situation in the western states. In Colorado, Patterson was unable to control the delegates at the Populists' state convention, who spurned his calls for a formal fusion with the Democrats. Instead, Patterson followed their lead after they nominated reform editor Davis Waite for the governorship, and he brought a large number of Colorado's Democrats with him. For the Republicans of Nebraska, it seemed that they were finally ready to treat the Populist threat seriously. After downplaying the Populists two years earlier, the Republican candidate had come in third in the gubernatorial race, giving the Democrats their first major state office. This time, they nominated noted railroad critic Lorenzo Crounse to head their party's ticket. In Washington, the Democrats were the first to respond to the new challengers. When the Populists selected a slate of farmers to lead their first campaign in the state, Democrats countered by giving their gubernatorial nomination to Henry J. Snively, a pro-labor prosecutor and advocate of railroad regulations. As a result, many of the party's conservative old-guard leaders endorsed the Republican ticket.[15]

A substantial component of the debates in the western states revolved around competing visions of progress. Despite some efforts to reshape the party's image in Nebraska, all western Republicans continued to declare that the Populists' very existence would scare off outside investment. Of course, the Populists were not opposed to investment, but they believed the current system privileged the rights of mortgage lenders, railroad stockholders, and mine investors over the rights of farmers and laborers—the producers. Populists, in turn, declared that the old parties had colluded with the wealthy to deprive common Americans of their political and economic freedom. The conspiratorial rhetoric they employed frequently combined suggestions of corruption with a critique of unequal regional development.

Colorado's Populists were especially eager to attribute the demonetization of silver to financial conspirators. Even before his break with the Democrats, Thomas Patterson had printed in the *Rocky Mountain News* the corroborating testimony of a man claiming to be an associate of Ernest Seyd—the supposed agent of the English money power.[16] Later that summer, after his move, Patterson explained that a third party was necessary because "the old parties have passed into the control of the money power." As a result of their policies, "a grievously unjust proportion of the wealth created by the productive population of the country is extorted from its rightful owners and forcibly diverted to the financial centers of the East."[17] Patterson's remarks were echoed by Davis Waite, who traveled around the state telling crowds that only the Populists could create an economic system free from the control of the Rothschilds.[18]

Washington State's leading reformers also used conspiracy theory to justify their move to a new party. Just in time for the campaign season, John Rankin Rogers—then just an Alliance organizer and local candidate—wrote a pamphlet titled *The Irrepressible Conflict, or an American System of Money*. In what was little more than a rehash of Emery's theories, he attributed the nation's policy of financial contraction to a small group of bankers based in England and New York.[19] It is difficult to determine whether Rogers was introducing the arguments to a new audience or repeating well-known tropes, but it is clear that the phrase "money power" rapidly entered the lexicon of Washington State Populists. Dr. O. G. Chase, a Populist candidate for the state house, published a series of articles in western Washington's small-town papers, one of them devoted largely to the story of senator and former secretary of the treasury John Sherman. Chase claimed that Sherman had been honest when he first took office but "went down before the money power" and would "be remembered by future generations as a tyrant and tool for Wall street and England."[20] Although the Washington reformers were late to the third-party movement, they used the same methods to explain the bankruptcy of their rivals.

Nebraska's Populists employed conspiratorial rhetoric throughout 1892 to solidify their new base. In January, in a series of print debates between Nebraska Populist Party founder Jay Burrows and Republican Edward Rosewater, Burrows attributed the demonetization of silver to the plot of the "bondholders." When Rosewater suggested that the Populists merely wanted to "scale their obligations" by using inflationary currency to cut their debt in half, Burrows responded, "Every man at all posted on the question knows that the money power of this country and the world performed on two occasions the most gigantic job of scaling the world has ever seen" by changing the debt obligation to "coin" and demonetizing silver.[21] While the party's gubernatorial candidate did not discuss the conspiracy in any detail that fall, he did declare that scarce money had been demanded not by "the toilers or the yeomanry" but by the "Shylocks of Europe."[22] As was typical of all their conspiratorial language, he blamed national politicians for enacting policies that redistributed wealth from the producers of the West to foreign and eastern financial interests.

The results of the 1892 election showed tremendous gains for the Populists in much of the West but also suggested limits to their success. Cleveland triumphed over Harrison and Weaver, although the Populist candidate won the electoral votes of Colorado, Idaho, Kansas, and Nevada, as well as one of the votes of both North Dakota and Oregon. No other candidate from a new party had managed to win electoral votes since the antebellum period, and in the process, Weaver received more than a million popular votes. But the single electoral vote from Oregon was the only one he captured from a state that had been admitted to the union before 1860, and his million popular votes amounted to less than 10 percent of the total cast that year. An examination of regional results showed some promise, but it also suggested that a change in strategy would likely be required if Populists were to hold more than a handful of offices. In Washington, for example, where the party had been formed less than one year earlier, the Populist gubernatorial candidate received 26 percent of the vote, suggesting that, given more time, electoral success was possible. Yet in Nebraska, the Populist vote actually declined from the total two years earlier, and Crounse was elected by a narrow margin. The rare Populist victories were usually a result of fusion. Only eleven Populists were elected to the US House of Representatives (all from the West), and a majority of them had been aided by the Democrats. In Colorado, where just two years earlier the Alliance ticket had struggled to gain more than 6 percent of the vote, Davis Waite won the governorship with just under half the votes cast. Though there was no formal fusion arrangement in the state, it is difficult to imagine such a rapid transition without the pro-silver Democrats. Similar results were recorded in Kansas, where Populists and Democrats fused to elect Populist Lorenzo Lewelling as governor. Pop-ulists themselves understood this situation, and it clearly influenced their thinking in the years that followed.[23]

DEPRESSION POLITICS

As 1893 dawned, the national situation was, from the Populist viewpoint, unchanged from that of the previous year. Grover Cleveland and the Dem-ocrats were about to take over the presidency and Congress but as the Populists saw it, the primary difference between the Democrats and the Re-publicans was a few percentage points on the tariff. So long as the national government remained in the hands of the two old parties, Populists devoted their energies to the reform of state governments. They were still too weak in Washington State to make an impact, where factions in the Republican legislature fought each other for the right to select a senator—which the 1893 session eventually failed to do.[24] In Nebraska and Colorado, in contrast, Populists held a large portion of seats in the state legislatures (as well as the executive offices in Colorado), and they would be held accountable for the governance of those states.

Populists did not hold a majority of seats in the Nebraska legislature, as they had in 1891. No one party held a majority, but the Democrats claimed the balance of power. Two years earlier, the Populists had passed a law limit-ing "all classes of mechanics, servants, and laborers" to an eight-hour work-day, enacted legislation for the protection of the union label, approved a secret or "Australian" ballot law, and passed a sweeping railroad rate bill. Additionally, they placed a constitutional amendment on the next ballot that, if ratified, would replace the members of the ineffective Board of Trans-portation with an elected commission. Even though the railroad bill was ve-toed by the Democratic governor and others were challenged in court, it was not a bad first effort.[25] There were substantially fewer expectations for the 1893 legislature, but surprisingly, the Populists were able to pass legislation by working with and applying pressure on like-minded or politically threat-ened Democrats. The two parties were first brought together to elect district judge William V. Allen to the US Senate. He would go on to become one of the leading Populists in Congress over the course of the decade.[26] Following their cooperation in the Senate election, Populists and Democrats worked together to pass the Populists' 1891 railroad legislation again, and this time the governor signed it. It was a substantial triumph for the state's reformers, but it was soon held up in the courts. The legislature rounded out the session by adding another pro-labor law to those passed the previous term. This time, it was an anti-Pinkerton bill, which would be enacted just months after the dramatic battle between strikers and mercenaries at Homestead, Pennsylvania.[27]

The Colorado Populists had far less luck in passing reform legislation. Like the Nebraskans, they did not hold a majority, but they could control the state senate if they worked with the Democrats. Their greatest challenge came in a series of fights over railroad legislation. Populists succeeded in repealing the old inadequate regulations, but they ultimately failed to develop an alternative, leaving the state without any substantial regulatory measures. When Waite rejected the repeal bill, the legislature (with Populist support) overrode his veto. Afterward, the impatient governor compared the legislators unfavorably to Judas Iscariot, who at least "went out and hanged himself" following his transgression. The Populists' one substantial achievement involved their decisive support of a women's suffrage amendment that ultimately appeared on the 1893 ballot. If not for this, the legislative session would have been universally recognized as a complete fiasco.[28]

As the Populists began their push for reforms in the West, the national economy went into a sudden tailspin. The explanations for the collapse are complex, but most agree that it was connected to the combined effects of a stock market crash and increased gold transfers overseas in the year leading up to the crisis. The crash, which began in the first days of May, led to greater stress on the gold supply and fear that the banks could not make good on deposits. The Treasury's gold reserve was significantly affected by this withdrawal of specie, and depositors, bondholders, and investors seriously questioned the stability of the whole American finance system.[29]

President Cleveland attributed the calamity to a recent Republican sop to the silver heretics: the Sherman Silver Purchase Act. Passed in 1890, the act required the monthly purchase of 4 million ounces of silver by the federal government at the market price and the subsequent issue of silver certificates backed by the white metal. But the certificates were imperfect; they could be exchanged for gold at any time, and given that gold was rapidly leaving the reserve, this created just one more strain on the system. Cleveland had railed against silver for months, and he had already declared his interest in repealing the law. Eastern business leaders and financiers had fed his suspicion of the act, and when the Panic of 1893 struck, he wasted little time assigning the blame. When the president called for a special session of Congress to convene in August, everyone understood his intent.[30]

All westerners who were committed to the cause of silver currency united to oppose the president. At a Denver convention of silver advocates, Davis Waite delivered his famous "Bloody Bridles" speech, in which he told his audience that the president's proposal would be yet another act of barbarity by "monarch and monopoly against the right of the people to self-government."[31] Those who considered Waite a wide-eyed radical could merely dismiss his remarks, but the response by the venerable Henry Teller could not be so easily ignored. In Patterson's *Rocky Mountain News* under the headline "Traitorous," Teller warned that the gold monometallist position Cleveland hoped to force on the nation would work for the benefit of the "financiers of England." He declared the struggle for silver currency to be the "FIGHT FOR COMMERCIAL AND FINANCIAL INDEPENDENCE, FOR PROGRESS, PROSPERITY, FREEDOM AND HAPPINESS OF 99/100 OF THE RACE." He made no reference to local mining interests but instead defined the debate in terms similar to those used by many Populists—as a struggle between those who held wealth and influence and those who merely sought to maintain their economic independence.[32]

The threat to silver also served to unite westerners in Congress. Young Populists such as Senators Kyle of South Dakota and Allen of Nebraska used the event to draw attention to their cause, and this time the western press did not dismiss them as mere cranks.[33] Western Democrats joined the Populist cause against a Democratic president, and some even publicly accepted the Populists' conspiratorial analysis. William Roach, a freshman Democratic senator from North Dakota, agreed that "a conspiracy existed, and that it was known that agents of England were here to force this Government to issue bonds."[34] California's new Democratic senator, Stephen White, went on to make insinuations regarding several older members of Congress and agents of the money power. Although stern rebukes by Senators Hoar and Sherman led him to publicly disclaim his remarks, White later sent a letter to Teller to convince him of the story's veracity.[35]

It was in the midst of the debate over repeal that a new leader emerged. William Jennings Bryan had first become a member of the House of Representatives in 1891, but he did not study the money question seriously until he was about to enter his second term. Of course, it was certain from the beginning which side he would take. He would not speak in defense of a metal, but he defended a way of life that was threatened.[36] In what some considered the finest speech of the whole debate, Bryan provided both the material and the moral explanation of his position. For those who demanded sound

William Jennings Bryan. Courtesy of the Library of Congress

money, he said, there was no such thing. The value of both gold and silver had fluctuated wildly over the course of the last century and would continue to do so. Bryan's strongest contentions focused on the inherent rights of the people. In reply to a congressman from Massachusetts who suggested that "the money loaner was entitled to the advantages derived from improved machinery and inventive genius," Bryan said, "He is mistaken. The laboring man and the producer are entitled to these benefits." American democracy was a pointless exercise if government did not express the popular will, and surely "free government can not long survive when the thousands enjoy the wealth of the country and the millions share its poverty in common. Even now you hear among the rich an occasionally expressed contempt for popular government." Bryan concluded by stating, "We have come to the parting of the ways":

On one side stand the corporate interests of the nation, its money institutions, its aggregations of wealth and capital, imperious, arrogant, compassionless. They demand special legislation, favors, privileges, and immunities. . . . On the other side stands that unnumbered throng. . . . Work-worn and dust-begrimed, they make their sad appeal. They *hear* of *average* wealth increased on every side and *feel* the *inequality* of its distribution. They see an overproduction of everything desired because of the underproduction of the ability to buy.[37]

As was common among the bimetallists, Bryan came to view the currency question as an aspect of the conflict between producers and predatory wealth. Whereas monometallists spoke as if the gold standard were neutral or natural, Bryan understood money to be a creation of humankind and that its form and function had a real-world impact that could not be ignored.

It was for this reason that many Populists came to view Bryan as one of their own. The core of Populist ideology did not stem from their views of the railroad or silver or any other tangible thing. Populist thought began with the premise that the industrial economy must be responsive to the popular will and the needs of "the people." Although some westerners thought primarily of the boon to regional development that would come with free silver, Bryan and many other western Democrats and Republicans recognized an aspect of the issue akin to the Populist understanding of it. The widespread adoption of this cause set in motion the chain of events that led to Bryan's nomination by three parties in the 1896 presidential race.

In a few short years, Bryan would lead a movement for reform, but in 1893, Cleveland still held the upper hand. Before his inauguration, a majority of congressmen had declared their support for free silver. But that was before the economy went into a free fall. Cleveland also plied undecided legislators with the promise of patronage. Less than two weeks after Bryan's speech, the House overwhelmingly passed the repeal bill by a vote of 239 to 108. Despite greater challenges in the Senate, it passed there by a vote of 48 to 37. Two-thirds of Republicans supported the bill, while the Democrats were evenly split. Westerners almost unanimously opposed repeal, and section was more significant than party in settling the results. Cleveland signed the repeal bill into law on November 1. It was a masterful job of political management by the president, but his victory seemed to confirm the suspicions of those who claimed that the American political system failed to represent the voting public.[38]

Cleveland believed that normal business would resume after the repeal was secured. In spite of this optimism, his predictions proved false. Worried by the dwindling gold reserve, the president ordered huge bond sales—equaling more than $200 million—between early 1894 and the first months of 1896, without the consent of Congress.[39] Although the fall in stock prices ceased, economic activity remained stunted for the rest of the year and would not return to normal levels for several years.

The depression unleashed the pent-up discontent of the 1890s. Labor clashed with capital in a way not seen since the 1870s, and sites in the West were not excluded. In the gold mining districts around Cripple Creek, Colorado, late 1893 saw a struggle between owners and members of the newly organized Western Federation of Miners over the latter's demands for uniform wages and an eight-hour workday. As the confrontation continued into the spring of 1894, some mine owners gave in to the demands, while others considered the use of force. In May, with the financial backing of the mine owners, the El Paso County sheriff gathered a force of 1,200 armed men to drive off the strikers. When the outbreak of violence appeared imminent, Governor Waite ordered the strikers to lay down their arms, but he also declared the sheriff's army to be illegal and ordered it to disperse. The governor acted for the miners in negotiations with several owners, and he eventually called in the National Guard to hold back and then disarm the deputies. With this act, the Populists gained the loyal support of organized labor in the state.[40]

The state conventions of 1894 showed that, despite the growing significance of national issues, local concerns continued to shape the course of events. In Colorado, Governor Waite himself became the issue of the day. His support of the miners got a mixed reception outside of labor circles, and his use of the National Guard in a Denver patronage dispute and his proposal to coin the state's silver in Mexico caused some to see him as unhinged. Despite the many questions raised by moderate Populists regarding Waite's temperament and Tom Patterson's attempts to bump him from the ticket, ultimately, the governor's support among laborers made him impossible to replace. Patterson and the *Rocky Mountain News* endorsed the entire Populist slate with the exception of Waite, but the Democrats refused fusion under any terms. Charles S. Thomas, Patterson's former law partner, was nominated by the Democrats, but he received little attention during the campaign. Republicans selected an obscure judge, A. W. McIntire, for the governorship and devoted their campaign to the divisive Waite administration—even blaming him for the depressed local economy while ignoring the national crisis.[41]

While fusion hopes died early in Colorado, it was finally given an opportunity in Nebraska. Interestingly, the chain of events that contributed to the alliance may have been initiated by the Republicans. When their convention nominated Thomas J. Majors for governor—a man suspected of corruption and believed to be a member of the nativist American Protective Association—prominent GOP editor Edward Rosewater of the *Omaha Bee* left the convention and temporarily abandoned his party. Before the other party conventions took place, Rosewater let it be known that he would support a Populist judge, Silas A. Holcomb. The Populist convention gave Holcomb the nomination on the first ballot when it met just days later. When it was the Democrats' turn to nominate, Bryan added Holcomb to the list of candidates, and he was quickly accepted by the delegates. It was the perfect year for Bryan to pull off the fusion arrangement he had been contemplating, as evidenced by his recent placement of key allies into prominent party positions. The Republicans simply did him the favor of nominating a candidate who offended both sides of the newly minted fusion alliance.[42]

Washington State's executive officers were elected to four-year terms, so instead of centering on a gubernatorial race, the campaign there focused on the state legislature and the two US House seats (which were elected at large in statewide contests). Still, the depression and the national policies of the two old parties provided an opening for the state's Populists. Although the main contests were for the state legislature, that body would have to elect a US senator (which the 1893 legislature had failed to do). In the 1894 contests, Populists put a greater emphasis on silver than they had in the past, yet they also continued to campaign in support of direct legislation. They also rejected growing talk of fusion, ruining the Democrats' hope of winning any significant offices. At the state Republican convention, Spokane lawyer and businessman George C. Turner eventually forced the convention to accept a free silver plank, and their campaign would revolve around their attempts to usurp the free silver issue and their denunciation of the Cleveland administration.[43]

Despite suggestions by historians that Populism was a movement born of economic decline and crisis (and thus was doomed by the return of "good times" later in the decade), the outcome of the 1894 elections suggests otherwise.[44] The results were determined more by tactical factors than by the state of the national economy. In Colorado, where the economy was in utter ruin, Populists were branded with the image of Waite, while Democrats were burdened by the presidency of Cleveland. The Populists garnered a substantial vote from organized labor in the state, but Republicans won the governorship and a majority in the state legislature based on support in the agricultural counties. In Nebraska, where Populists and Democrats had partially fused, Republicans linked them both with the increasingly unpopular president. The fusion candidate for governor, Silas Holcomb, managed to win a narrow victory, but the rest of the ticket fared poorly, and the legislature was again in Republican hands. Washington State Populists, in contrast, had never held power and had made no agreements with the other parties. As a consequence, the new party was defeated but actually made substantial gains throughout the state. Populists received more than one-third of the vote and now ranked ahead of Democrats in the state.[45]

Having achieved victory, the Republicans returned to business as usual. The legislatures of Nebraska and Colorado largely failed to pass any significant legislation, except for a subsidy for Nebraska's sugar beet refiners (which had previously been repealed by the Populists) and a Colorado act imposing harsh penalties for "train wrecking" (a law most likely to be used against striking workers).[46] In Washington, the legislative session was also dominated by conservatives, who succeeded in blocking railroad legislation. One notable piece of reform legislation did slip through, however. John Rankin Rogers, then a Populist member of the state house, authored a bill that would redistribute educational funds to districts based on the number of students in the district, essentially apportioning the money based on need rather than the wealth of the community. The bill was opposed by representatives from the wealthier urban counties, but popular support forced enough Republicans to vote for its passage.[47]

The Republicans' inability to pass substantive legislation should not be viewed as an indication of their indifference. Their lackluster record before the Populist emergence made the western Republicans vulnerable to reform advocates. Yet after the Populists proved to be a significant threat, regional Republicans tenaciously opposed any restraint on corporate power. At a fundamental level, to do otherwise would be to accept the Populist argument and reject their own model of development.

Though unable to support strong reform measures that threatened the region's capitalists, western Republicans were receptive on one front. By 1894–1895, nearly all western Republicans gave at least token support to silver. For some, such as Senator Henry Teller, silver was the key to wealth redistribution in America. For others, it was a convenient tool that could boost the region's economic base without directly challenging the powerful corporations that influenced state politics. Silver became so important to state parties in the West that one's availability for high office was directly related to advocacy of the cause. John Thurston, a prominent Nebraska Republican and railroad lawyer, proclaimed that the Republicans were the true silver party during his campaign tour of the state in 1894. He was rewarded months later when the legislature elected him to the state's vacant US Senate seat.[48] Colorado Populists and Democrats accused their US senator Edward Wolcott of being a gambler, a philanderer, and, worst of all, a corporation lawyer who was too favorably inclined toward big business. Despite the criticism, the Republican majority chose Wolcott on the first ballot, and they did so with the sole justification that he had always been a staunch advocate of free silver.[49] Washington's biannual fight for the Senate was not determined by the free silver debate, but those who were known advocates of the gold standard were rejected out of hand. The man selected, Congressman John L. Wilson, evaded questions on the subject and may have encouraged the circulation of rumors that he favored free coinage.[50] Western Republicans did not yet appreciate the danger that came with the creation of a silver consensus.

THE BATTLE OF STANDARDS

Among historians of Populism, 1896 is usually described as the year the movement collapsed. They suggest that Populists—particularly new converts and those who had only a partial understanding of the party's doctrines— were wooed by Bryan's dramatic oratory and fell under his spell, only to be destroyed. But fusion was not a new concept; nor were the fusionists somehow less "Populist" than those who opposed it. By creating a party that could legitimately champion silver at the national level, they changed the western political landscape and forced others to incorporate that view as well. Though they embraced a wide spectrum of reforms, money had been central to the movement's agenda from the beginning. Now it appeared that a majority of voters would be on their side. For most western Populists, 1896 was a year of opportunity, not a year of cataclysm.[51]

The growing sentiment in the West in favor of free silver created divisions within the old parties. Senator Teller and others began to insinuate that the Republican Party's refusal to accept currency reform would lead to their withdrawal from the organization. Despite these warnings, the man who was almost universally favored to receive the Republican nomination for president, Governor William McKinley of Ohio, had made his career straddling the monetary issue. He was better known for advocating (and in one case, authoring) a more traditional Republican economic policy: the

William McKinley. Courtesy of the Library of Congress

strong protective tariff. As events unfolded, however, McKinley and the head of his campaign, Mark Hanna, decided that some statement on the currency matter was necessary.[52]

The basic presumptions of many—and, for most western Republicans, their worst fears—were realized at the Republicans' St. Louis convention. The required majority of delegates was already committed to McKinley, and the single ballot taken on the final day of the convention was a mere formality. Earlier that day, a more genuine drama had played out on the convention stage. The monetary plank called for "sound money" and denounced "free coinage of silver, except by international agreement." It was as close to an unequivocal statement as anyone in the party cared to offer, and Teller would not stand for it. He offered the minority report as a substitute and begged the delegates to accept it; otherwise, he said, "I must, as an honest man, sever my connection" with the party. As he stood with tears streaming down his face, his request was rejected by the overwhelming majority. As he and other westerners walked out of the convention, they were hooted and heckled, with Hanna openly leading the worst of it. In expectation of such a bolt, Populist leaders were on hand to consult with the disaffected Republicans, and the two groups quickly decided to cooperate for the remainder of the campaign.[53]

Notwithstanding the departure of the silver men, the gathering in St. Louis was the most orderly of the three significant conventions of 1896. That of the Democrats—with the uncertainty that preceded it, the conflicts that defined it, and the energy that followed it—has received the most attention. But as the best recent scholars have emphasized, Bryan's selection was no accident, and the adoption of a free silver platform was just as inevitable as McKinley's nomination had been. The overwhelming majority of delegates from the West and the South supported silver, as did substantial numbers from the Midwest. Though the representatives from New York had been allowed to dictate the choice of candidate in years past, their control had already been broken.[54]

Bryan had long understood the possibilities available at the 1896 convention. With few truly established pro-silver party leaders, he perceived an opportunity for a dark horse to win the nomination. With this in mind, the Nebraskan wrangled a place for himself in the scheduled debate over the party's platform. It was his task to provide the final response to the arguments of the gold standard delegates. In his address he denied having any sectional animosity and then rebutted the statements of the gold men, who had asked the delegates to consider the impact silver would have on business. These same men had already "disturbed our business interests," he claimed, for the "business man" who worked for wages or farmed had an equal right to profit from his own labor as any financier or industrialist had. The financial policies of the East had placed that region's benefit over the good of all others. To the man who said he feared the coming of a Robespierre, Bryan declared, "What we need is an Andrew Jackson, to stand, as Jackson stood, against the encroachments of organized wealth." He attacked the national banking system and stated that "the banks ought to go out of the governing business." He then tore apart the Republican plank that suggested "bimetallism is good, but that we cannot have it until other nations help us." By the time he laid an imaginary crown of thorns upon his own head, Bryan had explained why the nation must strike out on its own to create a system under which farmers and laborers could prosper.[55]

While the speech brought a thunderous response from the convention in Chicago and allowed Bryan to secure the Democratic nomination, it also made him the logical candidate of the Populist Party. Populists had scheduled a late convention in the hope of collecting the bolters from the major party conventions, but the strategy backfired. Of course, some Populist leaders suspected that the Democrats would actively support silver currency, and a few of them had already been in communication with top Democrats. The Populists had advised them that silver advocates with a conservative streak would be unacceptable. Bryan's selection obviated any fear of that. He did not support government ownership of the railroads or the establishment of a subtreasury system, but he did believe that prosperity was illusory if those on the lowest rungs of society could not profit from their labor. As much as any Populist, he believed in popular control of the economy, and that was good enough.

At the Populist convention, the West and the South divided on the best option to take.[56] Westerners wanted Bryan and had no reservations about accepting him. Southerners, however, were hesitant to accept unconditional fusion with the Democrats. In this regard, it is difficult to define many of the key participants as representative of the "middle of the road" faction, as the antifusionists came to be known. Before the convention, Populist leaders had conferred with the Bryan camp about the selection of a vice presidential candidate. Bryan's Democratic running mate was Arthur Sewall, a wealthy shipbuilder from Maine, and neither Bryan nor Democratic campaign chairman James K. Jones wanted him to withdraw. Eventually, pressure from the southern wing of the Populists led to Bryan's nomination for president and a separate vice presidential nomination of Tom Watson, an ex-congressman from Georgia. This was done without Bryan's approval. The separate ticket was especially vital to those in the South who feared unconditional fusion with the Democrats. Even though a clear majority at the Populist convention demanded Bryan's presidential nomination, southerners believed that a separate ticket would allow them to maintain their party's independence. At the same time, all party leaders were sure that the party's rejection of Bryan would be deadlier to their movement than fusion.[57]

It was a strange solution for what would be a unique campaign. Bryan was left with two "vices"—as Republicans liked to joke—and eventually won the nomination from four parties—Democratic, Populist, Silver Republican, and National Silver. Despite the support from so many quarters, he was soon abandoned by many members of his own party. Democrats who remained committed to the gold standard (especially in the East and Midwest) formed the National Democratic Party and nominated the aging John M. Palmer for president. Their goal was not victory but to deprive Bryan of triumph. They claimed to control several hundred thousand votes right up to the time of the election, but if this were so, most of those voters apparently switched to McKinley in the end.[58]

Throughout much of the West, the popularity of Bryan's nomination aided fusion arrangements. Both Bryan and western Populist leaders favored this move, and Bryan tried to use his newfound influence in the West and South to encourage mutually beneficial arrangements. In Nebraska, Democrats and Populists agreed to a division of offices, and Silas Holcomb was renominated for governor. Despite their antifusion sentiment before 1896, Washington's Populists reluctantly accepted a division of offices as well. John Rankin Rogers was selected as the gubernatorial candidate, and the two US House seats were divided between the Democrats and the Silver Republicans.[59]

The situation was more complicated in Colorado, as it was throughout the Mountain West. There, nearly the entire Republican organization abandoned McKinley to support free silver. Thus, neither Bryan nor silver were useful in creating local fusion tickets. It was agreed that the Silver Republicans, Democrats, and Populists would support the same presidential electors, but it proved impossible to divide the other offices among the three parties. In the final arrangements, the state's Democrats and Republicans fused, nominating former Democratic governor Alva Adams for the highest state office. That left Patterson's Populists without a significant partner, while Waite led a die-hard antifusion Populist faction on yet another ticket. The "fusion" Populists nominated Morton Bailey, and Waite's backers chose him to run for governor yet again.[60]

Whatever the challenges of fusion, McKinley's Republican campaigners in the West were in an especially difficult position. Many had declared the necessity of free silver in the years leading up to 1896, but a few subsequently decided to completely reverse course and follow the party line. They issued statements that bimetallism would destroy wages, drive off international investment, and lead to a return of the worst conditions of the depression. Some admitted that free silver could provide aid to farmers but declared that this amounted to class legislation and the repudiation of debt—something they characterized as "dishonorable." Others suggested that those who favored silver were really in the employ of mine owners.[61]

Instead of walking back from their earlier support of free silver, many Republicans chose to read the party's platform literally. Some claimed that the problem with silver proposals involved the ratio of sixteen to one; others said the problem was the free coinage element, which would allow anyone to coin silver at the mint without limit.[62] But the most common statements focused on the fig leaf of international bimetallism—an arrangement that thinking people would have understood to be impossible. One newspaper, the *Colorado Springs Gazette*, actually made that very point but still backed Senator Edward Wolcott as he campaigned throughout the state preaching the necessity of an international agreement.[63] Senator John L. Wilson of Washington, who had previously been mute on the subject, said, "I am and always have been a bimetallist," but he also had "serious doubts as to the ability of the United States to maintain the free coinage of silver without the cooperation of at least two other great European commercial nations."[64] Silver proved to be a difficult issue to let go of.

The western Republicans' unwillingness to embrace the gold standard was a product of the political climate in the West. They understood as well as their opponents did the appeal of reform, and if not for silver, they would have had little to offer farmers and miners of their region. The Democrats, Populists, and breakaway Republicans, however, did not allow the claims of McKinley's supporters to stand.[65] Most observed that no eastern paper (regardless of affiliation) had taken the international bimetallism plank seriously, and they also noted that McKinley had said so little on the subject that there was no reason to believe he wanted it.[66]

For westerners, the results of the election were remarkable on all counts. Reform coalitions that included Populists swept all major offices in Nebraska and Washington, as well as in Idaho, Kansas, Montana, and South Dakota; reform candidates also won sixteen of those states' US House seats. In Colorado, Populist-backed congressmen John Calhoun Bell (Populist) and John Shafroth (Silver Republican) also won easily. However, Populists found no success in Colorado's state elections. Democrat Alva Adams defeated the primary Populist candidate by more than 15,000 votes. Still, the Populists managed to gain nearly 40 percent of the total vote. As soon as the Republican-Democratic coalition broke down, as it inevitably would, Colorado's labor vote would emerge as the largest bloc in the state. Even if reform was stalled in the Centennial State, the general outlook in the West was promising.[67]

Yet the Populists' overarching goal proved just beyond their reach. Bryan's whirlwind campaign through the Midwest and East became legendary, but ultimately, he could not overcome the wealth arrayed against him and certain geographic obstacles. Just as he would have expected, Bryan won the electoral votes everywhere the Populists held a substantial statewide presence. Of the states that had entered the union after 1860, he lost only North Dakota. To these victories he added the states of the solid South. But outside of these regions, he had no success. The strength of the old parties and their old ideas remained largely unchallenged in the Midwest and Northeast, and although Bryan had drawn large audiences, he not could totally reshape the political balance of these states in a matter of mere weeks.[68]

Still, Bryan's defeat in 1896 would not be the final word on reform. He certainly indicated as much when he titled his account of the campaign *The First Battle*. Bryan (somewhat arrogantly) viewed the fight for silver in 1896 as the opening engagement in a struggle against accumulated wealth. He donated the proceeds of the book to his allies, including leaders of the Populists, so that they might use the funds to strengthen their organizations. He did not believe that his defeat in 1896, or the fusion arrangement that had brought him so close to victory, would destroy the movement for reform.[69]

In this regard, his views were shared by many in the West. There, few Populists believed their party was on the verge of collapse in late 1896. In the immediate aftermath, even a southern Populist like Marion Butler could predict that in four years' time the Populists would be the core around which the forces of reform would coalesce. In fact, over the next two years, western Populists frequently expressed their belief that either the Democratic Party would collapse and a new party would take its place or, failing that, all reformers would voluntarily join the Populists. Their predictions were based on a few assumptions. First, when the powerful leaders of the gold Democrats returned to the fold, Populists believed that Bryan and others like him would be forced to either compromise on reform or abandon the organization. Populists also remembered the strife created by fusion, and they believed a new party would streamline reform without the necessity of awkward multiparty arrangements. Though southern Populists struggled to maintain their independence in the wake of the contest, the movement in the West could continue unabated.[70]

Of course, failure to enact reform once Populists took office could also prove fatal to the movement. This was especially true in Nebraska and Washington, where Populists held the governorships and pluralities in the legislatures. In Colorado—where Populists held only about one-third of the legislative seats, a Democrat had been elected governor without their aid, and the laborers they represented had not yet formed an effective lobby—any hope of reform proved illusory.[71]

In Washington, the session began with a typical fight over the Senate seat. Populists had hoped to elect one of their own but remained divided on the candidate. Governor Rogers acted as if he were neutral, but he had a man in mind and applied light pressure at the right moment. The less partisan Populists eventually joined with Silver Republicans and Democrats to elect George C. Turner, a Silver Republican from Spokane with a solid reform record. He was a former justice of the territorial supreme court with a record of ruling against the railroads; during the ARU strike in the summer of 1894, he had even advocated government ownership of the railroads and control of all "natural monopolies." As leader of the state's Silver Republicans, his selection also gave Rogers a powerful ally as he attempted to forge a permanent coalition.[72]

The bickering and disputes that had characterized all first-term Populist legislatures plagued Washington lawmakers in 1897, but they managed to compile a solid record in spite of themselves. The loudest complaints came from mid-roaders, who were angry that Rogers had awarded offices to Democrats and Silver Republicans. This group proved to be obnoxious during the entire session, and they even killed a bill to create a commission to oversee the state's railroads. Despite this failure, coalition legislators managed some significant accomplishments. They passed a workers' lien law, authorized a system for mine and factory inspections, restricted wage garnishment, and established a state bureau of labor. They also passed a railroad rate law, but the reductions were modest, and without a railroad commission, enforcement of the law could be held up through judicial injunctions. Still, when compared with its predecessors, the 1897 session accomplished a great deal.[73]

At the twenty-fifth session of the Nebraska legislature, Populists and Democrats managed to assemble a respectable record. They passed new stockyards regulations, abolished the bounty for the manufacture of beet sugar, and passed a municipal referendum law. To these they added three laws designed to outlaw trusts and combinations in restraint of trade. A local company found to be a trust would forfeit its charter of incorporation; a business chartered out of state could find itself completely banned from operations within Nebraska's borders. Although the failure of a bill forbidding free railroad passes for public officials diminished the legislators' image, their successes represented a dramatic transformation in the politics of the state from the time of the party's founding.[74]

During the 1890s the struggle for reform in the West was a difficult one, but the Populists changed all that. Not so long before, the region had been a bastion of conservatism. The Republican establishment emphasized that pro-business policies were a vital part of regional development, and many voters likewise linked western prosperity with the protection of opportunities for eastern investment. That, along with a healthy dose of national patronage, had entrenched the Republican Party throughout the region. The Democrats of the West were strictly a laissez-faire party, breaking with this trend only to give occasional lip service to the needs of frustrated laborers. Their campaigns were fought largely on cultural grounds, not on matters of political economy. Neither Republicans nor Democrats were prepared to become vehicles for substantive reform agendas, and neither were responsive as the voters grew restless.

The emergence of a new party dramatically shifted the region's political landscape. As the Populists overtook them in some states and threatened their position in others, Democrats with a more expansive view of government's role soon rose to prominence in local parties. Republicans, too, adapted to an extent, eventually placing a renewed emphasis on free silver coinage as an economic remedy to the region's ills. These transformations were necessary precursors to Democratic-Populist fusion campaigns and, ultimately, William Jennings Bryan's nomination by the national Democratic Party in 1896. Regional Republican parties fractured over the coinage issue, adding to the western fusion coalition. The fusion victories in much of the West provided consolation to those dejected by Bryan's defeat.

The foundation for a long-term reform movement appeared to be set. Populists, Democrats, and Silver Republicans held office throughout the region. Despite squabbles, they succeeded in enacting the most significant local regulatory legislation in the region's history. State executives also offered the kind of protection to labor unheard of in previous years. Bryan's loss was painful for those who had united to support him, but he appeared set to use his base in the West to launch another campaign in four years' time.

In early 1897 there were only subtle hints that something new was on the horizon. In the Nebraska legislature, a Populist in the state house named Addison Sheldon introduced a resolution in praise of the people of Cuba, who were "now struggling to free themselves from 400 years of Spanish misrule, oppression, and cruelty." It went on to say that all citizens hoped "the day may soon dawn when Cuba shall be free and European domination and intrigue shall be banished from American soil." To that end, the resolution asked the president and Congress to take action on Cuba's behalf, and it was adopted with little debate.[75] Such discussions were taking place in state legislatures nationwide, just as they were occurring with increasing frequency in the halls of Congress, in the national press, and undoubtedly among ordinary citizens as well.[76] Those like Sheldon who hoped to bring change to the country could not have fathomed what was to come.

3. THE MONEY POWER AND THE WAR OF 1898

By the beginning of 1898, Spain's war to maintain control over Cuba had been raging for three years. McKinley's cautious dealings with Spain had left many exasperated. Western Populists, Democrats, and Silver Republicans were some of the most vocal advocates of Cuban independence, and these enemies of the administration thought they understood the source of the president's hesitance. Frank Cannon of Utah, part of the close cohort of Silver Republicans in the US Senate, outlined the western reformers' view of the administration's position:

> If there be any policy on the part of the United States, it is one of affiliation with this movement, by which Spain shall be enabled to saddle upon Cuba the vast mass of debt incurred in the vain endeavor to conquer that island. . . . Mr. President, I charge now that the purpose of the Administration in delaying action is in consonance with, if not in direct copartnership with the will of the Spanish bondholders.[1]

As the debate raged on over Cuba, many Populists, Democrats, and Silver Republicans became increasingly certain that greater forces were at work.

Western reformers made their presence felt in the Fifty-Fifth Congress. Their numbers were not inconsequential: fourteen in the Senate and twenty-five in the House.[2] In the Senate, no one party held the majority, so the power of such a coalition could be magnified.[3] Although the cooperative effort among them was certainly new and fragile, administration policies began to drive many of these westerners closer together. In their eyes, McKinley's positions were exclusively favorable to moneylenders and large corporations at the expense of the producing classes. The second session of Congress had even begun with a proposal by Secretary of the Treasury Lyman Gage to "commit the country more thoroughly to the gold standard," reigniting the smoldering embers of 1896.[4]

Suspicion of the administration grew as the session went on, eventually encompassing McKinley's foreign policy as well. It would be inaccurate to suggest that westerners' frustration spilled over into their interpretations of foreign affairs; Populists especially had always believed that the forces behind international finance held sway throughout the world. By 1898, however, increasing numbers of westerners were arguing that a handful of economic elites constituted the driving force behind American foreign policy. It was this belief that led them to criticize McKinley's inaction early in the year, and that same belief remained at the core of their later critique of American empire.

MCKINLEY AND THE MONEY POWER

McKinley's complete alienation of the western reform delegation in Congress began shortly after he assumed office. Despite the plank in favor of international bimetallism that was part of his campaign, the president immediately denounced the policy in his inaugural address. He also spoke of the "embarrassment" caused by the "several forms of paper money," then stated a desire to withdraw certain notes from circulation.[5] His choice as secretary of the treasury, Chicago banker Lyman Gage, was a vocal gold advocate. Even before he was sworn into office, Gage had told members of the press about his plan to retire greenbacks and treasury notes and institute more flexible rules pertaining to the amount of backing national banks required for their own paper notes. The reaction in the West was overwhelmingly negative, and even the staunchly Republican *Omaha Bee* called Gage's plan to remove certain federal notes from circulation "unpopular and disappointing" and likely to cause currency contraction.[6]

The short session after McKinley's inauguration provided no time for such proposals, but in the middle of December 1897 Gage presented his plan to members of the House Committee on Banking and Currency. Despite the earlier criticism heaped on his proposals, the bill he brought to the House seemed even more extreme. Gage opened by stating that he intended to "commit the country more thoroughly to the gold standard . . . and thus strengthen the credit of the United States both at home and abroad." Next, he called for a reduction of the Treasury's "demand liabilities, in which are included greenbacks, Treasury notes, and the incidental obligation to maintain on a parity, through interchangeability with gold . . . the present large volume of silver certificates and silver dollars." In total, the bill authorized the resumption of $200 million worth of currency, to be paid for in gold obtained through a massive sale of bonds. In trying to justify this most controversial provision, even Gage admitted that the plan involved "a contraction of the currency at this time so violent that nobody could endure it." But Gage believed that by loosening restrictions on the national banks, privately issued currency could take the place of greenbacks.[7]

Again, the reaction from the West was overwhelmingly negative. A few orthodox Republicans looked forward to the entrenchment of hard money, but even some of them feared the consequences of this plan. Weighing the merits of Gage's bill, a writer for the Omaha Bee argued that it would "strengthen the treasury in relation to demand liabilities," but "in regard to contracting the circulation it is by no means certain that this would be avoided."[8] Of course, Populists and their allies were vehemently opposed to the plan, which in their eyes would entrench the gold standard, supplement the power of the national banks, and increase government debt for the benefit of moneylenders. Suggesting that the great issue of 1896 would again determine the contest in 1900, the editor of the Yakima Herald reminded farmers of the consequences of such legislation: "the single gold standard means contraction of the currency, increase of our interest bearing debt, and yet greater reduction in the price of the products of your labor." Embracing the coalition's calls for national rejuvenation, he asked readers to "hold patriotism above party and choose as becomes a free born American citizen."[9]

Opposition in Congress was just as fierce. William Allen, Nebraska's Populist senator, was certain that—if given the power to do so—the national banks would ruin the economy for their own gain. "They would be guided solely by the consideration whether they would make money by contraction or expansion, and thus the power would be placed in their hands to contract the volume of money and thereby throw millions out of employment, shrink the value of property to a point where they might buy it for one-half, or less." Giving private banks the power to issue currency was a threat to representative government. Already, Allen claimed, "the money power dominates every branch of the Government. . . . It is a government by the few and for the few." If the president had his way, and private banks managed the economy as they saw fit, "it would be but a comparatively short time until the masses would be practically deprived of their right to vote or to participate in the Government in any form, and we would pass from the semblance of a Republic into a complete aristocracy."[10]

Nearly every portion of the proposed monetary reform was offensive to western reformers, but they focused on the issue of bonds. Bonds were, after all, the linchpin of Gage's plan. No government-issued currency could be retired without bonds to maintain the federal gold reserve, and the repayment of bonded debt in gold would further commit the nation to the gold standard.[11] Fearing that the Treasury would adopt that policy regardless of legislation, Senator Teller proposed a resolution declaring that any federal bonds were payable in silver, at the option of the government. Western reformers in Congress came out in force to defend Teller's resolution and attack the system advocated by the administration.[12]

When he took to the floor of the Senate in support of his own measure, Teller accosted the Republicans for claiming to support international bimetallism during the 1896 campaign and them immediately abandoning it. True, he admitted, a commission had been sent to Europe to negotiate with the other major financial powers in 1897, but Gage's remarks had guaranteed its failure. This was no accident. "We knew that the power which created this Administration would not let it back out if it wanted to; we knew that the power which created it would control it; and we knew it would control it for the gold standard." Shifting tack, Teller now claimed that the same forces were also in command of American foreign policy. "The money power is the great power that has been felt all over the world. . . . It is the power that allows the wickedest war that was ever carried on against men to be carried on in sight of our shores, because it is feared that to do otherwise would disturb commerce and trade." Because of the influence of the greedy few, "the maintenance of a steady market for stocks and bonds render it impossible for the American people to assert their manhood."[13] Independent men saw the situation in Cuba and knew what justice required, but the money power stalled any action in Congress.

Teller voiced a belief that was rapidly gaining favor in Congress: the president was completely under the spell of the money power. While the administration's monetary reforms sputtered and died, those who already distrusted McKinley were making up their minds. Another Silver Republican, Senator Richard Pettigrew of South Dakota, told a close friend that "McKinley has absolutely gone over to the gamblers of Wall Street." The senator had even come to despise McKinley more than the previous chief executive. "Cleveland had something of a brutal tenacity and corrupt independence about him that stamped him as an individual," he said, "but this jellyfish of a fellow has none of these qualities, which marks him as possessed of no element of manhood."[14] The commander in chief was seen as little more than a tool for

Senator Henry M. Teller. Courtesy of the Library of Congress

the powerful. Westerners believed he was in no position to stand up for the oppressed in his own country or in any other.

CUBA, COLONIALISM, AND WAR

Populists and their allies increasingly viewed the actions of McKinley with skepticism. As Teller's statements made clear, the president's foreign policy was certainly not exempt from their suspicion. However, the complexity of their views of the Cuban issue must be understood in order to determine the connection between the western reformers and American intervention. Un-

like the stereotypical depiction of them, it was not with a "whoop and a holler" that ignorant Populists unleashed their pent-up frustrations.[15] Instead,
their interest in the Cuban issue had much deeper roots, and the course they
pursued vis-à-vis the Cuban crisis was influenced by the broad elements of
their worldview and their distrust of the administration.

Up to 1898, neither the Populists nor their western allies had developed
a cohesive analysis of colonialism or imperialism. That is not to say they
did not care about events overseas; in fact, the Populists frequently referenced world affairs in their tracts and speeches. However, as they discussed
Europe's colonial policies, their real purpose was always to illustrate points
about issues closer to home. For example, when they noted that Egypt's
debt to London banks had been the justification for the British attack and
takeover of that country, they were just pointing out the dangers of owing
perpetual obligations to European financiers.[16] And when India closed its
mints to silver in 1893, Populist statements attributed the policy shift to the
money power's desire to strangle the producers of South Asia and America
for the benefit of Britain's trade balance sheet.[17] Populist papers were also
littered with cartoons lampooning the failures of colonial powers or pointing
to European attempts to dominate the free peoples of the world.[18] Of course,
nearly all these remarks and images suggested that empires were often brutal
in their treatment of subject peoples, but this should not be misconstrued as
a unified critique of colonialism.

Cuba's war for independence became a watershed moment, forcing large
numbers of Populists and western reformers to intellectualize the meaning
of empire. A few took to the rebel cause almost immediately, within months
of the first shots being fired in early 1895. In December of that year, Senator
Allen delivered a speech that explained both his sympathy for the Cubans
and his vision of American internationalism. Allen contended that it was
"the true policy and the true doctrine of our country that wherever a people
show themselves desirous of establishing a republican form of government
upon any territory adjacent to us they should receive our encouragement
and support." Although he suggested that American strategic interests in the
Caribbean should shape policy as well, he argued that America must not "be
possessed of greed for territory, or the glories of conquest." He believed the
Cubans wanted genuine independence and proposed a resolution calling for
the swift recognition of the revolutionary government. Recognition would
grant the Cubans certain rights, such as the right to purchase arms from
a neutral power and thus win freedom for themselves. Despite the misgivings of some—namely, that the Cubans "are not of our race or tongue"—he

thought "it ought to be sufficient for us to know that they belong to a race of people who are striving for liberty."[19] Allen's statements seem remarkable when contrasted with the bombast coming from Senate Republicans. Just a few months later, Henry Cabot Lodge would deliver a speech that listed the strategic benefits of Cuban annexation and highlighted the racial logic of a war with Spain.[20] The Populist Allen, however, called for a foreign policy that combined national interest with American ideals.

Shortly after the outbreak of war in Cuba, media outlets of every size began covering the conflict with unusual ardor, and public speakers and reformers of all stripes soon joined the fray as well. While typical accounts have covered the Pulitzer-Hearst rivalry in New York, newspaper coverage was just as thorough in the West. Western newspapers began reporting on the revolution within days of its outbreak, and soon stunning headlines were dotting the pages of nearly every small-town weekly in the region.[21] Articles titled "The Cruel Spaniard" and "Butcheries in Cuba" described atrocities that were all but guaranteed to make readers' blood boil.[22] After a pause in the summer of 1896, the stories resumed with even greater intensity, just after Spain initiated its "reconcentration" policy in Cuba.[23] By late 1897, bloody outrages were so easily attributable to the Spanish that when the *New York World* published an article claiming that one general was responsible for more than 400,000 Cuban deaths (out of a population of 1.5 million), the *Spokane Daily Chronicle* found it creditable enough to reprint.[24]

The outrageous stories of atrocities in Cuba must be put in context. Most frequently, academics have classed the American response to events in Cuba into one of three categories: as a xenophobic reaction against Catholic, monarchical Spain; as parochial excitement whipped to a frenzy by the yellow press; or as an opportunity to exert national power.[25] Although these explanations suggest that the sympathy of common Americans was irrational or misguided, it should be kept in mind that real atrocities were happening in Cuba, and there was nearly as much truth in the accounts as exaggeration. One recent historian has pointed out that Spain's *reconcentrado* policy was responsible for the death of at least 100,000 people, and he considers 150,000—or one-tenth of the island's population—to be closer to the full truth.[26] Ultimately, public response to the stories coming out of Cuba spurred the country to action, but not all the sentiment should be considered unreasonable.

In the halls of Congress and in the media, there was often a partisan tone to critiques of the administration's Cuba policies. When Cleveland held office, the majority of criticism came from Republicans and Populists.

Later, following Bryan's rebuke of the administration in the summer of 1896 and, later, McKinley's victory, Democrats and Populists joined together to attack the policy of inaction. The new alignment also followed the divide that appeared during the "battle of standards." McKinley initially continued Cleveland's policy of nonintervention, denying the Cubans recognition while ordering the capture of any ships carrying contraband to the rebels. Popularly, these actions came to be seen as a show of callous disregard for the plight of a suffering people. As they sought to explain the apparent indifference of the two administrations, western reformers attributed this timidity to vested economic interests.

The most moderate of the Bryanites found fault with those who put commerce above all else and simply accused their rivals of possessing improper priorities. The *Aspen Daily Times*, for example, censured the president for refusing to do more to protect Americans imprisoned by the Spanish in Cuba. It attributed the dithering tendencies of the McKinley administration to "conservative business interests which have dominated bygone administrations" and "an incredible degree of cowardice in the department of state."[27] Editors of the *Omaha World-Herald*, a Democratic paper run by a close Bryan ally, described the situation in much the same way. By May 1897, they excoriated the Republicans for ignoring their party's 1896 platform, which had vowed more forceful action in favor of the Cubans. The difference between the party's promises and its actions was attributable to "cowardly leaders who are brave in the face of trembling and cowering humanity and terror stricken in the face of Wall Street influence."[28] In a later piece, the editor attacked a conservative paper for supporting Secretary Gage's assessment that talk of war "would quickly drain the treasury of its gold" and, worse yet, embolden the supporters of the free coinage of silver. The *World-Herald* writer noted that this was an example of "commercialism once more demanding that it be favored at the expense of justice and humanity." It was heartless to support the "oppression of patriots striving for liberty in order to maintain the gold reserve."[29] Although this attribution of inaction to greed was harsh, the comments of moderates paled in comparison to the statements of their more radical colleagues.

Some bellicose reformers began depicting the rebellion in Cuba as a conflict with the same great power facing America. William "Coin" Harvey laid out the global reach of predatory finance in one 1895 speech. He opened his address by telling the audience that a growing awareness of the immoral structure of finance was about to transform human societies. "Hope, comfort, and relief are coming. Manhood in this country is again going to be revived. We are going to force this country by the shere [sic] influence of intelligence to cease its worship of property and money as of greater value than humanity." This movement was not only national but global. "To-day liberty is appealing to us from all over the world. Cuba is to-day striking for liberty against the oppressor, Spain. . . . It is to liberate those people, it is to end their oppression that comes with your money power, that the liberty-loving people of Cuba are to-day striking for liberty." He believed the United States should have already recognized the Cuban revolutionaries and that by refusing to do so, "The president of the United States, the willing implement of the money power and tyranny and oppression, has given every assistance to Spain." According to Harvey's characterization of the money power, "The tail of that serpent rests in Egypt and India, its body in Europe, and its head is raised in this country." Essentially, he argued that colonialism was a product of the financial and political power wielded by an elite clique and that the United States (or a portion of it) was in much the same position as others on the global periphery. Harvey concluded, "We need a second declaration of independence in the United States."[30] In their attempt to liberate themselves from the political and economic domination of Europe, the Cubans were only doing what America should have done already.

Few developed such an elaborate picture of how the revolution in Cuba represented the fight against economic domination, but some saw presidential indifference as evidence of the money power's influence. The editor of Washington State's *Aberdeen Herald* used it to remind readers of the executive's real priorities:

Patriots at our very doors may be massacred in cold blood, Liberty and Freedom may plead in vain for recognition, the shrieks of murdered women and children may not move the hearts of the powers at Washington, but all this is being stored up in the memory of the American people who are not wedded to the worship of Mammon and will be brought forth and used in crushing rebuke to those who are, now in the great hour of need, unmoved by the slaughter in the fair island of Cuba, so say nothing of the want and misery in their own land.

Could Americans still recognize right, the author asked, or "will the next four years more firmly fix their fetters and subjugate them to the money power?"[31]

The employment of the money power conspiracy to explain American inaction was common throughout the West. Colorado newspapers were filled with editorials to that effect throughout 1896 and 1897. The *Aspen Tribune* claimed that even though the public and Congress favored Cuban independence, "the administration is representing the money power, which isn't patriotic," and in the contest between democracy and wealth, "the money power always wins."[32] A few months later, the *Ouray Herald* reminded readers of the broken promises of the Republican president. "Bloody deeds indescribable in horrid cruelty have been of daily, hourly occurance [sic] for two years. McKinley knows it; the money power knows it. The former may be in sympathy with the wishes of the masses but his Cuban policy thus far allies him with the money power which opposes intervention and consequent, perhaps, trouble with Spain."[33] Worse yet, suggested the *Silverton Standard*, the tendency of the money power to strangle American manhood had forestalled any national action. "The sympathy of American manhood is with her [Cuba] in her struggle, but the hand of that arch enemy of liberty, goldocracy is upon the throat of American manhood, and it is powerless to act." The author ended by stating, "The Cuban patriots will pass through fire and blood to freedom from Spanish tyranny long before the boasted free American will shake off the degraded manacles doubly riveted upon his limbs by the trusts, combines and aggregated capital of his country."[34] The money power would continue to restrain American manhood, while the Cubans demonstrated their freedom from the money power by fighting for liberty.

Talk of the money power's influence spread in unexpected ways. The general American public was not alone in its growing frustration with the president. The Cuban junta, operating out of New York, helped spread the message of the revolutionaries throughout the United States, but its members may well have been responding to the American media in late 1897, when the American secretary of the junta issued a letter to McKinley and made the contents available to the press. The junta claimed that the American government had stymied its efforts to fight through measures such as the US Coast Guard's antifilibustering patrols, without which "the patriots would be further advanced in their struggle." More damningly, the junta declared, "A majority of the people of this country desire to see a free and independent Cuban republic. An opposing factor of great force is the money power." The secretary elaborated, stating "that a majority of our people believe that the assistance of our Government till now has been given to Spain and withheld from the republic on account of the influence that emanates from great financial interests."[35] When it adopted the language used by the reformers, the junta reinforced the economic analysis that westerners were keen to embrace.

Senator William V. Allen. From Stanley Waterloo and John Wesley Hanson Jr., eds., Famous American Men and Women: A Complete Portrait Gallery of Celebrated People *[Chicago: Wabash Publishing House, 1896], 117*

By the opening of the second session of the Fifty-Fifth Congress, western reformers were more committed than ever to recognizing the Cuban republic. Speeches detailing the devastation of the island became a near-daily occurrence in one house of Congress or the other. Although most still favored nothing more than recognition, some wanted more direct involvement. When McKinley declared in his December 1897 message to Congress that recognition of the Cubans was "unwise and therefore inadmissible," Senator Allen detailed his frustration. The Populist senator stated that he "would not be content or satisfied with a simple acknowledgment of the belligerent rights of the people of that island, but I would demand absolute and unconditional political liberty and a recognition of the government they themselves have formed and to whose sovereignty they owe allegiance." Allen was certain of the justice of the Cuban struggle, and he expressed his frustration in his explanation of the administration's inaction:

> Unfortunately for the advancement and elevation of the human race and for the glory of our country, we have entered an era of cold and merciless commercialism that freezes the blood of patriotism in its veins and that is willing to sacrifice human rights, the honor of women, and the lives of children, if need be, that the course of business may not be checked. . . . If I should be asked what I mean by this expression, I would answer without hesitation that the owners of Spanish bonds in this country . . . and the carrying trade and the commercial interests of the world . . . have joined to prevent Cuban recognition, and their influence is sufficiently powerful in official circles to prevent anything further being done in the interest of those unfortunate people.[36]

It was the profit seekers who had stayed the president's hand.

Allen's talk of Spanish bonds would not have surprised western advocates of reform.[37] Since shortly after the start of the war, business-oriented newspapers like the *New York Times* and regional papers like the *Omaha Bee* had been reporting on the financial standing of special Spanish bonds backed by revenue from Cuba. A report by the *Times* in early 1898 even predicted that the war in Cuba would end if Spain could guarantee repayment—perhaps with American backing.[38] It should be pointed out that when Allen attacked those who were allegedly protecting the value of these Spanish bonds, he avoided any overtly conspiratorial language. Yet, given the extent to which bonds played a central role in the conspiratorial writing of Sarah Emery and in other texts of the genre, he may not have needed to spell it out.[39] When he suggested that those expressing indifference to the freedom of Cuba were doing so at the behest of bondholders, many Populists, Democrats, and Silver Republicans knew that they were facing their old enemies on yet another front.

Following Allen's lead, two Populists in the House attacked the president's policy, but this time they put a clearer emphasis on a single enemy. Congressman Jerry Simpson of Kansas connected the hesitancy of the current administration with that of its predecessor and, ultimately, to the financiers. Why, he asked, had Cleveland been so unwilling to acknowledge Cuban belligerency? Answering his own query, he stated, "Simply because

Mr. Cleveland and his Administration and his Cabinet were the agents . . . of the bond-holding interests of the country, and the $400,000,000 of bonds that Spain has issued to carry on the Cuban war were the one great factor. . . . It is my opinion then, and is now, that the Republican party will follow the same line of action."[40] Curtis Castle of California went so far as to describe the administration as little more than a puppet government: "Rothschild and his American agents, Belmont, Morgan, & Co., hold $200,000,000 in Spanish bonds. . . . Rothschild controls Morgan, Morgan controls Hanna, and Hanna controls McKinley, the Supreme Court, the Senate, and the House of Representatives. Hanna is America and America is Hanna."[41] Simpson and Castle honed in on just one element mentioned in Allen's speech: the Spanish bonds. They suggested that Cuban independence would void the bonds, potentially ruining the financiers who held them.[42]

The story picked up momentum in the following months. Frank Cannon made his speech on the subject in early February, the day after he proposed a resolution granting belligerency status to Cuba (with a rider that likely would have led to recognition of its independence). At the same time, publications sympathetic to the reformers ran articles on the subject with increasing frequency.[43] While conservatives did not accept the conspiracy narrative, some of them also questioned the basis of the administration's hesitancy. One of the administration's most ardent supporters, Senator John Thurston of Nebraska—chair of the 1896 Republican National Convention—admitted that "against the intervention of the United States in this holy cause there is but one voice of dissent; that voice is the voice of the money changers."[44]

Following the destruction of the battleship *Maine* on the night of February 15, the restless voices in Congress only grew louder. Most suggested that the ship's destruction had been the work of a Spanish mine, but nearly all concluded that Spain bore responsibility, regardless of its involvement. Washington's Silver Republican senator, George Turner, declared that it did not matter "whether the hand that exploded the mine was that of a duly accredited and authorized agent of the Government of Spain or whether it was that of a maddened and lawless fanatic. . . . The hand that intended to explode that mine in some well-understood contingency was the hand of Spain, and it is immaterial whose was the hand that sent the electric spark on its fateful mission of death and destruction."[45] Westerners continued to voice fears that McKinley would not act, and there was apprehension that even justice for the dead would be overlooked to keep business interests satisfied. In the House, James Hamilton Lewis claimed that he had heard of a young banker who had sent "a letter to the President of the United States . . .

This cartoon from the front-page of the February 27, 1898, edition of the Rocky Mountain News *originally contained a caption referring to the vessel in stormy seas as the "Ship of State." Spain's animosity and the influence of moneyed interests are depicted as equivalent threats in the rough waters ahead. Published within days of the* Maine *disaster, it could also be read as placing blame for the tragedy on Spain and its financial backers. Courtesy of the Denver Public Library*

calling upon him for an answer as to 'why should the mere loss of 250 lives be of consequence enough for him to unsettle all the stable values of this country by irritating Spain to conflict.'" This led Lewis to declare that it was not only "appropriate but most onerous upon us that we do something to instill a patriotism into the youth of this country."[46] The fallen dead of the *Maine* had to be avenged, commercialism be damned.

By the time the navy released its official report on the *Maine* disaster in late March, the Republicans' patience had reached its limit. The report suggested that the cause of the explosion had indeed been an external mine, but it blamed no parties specifically. Western Republicans joined the rapidly growing number of their partisans in expressing their rage. Senator George Perkins of California was positive that "the Maine was blown up from the outside. . . . The fact is established beyond the possibility of a doubt by the position of the bow and that of the iron from the bottom where the mine first took effect." The only issue left, then, was the identification of those responsible. "Surely," he said, this was "not by the act of friends. Neither by accident." Spain needed to be held to account. He also claimed that Spain possessed an "officially organized plan for the starvation of more than a million people, and of this number it saw 600,000 die according to the programme," although these facts had apparently been irrelevant to him not long before. As mainstream Republicans echoed the call for war, the president was forced to respond.[47]

On April 11 President McKinley finally asked Congress for permission to intervene in Cuba. Although this action had been widely anticipated, the content of his message only made McKinley's opponents more convinced that a plot was afoot. McKinley did not ask for a declaration of war against Spain; instead, he asked for permission to intervene as an impartial neutral. According to his message, merely ending the bloodshed was the goal. He said little about Cuban liberty, and the president explained that he continued to oppose any form of recognition of the rebel government or even the semblance of an alliance with it. For those who had long demanded a free Cuba, the call to action by the commander in chief was a complete disappointment.[48]

The reaction was immediate. The reading of McKinley's message in the Senate chamber had barely ended when William Stewart of Nevada and Marion Butler of North Carolina (the South's lone Populist senator) responded. Stewart declared that intervention without recognition of Cuban independence "looks like a war of conquest. It would be difficult to find a precedent for such intervention outside of the conquest of Egypt or the dividing up of China among the great powers of Europe"—cases of overt imperialism. The international community would never support such an action. Stewart also suggested that there would be other ramifications associated with the apparent conquest of Cuba. "What will you do with the island when you take it? There is some talk about responsibility. As I read international law, the responsibility upon us would be very great if we should take the island." Butler outlined Stewart's interpretation more clearly: "If we intervene in Cuba and take possession of the island, we can not liberate it from the lien which the bondholders have upon it. . . . Our interference will not be paramount to the mortgage under international law"—essentially, the conquest of Cuba would not invalidate Spain's bonds—"but the right to liberty and independence, for which the Cubans have fought, is paramount to a mortgage made to obtain money to subdue them." An independent Cuba could not be expected to pay the debts of those who sought to destroy it, but the acquisition of the island by the United States would make America liable for the payment of Spain's debt.[49]

A similar message was delivered by one of their colleagues in the House. The next day, Nebraska Populist William Greene explained the many complications associated with the executive's aloof policy: "I say that if we simply intervene we admit that Spain is a friendly power. We say there is no government in Cuba that we can recognize except the Spanish Government." Added to this was Spain's recent announcement that it was willing to participate in an armistice, potentially negating any need to pacify the colonial occupation force. "What is there left for us to do if what I have said should occur, except to turn our guns upon the Cuban patriots and compel them to lay down their arms!" And, he asked, what would happen after American troops had pacified the island? A Democrat from Michigan replied, "Give it a carpet-bag government under quasi-military rule." "I fear that will be the result," responded Greene. The Nebraskan was also afraid of the influence of financiers in the international community. "There are held by the people of foreign governments large sums of bonds issued by the Spanish Government and predicated largely upon the revenues which Spain derives from Cuba." If Cuba were granted its independence while simultaneously "admitting Spain to be a friendly power," the international community would be up in arms. "Do you not know that France, Germany, and England would step to the front and say to this country, 'You can not steal the territory of a friendly power unless you make the obligations good'?" Critics of the administration agreed that, without prior recognition of the independent government of Cuba, US intervention would only transfer Spain's debt to America.[50]

The assumptions of Stewart, Butler, and Greene fit the conventional reading of international law at the time. Historian H. Wayne Morgan has demonstrated that Spain's Cuban bond debt was a major concern of the Spanish regime, and its attempts to saddle the United States with a portion of it actually held up negotiations after the war.[51] Even media reports after the cease-fire described the attempts of Spain and France (whose citizens owned a large share of the bonds) to recoup their losses by suggesting that the United States was obligated to pay as the new sovereign power in Cuba.[52] Whether or not they had correctly judged the goal of McKinley and his allies, these critics of the president were not misreading the international situation at the time.

While the aforementioned opponents of McKinley argued that the president's policy was mistaken and that Cuba had to be recognized, they did not initially attribute that policy to the scheming of conspirators. But Allen and soon Butler went further. Allen wanted it stated on the record that the course laid out by the president would mean "that we will be called upon hereafter to pay the Spanish-Cuban debt." He also accused some of his fellow congressmen of playing a part, suggesting that "that is the fixed and settled policy in some quarters in this city."[53] Butler was certain that the

Cubans would be forced to pay for their freedom. "The great Republic of the United States," he said, "has turned its back on the brave band of patriots in Cuba. . . . Our Army and Navy is to be used to force them to surrender to a gold and monopoly syndicate. . . . We are to force them to submit to an industrial slavery worse than Spanish rule."[54]

A few took the bond conspiracy rumor to an even greater extreme. Earlier in the session James Hamilton Lewis, Washington's flamboyant Democratic congressman, had decried the "flock of these vultures wheeling around the head of the President." He claimed that a collection of powerful bankers had applied pressure on McKinley, seeking to take advantage of "the weakness of an emergency and now demand that the honorable President of the United States shall sell the liberties of the Island of Cuba to them for $200,000,000 and allow these men a mortgage upon the tax facilities of Cuba." If McKinley refused, according to Lewis, they would call back their loans from the government and cripple it before it could act against Spain.[55] Fears of this sort lingered for some time, perhaps intensified by the unclear motives of the president. Just days after McKinley called for intervention, Senator Allen again demanded recognition due to his growing suspicions that "the Island of Cuba is to pass into the hands of a syndicate of financial cormorants, financial buzzards, financial vultures, unless the United States takes prompt steps to check that conspiracy."[56]

Allen and Lewis did not invent such a story out of nothing. Rumors of Cuba's freedom being purchased by an independent syndicate had circulated throughout 1897 and into 1898, and evidence suggests that several bankers did propose a plan to purchase Cuban freedom (although it is unclear what terms they proposed).[57] As far as Cuba was concerned, the speculation surrounding the island's fate was intense during the three years of conflict, and in no way was this speculation limited to Populists.[58] Seemingly wild schemes abounded, and looking back, it is difficult to separate the totally irrational stories from those that were simply inaccurate.

Even though they questioned the methods proposed by the president, it must be emphasized that western Populists, Democrats, and their allies were consistently among the strongest advocates of an independent Cuba. Yet historians have struggled to explain why this was the case. One of the few focused works of scholarship on the subject concluded that their anti-imperialism was based on the bond conspiracy itself. According to historian Paul Holbo, Populists and their allies supported independence for Cuba rather than annexation as a means to strike at European bondholders. In his view, the Populists took the Cuba issue seriously from a relatively early point, shifting their domestic frustrations to troubles overseas by 1898. By that time, they had convinced the Bryanite Democrats and Silver Republicans of the seriousness of the money power threat. Together, they collectively attacked the administration for its idle stance on Cuba, and their irrational embrace of the conspiracy theory and their desire to void the bonds eventually forced them to reject the acquisition of Cuba.[59]

Holbo's reading of the situation ignores the fact that the bond conspiracy rumors were new in 1898, but Populist calls for a free Cuba were not. The evidence demonstrates that westerners used the bond conspiracy only to explain the puzzling actions of a president whose known primary objective was the maintenance of friendly relations with domestic capitalists. Westerners did not argue that Cuba should be free in order to devastate certain bondholders; rather, they tried to understand why anyone would be opposed to Cuban independence. For someone like Allen, the independence of Cuba was of supreme importance in its own right. In a speech in which he acknowledged that the press had labeled him the "the jingo of jingoes," Allen emphasized, "From the time the war broke out between Spain and Cuba I have been the steadfast and uncompromising advocate of independence. . . . We have no greed for Spanish territory," he continued, "nor for Spanish gold. . . . We do not want Cuba. We do not even desire to be her guardian. But we are determined she shall be free."[60] Although his analyses commonly incorporated his views on the political power of a capitalist elite, he simply stated his belief that this group was a hindrance to a humanitarian policy. Just as tellingly, Allen's 1895 speech had nothing to do with the holders of Spanish debt, but even at that early date, he was no less vigorous in his support of Cuban freedom.

Five days after the president issued his controversial call for intervention, Henry Teller offered his famous amendment, which stated clearly that "the people of the Island of Cuba are, and of right ought to be, free and independent." It included a disavowal of self-interest by "disclaiming any disposition or intention to exercise jurisdiction or control over said island except for the pacification thereof." It also demanded that Spain withdraw its military units from the island or face expulsion at the hands of American armed forces. The amendment significantly changed the complexion of the resolution for intervention. By specifically pointing to Spain as the aggressor, renouncing territorial aggrandizement, and calling for an independent Cuba, it alleviated the fears of those who distrusted the president. Teller's amendment was quickly adopted, and both houses passed the joint resolution on April 19. McKinley signed it the next day. On April 23 Spain replied with a declaration of war, and Congress responded in kind two days later. The United States was at war, but the battles in Congress only intensified.[61]

THE WAR REVENUE BILL

When America went to war in 1898, many hoped that a sense of patriotism would smooth over the conflicts that had divided the nation politically.[62] Despite such desires, conservatives and reform advocates continued to do battle with each other. Such contests were inevitable, as both sides believed the war could be a vehicle for their policy objectives. Their greatest fights took place during the first six weeks of the conflict, over what would come to be called the war revenue bill. Although western reformers once believed that intervention in Cuba had been stymied by the money power, they soon became convinced that the administration was seeking to placate that same power through a war measure.

On April 25 the bill was proposed by Congressman Nelson Dingley, a Republican friend of the administration best known for his authorship of the most recent tariff regulations. Dingley stated that, after several years of deficits, revenues (largely coming from the tariff) had just reached the point where they matched expenditures. However, while only $365 million had been spent in 1897, war expenses had raised costs another $300 million per year. To make up for these additional expenses, his new bill provided for two forms of supplemental revenue. The first involved an additional $100 million of internal taxes, primarily on the consumption of popular items such as beer. The second and more controversial part of the bill empowered the secretary of the treasury to sell up to $500 million of "3 per cent coin bonds, to be disposed of as a popular loan." The bonds were to be sold to the public in post offices in multiples of $25.[63]

The Populists and their allies in Congress could not believe what they were hearing. They had defeated one bond measure at the beginning of the session only to have another one thrust upon them, and the system of taxation created by this bill was nearly as preposterous. As they came out in opposition to the revenue plan, however, their arguments were often divided into attacks that focused on the "money power" (for the bond portion and its implications for currency) and those that derided Republican subservience to "plutocrats" more generally.

First and foremost, western Populists and their allies said the bond measure was completely unnecessary for a war that everyone knew would be of short duration. Representative John Kelley, a South Dakota Populist, declared that "even if Spain were a second-class power instead of what she is, there would still be no excuse for this fabulous bond measure."[64] Senators Allen and Teller likewise criticized the size of the bill and suggested that the administration had an immediate need for the money.[65] It had been spending more than the tariff was bringing in, they claimed, and this was an attempt to cover up the shortfall.

Beyond criticism of the sheer size of the bond issue, most who attacked the bill called it a sham that was being pushed through in wartime for the profit of a few. Kelley claimed his colleagues had been "rudely awakened to a realization of the fact that the spirit of patriotism which is aroused throughout the country has been taken advantage of . . . to satisfy the maw of the money changers."[66] Lewis of Washington also warned against being "buoyed off upon an imaginary patriotism to wrong the people by deluding them and robbing them." War, he said, "has ever been the pat time for the pilferers of public confidence and the plunderers of the public Treasury to do their destructive work."[67] Later, Lewis would claim that the bill itself had been drawn up at the instruction of Wall Street bankers.[68]

A few of the most radical Populists attributed the bond issue directly to the money power and then connected it to Secretary Gage's proposals. William Stark of Nebraska told the House that "there may be a sinister motive in the proposition to issue so large an amount of interest-bearing obligations at this time; that when negotiated the war may suddenly be brought to a close and the remainder of the bond issue utilized to retire the present legal-tender notes." He remained skeptical that even his partisan rivals would do such a thing, yet he could not allay his fears that "the emissaries of Shylock can always be depended upon to do his will."[69] Jerry Simpson was certain that the bill demonstrated an intent "to carry out a programme mapped out some time ago in the interest of the money lords of this and other countries to take advantage of the people, appealing to their patriotism to authorize for war purposes an issue of bonds the authority for which has been sought in vain in times of peace." The great purpose behind it all, he said, was to bolster the national banks. Aside from the profit they gained from interest, bonds were required as security on the notes the bank issued. "Bonds are to national banks the blood of life," he said. For Gage to initiate his plan to privatize the issuance of money, he first required these bonds.[70]

As the statements of Stark and Simpson demonstrate, a number of westerners incorporated portions of the classic conspiracy narratives into their counterattacks against the administration. In most of the apocryphal histories of finance that were popular in this era, the Civil War was cast as the pivotal moment at which the money power used a national crisis to its advantage.[71] It is not surprising, then, that some Populists and others believed they were living through a similar moment. Populist representative Charles Barlow of California contended that the "policy of the present Administration is to retire the whole noninterest-bearing debt [greenbacks] and replace it with an interest-bearing debt." It was a continuation of a phenomenon that had haunted the country for more than thirty years. "This bond craze of to-day is a legacy of the civil war," he said. "While the brave men on both sides were sacrificing themselves in a struggle of principle, which resulted in the liberation of 4,000,000 slaves, these shylocks and coupon clippers were completing their nefarious plans."[72] Just as that great struggle had been hijacked by the money power, many Populists feared the war for Cuba was experiencing the same fate.

The Civil War also provided a powerful example for those who desired monetary reform. The money power had made its greatest impact during the war, but it had also been a time of creative experimentation in national finance. In Populist narratives, one of the most important developments was the introduction of greenback currency. As the nation again went to war, many believed the same kind of creativity, and maybe some of the same solutions, could work again.

One after another, western reformers made speeches demanding that the Treasury issue new currency to pay for the war effort. Significant numbers of Populists in the House called for the addition of greenbacks to the revenue bill. South Dakotan Freeman Knowles and Nebraskan William Greene were Populists who held similar views regarding the utility of greenbacks. Knowles believed greenbacks had saved the union, but "after the war was all over and the danger past, then it was that the money devils began to cry 'dishonest money' and 'rag baby.' . . . And from that day to this it has been bonds, bonds, bonds." Greene also blamed "men outside of Congress" who "have taken advantage of conditions of war to secure legislation in their interests," just as they had in the 1860s.[73] Both men developed counterproposals to the bond plan; Greene called for $150 million in treasury notes, while Knowles demanded $250 million.[74]

While some Populists advocated for greenbacks, other western reformers saw the war revenue bill as a useful measure to push silver legislation through Congress. John Calhoun Bell of Colorado stated that he wanted the silver seigniorage held by the Treasury to be coined.[75] Yet, like those Populists who called for greenbacks, he did not do so because he believed in the inherent value of the metal. "The Supreme Court of the United States says gold is not money; it says silver is not money; it says paper is not money, but that a legal decree of a legislative body makes the money of the realm."[76] His Senate counterparts were eager to coin the seigniorage as well, but like Bell, they understood that all currency was fiat currency. Senator Allen called for the coinage of silver during one of his attacks on the bond measure, and he expressed his disdain for "that class of pseudo financiers who argue that the value of money resides in the commercial value of the material employed. We can displace every dollar of silver and gold in the United States and replace them with full legal-tender paper money, and if we limit that volume, every paper dollar will be equivalent in value to a dollar in gold."[77] Even the relatively conservative Silver Republican Henry Teller was willing to listen to the fiat money proposals of his friends. He flatly stated, "I have not been one of those who have been in favor, as a general rule, of issuing paper money," but added, "I know that the authority of the United States exists to issue paper money." But those who oppose paper money "can not defend this proposition here or elsewhere by saying that with $42,000,000 of silver in the Treasury, which will make as good money as gold, we are to keep it locked up there and then borrow an equal amount and pay interest upon it."[78]

The Senate succeeded in adding an amendment to coin the silver seigniorage, but neither Allen nor Teller nor any of the other reform senators could take credit for it. Instead, that honor went to Senator Edward Wolcott. The junior senator from Colorado had already been rewarded for his loyalty to the McKinley administration with the top position on the fruitless international bimetallic commission that was sent to Europe in 1897. With a few more feathers in his cap, perhaps the state legislature would forget that he had chosen his party over the silver cause in 1896. Wolcott's was one of the few amendments of the war revenue bill that westerners supported, but for those opposed to the administration, it hardly felt like a victory.[79]

Western reformers relentlessly attacked the war revenue bill for its bond measure, but they were nearly as offended by the components covering taxation. Republicans claimed that broad-based taxation was the only fair system, while Populists, Democrats, and Silver Republicans retorted that the bill's regressive forms of taxation did not match growing disparities in wealth. Some of these debates pertained to seemingly trivial matters, but they effectively demonstrated the sense of class division. One such conflict focused on something as mundane as a tax levied on beer consumption. Congressmen Castle and Maguire, joined by Senator White (all of California), objected to the provision that taxed beer, which they all identified as "the drink of the

Senator Edward Wolcott. Courtesy of the Library of Congress

poor." Castle further noted that champagne, an item "used only by the rich," was specifically exempted from taxation. The amount of expected income from the beer tax—$33 million—was one-third of the total amount to be collected through taxation. To those already suspicious of the administration's intent, this was further evidence that the bill represented upper-class disdain for common Americans.[80]

Western reformers were most angered by the bill's system of taxation—a levy on consumption—which they claimed would inevitably take more from the poor than from the rich. The bill was designed to impose a consumption tax on a number of popular items, but it contained no personal income tax or corporate tax provisions. Western reformers asked their partisan rivals how this was possible. Congressman Newlands of Nevada asked whether the "accumulated wealth of the country" was to be excused of its wartime obligations. Senator White of California asked, "Ought the wealth of this country to bear any of the ills of this war? . . . If not, what excuse is there for the bill as it came from the House, and what excuse is there for those who are seeking to exempt the rich?"[81] Some explanation was necessary to justify these unequal taxes.

More so than their allies, the Populists argued that there were few limits on the federal power to marshal resources in times of crisis. Congressman Simpson mocked Republicans who had claimed that "the wealth of this country is something sacred." "Why, sir," he said, "do you know that when war exists in this country, the Government can take a man from his home, his fireside, his family, and put him in the front rank of the Army and have him shot for the benefit of his country?" Why is it, then, that "we can not invoke an income tax to touch the wealth of the wealthy classes," even in time of crisis? Congressman Castle made a nearly identical comparison. He decried the new "age of commercialism," saying that greed had "dethroned man and enthroned property." A man "can be taken from the bosom of his family and be shot to death on the field of battle . . . but when it is proposed to lay the heavy hand of Government on property we are told that the property of the wealthy classes can not be touched." No individual's wealth could be withheld from the government, they argued, especially in time of war.[82]

Western Republicans avoided the debate over the revenue bill, with two notable exceptions. Colorado's Edward Wolcott fought with William Allen over the viability of an income tax, arguing that an inheritance tax was preferable because the living were too effective at dodging assessments.[83] The only other participation by a western Republican came during the debate of a proposed corporate tax. Democrats in the Senate were working to add a tax on the nation's largest businesses, but they struggled to develop a satisfactory amendment due to squabbles over its particulars. Following the rejection of yet another proposal, Stephen White offered an alternative. Rather than a tax on all corporations, he suggested a modest levy—amounting to one-quarter of 1 percent of gross revenues—"upon the business of oil refining and sugar refining, so that the Standard Oil and the sugar trusts will be able to pay taxes under the bill." Given that these were the two most identifiable monopolies in America, the tax was targeted at businesses he believed few would be willing to defend.[84] Challenging White's presumption, Senator John Wilson of Washington denied that the trusts could actually be made to pay. While he agreed with "the honorable Senator from California

[Mr. White] that this tax, if imposed, would be a tax upon those who can afford to pay it," he argued that it would provide them with an excuse to exponentially raise the price paid by consumers. Despite claims that he would have liked to support the amendment, portions of Wilson's speech also suggested an appreciation of the monopolies. He reminded White that "when he was a boy the consumer of oil paid 50 cents a gallon for it, and to-day it is only 8 cents at retail, and less than 4½ cents at wholesale." Wilson acknowledged that these companies enjoyed near complete control of the market, but he did not consider that regrettable.[85] Following White's vociferous response, his amendment passed in the Senate by a vote of 33–26, with no western reformers in opposition.[86]

The class dimensions of the portions of the bill pertaining to taxation were so flagrant that opponents attempted to counter them any way they could, often with symbolic proposals that had little chance of passing. Thus Senator Richard Pettigrew offered a truly ambitious amendment. Its first component would have defined the word *trust* in rather broad language. All organizations found to be trusts would then be subject to a tax of 5 percent on the total value of their manufactures. His purpose was "not so much to obtain revenue as to destroy trusts. Trusts have grown up covering almost every article of manufacture in this country . . . with the object of plundering the consumer." He cited Republican George Hoar of Massachusetts as one of the many who defended trusts by arguing that such a tax "punishes the innocent purchaser of all the sugar or any other article manufactured by a trust in this country." Pettigrew knew his proposal was extreme, but he believed the war funding measure was already being used for the benefit of the few. The choice, he said, was between "the continuance of plutocracy or absolute socialism. I am in favor of neither, but I am in favor of socialism before I am in favor of plutocracy." Even though nearly all the western reformers in the Senate voted for his proposal, it went down to defeat. Pettigrew's last-ditch effort to make the financing of the war fit the reformers' agenda failed. The victory of the administration's party was nearly complete.[87]

After a long fight in both houses of Congress, the conference committee reported back the final version of the war revenue bill in early June. Ultimately, the bill was not much different from its original form; the vicious debate had forced only cosmetic changes.[88] The House vote was held on June 9, and the results were as partisan as the debates had been. Not one western reformer voted for the measure, and not one western Republican voted against it. The bill passed by a vote of 154–107, with 87 counted as absent. The vote in the Senate the next day played out in much the same way. Western Republicans provided unanimous support for the bill and were joined by only two of the least dependable reformers: Silver Republican Lee Mantle of Montana, who would soon return to the administration's party; and James Kyle of South Dakota, a former Populist who had been drummed out of his state party after consummating a corrupt bargain with Republicans to secure reelection in 1897. The bill passed by a 43–22 margin, with 24 senators absent or abstaining. With McKinley's signature, the war revenue bill became law on June 13, 1898.[89]

The Populists, Democrats, and Silver Republicans who represented the West in Congress had little reason to trust the McKinley administration in early 1898. The president had promoted entrenchment of the gold standard from the moment he was elected, and his secretary of the treasury had declared his intent to secure its place and destroy alternative currencies through a massive bond sale. McKinley was no friendlier to the Cuban revolutionaries, whom the reformers viewed as foot soldiers in the battle against European economic power. Reformers soon linked Spain's dependence on financiers to fund its war effort with McKinley's inaction, developing it into a conspiracy theory that would shape their views of both the international situation and the president's actions thereafter.

As McKinley took the first steps toward intervention in Cuba, the Populists and Democrats remained skeptical of his motives. Maybe he wanted to force the American people to pay the financiers who had funded Spain's bloody war, they reasoned. Or perhaps he was interested in suppressing the Cubans themselves. When war did come, they were presented with a bond measure remarkably close to the one pushed by the administration earlier in the year. Again, they saw the hands of the financiers in McKinley's actions, and again they opposed him.

The success of the administration's war revenue bill highlights the diminishing fortunes of the western reformers once the war commenced. They may have ultimately succeeded in applying pressure on the administration and their conservative rivals when it came to Cuban independence. However, once the war began, they were unable to rein in the forces they had unleashed. The president they despised was now a wartime commander in chief. The bonds they opposed were now seen as vital to the war effort, and too many others refused to take a stand against them. In spite of the westerners' hopes, they proved unable to use the war to simultaneously liberate Cuba and reform America. Quite to the contrary, the war was paid for with bonds and consumption taxes, and it was managed by an administration with little fervor for ideals such as political freedom or economic justice. McKinley had called for intervention in order to return stability to the region, not to aid the revolutionaries. American interests were his primary concern, and this would soon become apparent in other areas. The war for humanity that the Populists had hoped for was about to become a war for empire.

4. HAWAIIAN ANNEXATION AND THE BEGINNING OF THE DEBATE OVER EMPIRE

On May 4, 1898, Congressman Francis G. Newlands, the only member of Nevada's Silver Party in the House, submitted House Resolution 259, "to provide for the annexing of the Hawaiian Islands to the United States."[1] The resolution was immediately forwarded to the House Committee on Foreign Affairs. Although it did not create much of an immediate stir, it did catch the eye of the McKinley administration, which would use its influence in the committee to garner Republican support for the measure.[2] That it was sponsored by one of the western reformers likely added to its appeal.

Newlands was hardly a logical ally of the administration. His devotion to free silver was as strong as that of any member of Congress, and he had referred to the Republicans' war revenue bill as a scheme to satisfy the "rapacity" of the national banks.[3] At the same time, he was a man of no small ambition. He may have been attempting to make a name for himself in order to challenge Senator William Stewart's control of Nevada state politics.[4] Even more likely, he may have simply believed the time was right to take the islands.

The reintroduction of Hawaiian annexation in the midst of the war with Spain took a politically charged topic and made it explosive. Seeing this as a chance to take action on an issue that had been delayed since the second election of Grover Cleveland in 1892, Republicans almost universally supported it. Western reformers, however, were divided over the measure. This is hardly surprising when one considers the diverse individuals who had been pulled into the free silver coalition. A few who had been in Congress earlier in the decade had supported Hawaiian annexation then, and some among them—such as the widely admired Henry Teller—had a truly expansive vision of what America could become.

Though this was not the first time western reformers were forced to take a stance on the question of empire, Hawaiian annexation proved to be an

94

intellectual turning point for many in the movement. As troopships prepared to depart for Puerto Rico and the Philippines, there was little doubt that expansion was about to become a serious matter of debate that no one could ignore. Those opposed to annexation began the process of developing a foreign policy to fit the existing Populist worldview. Their arguments would be carried over and refined in the debates that followed.

WESTERN REFORMERS AND THE AMERICAN EMPIRE BEFORE 1898

The Populists, Democrats, and Silver Republicans of the West had occasionally dealt with the matter of American territorial expansion before 1898, although they had largely failed to consider it in any systematic way. Like nearly all residents of the western states, they did not question the propriety of continental expansion. However, many who would join the western reform coalition had some misgivings about the potential annexation of the far-off islands well before 1898.

Like their Republican neighbors, western reformers accepted the original premises underlying earlier American expansion. Given their own emphasis on the political independence of small property holders, they could hardly critique the basic outlines of the continental "empire of liberty." They did not, however, presume that the Indians should be dispossessed with callous disregard for the interests of the native peoples. Nearly all supported allotment under the Dawes Act to provide opportunities for Indians to emulate their white neighbors—a policy they viewed as uplifting. When evidence of land swindles surfaced, Senators William Allen and Richard Pettigrew even intervened to protect the land rights of certain tribes. Pettigrew was also one of the leading advocates of substantial spending for Indian education, but one of his statements on the subject acknowledged the imperial reality. Despite the high cost of such education, he declared it to be "but a paltry sum for the price of a continent."[5]

The westerners' unanimity on continental expansion broke down when they were faced with the potential annexation of overseas territories. In particular, the status of Hawaii troubled some of them for much of the 1890s. In January 1893, when the islands' last native monarch was overthrown by the plantation-owning sons of American missionaries—aided by marines from a nearby American warship—President Benjamin Harrison presented a treaty of annexation to the Senate. With Harrison's term about to expire, and with President-elect Grover Cleveland questioning the legitimacy of both the revolution and the treaty, the Senate held off on ratification. Upon assuming office, Cleveland withdrew the treaty and, following an investigation by former congressman James Blount, declared that American involvement had been inappropriate. However, despite his belief that the revolution would not have succeeded without the aid of American arms, Cleveland refused to reinstall Hawaii's queen. Instead, the president entrusted the question to the "extended powers and wide discretion of the Congress" and washed his hands of the matter.[6]

Congress had already begun the discussion without Cleveland's permission, and it continued without him. For more than a year after the submission of the treaty, members of Congress deliberated on the future of the islands. A number of western senators who would go on to support William Jennings Bryan in 1896 became involved on both sides of the annexation debate, and they were deeply divided on the subject of expansion. Democrat Stephen Mallory White of California was one of the most vociferous opponents of annexing Hawaii, emphasizing the impropriety of American involvement in the revolution and the native inhabitants' unfitness for democracy.[7] He was joined in opposition by Pettigrew of South Dakota, who declared that annexation was being pushed by big business interests, especially the sugar trust.[8] Pettigrew hinted at the worldview that many western anti-annexationists would later adopt, but most of his colleagues had not yet integrated their views of domestic and foreign affairs.

The Populists in the Senate held mixed views on Hawaii. Kyle of South Dakota defended American involvement in the revolution and supported annexation, but, sensing controversy, he worked primarily to pass resolutions that would delay the question of expansion to a future date.[9] Allen, in contrast, deplored American interference in Hawaiian affairs and initially called for the reinstatement of Queen Lili'uokalani by force. He further condemned the rise of a new aggressive spirit in American foreign policy "which has induced this country within a comparatively short time to 'bully' small and semibarbarous powers." But by 1895 he believed that the annexation of Hawaii to the United States or some other power was inevitable.[10]

Perhaps the loudest proponent of territorial expansion in Congress was the senior senator from Colorado, Henry Teller. Teller made no secret of his "spread eagle" Americanism. In one speech he declared: "I am in favor of the annexation of those islands [Hawaii]. I am in favor of the annexation of Cuba; I am in favor of the annexation of that great country lying to the north of us."[11] He envisioned a time when nearly the whole of the Western

Hemisphere would be in American hands. For Teller, there was no limit to the territory that could become part of the American union.

Congressional debate over Hawaii began to die down after the spring of 1894. With annexationists stymied as long as President Cleveland was opposed, all sides looked for a short-term solution. A number of resolutions were proposed that declared the American position toward the islands. Democrat David Turpie of Indiana submitted a Senate resolution declaring that the domestic politics of the islands was wholly the concern of the people already living there, but simultaneously warning that any interference by an outside power would be regarded as "unfriendly" by the United States. It passed easily, but all understood it to be only a temporary respite. The debate would be reignited in 1898.[12]

NEW BEGINNINGS

By the time William McKinley was inaugurated, the situation was largely unchanged from 1893. Hawaii remained independent, but a greater share of those in power sought incorporation as the best avenue to financial security. Although the Republican Party's platform in 1896 had called for the annexation of Hawaii, the new president initially tried to keep silent on the issue, telling representatives of the Hawaiian government in late 1896, "I have my ideas about Hawaii," but "it is best at the present time not to make known what my policy is." It is likely, however, that he wanted annexation from the beginning. Events soon provided McKinley with an opportunity to act. When the Hawaiian government began turning away Japanese immigrants (most of whom were coming to work on the islands' plantations), Japan responded by sending a warship to the islands. McKinley claimed that the rising tensions between Hawaii and Japan demanded a change in the status quo. In June he sent a message to the Senate stating that the annexation issue had always been "merely a question of time," and that time had finally arrived.[13] Although no action could be taken during the short opening session of the Fifty-Fifth Congress, a new fight over annexation was certain to arise when the second session began in December 1897.

Several westerners played a significant role in the fight against Hawaiian annexation. Senators White and Pettigrew, who had been against the treaty during the Harrison administration, became leaders of the opposition to the new treaty. In early February 1898 White introduced a simple resolution calling for Hawaiian self-rule, very similar to the one Senator Turpie had proposed in 1894. He claimed that he expected it to pass with little oppo-sition, but when the debate over annexation became more serious, White dropped the resolution altogether. It seemed the annexationists were more determined than they had been in the past.[14]

At the same time, Senator Pettigrew worked quietly. He wrote a letter to the Japanese minister in Washington, suggesting that it would be useful "for the Japanese Government to propose to join the United States in guaran-teeing the independence of Hawaii." Such an action would surely "prevent the passage of this bill or resolution for the annexation of Hawaii, there is no question about it."[15] The senator from South Dakota also maintained ties to an ex-colleague—former Silver Republican senator Fred T. Dubois of Idaho—who remained an active opponent of the acquisition of Hawaii. Pet-tigrew had two of Dubois's anti-expansionist speeches printed and sought to use the ex-senator's influence with other Silver Republicans in Washington.

Pettigrew also made contact with Hawaiians who were working to main-tain the islands' independence. He wrote to Joseph Carter, a close personal friend of Queen Lili'uokalani who was working to help her restore the mon-archy, and asked for financial aid to support Dubois in Washington. "He has a great deal of influence with Senator Cannon [of Utah] and Senator Mantle [of Montana]," he noted, "but he is poor and unable to come to Washington without assistance."[16] Carter may have provided a link to other opposition groups from Hawaii. Pettigrew and Senator George Hoar of Massachusetts welcomed representatives of native Hawaiian anti-annexation organizations, and Pettigrew invited them to the opening ceremonies of the session in early December 1897. These groups brought petitions designed to show the na-tives' preference for an independent Hawaii. One, which contained more than 17,000 signatures, was given to Hoar, whom the Hawaiians believed was opposed to annexation despite his earlier support for it. Another petition, which asked for restoration of the monarchy, was given to Pettigrew.[17]

Despite the administration's efforts, opposition to the treaty persisted throughout early 1898. Members of Congress were soon too distracted by Spain and Cuba to deal with the treaty, but McKinley would not have long to wait. With Commodore George Dewey's victory in the harbor of Manila at the beginning of May, Hawaiian annexation came to the forefront again. Hawaii, claimed the expansionists, was the most logical stopover point for voyages from the West Coast to Asia, and Dewey would need to be resup-plied if he was to hold the bay. Even more importantly, volunteers from the western states were already being sent to California in preparation for an expedition to the Philippines, and the troopships would require a place

Senator Richard F. Pettigrew. Courtesy of the Library of Congress

to stop and resupply. To vote against Hawaiian annexation would therefore jeopardize the American war effort.[18] Furthermore, in a rapidly changing and dangerous world, Hawaii was the key to any defense of the Pacific coast and a future isthmian canal. Others calculated that Hawaii would be necessary if the United States were to hold the Philippines in the long term.

THE ANNEXATIONIST ARGUMENT

Even before the debate over the war revenue bill died down, the discussion of Hawaii's future began to move toward center stage. Interestingly, those who had been the strongest proponents of Hawaiian annexation earlier in the decade were remarkably quiet. Some members of the western congressional delegations did go on record to explain their support for the Newlands resolution, but clear differences emerged between Republicans who supported aggressive foreign policies and western reformers who saw the annexation of Hawaii as a necessary adjunct of the war effort.

Though they gave few speeches on the subject in 1898, it is worth noting the arguments of the two foremost advocates of Hawaiian annexation during the 1890s: Senators Henry Cabot Lodge, a Republican from Massachusetts, and John Tyler Morgan, an Alabama Democrat. They had advocated annexation for years, and their statements from earlier in the decade continued to shape the discourse on both sides of the debate in 1898. First, they emphasized the strategic value of Hawaii. "All the great routes from San Francisco and from Vancouver, all the great routes to the East, to and from the [hypothetical] Nicaraguan Canal, pass those islands," Lodge declared.[19] Similarly, Morgan went so far as to suggest that "it would be folly for our citizens of this country to build the Nicaragua Canal, or for our Government to sanction the scheme," if some other power held the islands.[20] The duo also frequently declared that America had to act immediately, because others would not wait. In the early 1890s both Lodge and Morgan claimed the British were interested in Hawaii, despite statements from Britain to the contrary.[21] But the senator from Massachusetts did not focus all his attention on the potential British threat. Following its 1894–1895 war with China, Japan seemed to be the increasingly dominant power in East Asia, and by mid-decade, Lodge identified the Japanese as the real threat.[22] In one speech, Lodge openly fretted about the threat posed by a growing Japanese navy—at a time when many senators still had passages from Alfred Thayer Mahan's *Influence of Sea Power* floating in their heads.[23] A Japanese conquest of Hawaii would make that nation's strategic advantages in the Pacific impregnable, the expansionists said.

The annexationists of 1898 would combine the old rhetoric of national power with the kind of patriotic flag-waving that is possible only in times of war. Republican congressman John Barham of California spoke of the value of Hawaii as both a domestic trading partner and a place "of great importance from a military point of view," as "demonstrated by facts developed during the pending war with Spain." Barham was also sure that the islands could not maintain their independence. Those who opposed annexation preferred "quietly sitting by [to] see England, Japan, Germany, or some other nation take the islands and their trade and military advantages." He brushed aside suggestions by editors and politicos who claimed that the islands were unnecessary, saying that he preferred the arguments presented by military men. Just as one went to a doctor for medical problems, "So it seems to me, in military and naval affairs, that we should be largely guided by the opinions of men learned and trained upon these subjects." Worse still, those who would neglect the islands today would "sacrifice the unparalleled achievement of our arms upon the seas, so heroically won by Admiral Dewey and his men at Manila, and endanger him, his men, and our soldiers."[24]

Barham followed the typical expansionist script in his speech, but he remained focused on the value of Hawaii itself. Another California congressman, Samuel Hilborn, believed that annexation was about much more. Dewey's victory had changed America's place in the world. Before then, he said, "We were content to build up and develop this continent," whereas "the world looks upon us now as a martial nation, ready to participate in the struggles which change the map of the world." The spot on the map that most concerned Hilborn was an archipelago just off the coast of Asia. Americans were heading to the Philippines already, and many would certainly meet their ends there. "Miles of headstones will mark the burial place of soldiers from every State of the American Union. . . . No foreign flag will ever wave over an American burial ground where rest America's brave defenders." Before the American flag had even been hauled up in Manila, he denied anyone's right to take it down. Hawaii was needed as a stepping-stone to "reach our more distant possessions in the Orient."[25]

Barham and Hilborn were quite typical of congressional Republicans during the debate. Barham spoke of an immediate need due to the war. Hilborn spoke of new international responsibilities as a consequence of the war. Anti-expansionist fears of colonialism and militarism were brushed aside. Barham obviously believed that the military leadership should be followed, not instructed, while Hilborn thought a larger military establishment was "already necessary." As America took its place in the world, "we have been irresistibly swept into a position where we must become a warlike nation," he said. These remarks conflated national greatness and national power, both of which required annexation.[26]

None of the western reformers in the House went so far in their remarks. Those who favored expansion believed in limits, and for many, Hawaii represented that limit. The author of the controversial resolution, Congressman Newlands, gave a lengthy speech on annexation in which he laid out many of the same arguments made by certain Republicans. He spoke of the need to secure access to and from an isthmian canal, just as Senators Lodge and Morgan had throughout the 1890s. The islands also had strategic utility for both offensive and defensive operations. Unlike the two senators, however, he argued that possession of Hawaii would be such a deterrent to American enemies that annexation would "minimize the necessity of militarism." He also hoped the issue would not be "considered in the public mind in connection with the Philippine question." Hawaii had a small population, but in the case of the Philippines, the "acquisition of such a population may entirely break down and destroy our industrial system." Annexing those islands would only complicate the American legacy of "individual liberty, individual representation, and industrial and commercial laws." For Newlands, true colonialism was to be avoided at all costs.[27]

In the Senate, administration Republicans spoke rather sparingly, frequently leaving Democrats, Populists, and Silver Republicans to fight amongst themselves. In these fights, Nevada's William Stewart and the venerable Henry Teller took up the role of the chief defenders of expansion. The West's two elder statesmen specialized in tearing down the constitutional arguments against annexation.

Stewart did not lay out any ideological basis for his support of expansion. His longest speech essentially declared that the US Congress could do as it wished, annexing or ruling lands without constitutional restrictions. Treaties were not the only legal means to achieve annexation, and consent of the governed played no part in the matter at all. When pressed by an opponent to admit that he must believe in *some* limits to the power of Congress, Stewart assured him there were few. "There is no lack of power to pass an act," he said, and very little that could not be done through one. If Congress would "pass an act tomorrow extending our boundaries 300 miles down into Mexico, our courts would have to follow it." In that case, even the consent of the newly added inhabitants would be legally superfluous. From there, the question of ultimate statehood for a territory rested with the "sound discretion of Congress. It may take a century or two. . . . The decision holds that Congress must also exercise a sound discretion when it will cease to treat it as a colony or Territory. That is a question we may not live to see disposed of."[28]

While Stewart's precise motivation for supporting expansion remains unclear, Teller's views are less murky. Teller was, in no uncertain terms, a fervent expansionist. His desire to add new land to the American republic had in no way diminished, and his statements in 1898 were little different from those he had made in 1894. Most of his speeches focused on historical examples of expansion—and opposition to expansion—from the earliest days of the republic. He especially liked to speak of Thomas Jefferson's doubts about the constitutionality of annexing the Louisiana country. Though troubled right up to the last moment, "He solved that doubt, Mr. President, in favor of bringing it in." Teller considered it Jefferson's greatest contribution as president, an act that ensured American greatness by providing property and a livelihood to future generations.[29]

The senator from Colorado did not speak only of the past. Teller was sure that America's future lay in the Pacific. America's population would only grow, he said, and trade would be necessary for continued prosperity. Trade with Asia would become "the great trade of the world and a great boon to this great population when it shall be overflowing and filling the land with just such people as we have to-day, only, I trust, a little better." Hawaii was part of that link across the Pacific. But Teller's ambition did not stop there. Some thought it would be ignoble to take land in a war fought for humanity's sake, but Teller believed the nation had entered this war "in the interests of freedom," and nothing could tarnish that fact. "I do not believe that will be possible, though we may take in Cuba, Puerto Rico, the Hawaiian Islands, and the Philippine Island." He was confident that such acts by the United States would never become sordid because those islands would be governed in the interest of "every one of the people whom we invite or bring under the influence of our flag."

Teller's reference to an "invitation" to join America hinted at a principle he had emphasized in his 1894 speech in favor of Hawaiian annexation. Back then, he had even been "in favor of the annexation of the great country lying north of us," but there was a condition: "If the Canadians will never choose to come to us we shall never get them," he said. If the United States could "manage [its] affairs [so] that they [the Canadians] can see ultimately that it is [in] their interest to become a part of the United States," then Canada would voluntarily join the union.[30] He used Canada as an example, but he made it clear in 1894 that the principle was the same for any country. Perhaps Teller forgot about these earlier remarks, because by 1898, he no longer spoke of consent of the governed. Yet he still believed that America would rule these lands with justice and that they would be shown the benefits of a connection to the United States. Teller never abandoned his rather idealistic image of American progress, although he would eventually remember his devotion to liberty.

WESTERN OPPOSITION

While Teller, Stewart, and Newlands fought to annex Hawaii, many of their closest partners fought against them. It was awkward for western Populists and their allies to work with southerners who had ruthlessly stamped out their third-party efforts and with New Englanders such as George Hoar who had derided them since their appearance in the national legislature, but they had little choice. The western reformers raised a number of the same issues and concerns as their colleagues from the South and Northeast, and their statements regarding race and citizenship were based largely on the same assumptions as their counterparts from other regions. In many ways, this fact is unsurprising, as the basic components of the anti-imperialist argument had been honed for nearly half a century by intellectuals such as Charles Schurz and laid out in well-known tracts such as his article "Manifest Destiny," published in 1893.[31] The occasional similarity of their remarks partly explains why previous historians have overlooked the western opposition to expansion and imperialism. However, when western reformers discussed the ultimate implications of empire, or when they connected domestic structures of power to the renewed push for territory, their language demonstrated an interpretation rooted in Populism's republican ideology. They spoke of traditional fears of centralized authority, militarization, and diminished economic opportunities that would ultimately bring about the end of free government. The exploitation of distant colonies could break the back of American democracy, they claimed.

The speeches of all anti-annexationists expressed the belief that Hawaiian annexation would only set the stage for wider expansion. Congressman John Shafroth of Colorado attacked New York Democrat William Sulzer for saying that America "should not only annex Hawaii but should extend its power and dominion across the Pacific and forever hold possession of the Philippine Islands." In fact, Shafroth claimed, "four-fifths of those Representatives who believe in the annexation of Hawaii" also called for the acquisition of the Philippines. Senator White claimed, "If we consummate this scheme, it will be urged that we must have the Philippines because Hawaii is not of great value unless in connection with other possessions," and the result would be a flood of "Polynesians, Malays, Chinese, Negritas, and semi-orang-outangs [who] will demand our care." These western critics were attacking not only Hawaiian annexation but also the later annexations they feared would follow.[32]

Opponents of annexation took turns ridiculing and dismantling the arguments of their rivals. Most commonly, they pointed out that Pearl Harbor had already been ceded to the United States via treaty, and the rest of the islands added little of military value.[33] After thoroughly researching the matter, Pettigrew pointed out that an alternative base was available, and it was already in American hands: "The harbor of Kiska [in Alaska] is a noble bay, perfectly protected from all winds. . . . There are no hidden dangers, and the depth of water is sufficient for any vessel." Others had dismissed Alaska's harbors as too icy or too far afield. Pettigrew threw these claims aside, citing sources that his foes could not reject. Senator George Perkins, a conservative Republican with close ties to the Southern Pacific Railroad, had informed him that "there never has been ice known in the harbor but once, and his ships have gone there for the last quarter of a century." Additionally, information that came directly from the Department of the Navy demonstrated Hawaii's limitations as a coaling station. In a letter he received in January, a respondent from the navy explained that the new battleship *Massachusetts*, "steaming at the most economical rate, can sail 4,797 miles. She can just get from Honolulu, by the shortest route, to Manila if nothing happens." But, he continued, "this distance that she can travel is from the official trial. She can not do it in practice. . . . She would be 3 miles short with every favorable circumstance, with no adverse winds or storms." By comparison, Kiska was only 3,700 miles from Manila.[34]

Other western anti-imperialists discredited claims that Hawaii was vital to American security. North Dakota's senator William Roach, a Democrat, delivered one of the most stinging speeches, sarcastically admitting, "for argument's sake":

> [If] we were in trouble with any European power that country would send its ships to Asia and then across the Pacific Ocean in order to attack our western coast. I will even admit that Hawaii is so large and so strong that such European power could not possibly send its ships around Hawaii, but must inevitably have them stopped as soon as they struck our coaling station in Pearl Harbor. I will admit, Mr. President, all of these things, notwithstanding the historical fact that Gibraltar is as strong a fortification as Honolulu, and not much farther distant from the United States coast; and yet we have never had trouble by reason of England's owning Gibraltar.[35]

Roach could not envision how an island thousands of miles from American shores could be essential for national security.

His colleagues continued in the same vein, if with a less sardonic tone. Senator William Allen noted that "a child capable of locating the Hawaiian Islands on the maps would be convinced at a glance" that they had no defensive value. "They have no significance whatever and not the slightest value for defensive purposes. They will only add to the burden of our country in defending its coast."[36] Stephen White of California also questioned how a defensive perimeter so far from the mainland could be of any use against a real-world foe. San Francisco and San Diego were already fortified, and there were few powers capable of attacking those cities. For those who claimed that Britain was a threat, he pointed to British fortifications and bases in British Columbia as a greater danger than any that might come from Hawaii. "There she is right in sight of the smoke of our civilization. She is not compelled to go 2,100 miles from anywhere and be dependent upon a precarious supply of coal and provisions." For those who claimed that Japan was the primary threat, White observed that Japan had made only friendly overtures to the United States and was not even a threat to Hawaiian independence. "If her actions toward Hawaii excite doubt, negotiation—friendly, manly negotiation—will solve all." With only Japan and Britain mentioned by expansionists as threats to the West Coast, the Pacific seemed to be safe for the foreseeable future.[37]

While critics were sure that Hawaiian annexation would do little for national defense, they also suggested that distant colonies were a point of strategic weakness. White asked simply, "If our coast is not well protected now, will we make its protection easier by obtaining an addition that also must be fortified?"[38] Congressman Shafroth of Colorado pointed to recent examples from the war with Spain: "We have attacked Spain at her weakest points, namely, in her outlying possessions. If we acquire colonies, the first attack upon us will be through them." As extensive as America already was, he said, it was an integrated state that provided no easy avenues for attack. "There is no way of holding a slice of territory cut from a nation located such as ours. . . . When nations find that nothing can be gained by war with such a country the idea of conquest vanishes even if they covet our possessions. We should not exchange concentration for diffusion."[39] His fellow Coloradan agreed. "If you pile up mountains of coal during times of peace from the territory of some of the friendly powers," said John Calhoun Bell, "that will simply make the island a more inviting object of attack should we become involved in a foreign war." If Hawaii were annexed, attacks would come "at this vulnerable point, in mid ocean, some six or seven days' sail from our nearest home port." The only possible defense would be from a greatly enlarged navy—hardly a solution that Bell would endorse.[40]

Anti-annexationists in Congress also attacked the Newlands resolution because of the threat it posed to constitutional restraints on power. Allen argued that only a treaty could be used to annex territory, pointing out that a joint resolution had no more power than any other law passed by Congress—and like all other laws, it was applicable only within the sovereign bounds of the United States itself. He went further, emphasizing the strict constructionist viewpoint that many Populists were committed to. The Constitution provided for a limited grant of power, he said, and "powers not expressly granted or not necessarily implied or proper for the execution of granted powers do not exist and can not be constitutionally employed."[41] Senator White agreed that the Newlands resolution went beyond the mandated limits of power, claiming that "there is no precedent for such legislation." When expansionists reminded him of the example of Texas, he denied that there was a parallel. Texas had been admitted as a state, but few of his contemporaries even spoke of a day in the distant future when Hawaii would become a full member of the union. It would remain, he was sure, a mere colony.[42]

Beyond their attempts to compare the addition of Hawaiian to earlier expansion, annexationists claimed rather broadly that expansion was part of America's fate. Again, opponents of annexation united to refute this suggestion. Pettigrew attacked the conceptual basis of manifest destiny, calling it "the murderer of men. It has committed more crimes, done more to oppress and wrong the inhabitants of the world than any other attribute to which mankind has fallen heir." It was, he said, "simply the cry of the strong in justification of their plunder of the weak."[43] Like Pettigrew, Congressman Bell believed manifest destiny was a policy of brute force. Perhaps "the time has come when manifest destiny shall automatically decree that this exemplary Government shall shed its gabardine of justice, impartiality, and equality, and shall join the Old World in gormandizing its national greed by absorbing all the smaller governments that come within its reach." But he certainly hoped that such a time had not yet arrived.[44]

Along with his critique of manifest destiny, Bell questioned the legitimacy of the government of Hawaii. He noted that the Hawaiian senate practically controlled the affairs of the islands, but that high property qualifications prevented the vast majority of inhabitants from voting for its officers. The land losses of indigenous Hawaiians ensured that few of them could vote, while white planters maintained a monopoly on political power. "The best of evidence has been secured by a personal canvass of the natives and of the non-American population, and it has been found that at least 90 per cent of the population are praying for an independent government." The takeover of Hawaii by the descendants of Americans was not, as one expansionist congressman had suggested, "the bold assertion of American manhood"; rather, it was a wrongful usurpation of authority.[45]

Bell hit on the central issue that nearly all anti-annexationists (and later, anti-imperialists) focused on: consent of the governed. Senator Allen struck just such a chord when, during a heated debate, he asked a colleague, "Suppose Congress should declare that it was a necessity to annex England and the President should approve it, would that annex England to the United States?" Certainly, Allen continued, Congress had no legal authority to do that without some kind of popular referendum, and even Parliament lacked the authority to approve such a proposal. When his colleague declared that yes, in fact, Congress did have such authority, Allen asked how it was possible that the United States could "bind the people of England" in such a way. If this were legal, "then we can annex the world."[46]

All anti-annexationists were united in their belief that expansion and colonialism would violate the basic principles of American government. They were sure that Hawaii would not be made a state, largely due to the racial makeup of the people who lived there. Shafroth reminded his fellow House members that the Hawaiians "belong to an entirely different civilization, to an entirely different race. They know nothing of republican institutions."[47] Race was tied to democracy, and in this view, most members of the opposition agreed with the expansionists. Hawaii would never have the right population to make it suitable for full partnership in the American political system. This assumption was based on both the islands' racial demographics and commonly held beliefs that tied together mental acuity, health, and the environment. Underlying it all was a confidence that whites—living in lands to which they were well suited—had attained the highest level of civilization. In his speech in mid-June, Congressman Bell integrated both the racial and the environmental elements into his argument against expansion. At one point he broke down the population of Hawaii into racial categories: "There are 40,000 Hawaiians and mixed bloods, and probably 8,000 of these are over the age of 21 years; 24,000 Japanese, mostly all males, and probably 16,000 of them above the age of 21 years; 15,000 Chinese; 8,000 Portuguese," and so on. His focus on demographics was just part of his overall argument about politics—namely, that the islands were, due to their population, unfit for incorporation into the American political body. American freedom was based on citizens' equal access to the ballot box. "If we annex Hawaii, we must treat all of the citizens thereof as political equals and give them the privilege of the ballot, or must make another radical change in the policy of our Government." Just over 3,000 residents of the islands had been identified as "Americans" in the last census, and this tiny fraction of the population would have no control if true democracy followed the flag.[48]

Bell and his allies went further, declaring that American civilization could not survive in the tropics and that products of such an environment were unfit for citizenship in a democracy. "There is not a case in history where this civilization has thrived under a tropical sun." In Africa, he said, the "torrid sun has never allowed the front brain to develop." These facts were immutable, he explained. "Take the extreme north; the government that has always controlled best is force. Take the temperate climate . . . and they tell us that reason is the controlling force there; but take the case of those within 30 degrees of the equator, and nothing else has ever governed them so well as superstition." Senators Allen and Roach voiced similar concerns. According to Roach, it was a "notorious fact that out of the 90,000 inhabitants of the Hawaiian Islands there is not to exceed 5 per cent of them capable of taking any part in government. A government of that kind of people and by that kind of people would be irrepressible conflict, while a government for that kind of people would of necessity have to be a very strong one."[49] Certainly, the anti-annexationists said, these were not people who could be incorporated into the American body politic.

The opponents of Hawaiian annexation feared the incorporation of distant lands and their peoples, but they had no desire for less democratic alternatives either. Regardless of region or political affiliation, all the anti-annexationists—as well as the anti-imperialists who followed them—believed it was impossible to reconcile a colonial system of rule with the American political tradition. Shafroth asked, "Are we going to violate the very principle for which our fathers fought the Revolutionary war? Are we now going to deny the principle that 'taxation without representation is tyranny'?" He also mentioned the "monster petition against annexation, signed by more than a majority of the Hawaiians" and presented by Pettigrew earlier in the session. Bell, Pettigrew, and Roach joined Shafroth in denying that the Hawaiians had consented to annexation. If the people of Hawaii were incapable of participating in a democracy, the islands should be excluded; if they *were* capable, their voices should be heard.[50] Allen went further, demanding that Hawaii, the Philippines, and Puerto Rico be granted freedom on the same basis as Cuba. "On all those islands that dot the sea I would erect and sustain an independent republican form of government," he said, "giving them moral aid and support, as we have other islands in the past, and I would demonstrate to the world in time that all the Western Hemisphere was dedicated in different sections and in different republics to the cause of a government by the people and for the people."[51] Allen was every bit the American exceptionalist his opponents were, but he thought that American influence should remain persuasive rather than coercive.

Commonly, both eastern and western anti-annexationists claimed that undemocratic systems under the American flag were a threat to democracy at home. However, it was on this point that the arguments of conservative opponents of expansion fell flat. They suddenly claimed that a single change would endanger the entire system on which American freedom was based, while few among them questioned the economic or political structures of power that had taken hold domestically. For Populists and their allies, in contrast, government by the people was already under threat. The growth of huge economic empires at home and an apparent alliance between political and corporate America had convinced many of them to leave the two-party system earlier in the 1890s. These western opponents of annexation most clearly differentiated themselves from their eastern counterparts when they discussed the far-reaching consequences of a colonial policy.

For all anti-expansionists, the proposed "new possessions" were a threat to the American racial, political, and industrial order. But because westerners viewed the existing governmental and economic systems as hugely flawed, they were particularly sensitive to the ways in which an unequal colonial system would accentuate those flaws. An examination of the remarks of the most outspoken among them—notably, Senators Richard Pettigrew and William Allen and Congressman John Calhoun Bell—provides a clear example of the Populist view of annexation.

Though still nominally a Silver Republican, Pettigrew had quietly joined the Populist caucus at the beginning of the year.[52] Like his fellow Populists, Pettigrew was sure that economic opportunity was dying, and with it, American democracy. For that reason, he emphasized the economic threat posed by the influx of Asian workers that would come with a Pacific empire. Despite his favorable remarks about Japanese civilization and the intelligence of native Hawaiians at other points in the session, in June he described the inhabitants of Hawaii as the worst kind of degraded laborers.[53] Pettigrew believed that the founders had envisioned a government supported by independent property owners, but he contended that Asian labor posed a danger to the American yeoman. He considered "the Asiatic races" to be "people with a low vitality and great tenacity of life, human machines who could subsist upon the least of food and perform the most of work."[54] They would destroy the freedom of the white laborer who was the backbone of American democracy; he stopped short of saying that only whites were capable of the requisite independence to maintain such a government.

Pettigrew also saw the concentration of power necessary to control an empire as the death knell of American freedom. Because he believed that "no one for one moment pretends that we intend to admit the Asiatic people of Hawaii or of the Philippines into full citizenship under the Government of this country," the consequence would be colonial rule and government by decree. For Pettigrew, the only safeguard of freedom had been a "government of limited powers" established by the Tenth Amendment, but he was sure that colonialism would destroy that barrier as well. Already the centralization of power in America had become too great. Growing inequality was the consequence: "The wealth of the United States, which was once fairly distributed, has been accumulated in the hands of a few; so that, according to the last census, 250,000 men own $44,000,000,000, or over three-fourths of the wealth of this country, while 52 per cent of our population practically have no property at all and do not own their homes." Pettigrew argued that, by using their power to control the votes of those in desperate circumstances (as he believed had occurred in 1896), the elite had "usurped the functions of government and established a plutocracy." Imperialism was the scheme of all plutocracies, and while he believed that expansionist policies would benefit the commercial elites, he also saw how imperialism could be used to rationalize militarization. "Whenever all power and all property have been gathered into the hands of the few and discontent appears among the masses, it has been the policy to acquire foreign possessions, to enlarge the army and the navy, to employ discontent and distract its attention." Colonies would be a white elephant providing further justification for the centralization of government power.

Senator Allen had a similarly negative view of annexation, but he focused on different perils that would accompany it. In a speech on July 4, he likewise emphasized the threat posed by immigration. With regard to Hawaii, the Philippines, and all the other lands the most aggressive expansionists dreamed of acquiring, he said he could not "incorporate in our population, as citizens of the United States, 15,000,000 people belonging to alien races, the most of them ignorant, brutal, hostile, and savage," who would "reduce the standard of our home civilization to that of a low and brutal Asiatic population." He did not want them as citizens, but he believed nothing else was possible under the Constitution. Once those islands were annexed to the United States, "there is no power in Congress by legislation to prohibit the Malay of the Philippine Islands from coming to South Dakota or Nebraska or New York; and, sir, they will come by the million," he warned. Once here, they would compete with "the farmers and laborers of your State and of my State. They will come to reduce the standard of civilization in all the occupations in this country among our legitimate population. The Japanese cooly [sic] and his son will become farmers in your State and in Nebraska, and they will lower the prices of farm products there. . . . So, sir, the Japanese cooly's wife and daughter will become competitors with the wife and daughter of the American citizen." Allen framed the threat as a direct attack on American manhood and men's role as providers and protectors of their families. That economic threat would destroy the entire American way of life. The struggle to maintain American freedom would be lost, as he forecast that "out of it all will grow a landed peasantry with a few thousand landlords, who will own millions of acres of our country." Ultimately, the demise of free labor in America portended the failure of democracy. The nation "will pass from a Republic, which was framed by the founders, into an oligarchy, if not into absolute monarchy itself."[55]

In another speech made just two days later, Allen shifted his focus to two of the other major concerns of western reformers. First, he pointed out that the addition of new territories would require a military buildup to defend the islands from external threats and "to keep the natives in subjection." He said, "our Navy must be increased; our standing Army must be increased to at least 200,000 soldiers, and all the burdens of taxation are to rest upon the people of this country, for we can expect nothing from the Hawaiian Islands or the other islands that we shall annex." The taxes to pay for it all would have to be wrung from American farmers and laborers via consumption taxes and the tariff, as the Supreme Court had invalidated the federal income tax. Allen was no lover of the professional military, but the costs associated with this kind of expansion would be ruinous.[56]

Second, Allen was sure that the yearly expenses associated with such a military would exceed revenues in many years. The addition of overseas colonies was "one step, and an important step, in the interest of the perpetuation of a national debt. I have no doubt in my own mind that every man who has the money and desires to own Government bonds and draw interest from the people in the form of taxation is in favor of this scheme of annexation." With new expenses, the government would be influenced by "these interest-eating patriots." Then, with debt dragging the government down, control "will pass from the masses of the people, from the debtor class to the creditor class, and the Republic, if it exists, will exist in name only. . . . Every one of these men is in favor of annexation." Harking back to earlier conspiracies, he claimed that financiers and bondholders would destroy representative government.

While Allen believed that militarism would weaken democracy through backbreaking taxes and perpetual debt, Congressman Bell saw even more direct links between the military establishment and the economic elite. He ridiculed the arguments of those "high in the Army and Navy ranks" that the acquisition of Hawaii would extend the American defensive perimeter. These leaders knew the military would have to be expanded in order to defend and, more importantly, control the islands. Over time, the American public would become accustomed to rule by the bayonet. Worse yet, if present conditions were any sign of things to come, Bell expected the military to become more closely tied to a select elite. "Every year we draw nearer and nearer to the caste system of the Old World. No man can look over the military appointments recently made because of the social, political, or financial standing of young men . . . without being convinced that an invidious distinction was made against the efficient trained soldier from the ordinary ranks of society." He even proclaimed, perhaps facetiously, the widespread belief "that applicants for office in the Army or Navy must now present their pedigrees, strains of blood, or social standing rather than their qualifications."[57]

For those at the bottom of American society, the annexation of Hawaii would lead to greater deprivations. Unlike expansion during earlier times, which had provided land and resources for the use of all Americans, only a "few wealthy Americans and European whites will own all the valuable possessions of these islands." Just like Pettigrew and Allen, Bell was confident that, rather than hiring white Americans (who were, according to Bell, unfit for the tropical climate), these great property holders "will inevitably employ the natives or the poorly paid labor of like climates, and will produce untold quantities of the necessaries of life, and will pour them into our channels of trade in competition with our laboring classes." Annexation would bring "the return of slavery to this country," he said. The support in Congress for expansion indicated to Bell that "the United States will unfold itself in the early morning of the twentieth century into the greatest military and naval power and into the most regal and resplendent aristocracy that the world ever beheld." Whereas expansion had once been a guarantor of freedom for Americans, annexation in the era of unrestrained capitalism would certainly destroy it.

The Populists' critique of Hawaiian annexation was mild compared with their later anti-imperialist arguments, but they were beginning to demonstrate an understanding of the alignment of domestic and foreign affairs. The economic opportunities and political independence that had defined American freedom would be challenged by the incorporation of lands that were unsuitable for homesteads and peoples who were easily exploited.[58] Colonies also provided opportunities for militarists to demand greater resources and for federal authorities to rule without democratic mandates. Both were inappropriate precedents for American governance.

The rhetoric that had been at the heart of so much of the Populist analysis was largely absent from this debate. Allen spoke of his fear that annexation was part of a scheme to create permanent public debt, but almost nothing was said about the money power.[59] Western reformers of all stripes freely brought up the conspiracy at other times during the session, and the early debate over Hawaii actually overlapped with the last discussions of the war revenue bill, the most onerous measures of which were attributed to international financiers. One explanation of the difference may involve the limits of the money power conspiracy itself. The term *money power* was, after all, aimed only at financial interests, and surely they were not the only ones interested in expansion, the Populists reasoned. Increasingly, they focused their outrage on other targets. Whereas the battle of 1896 had been waged almost solely against banking interests and monetary speculators, later campaigns were in opposition to "aristocracy" and "plutocracy."

Another possible explanation relates to divisions among the western reformers themselves. Although many of their most important leaders in Congress opposed annexation, there were notable exceptions. Senators Henry Teller and William Stewart—the latter a regular promoter of the money power conspiracy—were among the supporters of the administration's initiative. On the one hand, Stewart was beginning to shift back into the Republican Party, a more fitting place for the mine operator and friend of big business. Teller, on the other hand, would undertake a convoluted political journey that continued for the remainder of the debate over expansion.

The joint resolution for annexation came up for a vote in the House of Representatives on June 15. It passed by a margin of 209–91, with six members counted merely as "present" and an additional forty-nine not voting. Among the supporters of the resolution were twenty-two westerners, ten of whom were Republicans and the rest reformers. No Republicans from the western states voted in opposition to annexation, while six Populists, Democrats, and Silver Republicans did. Interestingly, no Republicans were absent for the vote, but six Populists were. Others spoke up for them, claiming that several would have voted for the resolution had they been there. Yet it seems no mistake that they were not present.[60]

The day before the Senate vote, scheduled for July 6, Senator Hoar announced his reversal on the subject. He cited the points made by the opponents of annexation—that military enlargement would be necessary, that the country would be swept into competition with the great powers, or that expansion would continue because of it—and then claimed that it was all "needless alarm." Hawaii was small, its addition would aid the war effort, and although he had no desire for colonial adventure, there was nothing to worry about in the case of Hawaii.[61]

Pettigrew was furious. The Hawaiian delegates seeking to maintain the independence of their homeland had met with Pettigrew and Hoar, and now the latter was choosing to ignore their pleas and maintain party loyalty. "The Senator from Massachusetts says that this is wrong," declared Pettigrew in the minutes before the vote, "that it is a sin; that it is wicked; but the islands are so little that if we will forgive him for taking that country, he will sin no more; he will be virtuous and resist a like crime if it involves a larger acquisition of territory." He scolded Hoar for forgetting that "the first step in wrongdoing is the dangerous step. If we set the example, regardless of honor, of acquiring title to a territory from puppets that we have set up, what will we not do?" Hoar's earlier talk of moral action rang hollow.[62]

The vote in the Senate was much the same as that in the House. The aggregate vote was 42-21, with a remarkable twenty-six members not voting. Ten western Republicans were joined by two Silver Republicans (Teller and Cannon of Utah) and one Populist (Kyle of South Dakota, whom Pettigrew believed was now trading votes for patronage). Five western members—Allen, Pettigrew, Roach, White, and the Silver Party man from Nevada, John Jones—voted against the measure. Seven more westerners did not vote at all. Only one of them—John Thurston of Nebraska—was a Republican. Thurston was likely the only nonvoting member present that day to state his opinion on the subject. He declared that he was against annexation, but because he was paired with an absent member who was likely to vote in favor of it, he sat out the voting. Six western reformers absented themselves from the vote.[63]

It is almost certain that these nonvoting members sensed the importance of the issue to their allies, men with whom they intended to work again. It is just as likely that they did not want to be on record as voting against a wartime measure that seemed quite popular. These members sensed the powerful emotions stirred up by expansion and the war, but they felt ambivalent.

The remarks of Newlands, author of the resolution, demonstrated as much. Pettigrew, Allen, and other reformers exhibited no hesitance in their opposition. They acted with a sense of moral certitude, and they believed they were defending the foundations of independence in republican America.

The debate over Hawaii in 1898 was the culmination of the conflict that would determine that archipelago's future, but it was the opening salvo in the contest to determine America's future course. Expansionists and their opponents had spent more than a generation fighting over foreign policy, and the struggle rapidly intensified in the last years of the century. Western reformers were initially divided over the issue, unsure of how to proceed as the loyal opposition in wartime.

Those Populists, Democrats, and Silver Republicans who opposed expansion found themselves with unusual bedfellows. Carl Schurz and men of his ilk were among their harshest critics in 1896. Logically, although they borrowed some arguments from the mugwump repertoire, they largely developed a critique of expansion rooted in their own worldview. The concentration of power that must inevitably follow imperial expansion could not be taken lightly, they said. The benefits of empire would accrue only to wealthy investors and plantation owners, not independent laborers. Colonies—especially those with populations deemed to be of uncertain quality—posed a new threat to the broad-based economic and political system traditionally championed in America. Their arguments in the summer of 1898 provided the first formal Populist renunciation of empire, laying the foundations for their later positions.

Yet their vision of America was not the only one offered by westerners at this time. Conservatives embraced empire, if sometimes with hesitation, but so did a number of prominent reformers. Many former Republicans with expansive views of national greatness drifted back toward their old allegiances. Others believed that the president should be supported in wartime, or that Hawaiian annexation was too popular to oppose. Many of these same annexationists had no stomach for further expansion, and they drew the line at Hawaii without acknowledging that their votes would help their opponents at a later date.

As the summer wound down and Congress prepared to adjourn, both sides readied themselves for the next test. The reformers had fought the administration all spring and into the summer, but they had helped make

McKinley a wartime president. They had challenged the policies and initiatives of the commander in chief, and conservatives wanted to hold them to account for it. Late summer marked the beginning of another campaign season, and the winner would hold the upper hand in the struggles that followed.

5. PATRIOTISM AND THE ELECTIONS OF 1898

Western reformers had begun 1898 with high hopes. In the first months of the year they succeeded in stifling the administration's new banking plan and demanded in its stead a financial system that was directly accountable to the people. They were confident that, at least in their home states, they had popular support on their side. Just as they had in 1896, many of them believed they would campaign in the fall on a platform that demanded economic justice. But then the war complicated the situation. It was waged on terms chosen by the commander in chief, and the reformers were unable to stop the war revenue bill or the annexation of Hawaii. Could their old agenda still take precedence over these new issues?

It was an especially difficult time for politicians in the West, and no one was more aware of the challenges faced by reformers than Richard Pettigrew. The South Dakota senator was also the most well-connected politician in his state. In early 1898, as Congress debated Secretary Gage's monetary restructuring and the discussion of Cuba's suffering intensified, Pettigrew was simultaneously working to cement another fusion coalition in South Dakota for the fall campaign. He tried (and failed) to prevent South Dakota Alliance founder Henry Loucks from returning to the Republicans.[1] He also informed his friends that although he was now a Populist, that news should be kept quiet so that he could maintain the Silver Republican organization "as a half-way station" for those who were not ready to move directly into the Populist Party.[2] He also demanded that members of all parties be given places on the ticket in order to bind the Democrats, Populists, and Silver Republicans together. His ultimate goal was to bring everyone—including Democrats—into the Populist ranks or, failing that, to form a new party for all reform forces.[3]

Pettigrew believed that the key to success was holding firm to a message of economic justice. As he explained to one confidant, the object was to "rally the people who protest against government by injunction, government by trusts, government by the banks—in fact, against the domination of plutocracy."[4] Shortly before the outbreak of war, he told an associate that the campaign must focus on national issues: free silver, government control of the currency, and opposition to the trusts. Pettigrew was sure that the president's subservience to the economically powerful would be at the heart of the fall campaign.[5]

The senator's tone changed just two months later. While he had initially believed that the war would be over quickly and not affect the elections, he now sensed the growing possibility that it would indeed interfere.[6] On June 20 he wrote to Governor Andrew Lee and told him it was now necessary to "make State issues prominent" in the coming fusion campaign. While he hoped his Populist colleagues in the House would hold on to their seats, "I am a thousand times more anxious for your election," he admitted to Lee. Pettigrew stated rather bluntly that all future success required the continued control of state offices.[7] A week later he wrote to Lee again and provided some insight into his thoughts. "The Anglo-Saxon has an inherent greed for land," he noted, and the desire "to reach out and conquer the world is bred in his blood and bone." Americans did not realize, however, that conquest no longer offered the benefits it had in past generations. Imperialism would allow the "plutocracy" to be "thoroughly enthroned in this country."[8] Yet he also sensed that most Americans were not ready to reject the temptations of empire. The excitement of war had captured the public mind, and it was too soon to take that fight to the campaign trail. The same excitement had also transformed what Pettigrew had once seen as a favorable contest in the fall into a totally uncertain quantity.

The difficulties Pettigrew faced were the same ones challenging reformers throughout the West. The reformers who had reshaped the dominant political rhetoric of the region were in many ways unprepared for a contest fought on different terms. Early in the year, their economic platform had looked as strong as ever. The war changed everything, and their rivals were soon battling to make the election a mandate on the wartime president. By shifting the debate back to matters of patriotism and loyalty, Republicans turned near-certain defeat into a significant victory.

POLITICS AND PATRIOTISM

Over the course of 1898, the very definition of *patriotism* became a subject of substantive debate. Populists and their allies attempted—as they had for much of the decade—to appropriate the concept of patriotism to bolster the cause of reform. By the summer, that objective was slipping away from them. When war came, militarized valor and unquestioned loyalty became the synonyms of patriotism, and opponents of the commander in chief found themselves defending their right to object.

Early in the year, the reformers deployed the language of manly patriotism to unify the coalition of parties that had come together in 1896. In February representatives of the Populists, Democrats, and Silver Republicans in Congress issued separate statements to their members, calling for united opposition to the Republican Party and the financiers who backed them. All three invoked patriotism as the motive to animate the people's support of reform. Most emphatic of all were the Populists, who proclaimed that "patriotism and manhood are not dead," highlighting their belief that the American people were finally awakening to the threats to their freedom. "The spirit of '76 is abroad in the land and the friends of liberty everywhere are awaiting the patriotic call to fight a common battle against a common foe. Let this be done, and we can crush every traitor as did the men of the American revolution." The Populists also flayed the foreign "gold syndicate"—the money power in one of its many guises. Any man who opposed them was little more than a "tory," they said.[9]

One of the largest congressional battles at the beginning of the year involved Secretary Gage's proposal to restructure the nation's financial system, a move that included selling government bonds and replacing greenbacks with national bank currency. The response from westerners had been overwhelmingly negative, and again they claimed that theirs was the patriotic position. When a writer for the *Yakima Herald* asked Republican readers to "hold patriotism above party and choose as becomes a free born American citizen," they defined the goldbug position as submissive or un-American.[10] William Allen said much the same in Congress, calling any man who would hand over the power to coin money to private firms "the enemy of his country." While he had no problem with honest bankers, generally "the rule is that such men know no nation, no patriotism, and but few have knowledge of any God save the gold they horde and worship." Handing over power to such individuals was not just dangerous; it was disloyal.[11]

Patriotic and masculine rhetoric was also utilized by the western reform-ers as they called for intervention in Cuba. In this context, they claimed their adversaries were feeble when love for country ran afoul of the money power. As a writer for the *Denver Times* put it, "Justice may be outraged, our president may be traduced and villified [sic], our national honor may be im-pugned," but the country remained bound "to the interests of the Spanish bondholders."[12] When fifty of the leading residents of Colorado Springs (who self-identified as "patriotic citizens") called for peace in the wake of the destruction of the *Maine*, local newspapers attacked them mercilessly. One sarcastically stated that while their patriotism was not "the sort that enabled this country, in 1776, to declare its independence . . . they are still patriots; they are patriotic to the vast interests of wealth at home and abroad."[13] Pop-ulists and Democrats did not equate patriotism with violent action, but they did suggest that it should be unfettered by greed.

When war did come, the position of the administration's opponents be-came much more complicated. To fight McKinley now would be to question the decisions of a wartime commander in chief. Conservatives sensed the opportunities this presented and leaped at them, the first of which was west-ern opposition to the war revenue bill. Eastern congressmen and newspapers attacked those attempting to stop the bill, suggesting that the westerners were ignoring the need for wartime unity. Western reformers proved remark-ably sensitive to these slights, and they began to defend their patriotism in nearly every speech they made. Henry Teller lashed out after seeing that some newspapers characterized "senators who do not believe in a bonded debt . . . as the 'assistant Spaniards.'" Certainly, the once quiet friends of the administration did not have a monopoly on patriotism, he said.[14] A Pop-ulist congressman from Kansas, Nelson McCormick, likewise claimed that although all "Populists, Silver Republicans, Democrats, and Republicans are willing and ready to assist our President in this war with Spain," he feared Republicans would now accuse the rest of "disloyalty because we exercise our judgment as well as our rights as Representatives."[15]

Other westerners counterattacked, claiming that patriotism was being used as a shield to pass outrageous measures, such as huge bond sales and new regressive taxes. Congressman John Kelley said that "the spirit of patri-otism which is aroused throughout the country has been taken advantage of" to pass the war revenue bill and "satisfy the maw of the money chang-ers."[16] Representative James Hamilton Lewis likewise warned against being "buoyed off upon an imaginary patriotism to wrong the people by deluding them," and he reminded his audience that "war has ever been the pat time for the pilferers of public confidence and the plunderers of the public Treasury to do their destructive work."[17]

Western newspapers printed similarly skeptical analyses of the war revenue bill. The editor of the *Yakima Herald* wrote that the Republicans had "at last found an opportunity to silence all opposition to their policies." Indeed, the Republicans had "issued their ultimatum that to criticise [sic] republicanism is treason, and that the definition of the word patriotism shall for three years, or during the war, be changed from that given by Webster to read: 'Love of the republican party; devotion to the welfare of the republican party; the passion which inspires one to serve the republican party.'" Those who resisted were branded "traitors and copperheads."[18]

Some continued to fight for definitions of patriotism tied to independence and character rather than simply strict loyalty to a party or a political figure. One writer declared that any "senators who surrender their principles, betray their constituents and abjectly surrender to the money sharks should be branded with the scorn and contempt of every patriotic citizen."[19] Another stated, "Patriotism does not consist of falling in with every nefarious financial or taxing scheme that is put forward by designing politicians under the guise of patriotism. The truest patriot is the one who forgets self in his desire to stand up for the common good."[20] Such statements fit well with the earlier attempts by Populists and their allies to meld political independence with manly and patriotic virtue, but their local rivals had a counter.

In the opening months of the year, Republican congressmen and newspapers from the western states were in no position to attach additional partisan meaning to the term *patriotism*, demonstrating how the appropriation of nationalist sentiment was influenced by regional political trends. Western Republican candidates had suffered major setbacks in the elections of 1896, when they had gone to the polls as the standard-bearers of gold money and the national banking system. When Secretary Gage proposed strengthening the gold standard and national banks at the beginning of the Fifty-Fifth Congress, western Republicans either remained silent or cautioned against such a move. Despite their affiliation, they could not attach the word *patriotic* with their party's economic program.

The war revenue bill was no more promising for western Republicans. Both pro-administration newspapers and members of Congress were silent. In the case of the typically partisan *Omaha Daily Bee*, there were occasional and very brief suggestions of reformer disloyalty, but the claims were always made without explanation.[21] The *Bee*, like many other western Republican journals, had nothing positive to say about the war revenue bill. In a series of articles, it joined the attack on the bond issue, calling it totally unnecessary and undesirable. Even though it was supposed to be a "popular loan," bankers and financiers were certain to end up with the majority of bonds. One writer for the *Bee* denied that anyone "assails the patriotism of the bankers" (apparently the author was not reading reports from the nation's capital) but added that the interests of financiers were opposed to those of nearly all other classes. Avid partisans though they were, these writers were in no position to make support of the bill a litmus test for patriotism. Theirs was a common refrain, as western Republican papers' response to the bill ranged from damning with faint praise to modest condemnation. Western Republicans remained fearful of the economic issues that had led to their decline throughout the region.[22]

As Congress moved from the debate over finance to wartime discussions of expansion, new opportunities arose. Though not yet ready to fight over bonds and taxes, western conservatives soon grabbed on to Hawaiian annexation as a tool to use against their enemies. Their congressmen and editorialists claimed that annexing the islands was somehow necessary to aid and honor the nation's brave combatants. Some, such as California congressman John Barham, said that Hawaii could serve as an adequate base only after it was annexed, and in the meantime, opponents were endangering the soldiers who sailed to Manila to secure the fruits of American victory.[23] Samuel Hilborn of California also tied Hawaiian annexation to the acquisition of the Philippines. Because American blood would be shed to raise the US flag in that distant Spanish colony, it would be inappropriate to ever lower that flag again. According to Hilborn, abandoning any of the Pacific islands would dishonor America's war dead.[24]

Although the anti-expansionists continued to support their own definition of patriotism as a defense against accusations of disloyalty, they remained sensitive to those charges. Several western congressmen all but admitted that they were cowed by the pressure to support annexation. James H. Lewis of Washington was late to take sides, but he admitted that he felt compelled to act contrary to his own desires: "My state, her citizens, my constituents, have in various ways expressed their desires, wishes, and preferences upon the issue," so he now had to ignore his "personal fears" and support expansion.[25] Freeman Knowles of South Dakota openly admitted that, despite his previous opposition to Hawaiian annexation, he now supported it because of the war. Surely, he succumbed as much to the annexationists' attacks as to their arguments.[26]

The western press demonstrated the same trends. In some places, especially the Pacific coast states, nearly all the media supported the acquisition of Hawaii, and some took pleasure in lambasting those who stood out in opposition. The editor of the *Oregonian*, one of the Pacific Northwest's most prominent conservative papers, demonstrated his impatience with opponents of the measure: "The privilege of unlimited talk in the senate is one of the abuses flagrant in that body. The country will not forever endure it. Meantime, while this obstructive talk is going on, there is no way to supply our sailors and soldiers."[27] Some in the fusion press accepted similar definitions of wartime patriotism, further weakening the position of the opposition. The editor of the Democratic *Yakima Herald* called the acquisition of Hawaii a "war measure" that was "of more importance than a fleet of battleships." The same paper even reprinted an article from an eastern paper titled "Stand by the President," which equated opposition to annexation with defiance of the commander in chief's orders.[28] With little thought for its greater political meaning, the *Herald* portrayed some of its allies as traitors. Clearly, the war brought certain challenges for dissenters.

THE WAR, EXPANSION, AND POLITICS IN THE STATES

The war necessarily had an impact on state politics and the discussion of issues at the local level. Western people and their state governments ended up playing a significant role in what would become a global event. Dewey's victory guaranteed that the military campaigns would not be confined to the Caribbean but would extend into the Pacific as well. All of a sudden, geography, expediency, and politics came together to put the people of the western states in a complicated position.

In April 1898 the regular army of the United States was unprepared to take on any foreign power. Instead, National Guard units from the states were called upon to carry the load. In addition to the existing guard units were a number of new (and hastily raised) infantry regiments and cavalry troops, all organized to fulfill quotas given to each state. Of course, many of the older units went through rather dramatic transitions, as unfit officers were replaced (frequently with men from the regular army) and unhealthy men were dismissed. The politics of a unit's home state continued to matter as well. Governors were given considerable discretion in the commissioning of officers, and in some of the newly formed units, the troops themselves

chose their officers in elections that resembled peacetime contests. This latter method helps explain how William Jennings Bryan—a man with neither
military experience nor military inclinations—found himself in command of
the Third Nebraska Volunteers.[29] Most of the regiments called into federal
service, including Bryan's Third Nebraska, would never leave the United
States. His unit was recruited after McKinley's second call for volunteers, so
it was not mustered into service until July. Shortly after it joined the federal
service, his regiment was sent to wallow in the miasmatic swamp that was
Camp Cuba Libre, just north of Jacksonville, Florida. There it would remain
until well after the end of combat operations.[30]

Yet a great many units from the western states experienced a different fate.
To follow up Dewey's victory, McKinley ordered a force prepared for the purpose of capturing Manila. Despite the protests of the top officer of this new
command (General Wesley Merritt), the force assigned this task was made
up primarily of volunteer units from nearly every state of the trans-Missouri
West. Hawaii, though still an independent "neutral," served as the primary
stopover on their trans-Pacific journey. Volunteers from the West therefore
got a firsthand look at the lands that would spark such major political debates over the next several years.[31]

The composition of volunteers from the western states was also noteworthy. Because of their prominence as local leaders, and because so many of
them had advocated intervention on behalf of Cuba, a great many Populist,
Democratic, and Silver Republican public figures felt obligated to participate.
Shortly after the war broke out, Bryan sent a letter to President McKinley
tendering his services. When the news spread, Bryan's friends bombarded
him with letters of their own, warning him of the dangers. As William Allen
put it, "You minimize you[r] position in the political world and place your-
self in the grasp of Hanna and McKinley whom I do not doubt would be
glad to expose you to every conceivable danger, get you out of the country if
possible, and have superior officers involve you in difficulty and possibly disgrace." Kansas congressman Jeremiah Botkin was also keen to remind Bryan
that "the war in which we are engaged with a certain jew and his cohorts is
a much more important war than that we are fighting with Spain." Bryan
was the only man that Democrats, Populists, and Silver Republicans would
unite behind, Botkin said, and as a servant of the people, he had "no right to
hazard [himself] personally or politically at this most important and critical
time."[32] Prominent Silver Republican Charles Towne nearly followed in Bryan's footsteps. "You must be crazy, and if you were near enough I would call
a commission of lunacy and send you to the asylum at once," wrote Richard

Pettigrew to his close friend. "What do you think the Goldbugs would do with you if they got you down in Cuba? They would see that you made no more silver speeches, or troubled further the political waters of plutocracy."[33]

Although Towne ended up following Pettigrew's advice rather than Bryan's example, others close to the reform leaders enthusiastically enlisted for the fight to free Cuba. Another friend of Pettigrew's named Jonas Lien, a recent college graduate who had left his studies to campaign for Bryan in 1896, joined the First South Dakota Volunteers when the war began and remained in contact with the anti-imperialist senator throughout his service.[34] Arthur C. Johnson, nephew of Colorado Populist leader and newspaperman Thomas Patterson, joined the First Colorado and acted as an embedded reporter for his uncle's paper over the months that followed.[35] John Rankin Rogers's private secretary, prominent Silver Republican John Ballaine, was also the adjutant general of the state's National Guard. He resigned his post in order to take a lieutenancy in the First Washington Volunteers.[36] Frank Eager, editor of the *Independent*, Nebraska's most important Populist publication, had been in the National Guard for years and became a captain in the First Nebraska.[37] These regiments, along with the Twentieth Kansas, First North Dakota, First Idaho, First California, First Montana, First Wyoming, and a scattering of other volunteer units, made up the bulk of Eighth Corps, the force assigned to capture Manila.[38]

As elements of the corps readied for their voyage, the question of expansion was already attracting attention in the western press. However, the lack of established partisan positions, combined with the president's silence, left many local political leaders unsure how the issue should be sorted out.[39] Newspaper editorials reflect the uncertainty that followed Dewey's victory at the beginning of May. As they scrambled to keep up with changing circumstances, some papers changed their positions by the day. The *Oregonian* of Portland, one of the most important Republican newspapers in the Pacific Northwest, vacillated wildly in its opinions over a surprisingly short time. On May 9 the paper informed its readers that, although the United States might need to control the islands for a time, any long-term possession of the Philippines "would be in every way to be regretted." The people of the islands were incapable of self-government, and although a coaling station might be of use, "the best thing that could happen to us concerning the Philippines is that we release them to Spain upon payment of a war indemnity." Three days later, another column in the paper largely supported the conclusion that a base was needed in the Philippines, and it emphasized that it was time for America to control the "avenues of commerce" to Asia. By May 14, with this new commercial focus in mind, the paper fixated on the masses of wealth flowing out of the islands and suggested that "an infusion of American blood and the introduction of the liberal principles of American law" were needed to improve the islands. Then, "in the course of 50 or 100 years the 8,000,000 or 10,000,000 simple-minded inhabitants of the Philippines may become fitted for the responsibilities of American citizenship." In less than a week, the Philippines had been transformed from an undesirable land into a future state.[40]

Despite any misgivings, most western Republican editors came to endorse an expansionist foreign policy. Papers such as the *Seattle Post-Intelligencer* proclaimed George Washington's warnings against aggressive foreign policies to be a dead letter in this promising new era.[41] Some, though, would not endorse expansionist policies until well after 1898. The *Omaha Bee*, for example, frequently included editorial remarks suggesting that the addition of the Philippines would be more of a burden than a blessing.[42]

While increasing numbers of Republican papers called for an overseas empire, Populist and Democratic publications remained divided. Nebraska's leading reform publications opposed expansion,[43] but the same was not true in Colorado or Washington, where many of the most important reform papers, led by Denver's *Rocky Mountain News*, the *Seattle Times*, and the *Spokesman-Review* of Spokane, talked of an empire in the Pacific. All justified the policy by claiming that connections across the Pacific would expand trade opportunities. As one writer for the *Spokesman-Review* put it, holding the archipelago and gaining the trade of Asia "may solve the perplexing problem of providing work for the unemployed, and markets for the surplus goods of American factories."[44] For many, empire appeared to provide remedies for the troubles of producers.

That so many newspapers in the Far West—regardless of political allegiance—supported expansion should come as no surprise. Newspapers are necessarily commercial and promotional enterprises, and western newspapers had a tendency to act the part of boosters that predicted a future of fame and wealth for their towns, cities, or states. This propensity was only accentuated by the political discourse of the West in the 1890s. Despite denials by greenback theorists and the more prominent minds in the Populist Party that overproduction was the source of America's economic difficulties, they still precipitated the shift of political discourse toward economic subjects. Now, when advocates of expansion promised that the nation's attention would be fixed on the Pacific and trade with Asia, the boosterism of many western editors overcame any hesitance they may have felt.[45]

There is also a great deal of evidence that these voices did not represent the majority of Bryan's followers. Weeks after the excitement of the first battle, the editor of Nebraska's *Independent* sent fifty letters to friendly members of the legislature and editors of reform newspapers in the state. One part of the questionnaire asked respondents to explain how the party conventions should respond to "consequences growing out of" the war. Thirty-one of the fifty unequivocally stated their opposition to new acquisitions or conquests; only three argued that the conventions should support expansion. As one newspaperman put it, "All populists should be too enlightened to doubt for a moment their duty to oppose land-grabbing, militarism, or any other appurtenance of royalty."[46] Another informal poll, this one by the *Denver Post*, produced similar results. Of the forty-five local lawyers, politicians, and businessmen asked—most of whom were Democrats—twenty-eight rejected permanent occupation of the Philippines.[47] Not all reformers quickly adopted anti-imperialism, but a great many considered expansion into the Pacific a dubious undertaking.

The debate had barely begun when the soldiers of the western volunteer regiments began their journey to the Philippines. The first western regiments departed for Manila in the last days of May. A second contingent left San Francisco on June 15, and a third followed near the end of the month. Ten thousand American soldiers were on their way to the Philippines, where they took up positions alongside the insurgent army that was already besieging the colony's capital city.[48]

A day before the second wave of troops went to sea—and just weeks before his own regiment would be mustered in—William Jennings Bryan took the opportunity to address the subject of imperialism. In Bryan's eyes, the topic had become too important to ignore, but he knew it would be improper to speak out on the matter after he became an officer in the American army. This would be his best opportunity. He opened his speech by declaring that "Nebraska is ready to do her part in time of war," but this did not "indicate that the state is inhabited by a contentious or warlike people." It merely demonstrated that "they do not shrink from any consequences which may follow the performance of a national duty." Their obligation was to protect the United States in time of war and liberate Cuba, both of which were honorable reasons to serve. But he believed there was no justification for the acquisition of far-off islands, which would transform the humanitarian struggle into a war of conquest and lead to "the charge of having added hypocrisy with greed." Dewey's victory had a purpose, and the defeat of Spain in the Pacific was a legitimate goal, but one triumph in battle must not determine the course of American policy. "Our guns destroyed a Spanish fleet, but can they destroy the self-evident truth, that governments derive their just powers, not from superior force, but from the consent of the governed?" Those who "clothe land-covetousness in the attractive garb of 'national destiny'" would gain no support in Nebraska, he said.[49]

At nearly the same time that Bryan was speaking, activists in Boston led the first formal anti-imperialist meeting organized in America. Bryan had no contact with its leaders at the time, but the basic sentiment was the same. The old mugwump Gamaliel Bradford led the gathering, and like Bryan, he and the speakers who followed condemned the wild dreams of empire that they feared had gained a foothold in the American psyche. While support for conquest had developed almost impulsively, opponents were urging Americans to consider the consequences both for their own nation and for those who were fighting for freedom.[50]

The war with Spain would last only two months more. On August 12 a peace protocol that suspended fighting was signed by the United States and Spain, with a formal peace treaty to be negotiated thereafter in Paris. On the other side of the world, Americans in the Philippines were totally unaware that the war had ended. The telegraph cable connecting Manila to the outside had been cut at the beginning of the conflict. In the meantime, the American commanders in the archipelago, General Wesley Merritt and Admiral George Dewey (recently promoted), had negotiated with their Spanish counterpart for a peaceful surrender of Manila. Without informing their Filipino allies, the "combatants" arranged a sham battle for the purpose of preserving Spanish honor and guaranteeing sole American possession of the city. When the faux attack began on August 13, not everything went according to plan. Some casualties were suffered, and the Americans did not occupy the Spanish positions quickly enough to prevent their former allies from entering the suburbs of Manila. Worse still was what followed. American officers were rather lamely forced to explain to Emilio Aguinaldo—leader of the Filipino revolutionaries—that American occupation of the city was required to preserve public order. Aguinaldo and his army did not disperse; instead, they continued to hold their positions surrounding Manila. The public debate over empire was about to move beyond conjecture.[51]

THE CAMPAIGN OF 1898

Although the war was still the primary focus of public attention in the summer of 1898, by July, at least some conversations had turned to the fall election. It was the first major contest after the upheaval of 1896, and it proved pivotal for the western states. In the eyes of Bryan and his allies, this election would allow Democrats, Populists, and Silver Republicans to perfect the fusion coalition and thus ease their favored candidate's road to the presidency in 1900. Every House seat was at stake, along with the senatorial positions held by William Allen, Stephen White, William Roach, and several other prominent westerners. Additionally, a large number of state positions were up for grabs, making this contest crucial for determining the political future of the entire region.

However, the issues of 1896 would not be the dominant ones in this election. Populists and Democrats in the West had hoped to continue their crusade for economic justice. Some Republicans considered co-opting the message of their opponents by taking up reforms of their own, but reality soon forced them back into the uncomfortable positions they had occupied two years earlier. Of course, the war would have an impact, but early in the campaign, its significance remained unclear. Questions surrounding expansion were present throughout the contest, but even in states where Hawaiian annexation was popular, the expansion issue was not yet the exclusive property of one side or the other. The two sides continually jockeyed for position, but the decisive issue emerged only in the last month of the campaign.

It is important to keep in mind that the western reformers had not expended their full energies in 1896. In both Washington and Nebraska, where reformers held the governorships and many of the legislative seats, they had compiled solid records in the sessions of 1897. Washington's Democrats and Populists had also succeeded in placing women's suffrage and single tax amendments on the ballot that November.[52] In Colorado, where Democrats, conservative Republicans, and a mixed bag of Silver Republicans had made up most of the last legislature, reform stalled. However, new organizational efforts on the part of Colorado's laborers soon shifted the balance in favor of change. Unions such as the Western Federation of Miners (formed in 1893) had been greatly influenced by the Populists. In addition, by 1896, several organizations had come together to establish the Colorado State Federation of Labor. At its 1897 convention, a majority of delegates declared the need for direct political advocacy, and in 1898, its leaders agreed that members must unite behind a pro-labor ticket. Federation secretary David C. Coates was a Populist, but he also developed a program to vet all local candidates so affiliates of the organization could endorse an appropriate slate. In such a way, they intended to secure a legislature that would pass an eight-hour law for miners.[53] In each state, then, reformers were well positioned to continue the fight over economic policy.

Conservatives soon provided further justification for a continuation of the reform coalition. In late 1897 and early 1898, Gage's monetary reform proposals caused frustration even among the editors of western Republican newspapers. Wolcott's international commission had already proved a colossal failure, in no small part because of Gage's public statements since assuming office.[54] Any thought that western Republicans could hide behind the fig leaf of international bimetallism was thus erased. Adding power to the reformers' arguments was the Supreme Court's March 1898 ruling in *Smyth v. Ames*. In one fell swoop, the Court threw out Nebraska's maximum railroad rates and threatened similar laws enacted in other states (such as Washington's recently passed rate regulations). Passage of the law in 1893 had represented Nebraska Populists' greatest victory, but now the Court had ruled that the rates did not offer a fair return to the railroads and represented confiscation without due process of law—a violation of the Fourteenth Amendment.[55]

The ruling was an attack on one of the more substantial gains made by the Populists and their allies, and at first it appeared that it would only bolster their resolve. Just the week before, Senator Allen had lambasted those who called for national regulation of the railroads. "We have Interstate Commerce Commissioners. We are paying them large salaries. . . . Pray, what are they doing for the country and for the shipper? Absolutely nothing." In the battle between the regulators and the regulated, the winner was clear. The commissioners were "as powerless and impotent as a babe in its cradle to control these corporations."[56] After the Court's ruling, the only other means of reining in the railroads' power was practically nullified. Any rate that a conservative court deemed unfair could be thrown out. Writers for the *Independent* lashed out at the Court in the weeks that followed. Even though the outcome had been expected, they were upset primarily because the "power of injunction" and "the evident bias of the supreme court" now made it "practically impossible to enforce any regulation of the railway rates except such as the roads themselves will agree to."[57] In several articles, the paper emphasized the Court's application of the Fourteenth Amendment and its identification of the railway corporation as a legal person. When the Interstate Commerce Commission issued a report in early April admitting that court rulings had crippled it, the *Independent* simply ran the headline "Regulation a Failure."[58] Allen and the writers for the *Independent* were in perfect agreement: only public ownership could solve the problem.

Before the war with Spain, Populists and other members of the reform coalition continued to hammer home the need for change. Whatever the future of their party, they offered alternatives that no one else did, and they promised a kind of economic equality that many Americans still dreamed of. Populism, they contended, was every bit as necessary now as it had been at the beginning of the decade.

While the Populists and their allies demanded substantive reform, Republicans did not remain static. Early in the decade, western Republicans had advocated silver, but that option was dead to them now. A new tack was needed. Of course, nearly all western newspapers were critical of corporations deemed to be monopolistic, and some, like the *Omaha Bee*, had developed a lengthy record of such criticism. Others provided occasional hints that the party should become a vehicle for reform. When the newly elected Republican governor of Michigan, Hazen Pingree, began to lash out against trusts in his public addresses, a number of western Republican editors responded enthusiastically.[59] Few of the region's prominent politicians followed suit, but some tested the waters. In a February speech to the Baltimore Union League, Senator John Thurston told easterners about the situation in his part of the country. There, he said, the "allied force of free silver, socialism, lawlessness, and anarchy" had continued to proselytize with great success, all in an attempt to "array every man without a dollar against every man with a dollar." There was only one way to put an end to the threats to national development posed by extremists from the West, he said. It was time for the Republican Party to "stand eternally against all unlawful combination and unjust exaction of aggregated capital and corporate power; it must smite with the mailed hand of law every combination formed to artificially decrease the wages of labor or increase the prices of necessities of life." Certainly, this was strange talk coming from a railroad lawyer and archconservative, but Thurston considered the situation in the West to be dire. In early 1898 he predicted that another campaign based on support of the economic status quo would lead to disaster.[60]

Thurston's prediction proved wrong on nearly all fronts. Though western Republicans were hesitant to emphasize their conservatism, they did not embrace reform in any substantial way. Calling for reform while running against the Populists would only provide ammunition for the opposition. Thurston believed his party could not survive if it did not accept change, but as it turned out, the Republicans did not have to change just yet. Public frustrations had not abated, but the war soon provided an alternative path to victory.

The campaign officially launched in August. The Populists, Democrats, and Silver Republicans of Nebraska met at separate conventions in Lincoln

on August 2-4. As usual, plenty of squabbling accompanied the cooperation, but there was no great struggle over ideas—only over candidates. Some
Democrats believed they deserved the governorship, but the Populists stood
firm behind William A. Poynter, an early Alliance leader and senate majority leader for the 1891 legislature. He was also a teetotaler, and Democrats
debated his merits nearly all night before finally accepting the Populist candidate.[61] The platforms of each party remained separate, but they were largely
focused on the same issues. None of the parties approved an anti-imperialist
plank. Instead of declaring a policy with regard to the Spanish islands, the
Populist platform acknowledged the importance of the issue but ultimately
stated that the wise course was for the government to "postpone consideration until the conclusion of the war, to be taken up for mature deliberation
by the people when no public excitement exists." All parties included planks
that praised the bravery of those fighting the war, attacked the bond issue
used to finance it, and expressed their disgust at attempts to bolster the gold
standard or destroy silver and paper currency. The Populists added another
demand for government ownership of the railroads and pointed directly at
the *Smyth v. Ames* decision as proof that it was necessary.[62]

The fusion forces of Washington State did not convene until a month
later, meeting again (as they had in 1896) in the town of Ellensburg. Washington's three parties had less to fight over than most other western fusionists in 1898 because of the state's four-year gubernatorial terms. James
Hamilton Lewis and William C. Jones, the first non-Republicans to win
congressional seats since statehood had been achieved, were also due to be
renominated. After a brief squabble over nominations for supreme court
judgeships, the three parties hammered out a general platform that included
planks demanding the free coinage of silver and federal control over the
issuance of currency, opposing any further sale of interest-bearing bonds,
praising the present governor and legislature for the first balanced budget
in state history, and calling for direct legislation. The Populists approved a
separate platform, pledging support for the women's suffrage amendment
that would appear on the ballot. They also condemned the actions of the
administration before and during the war, claimed that intervention had
been delayed and that thousands of Cubans had died as a consequence, and
accused the president and the cabinet of mismanaging the war, turning its
"unavoidable hardships" into "horrors" for the nation's soldiers. The platform concluded with a renunciation of the "aggressive policy of territorial
expansion," but it also rejected "the surrender to Spain of any of the territory
that has been acquired" and "the surrender to Spain's domination of the

people of any Spanish colonies who co-operated with our forces against our enemy in the late war." The vague wording could please expansionists and their opponents alike.[63]

Colorado's conventions were under way at the same time as Washington's. The organization of a fusion coalition in Colorado fared better than it had in 1896, but the situation had become much more complicated. The state's Silver Republicans divided into three parties, with Teller leading the only pro-fusion, pro-reform element.[64] Teller's Silver Republicans, Thomas Patterson's Populists, and the Democrats then proceeded to cement their alliance. Democrat Charles S. Thomas—a man with a mixed record on organized labor—was given the nod for the governorship, but only after a fierce protest from the Populist camp. All other state offices and the two House seats were split among the Populists and the Silver Republicans. Each convention also developed its own platform. The most prominent feature in all pertained to the money question: each emphasized the free coinage of silver. Of course, all went on to praise the heroism of the state's and the nation's soldiers, but the Democrats and Populists differed substantially on the consequences of the war. The Democrats claimed the soldiers' efforts had added to the "glory and power of the nation, and to the limits of our domain," and they now believed the new possessions represented the nation's "enlarged duties and responsibilities." The Populists said the islands should not be given back to Spain but should be protected "until such time as a majority of the people of these respective countries shall express a desire to establish a government of their own."[65]

The greatest commonality among the combined reform parties of the three states was their desire to continue the economic fight above all else. Imperialism was not yet a clear issue, and certainly not a unifying one. In Nebraska, even though Senator Allen condemned "land-grabbing" in the biggest speech of the fusion conventions, there seemed little need to make the campaign about anti-imperialism.[66] Their greatest opponents, such as Edward Rosewater of the *Omaha Bee* and Senator John Thurston, also opposed expansionist policies.[67] Although at least one Republican congressional candidate tried to challenge an incumbent Populist by supporting imperialism, the issue was not an integral part of the state campaign.[68] A fusionist stand against expansion in Nebraska would only serve to alienate certain voters. In the case of Washington, the situation was more ambiguous. The state's Silver Republican senator, George Turner, had absented himself from the Hawaiian annexation vote, and Congressman James Hamilton Lewis had recorded his own serious reservations before voting for the Newlands resolu-

tion. The state press, however, seemed to favor the acquisition of Spain's colonies, and Governor Rogers directly stated his own preference for holding all
lands taken.[69] The Populists' brief statement on the subject was ambiguous,
and none of Washington's party leaders considered expansion—either for
or against—an important issue for the campaign. Colorado newspapers supported the acquisition of the islands, and so did the Democratic platform.
Even so, Charles S. Thomas—the candidate the Democrats had forced on
their allies—was one of the most solidly anti-imperialist politicians in the
state.[70] Clearly, none of the fusion parties were ready to put issues of foreign
policy ahead of domestic reform.

In spite of their wishes, the war had stirred up too much sentiment and
created too many issues of its own for any of the reform parties to ignore.
In some instances, Republicans were trumpeting the military victories won
over the summer as the triumphs of Republican governance. The reformers
were forced to respond by noting that members of all parties had joined
the war effort, all the while reminding audiences that the administration
had practically been pushed into the war against its will. At the same time,
they frequently criticized the administration—especially Secretary of War
Russell Alger—for inept management of the army's supplies and the disorder
and disease that infested the military camps. Nearly all papers reported the
struggles of the War Department over the summer and fall, but as campaign
season began, the coverage was increasingly seen as partisan. In Washington
State, Congressman Lewis and Senator Turner made the administration's
incompetence a substantial part of their political campaigns. Lewis, who had
accepted a position as a military inspector (with the rank of colonel) late
in war, was especially harsh in his criticism of profiteering and negligence.
Their attempt to turn a popular war into a political scandal held as many
dangers as benefits.[71]

Increasingly, the reformers came to fear that the campaign was being re-
directed away from economic issues and toward the war, and some tried to
steer it back to the course followed in 1896. "Republican managers in this
state [Washington] are trying desperately hard in this campaign, so far as
national issues are concerned, to ignore the currency question and make
an issue of the war with Spain," wrote one editor.[72] Another pointed out
that when the reformers had attempted to remonetize silver, they had been
called "'cranks,' 'anarchists' and 'repudiationists,'" until those old epithets
lost their power. Now, Republicans were using "promises of military glory"
and talk of the opportunity to "join English Tories in schemes of oppressing
and robbing the helpless of the earth" to distract attention from domestic re-

form.[73] Senator Turner told audiences that it was a contest of "money against manhood, and gold against the teachings of Almighty God," yet both sides either allowed or encouraged the war issue to affect the campaign.[74]

Whatever difficulties the fusionists faced, western Republicans' challenges were at least as great at the beginning of the campaign. Because nearly all their state parties—including those of the three states in this study—had flirted with free silver at some point in the 1890s, they had been in a weak position to assail the Bryan campaign in 1896. Each state party had to adapt quickly, or its struggles would continue. In Colorado, change failed to happen. Wolcott took charge of a coalition of conservative Silver and McKinley Republicans, then secured the party's gubernatorial nomination for his brother. Almost no Republican newspapers in the state admitted that the party accepted the single gold standard, and both the Republicans and their opponents continued to champion silver as the primary issue. The campaign boiled down to a contest of personalities, and for that reason, the Republicans were again doomed to failure.[75]

In Washington and Nebraska, the Republican organizations were led by those closer to the party's national mainstream. By 1898, nearly all the mainstream Republicans in those states accepted the gold standard, but many were still unsure of this new position on the money issue. Of course, according to the typical narrative presented by historians, Republicans could count on the rising tide of prosperity to carry them to victory. Improved economic conditions have often been used to explain the rapid decline of Populism in the West, but those claims seem to be based largely on Republican claims after the fact.[76] All parties admitted that times were better in 1898 than they had been two years earlier, and they all tried to take credit for it. Republicans were much more willing to boast about national prosperity and the value of "100 cent dollars" in October than they had been even in April, and they tended to identify economic growth as an adjunct to their party—with no essential explanation of its source.[77] Washington's Senator John L. Wilson simply told audiences that throughout the "history of the republican party," good times "always attended it when in power." In a similar vein, Wesley L. Jones, one of the state candidates for Congress, responded to his opponent's suggestion that any economic improvement was an "accident," not a result of Republican policies. "I tell you," he exclaimed to his audience, "I am going to stand by the party that is struck by this sort of accident."[78] The talk was much the same among Nebraska Republicans. "No man of candor and honesty will deny that the United States is very much more prosperous now than it was two years ago," claimed a writer for the *Omaha Daily Bee*. "It is not necessary to discuss the causes of this fortunate condition. It is sufficient to know that it exists and inquire as to what is essential to its continuance." Republican control of Congress was the predictable answer supplied by the author.[79] One candidate on the state ticket attempted to perform some verbal sleight of hand to aid the party's chances. While claiming that prosperity had returned to both the state and the nation, he simultaneously informed his audience, "Capital has no confidence in populist rule and so long as that party remains the dominant one in this state so long will capital be slow to invest in Nebraska."[80] The speaker made no attempt to reconcile the two statements.

Something else was needed to bring a Republican victory. The war proved to be a powerful issue, and soon the victorious commander in chief would join the campaign. In early October, President McKinley embarked on a speaking tour of the Midwest that culminated in his arrival at the Trans-Mississippi Exposition in Omaha on October 12. Ostensibly, this was not a campaign tour, but McKinley knew he could make voters see the connection between a triumphant wartime president and local Republican candidates. His speeches have been characterized as broadly imperialist, and according to his biographers, he was warmly welcomed throughout the tour—especially when he made reference to America's new "duty" across the Pacific. Yet the president was not outlining his vision in any great detail. In signature McKinley style, his tone was inoffensive, and any policy remarks were carefully veiled so as to remain opaque to audiences. In his Omaha speech, the president pointed out that "hitherto, in peace and in war, with additions to our territory and slight changes in our laws, we have steadily enforced the spirit of the constitution. . . . We have avoided the temptations of conquest in the spirit of gain." Though he also acknowledged that "new and grave problems" faced the nation, instead of suggesting that the old traditions were outdated, he reaffirmed the sentiment by stating, "We must avoid the temptation of undue aggression, and aim to secure only such results as will promote our own and the general good." If his discussion of new responsibilities demonstrated his preference for a more robust foreign policy, he never clarified what that entailed. It was left to the listener to determine whether those responsibilities could be fulfilled with a tiny coaling station or would require the acquisition of an expansive island group of 7 million to 10 million inhabitants.[81]

The most important portions of the president's remarks pertained not to foreign affairs but to domestic politics. After praising the achievements of the soldiers who had fought the war, he asked the audience, "Who will dim the splendor of their achievements? . . . Who will intrude detraction at this time to belittle the manly spirit of the American youth and impair the usefulness of the American army?" Worse still, "Who will embarrass the government by sowing seeds of disaffection among the brave men who stand ready to serve and die, if need be, for their country? Who will darken the counsels of the republic at this hour, requiring the united wisdom of all?" All at once, he united his administration's objectives with the soldiers' service, making it seem craven to criticize either. Then he claimed that America still faced challenges and that unity was needed instead of partisanship. This last component had already become a significant element in the president's speeches delivered on this tour. Just the day before, he had told the residents of Boone, Iowa, "This is a solemn hour demanding the highest wisdom and the best statesmanship of every section of our country." He concluded by asking them to "remember at this critical hour in the nation's history we must not be divided. The triumphs of war are yet to be written in the articles of peace."[82] The emergencies of war were still facing the nation, he claimed.

McKinley told audiences that the crisis was ongoing, and partisanship (or at least the kind of partisanship emanating from his rivals) was inappropriate. Again, he was nonspecific, refusing to identify which emergency in particular concerned him. At that moment, the press had identified two situations as "crises." One pertained to the commitment of Aguinaldo's Filipino revolutionaries to independence—a major story for much of the summer. The other, which received much more press attention in the fall, was based on a rumor that negotiations with Spain could break down at any time and war could resume. The great fear was that Spain would not be acting alone, based on claims that the European powers—led by either Russia or Germany—were considering intervention on behalf of Spain. According to some, Europe was jealous of American claims to the Philippines, while others cited a fear that the American presence might upset the fragile balance of power in East Asia.[83] Rumors of European intervention had preceded the war and never really ceased.[84] In July, Frank Eager, a Populist editor and captain in the First Nebraska Volunteers, wrote a letter to his brother from an encampment just outside Manila, stating that rumors of a European intervention were spreading fast.[85] From September through the end of the political campaign, these rumors reached a new peak. Spanish negotiators were one potential source of these reports, and some in the press acknowledged as much.[86]

It is difficult to state for certain how believable these stories were to the American public, although suspicion of European intrigue was as old as the republic itself and—especially in the case of the Populist constituency—still significant in the 1890s. There was just enough recent history to make the stories plausible. A mere three years earlier, the unlikely coalition of Germany, Russia, and France had intervened at the conclusion of the Sino-Japanese War to prevent Japan from taking possession of certain Chinese territories. It was feared that the incorporation of these possessions would tip the regional balance of power too strongly in Japan's favor.[87] To many, it may have seemed possible for a similar scenario to play out again, but the administration should have known better. Spain had been attempting to gain allies from the months before the war right up to the negotiations. McKinley's lieutenants had kept in contact with the diplomats of the great powers throughout the process, and even as negotiations were under way, they received confirmation that no interventions were contemplated.[88] But such rumors could always be put to use at home.

Republican campaigners painted the situation as a potential national emergency that could be prevented only by following the lead of McKinley. Especially in the Nebraska campaign, Republicans emphasized the danger of the moment. The editor of the *Columbus Journal*, for example, advertised that all patriotic Americans should vote for the Republican legislative candidate because "he has been an earnest supporter and is in sympathy on all points with the administration" and would "act in hearty co-operation with the President in the peace negotiations now pending. That the present is a critical period in our history, all thoughtful Americans admit, and realize the necessity of electing a congress in full sympathy with the administration." To abandon the president now would be unpatriotic because "the statesmen of Europe are eagerly awaiting political events in this country."[89] The editor of the *McCook Tribune* told readers it was their duty to "endorse the administration" by electing Republicans to the state legislature. "They are all worthy and able men and believe that President McKinley should be upheld in the present crisis."[90] Another Nebraska paper went even further, claiming that the Populists and Democrats were acting on behalf of Spanish interests and sought to "embarrass the National administration as much as possible in the settlement of the questions growing out of the war, so that some or all of the advantages gained by this country in the war with Spain will have to be thrown away." Aiding them were "speakers from the east" who had been sent into the state and whose "utterances would indicate that they are in the direct employ of Spain." Traitors were afoot, and the nation must be defended. "Patriotism demands this course without regard to previous political opinions."[91]

The suggestion that Populists and Democrats wanted to throw away "all of the advantages gained by this country in the war" hinted at the expansionist subtext of the campaign. Rarely did any Nebraska editors directly express opinions regarding the American situation in the Caribbean or the Pacific. Instead, local Republican papers reprinted stories from the national media that discussed the inability of the Cubans, Puerto Ricans, or Filipinos to manage their own affairs and then described how American troops were keeping the peace. Then, on their political and opinion pages they wrote that patriotism required support for the president's policies—whatever they were. As one of these editors put it, if you were "a good patriotic American citizen, you indorse the policy of the president with reference to the Cuban, Porto [sic] Rico, and Philippine questions," without any further explanation. Patriotic duty required voters to put Republicans in Congress.[92] But it should not be assumed that all Republicans equated patriotism with expansion. Throughout the campaign, the Republican *Omaha Bee* continued to oppose what it regarded as imperialism. Still, like the rest of the state's conservative media, the *Bee* declared that "patriotism should rise above partisanship" and observed that "the main issue before the people at this time is whether the national administration under William McKinley shall be endorsed and upheld and the policy under which this country is enjoying exceptional prosperity shall be continued."[93]

In Washington State, the newspapers and campaigners used much the same material to support an identical conclusion: a vote against local Republicans would weaken the president at a critical juncture. It "could be interpreted in no other way and would have no other meaning than as a vote of national censure upon William McKinley." This issue was "first and foremost above all other issues," they claimed.[94] But in Washington, loyalty to the president was rarely viewed or described as an issue unto itself; although loyalty was a patriotic duty, it was also a prerequisite to territorial expansion. Consistently, the state's newspapers expressed the hope that voters would "favor upholding the hands of the noble administration at Washington in arranging the terms of peace to the permanent advantage of America, instead of neutralizing the grand victories of the magnificent war."[95] While some fusionists claimed that all parties in Washington supported the acquisition of Spain's islands, the records of their congressmen called that assertion into question.[96]

Local Republicans were not finished tying patriotic sentiment to the actions of their party. They criticized their rivals' untoward attacks on the War Department—and, indirectly, on McKinley—denying that a Democrat or a Populist could do so and still demonstrate patriotism. Nowhere was this truer than in Washington State, where Turner and Lewis continued to accost Secretary Alger's incompetence throughout the campaign. When Lewis attacked those managing the war as "tasseled society sapheads," the *Tacoma Daily Ledger* declared, "[those] are words intended to be expressive of the fusionist estimate of the brave men who scaled the heights of El Caney and others, many of whom now rest in their graves of heroes at Santiago."[97] Turner was blasted for criticizing "*without mercy the course of President McKinley during the late war, accusing him of weakness, cowardice and collusion with money kings.*"[98] Speaking before a large Republican crowd, Senator Wilson called Turner's language "unpatriotic and treasonable."[99]

In Nebraska, the talk of treason was often borrowed directly from the era of the "bloody shirt." Just weeks after the close of the state conventions, Republican gubernatorial candidate Monroe Hayward ended one of his biggest speeches by reading a campaign bill from 1864 that called for the "brave men who hate the rebellion of Abraham Lincoln and are determined to destroy it" to join the Democrats. The opponents of the administration in 1898 were little different from those in 1864, he proclaimed.[100] The rhetoric of a previous era was only amplified when it was discovered that the Populist state commissioner of public lands had been a "copperhead" member of the Indiana legislature during the Civil War. Republican papers soon put this revelation to use as further evidence of fusionist disloyalty.[101] This kind of language had dominated Nebraska politics in the years before the Populist uprising, and it was reincorporated into the political lexicon as if nothing had changed.[102] By the time Senator Thurston declared "patriotism" to be the true issue during his late campaign swing through the West, other Republicans had already made that point clear to voters.[103]

Western reformers thought they could defuse the contentions of their opponents and demonstrate their own loyalty by emphasizing their military service. James Hamilton Lewis made it clear that he had seen abuses while serving in the inspector general's office. Yet opponents claimed he had never been formally accepted in that position, citing as evidence the fact that he would have been court-martialed if he had made such slanderous comments while in uniform. Lewis eventually provided proof of his military service from the War Department, but Republican papers continued to accuse him of being a fake colonel right up to Election Day.[104] In Nebraska, a front-page article in the *Independent* recounted Senator Allen's brave military service as a young man during the Civil War, as told by the Iowa veterans with whom he had served. The headline of the article, "W. V. Allen as Private," even accentuated his position as a common soldier. Although the article made no reference to Allen's recent criticisms of the administration, the timing suggests it was a response to attacks on the senator's loyalty.[105] Yet such defenses inherently accepted their opponents' emphasis on the primacy of military service. Allen had endured personal hardships and risks at least as great as those faced by American soldiers during the War of 1898, but the *Independent* article suggested that he deserved credit because, as a patriot, he had followed orders while in uniform. Lewis's statements tacitly accepted that only those in uniform had the right to criticize the War Department, weakening the claim that civilians possessed a similar right. At a moment when patriotic sentiment was at fever pitch, western reformers did not fully challenge the growing tide of militaristic nationalism.

The results of the 1898 contests were far more decisive than most historians have realized. From a national perspective, analysts have pointed out that Democrats gained several seats in the House but remained in the minority, while Republicans picked up a few seats in the Senate. Instead of what some feared would be an off-year decline, 1898 represented a minor victory for the McKinley administration.[106] If the contests are examined from a regional perspective, 1898 was a clear disaster for the western reformers. In Washington State, Republicans captured the legislature and defeated both William C. Jones and James Hamilton Lewis, as their 13,000-vote majorities from 1896 were turned into defeats of more than 2,000 votes apiece. Similar results were recorded along the Pacific coast. Of the six Populist, Democratic, and Silver Republican House members from those states, only Marion De Vries of California won reelection. In Nebraska, there was some reason for celebration. Poynter won the governorship by less than 3,000 votes, and the fusionists held all the congressional districts they already controlled. Yet they too lost the state legislature, and Senator Allen would not be reelected.[107] Throughout the West, the defeats piled up. Governor Andrew Lee of South Dakota barely managed a victory but was left to face a hostile legislature, and Kelley and Knowles were not returned to Congress. Even in Kansas, that bastion of Populism, fusion forces were swept out of state offices and lost five of their six House seats.[108]

Only in the mountain states did the reformers have a measure of success. There, issues surrounding the war had largely been pushed aside during the campaign. Two years earlier, the local regular Republicans parties had all but collapsed, and their recovery was not yet complete. Consequently, fusion in Colorado proved an election-year success. Thomas was elected governor, Bell and Shafroth were sent back to Congress, and a more reform-minded group took charge of the legislature—a sweep unmatched even in the other mining states. Populist infighting in Idaho led to a successful Democratic and Silver Republican fusion ticket that excluded the Populists. In Montana, too, the fragile silver alliance broke down, as William A. Clark of the Anaconda mine pushed the state's Democrats to nominate a straight party ticket. The Populists and Silver Republicans who attempted a separate fusion ticket went down to defeat at the hands of the Democrats. Even in Nevada, single-party politics prevailed as the Silver Party remained dominant at all levels, but the victory just briefly masked emerging divisions that loyalty to a metal could not smooth over. Fights over the spoils threatened to tear apart the remaining reform coalitions in the states most opposed to administration policy.[109]

As they tried to explain the results of the contests, many on both sides contended that the war had played a significant part. In a letter to Jonas Lien in Manila, Richard Pettigrew attributed defeats in South Dakota to the difficulties accompanying local fusion arrangements and the "unlimited supply of money" held by their opponents. He added in conclusion, "The war sentiment is strong, and that had a good deal to do with our defeat."[110] In Washington, the Republican state committee chairman attributed the stunning reversal to two issues: his opponents' support for the single tax (which had more to do with Republican branding of the amendment than the reformers' espousal of the doctrine) and voters' realization that "the administration needed the undivided support of all parties" because of the ongoing negotiations with Spain. The attacks of Lewis and Turner only highlighted the president's call for unity.[111] Their state rivals largely concurred with this analysis.[112] Despite the election of Poynter in Nebraska, state Republicans believed the contest marked a dramatic shift. In 1896 Holcomb had been elected by a majority of more than 20,000, whereas Poynter's victory was by less than 3,000. State Republicans declared with no small amount of satisfaction that their victories in the West had killed silver as an issue. "There has been a wonderful change in sentiment in Nebraska," crowed another paper, "and Bryanism is doomed."[113]

Despite their limited victory, Nebraska Populists suffered the loss of Senator Allen, and at least one person commented on the connections between this defeat and the upcoming contest that would define America. Jay Burrows, an Alliance organizer and one of the founders of the state party, wrote a letter to the *Independent* in which he described the loss of Allen—"the greatest United States senator the state ever had"—as an incalculable disaster for the people because of the "new situations that confront the nation." Allen was a thoughtful analyst of American overseas policy, and Congress would have to decide the fate of the Philippines without him. A colonial occupation would mean "our complication in European politics" and a militarized society. A more inclusive form of expansion would "necessarily and unavoidably place the ten or fifteen millions of this half civilized Asiatic population upon absolute equality with our own people," essentially destroying American labor. The alternative, he said, was to tell the Filipinos to "establish a free constitutional government for your own people." If they did so, they would "have our moral support, our advice, and our armed assistance" if they needed it. According to Burrows, the ultimate decision among these three alternatives would determine the fate of not only the Filipinos but also the Americans. The American people must choose between the course of "rapacity and greed and thirst for dominion" or "national honesty, integrity and devotion to a God-given mission." While Nebraska's Populists and Democrats had avoided a discussion of imperialism during the campaign, the consequences of the war were yet to be settled.[114]

The elections of 1898 were far too confused to create the clear divisions and evoke the moral senses of 1896. The rhetoric adopted in the campaigns combined elements of that earlier contest with the type of discourse that became dominant over the next two years. Populists and their allies started the year hoping to cement their position or even expand their influence through a message that emphasized the economic and political empowerment of farmers and laborers. Western Republicans took a beating at the beginning of year as they were forced to defend the domestic and foreign policies of McKinley. The war had changed the situation, and conservatives now saw that their chance for success in November could be tied to victories won on the battlefield that summer.

The campaigns were just as messy as one would expect. In some states, such as Colorado, Republican parties could barely reassemble all their fractured pieces in time to wage a coordinated effort. The western reformers were somewhat more successful at reassembling their coalitions, but in the confusion of the war, they were unsure of their direction. They continued to focus on their economic platform, but most did not know what to say about the conflict with Spain, the conduct of the president, or the possibility of territorial gains. Although most Republican parties were only slightly more purposeful in their statements on the Philippines, they largely succeeded in depicting their opponents as disloyal in a time of war and international crisis. Finally, western conservatives changed the terms of a debate they had been losing for most of the decade. This was the greatest difference from the last presidential race, and one that promised to give Republicans the national mandate they had lacked.

As a consequence of the many defeats suffered by Populists and their allies in 1898, McKinley would have a solid majority of regular Republicans in both houses of the Fifty-Sixth Congress. It was this Congress that would determine the form of control the United States exercised over its "new possessions." In addition, although he preferred to push it through as quickly as possible, McKinley knew that if the lame-duck Senate of the Fifty-Fifth Congress did not ratify the peace treaty with Spain—which was still being negotiated—the next one would. His campaign ploy had worked, and now he could reap the rewards.

6. IMPERIALISM COMES TO THE FOREFRONT

"There is mourning in Nebraska to-day," said Senator William Allen on February 6, 1899. "There will be weeping at the hearthstone of many a Nebraska home to-night." The first reports of fighting around Manila had just arrived. The initial rumors claimed that the army led by Emilio Aguinaldo had attacked American positions, most of which were held by volunteer regiments from the western states. Allen said he had been informed that ten of the first twenty dead were from the Nebraska regiment. "I can not condemn too severely the assault, the treacherous assault, made on our troops," he continued. He went on to call the individuals responsible for the attack "savages as bloodthirsty and incapable of being reconciled as the Ogallala Sioux." Despite his anger toward those who had killed his friends and neighbors, he told the audience that "this ought to be a warning to us." At the close of his speech, he told all present that he looked forward to "the day when the Filipinos and the inhabitants of Porto [sic] Rico and Cuba may rise to a true conception of the duties and obligations of citizenship; when they too, with the encouragement of this great and powerful Republic, shall take their station among the civilized republics and peoples of the earth."[1]

The outbreak of a new conflict put Allen in a difficult position. Like a number of other western reformers, he favored ratification of the peace treaty but rejected the notion that the United States had inherited some obligation to conquer and hold people without their consent. Now, Allen acceded to the use of force to put down this wanton attack on the soldiers who had helped break the chains of Spanish oppression. But he still rejected outright a policy of aggression. Overseas conquests, colonialism, and militarism were, in Allen's mind, totally without precedent in American history and unacceptable behavior for a republic.

In early 1899 the battle lines that divided imperialists and their opponents were still incredibly convoluted. Some Republicans still had misgivings about the acquisition of overseas territories, especially the Philippines, but most would not publicly oppose the president. At the same time, two apostate Republicans from the West—Henry Teller and William Stewart—unreservedly supported the acquisition of all the lands occupied by American forces. Populists such as Allen distrusted McKinley but wanted to put an official end to the war with Spain before determining the fate of the islands. And of course, many others declared that the treaty must be stopped in order to safeguard liberty and the Constitution.

Despite this diversity of positions, harder ideological lines were appearing. Increasingly, Populists and Democrats demonstrated their firm opposition to imperialism. Whereas western reformers had been divided over Hawaiian annexation, nearly all opposed the permanent occupation of the Philippines. Some had considered Hawaii to be necessary for the war effort, while others simply saw it as too small to meaningfully alter American ideals or institutions. The same could not be said of the Philippines. To control and defend a distant archipelago with perhaps 10 million inhabitants would require a larger army and navy, a greater administrative bureaucracy, and—most ominously—a willingness to disregard the tradition of representative government.[2] This new policy, the western critics claimed with certainty, was demanded by the great financiers and industrialists. The reformers' crusade had been designed to put the interests of humanity before those of business. In 1899, as they tried to prevent territorial acquisition, that struggle expanded into a new field.

INTERREGNUM

Following the elections of 1898, much remained undetermined. The president's campaign tour had provided little insight into his foreign policy ambitions, and the final treaty was not signed and its terms made public until December 10. Although the treaty fulfilled the main purpose of the war—Cuba was recognized as being under American tutelage, pending the organization of a new government—it also included provisions for the acquisition of Puerto Rico and the Philippines. The latter was to be exchanged for the sum of $20 million.[3] The treaty lived up to the anti-imperialists' fears, but it did not provide a substantially clearer outline of American policy. While it differentiated between Cuba and the other islands, it did not state whether the United States was to hold Puerto Rico and the Philippines as colonies in perpetuity, as territories that would obtain statehood in the future, or as short-term protectorates that would become independent countries. McKinley chose not to clarify his plans, only adding to the controversy.

The closest the president came to a statement of policy was a document directed at the Filipinos and American military personnel on the islands, not Congress or the American public. It declared that Dewey's victory "practically effected the conquest of the Philippine Islands and the suspension of Spanish sovereignty therein." In a typically paternalistic manner, McKinley tried to assure the Filipinos that the Americans came "not as invaders or conquerors, but as friends, to protect the natives in their homes, in their employments, and in their personal and religious rights." Military commanders were to guarantee the "full measure of individual rights and liberties which is the heritage of free peoples, and by proving to them that the mission of the United States is one of benevolent assimilation, substituting the mild sway of justice and right for arbitrary rule." Yet every suggestion of benign intent was followed by a warning. Those who did not submit to the newly established authority, McKinley vowed, would be brought "within the lawful rule we have assumed, with firmness if need be," and to that end, "the strong arm of authority" must be maintained.[4]

The Filipinos themselves immediately saw through the doubletalk. After McKinley issued his proclamation in mid-December 1898, General Elwell Otis, the new head of the American army in Manila and titular military governor of the Philippines, provided a sanitized version of it to Emilio Aguinaldo. Otis apparently believed that the Filipino commander had no means of obtaining the original. The form Otis provided de-emphasized the American claim to sovereignty but still stated that the United States was there for the benefit of the inhabitants, suggesting little likelihood of an American withdrawal. Aguinaldo would not have been satisfied with the content of the sanitized version in any case, but the Filipino general was furious when he learned of McKinley's claim that the right of conquest entitled the United States to absolute control over the whole of the Philippines. The army under Aguinaldo's command maintained its position surrounding Manila but took no action that would provoke a response. Regardless of his course, the likelihood of a peaceful conclusion grew increasingly slim.[5]

As tensions were building in the archipelago, other opponents of empire were taking action in the United States. By November 1898, those who had organized the anti-imperialist meeting at Boston's Faneuil Hall had succeeded in attracting large numbers of prominent northeasterners (and a few others) to help them form a new organization. The Anti-Imperialist

League was officially created on November 19, with former Massachusetts governor and secretary of the treasury George S. Boutwell selected as its first president. The choice of a regular Republican by the heavily mugwump organizing committee was no accident; it was designed to demonstrate their nonpartisan approach to the issue. Honorary vice presidencies were bestowed on men such as businessman, economist, and gold standard advocate Edward Atkinson; former president Grover Cleveland; steel tycoon Andrew Carnegie; leading mugwump editor Carl Schurz; and former senator—and most recently, McKinley's secretary of state—John Sherman. They were joined by labor leader Samuel Gompers, but for the most part, the views of these men ran the (rather limited) ideological gamut from classical liberal to conservative.[6]

Of course, there were plenty of others who recognized the dangers that accompanied imperialism. Richard Pettigrew was thoroughly opposed to the acquisition of the Philippines, and in late 1898 he used his contacts inside the First South Dakota Volunteers to gain an unfiltered assessment of the situation there. The most important of these correspondents was Jonas Lien, a twenty-five-year-old reform speaker and editor who was serving as a lieutenant in South Dakota's regiment in Manila. It was Lien who informed Pettigrew in October that "the much heralded battle of Manila [the Americans' capture of the city in August] was a farce—cut and dried and prearranged." Lien also told the senator that if the Americans attempted to claim the islands for themselves, Aguinaldo and his army would fight. Worse still, "if they determine to fight it will be a prolonged struggle, ending either in the withdrawal in disgust of the United States forces or in the extermination of the native population." The best solution was for "you gentlemen who occupy seats in Congress" to "devise some scheme to get rid of it."[7]

Pettigrew was hoping to do just that. He responded to Lien by stating that militarism and "the conquest and government of unwilling people" were un-American doctrines that must be defeated. In a remarkable declaration of his commitment to the cause, he wrote, "If we try to occupy the Philippines I hope the native inhabitants will fight us, and then I hope they will whip our army, for I believe all governments derive their just powers from the consent of the governed, and we have no right to forcibly occupy that country." The Filipinos possessed every right to control their own affairs, and they should be allowed to "set up a government of their own and run it in their own way, without interference on our part in any particular."[8]

Pettigrew believed the best way to halt American ambitions in the Philippines was to defeat the Treaty of Paris. He was joined in this view by many members of the Anti-Imperialist League and by senators such as Maryland Democrat Arthur Pue Gorman and Massachusetts Republican George Frisbie Hoar. The two-thirds majority required to ratify the treaty was a high hurdle, and opponents believed that popular sentiment in favor of expansion would fade with the passage of time. Given a few months more, passions would calm and the public would again favor more traditional American policies, they argued.[9]

The opponents of ratification have often been depicted as the only real hope for American anti-imperialism, yet the possibility of "success" by this route was highly questionable at best. If McKinley was committed to ratifying the treaty, there was nothing they could do to stop it. The president could always call a special session of the newly elected Fifty-Sixth Congress just days after the sitting Congress adjourned, and it was a more solidly pro-administration body than its predecessor.[10] While a number of anti-imperialists believed the American public had become temporarily irrational, it is surprising that historians have accepted that claim. Popular opinion regarding the Philippines was due to become more emotionally charged, not less so.

One anti-imperialist outside of the Senate has been given considerable attention for his controversial role in the ratification debate. In mid-December, William Jennings Bryan requested and received an honorable discharge from the army, not long before his regiment was due to take up garrison duty on the islands now under American control. Freed from the obligation to follow the commander in chief, he could continue the anti-imperialist campaign he had begun in June.[11] Bryan disagreed with those anti-imperialists who favored rejection of the treaty, contending instead that America could handle the situation more directly through legislation than diplomacy. Peace with the Filipinos could be established by declaring that America's aim was to help them set up an independent government. But even such a simple declaration of policy would be hollow until Spanish sovereignty was erased.[12]

Both contemporaries and historians have described Bryan's position as complicated, contradictory, and incongruous with his stated goal. But those who left behind the most widely referenced accounts—including George Hoar and Andrew Carnegie—were opposed to Bryan on nearly every other issue.[13] Of course, these men had no reason to see any high motive in Bryan's actions, and both Hoar and Carnegie claimed the Nebraskan was only seeking political advantage. In his account (published well after the fact), Hoar claimed Democratic senators had informed him that their party "could not hope to win a victory on the financial questions at stake after they had been beaten on them in a time of adversity; and that they must have this issue for the coming campaign." Bryan was the leading force behind this line of thinking in Hoar's telling of the story, and he claimed Bryan encouraged seventeen of his "followers" to vote for the treaty.[14]

To suggest that politics played no part in Bryan's thinking would be inaccurate, but to say that the war had been conducted and portrayed in a nonpartisan manner up to this point would be equally erroneous. Additionally, Bryan clearly expressed to Carnegie his desire to downplay imperialism as a political issue, if at all possible. When, in December 1898, the steel magnate suggested that anti-imperialism could make Bryan a strong candidate in the next presidential contest, Bryan disclosed his hope "to see the question disposed of before 1900, so that the fight for silver and against trusts and bank notes may be continued."[15]

Whether or not Bryan believed the issue of imperialism could be taken care of before the election of 1900, there is reasonable evidence that he suspected the treaty's rejection would have dire consequences for those who opposed it. His letters to Carnegie reveal his fear that a backlash against the anti-imperialist movement would halt their efforts permanently. "Sentiment is turning our way," he said, so "why risk the annihilation of our forces by rejecting the treaty?" In any event, "To reject it would throw the subject back into the hands of the administration," which obviously could not be trusted on this matter. At the same time, those who stopped the treaty "would be held responsible for anything that might happen" in the interim. In a much briefer letter sent to Carnegie just two days earlier, he expressed a similar view of the situation: "Your plan is dangerous," wrote Bryan, "my plan is safe."[16]

Historians who have accepted the criticisms leveled by Hoar, Carnegie, and other conservatives have completely ignored the context of the moment.[17] As demonstrated in the previous chapter, the president himself had campaigned in 1898 by telling audiences that the nation faced a "crisis" and that voters needed to put loyalty to the administration above all else until the war was officially concluded. This rhetoric continued after the campaign as well, only compounded by rising tensions in the Philippines.[18] By January, Republican newspapers were occasionally running stories stating that Aguinaldo and his representatives in Washington were "getting encouragement from the anti-expansionists in Congress."[19] Another claimed, "By delaying ratification of the peace treaty senators hope to see trouble in the Philippines."[20] Even some Democratic papers ran stories suggesting that delayed passage of the treaty provided inspiration not only to "Aguinaldo and his followers, but to foreign nations to encourage opposition to the United

States."[21] An appreciation of this context necessitates a reappraisal of Bryan's position. Bryan's actions and private statements suggest that he considered the risk to be plausible, just as the voting public had in 1898.

It should also be kept in mind that the stakes for Bryan were quite different from those for conservative opponents of the treaty. Bryan's western allies had taken a severe beating in the recent elections by virtue of Republican entreaties to put patriotism above politics. Those who were most critical of his decision were a Republican senator who was unlikely to face such repercussions, a Republican businessman who was beyond caring about his own popularity, and mugwumps who had never held office or had not come close to positions of power since shortly after the end of Reconstruction. Bryan's actions were calculated to save the movement he had led in 1896, but in the process, he provided those who loathed him a convenient excuse when they chose to abandon him later.

Historians interested in discrediting Bryan have also turned to his ally, Richard Pettigrew. In his semiautobiographical account written twenty years after the fact, the former South Dakota senator claimed that Bryan had proposed making "ratification of the Spanish Treaty an act of political expediency," allowing reformers to save face in the short term while threatening the Republicans with the epithet of "imperialist" in the next election if they failed to support Philippine independence.[22] Historians have used this account to claim that Bryan politicized the process and tarnished the cause of anti-imperialism. In reality, the treaty fight was already thoroughly political, and Bryan understood that the threat of retaliation by the electorate is one of the few motivators in the American political system. Additionally, other segments of Pettigrew's account have been called into question, and portions of it that arraign conservative anti-imperialists (including Hoar) have somehow been ignored.[23]

Regardless of the claims of historians, anti-imperialism manifested itself in many forms during the last political battles of the Fifty-Fifth Congress. Although western reformers in Congress remained divided over methods, by this point, nearly all of them agreed that the new overseas policies advocated by expansionists posed real threats to freedom at home and abroad. For those who had suffered stinging defeats in 1898, this was their last chance to put their opposition to empire on record in Congress, and they made the most of it.

THE OPENING OF THE DEBATE AND
ARGUMENTS FOR EMPIRE

Before the president sent his proclamation of "benevolent assimilation" to the Philippines, and even before the Treaty of Paris was signed, opposition to annexation was forming in Congress. Senator George Vest, a Missouri Democrat, introduced a resolution stating that "under the Constitution of the United States no power is given to the Federal Government to acquire territory to be held and governed permanently as colonies." It went on to clarify that small quantities of land could be acquired as coaling stations, but it specifically defined colonialism as a European institution and one not suited for the United States.[24] Vest's resolution was only the first of many designed to force the administration and its allies in Congress to declare their intentions toward the Philippines, and these resolutions (not the treaty vote) became the clearest point of contention between supporters and opponents of empire.

Republicans were forced into a tentative position, largely by the administration's silence, and Populists and Democrats sensed the opportunity this presented. The most well-known Senate resolutions on policy, and the ones most seriously debated, were those by Vest, presented at the opening of the session; one by Augustus Bacon of Georgia, first offered as debate began in earnest on January 11; and one by Senator Samuel McEnery of Louisiana, proposed just before the final vote on ratification.[25] Despite the prominence of resolutions offered by southerners, western senators were no less active. Between January 11 and February 11, William Allen alone offered three different resolutions designed to put either the Senate or both houses of Congress on record in opposition to colonialism. The last of these was framed merely as a reaffirmation of the principles of the Declaration of Independence, but in reality, it was a thinly veiled criticism of those who believed that Puerto Rico and the Philippines should be ruled by Americans.[26] Allen claimed to be surprised at the opposition that arose over the resolution's statement that the doctrine of the Declaration "is universal and extends to all peoples, wherever found, having a distinct and well-organized society and territory of their own."[27] He was not the only westerner who used resolutions in an attempt to force some statement of policy out of McKinley's backers, but all proved ineffective.[28]

Western reformers had no lack of opportunity to voice their opposition to imperialism. The Senate devoted much time to debating the pending treaty and the resolutions designed to set American policy. House members normally would have had less opportunity to state their opinions, and they had no chance to vote on or even debate the merits of the treaty. But in this case, the administration handed them a gift. Secretary of War Russell Alger, Adjutant General Henry Corbin, and their ally in the House, Representative John A. T. Hull of Iowa, fashioned a bill designed to expand the regular army from roughly 25,000 men to 100,000 on a permanent basis, ostensibly to police the colonies. But resistance to an enlarged American army was stronger than the administration had supposed, and it soon became clear that the bill had little chance of passing. As they attacked the Hull bill, anti-imperialist congressmen used the opportunity to reflect on how colonialism and militarism threatened democracy at home.[29]

The president's western supporters were somewhat slow to organize a response, perhaps because of their own lingering ambivalence about expansion. In one case, Senator George C. Perkins of California asked the state legislature to instruct him how to vote on the Treaty of Paris. In his request, he clearly indicated his belief that the dangers associated with annexation of the Philippines were great, and he suggested his preference to vote against the treaty. Perkins was a former governor and, according to one historian, was known "notoriously as a servant of the railroad" and big business generally, but in the last lines of his letter, he awkwardly referred to himself as a mere "representative of the people of California" and acknowledged that it was his duty to "obey" the wishes of the state legislature. In this circumstance, he thought it wiser to abdicate his senatorial responsibility than to support a risky policy of his own volition.[30]

Eventually, western supporters of the administration did organize a response, but most remained hesitant. Most commonly, they declared that it was the wrong moment to state American intentions toward the "new possessions." Many were likely trying to follow the president's lead, but the chief executive proved too nimble for even his allies to pin him down on the subject. And so they were left to argue that no one should declare US policy. Senator Thomas Carter of Montana questioned the utility of an early declaration of policy. "It must be conceded by those who seek to determine the momentous questions presented by the resolutions, not questions of constitutionality, but questions of policy, that our information is of the most meager character." Greater knowledge would allow Congress and the president to better chart the nation's course. As for now, "Even the number of islands in the archipelago seems to be a matter of controversy and doubt. The number of dialects or languages spoken by the people is merely conjectural, so far as our information at present extends."[31] In a similar vein, Congressman Thomas Tongue of Oregon casually remarked that the situation would be much clearer in several years, and perhaps no decision should be made until then.[32] Such a time frame was supported by William Stewart. Nevada's gray-bearded senator thought any declaration would be "entirely premature." He continued, "Six months or a year or two or three years hence will develop the facts, and the American Government will be better able to deal with it when they have a full knowledge of the facts than they are now, with the limited knowledge they have."[33] Of course, this was tantamount to handing the subject over to the president, but it allowed expansionists to claim that their solution was the cautious, responsible one.

The imperialists' refusal to define the terms of expansion—such as whether it would be temporary or perpetual, or whether the peoples would be considered citizens or subjects—only led to greater criticism by their opponents. Jerry Simpson mocked a Pennsylvania Republican for what he branded a "new kind of statesmanship." As Simpson pointed out, "He did not tell us and he did not know what course the President is going to pursue with reference to expansion or the annexation of the Philippine Islands, but he finally said that he was willing at all times, in season and out of season, to stand by whatever his party wanted him to stand by." The Kansan imagined a circumstance in which a member of Congress had no thoughts of his own on a matter "until he read his paper and found what the President stood for."[34] The laughter his comments evoked could not mask the seriousness of the issue.

Imperialists were able to argue that the policy question could be put off until a future date because America had always been a country of freedom and justice, and there was no reason to believe it would behave differently now. Colorado senator Edward Wolcott was sure that Americans would not "put our hands upon that people [the Filipinos] except to bless them. American institutions mean liberty and not despotism, and our dealings with those islanders, be they brief or be they for all time, can only serve to lift them up nearer into the light of civilization and of Christianity."[35] Congressman Tongue assured the House that "it is safe to trust the representatives of the American people to establish a government in the Philippine Islands, not only much better than the people have ever known, but one that will give the fullest share of personal liberty and political privileges that the people are capable of receiving consistent with their own welfare." For Tongue, this was guaranteed because the Anglo-Saxons were a just race. In response to those who claimed the United States would act as Spain had, he asked how anyone could "compare America to Spain, Americans to Spaniards? The difference between these two races was demonstrated by Dewey at Manila. . . . Why not rather point us to our own race, to the example of our own history?" Along with America's own history of expansion was "the success of English colonial government," which proved affirmatively that Anglo-Americans were morally (and racially) fit to rule.[36]

The imperialists then took their arguments further and cited an American obligation to "protect" and govern those who could not yet govern themselves. Henry Teller did not believe "we should shrink from our duty because there may be difficulties attending it." The country had gone to war to free Cuba from tyranny, he said, and "when eight or ten millions more of men under like circumstances fall under our control, we can not avoid our duty by saying, 'We went to war to help Cuba. We will help nobody else.' That is cowardly." In his view, the Philippines needed to be freed from Spain and protected from outside enemies.[37] His fellow Coloradan Wolcott agreed, but he laid out the other possibilities in grimmer detail. "The course of events, unexpected and necessarily unforeseen, leave us at the conclusion of this war charged with a duty toward 9,000,000 people in far-off, distant seas," he said. "We found them cruelly oppressed by Spain. No man with bowels of compassion would want to turn them back to that country." To abandon them now would be to leave the diverse people of the islands open to "internecine strife, perhaps extending over a generation, with its accompaniment of bloodshed and murder and rapine." Surely it was clear that "the people there are as yet apparently unfitted for self-government." The only alternative, he suggested, was to take them under the American wing or leave them vulnerable to "the land-hunger and the greed of the countries of Europe that are now seeking to colonize land the wide world over," several of which might fight for the islands and "plunge the world in[to] war."[38] Teller and Wolcott demanded American control to fulfill an obligation to oppressed peoples and to maintain international order.[39]

The talk of America's benign mission was not totally new in late 1898 and early 1899, but it had been less apparent in earlier manifestations of expansionist sentiment. The language imperialists now adopted bore a closer resemblance to that used to justify intervention on behalf of Cuba than it did to the language applied to Hawaiian annexation just months earlier. Although this was certainly an appeal to the widely held faith in America's exceptional role in the world, the shift in rhetoric is telling. Its use in this case suggests—as many scholars have explained—that the rhetoric of a civilizing mission and paternalistic tutelage relied on a common vision of America as a powerful force for good. The nation's inherent morality then provided justification for intervention and colonialism.[40]

Of course, the language of benevolence and protection was mixed with other, less compassionate talk. Nearly everyone claimed that the acquisition of new territory would benefit the inhabitants, but several imperialists acknowledged that profit and strategic advantage were the real objectives. William Stewart was rather exceptional, in that he overtly rejected the supposition that the United States had any special responsibility toward the Filipinos. "When and where did the idea originate that it was the duty of the United States to go into the Philippine Islands to establish a government for those people and to prepare them for self-government?" he asked. "If it is our duty to give the people of the Philippine Islands good government, to educate them, and to establish a government suitable for them, is it not our duty to do so to every country in the world where they do not have a government suitable to our ideas?" Instead, he reminded his listeners, "There are many people who think they are valuable acquisitions." Possessions in the tropics would provide goods that could not be produced in the United States, thus reducing the flow of hard currency overseas. The senior senator from Nevada was also certain that America could capture a larger share of the Asian trade. "There is in the Orient an import trade which in round numbers amounts to a billion dollars a year. We have only 5 per cent of the trade of Asia and Oceania. If we had these islands, and were engaged in the trade there, we would have a nucleus for trade and have a chance to compete with England." He was confident that the Philippines would facilitate trade for the United States, just as Hong Kong did for Britain.[41]

Congressman Tongue was even more emphatic about the need to develop trade with Asia. The future of industrial America required it. "The productions of the United States are increasing year by year with tremendous rapidity," he said. Europe—especially Britain—and its colonies had provided the largest markets for American exports up to the present, but their demand would soon be outstripped by the supply of American goods. "The only remaining field is in Asiatic countries." The United States could "preserve and increase our trade and commerce in the Orient if we are prepared to defend them. . . . With a chain of naval stations in Hawaii, the Ladrones, and the Philippine Islands, the Pacific Ocean will become an American lake, and will bear American commerce, not only now, but in the future." The congressman from Oregon explained that the war with Spain had produced unprecedented opportunities, and America needed to secure its place while it could. Tongue's emphasis on American self-interest fit well with his belief that the doctrine of "consent of the governed" was a fiction. "The pilgrim fathers did not wait upon Plymouth Rock for the 'consent of the governed' before taking possession of this continent," he said. Consent had only occasionally been tied to the right to govern, and that fact remained true in the present time. "Mississippi and other States are disfranchising large numbers, if not a majority, of their male citizens without their consent." Although Tongue halfheartedly mentioned consent of the governed as an ideal that all governments should aspire to, he essentially described the principle as a fiction.[42]

Other westerners joined Tongue in recounting how democracy had been limited during the history of American expansion. Henry Teller claimed that Congress held nearly unlimited power over territories annexed to the union. The residents of lands conquered from Mexico had never been asked for their consent, and the relevant treaty had allowed Congress to deal with such lands at its own discretion. Even now, portions of those territories had been excluded from full admission, and he reminded his colleagues that, "in the case of the Territories of New Mexico and Arizona," the United States had ruled without the consent of the governed for fifty years.[43] Teller's remarks were echoed by Nevada's William Stewart later in the session.[44] Westerners knew all about government without consent.

Teller had little criticism for those allied reformers who differed from him on expansion. The imperialist Republicans were not as generous. Most suggested (as they had for much of 1898) that their opponents were essentially traitors. Frequently, McKinley's supporters claimed that any disagreement over the treaty emboldened the Filipinos to attack the Americans in Manila. Tongue claimed that "their ignorance and passions are being inflamed by fraud, by falsehood, by deceit, and by slanderers of Americans and American institutions, in the Philippine Islands, in the press there and here, and in both ends of this Capitol." Ultimately, he said, the anti-imperialists were "shotting guns to be fired into the ranks of American soldiers. They are whetting knives to be plunged into American bosoms."[45] Senator Wolcott of Colorado agreed. Those who wanted to debate policy were holding up the treaty vote and complicating the international situation. He complained that the Senate was left "wrangling day after day before the gaze of the whole world." Those who fought the treaty or questioned American policy were guilty of giving "counsel and aid" to "those people in the Philippines who might be inclined to question our authority." Furthermore, the war needed to be brought to an end before European nations decided to intervene on behalf of Spain. "Bar England, there is not a country in Europe that is not hostile to us," he said. "During all this war they stood in sullen hate, hoping for our defeat and that disaster might come to us." The Senate must act, or Europe would.[46]

THE RESPONSE OF THE WESTERN ANTI-IMPERIALISTS

Despite the attacks of Wolcott and others, the opposition continued to contest what increasingly appeared to be an imperialist policy. Their fight was not confined to any single topic, as western reformers leveled attacks against the undemocratic rule, economic exploitation, and militarism resulting from McKinley's vision. Populists and their allies charged their opponents with quashing democracy abroad while strangling it into submission at home. The republican independence they cherished could not survive alongside the machinery of a warlike imperial power. Conquest, they declared, offered no new freedoms; it served only to extend the reach of the industrial and financial elite.[47]

An examination of the moment at which nearly all Populists and reform Democrats united to oppose expansion reveals key elements of the debate that have hitherto been ignored by scholars. For example, some historians have claimed that the conflict between anti-imperialists and imperialists was a "narrow and limited debate on the question of which tactical means the nation should use to obtain commonly desired objectives"—that is, the expansion of overseas trade. This analysis was advocated most prominently by historians who attributed imperialism to economic motives—namely, William Appleman Williams and Walter LaFeber. According to them, nearly all Americans came to view overseas markets as a solution to the problem of "overproduction," so the only real difference between imperialists and anti-imperialists was the extent to which they believed overseas colonies would facilitate trade.[48]

Perhaps it is most useful to examine what Williams and LaFeber got right. Although they devoted large portions of their works to Americans' increasing desire to find new markets, they most usefully described the conception—embodied by many of McKinley's policies—of an empire based on trade and supported by a nearby military presence, when required. Whereas European imperialism of the era was based on the control of large populations to monopolize colonial resources and markets, McKinley and his forebears envisioned a smaller footprint, and certainly one without the trappings of colonialism. The situation in the Philippines altered the equation to some extent, but the constituent parts of America's new empire were already taking shape by then.[49]

Historians have had little difficulty finding evidence that the anti-imperialists of 1899 were part of a growing consensus in favor of greater international trade. A central component of the Democrat-mugwump alliance of the Cleveland years was an emphasis on low-tariff policies designed to improve trade prospects. Although Populists had officially labeled the tariff fights of the old parties a sham issue, many of them had also called for open trade policies to create new markets for American goods. Furthermore, several Populists had supported the development of coaling stations in the Pacific and Caribbean during their congressional careers as a means of promoting greater American influence and trade.[50] However, the western Populists and Democrats can be characterized as essentially imperialistic only if one misunderstands the most vital elements of their worldviews. Their opposition to the growing power of domestic capitalists and their fear of militarism guaranteed that they would fight relentlessly against the policies McKinley was already beginning to implement.

First, it should be noted that while some western anti-imperialists supported the acquisition of overseas naval bases, others had always seen them as unnecessary. In a speech in 1898, Senator Stephen White declared his opposition to any form of "territorial aggrandizement which would require maintenance by a naval force in excess of any yet provided for our national uses. . . . Even as simple coaling stations, such territorial acquisitions would involve responsibility beyond their utility."[51] In a similar vein, Richard Pettigrew wrote a letter to his brother informing him of his views on Cuba, Hawaii, Puerto Rico, and the Philippines. "I would not put a protectorate over any of them," he wrote, "neither would I have a coaling station at any of these points. . . . Plutocracy wishes us to enter upon the acquisition of distant countries to govern, and thus furnish food for discontent."[52]

Many westerners understood Pettigrew's point well—namely, that a larger global presence would likely lead to an increasing number of American interventions and wars. Their opposition to colonialism was not part of an otherwise expansionist program; they were just as opposed to the kind of armed entanglements that would accompany any militarist program. By early 1899, White considered his earlier suspicions confirmed. These island bases, combined with the proposed expansion of the military, were preparations "for not merely a war, but for wars." In the future, he asked, was it not likely that "our growth along the lines of conquest will enlist the opposition of other peoples; may it not be that other nations, seeing that we are attempting to interfere with them, will here-after, however friendly they may be to-day, challenge our superiority?"[53] Similarly, Simpson noted that his recent opponent in the election had claimed that the Pacific islands were "but a stepping-stone" and that "later on, when China was to be divided up amongst the foreign nations, we were to be on hand with a big army and a big navy to see that we got our part of it."[54] Nebraska Populist William Greene believed that Britain was encouraging the American takeover of the Philippines as a counter to the influence of other imperial powers in East Asia. Ultimately, Britain "wants us to form an alliance with her. Why? When the great struggle comes, England wants the United States to help her in her plan to steal the biggest portion of the Chinese Empire."[55] Western anti-imperialists did not merely oppose the extension of the nation's territorial boundaries; they fought imperialism because they perceived the acquisition of distant stations as the beginning of a new policy that would lead to perpetual conflict and the growth of militarism.

Certain western reformers expressed their desire for America to become more engaged in affairs overseas, but most opposed the military buildups required for the maintenance of a new empire. Although western reformers had a mixed record when it came to congressional proposals for military modernization early in the decade, by the latter half of the 1890s, they consistently opposed any substantial expansion of the nation's armed forces. In early 1898—when war with Spain seemed imminent—Simpson declared that he favored a limited naval construction program, fearing what others might do with an enlarged navy. Because he believed the purpose of the American navy was solely defensive, "we do not need a large number of seagoing battle ships." Instead of what is now referred to as a "blue-water" navy, Simpson wanted the American fleet to be constructed with coastal security in mind.[56] Such a force would be incapable of projecting global power, and it certainly could not be used to support the development of an overseas empire. At around the same time (early 1898), colleagues such as Coloradans John Shafroth and John Calhoun Bell dismissed permanent expansion of the regular army as unnecessary and undesirable.[57] In 1899 Populists and their western allies were even more emphatic in their opposition to any military enlargement. No form of imperialism would have been possible without a larger and more modern military establishment, but (as explained in greater detail shortly) western reformers detested everything associated with militarism.

By early 1899, western anti-imperialists had become even more committed to opposing the unnecessary use of force overseas. Sensing that enforcement of McKinley's "benevolent assimilation" proclamation could lead to a new war, William Allen proposed a resolution stating that "any aggressive action by Army or Navy on the part of the United States against the Filipinos would be an act of war unwarranted on the part of the President and the exercise of constitutional power vested exclusively in Congress."[58] The resolution went nowhere, and neither the commander in chief nor his generals paid such statements any heed.

Other westerners vented their frustration over a military occupation even closer to home: Cuba. When it appeared that American soldiers were settling in for a long occupation of the Caribbean island, the same members who had called for war a year earlier were furious. South Dakota Populist Freeman Knowles noted, "It is now six months since hostilities ceased, and no move has been made by the Administration to give the people of Cuba the independence and self-government promised them in the declaration of war." Cubans were "begging of the President to be permitted to call a convention of the Cuban people to form a government," but the administration was deaf to their cries.[59] Shafroth pointed out that some supporters of the administration claimed that the regular army needed to be permanently increased in order to police Cuba.[60] While some imperialists were reconsidering their pledge to make Cuba independent, western reformers were calling for an immediate end to American interference in the island's affairs.

Furthermore, opponents of the administration rejected its economic arguments. The profits accompanying militarized expansion would not ultimately trickle down to farmers and laborers. Populist representative Curtis Castle of California asked the expansionists, "Since the vast majority of our citizens are to have no share in the rich treasures of the Orient, I wish to inquire what portion of our population is to be permanently enriched?"[61] Traders, speculators, and manufacturers could hypothetically make a profit from imperialism, but it was hardly logical to argue that ownership of the Philippines would mean control of the Asian trade. Congressman Greene called the imperialists' talk of American trade domination in Asia "only dreams." It would be impossible to undercut the advantages held by others. "Do you think the Chinaman is going to buy American wheat unless he can get it cheaper than he can get wheat from India? Do you think he is going to buy American beef unless he can buy it cheaper than he can buy the Australian beef?" The best proof of that principle had already been provided by the War Department. "Where did the Government go to buy the beef and the sheep and the flour and the vegetables to feed our army at Manila?" he asked. "Why, we went to Sydney, Australia." Surely, American agricultural products were in no position to take over the trade in Asia.[62]

Whatever their hopes for increased commerce, the Populists' critique of imperialism was interwoven with their opposition to monopoly capitalism and the corrupted centralized authority it relied on. Western reformers believed they were witnessing the evolution of a growing infrastructure of political, economic, and military power. Imperialism represented the extension of that system for the benefit of economic elites. One of the best articulated

examples of this critique came from Castle, who claimed that the imperialists planned not only to "deny the Filipinos their well-earned liberty" but
also to "send over a horde of hungry exploiters":

> Protected by the strong arm of the military despotism to be given those
> unhappy people in lieu of their own government, [these exploiters] will
> seize all the natural resources of the islands, and under the guise of law,
> through charters granted by the Government, all kinds and descriptions
> of monopolies are to be farmed out to these ravening harpies. With the
> land sequestered and the instruments of production monopolized, the
> natives must ever remain a subject people, whose cry for liberty will be
> answered with the lash.

The administration was working to complete a global system of exploitation.
"Nowhere upon the earth does labor secure the results of its efforts," and Filipino laborers would now be exploited even more fully than their American
counterparts, to the detriment of both. Economic opportunity, the hallmark
of American freedom, was being eliminated through a process that concentrated wealth and power. "The monopolization of the natural resources of
all countries and the monopolization of the instruments of production, together with the monopolization of the means of distribution, forever bar the
poor from any portion, however small, of the stolen wealth wrung from the
unrequited toil of subject nations."[63]

Castle described this centralization of power in international terms, but
his explanation of America's place in the system was complicated. He would
have characterized America as part of that global periphery of "subject nations," but he was also sure the nation's elite were part of the scheme: "The
American plutocracy, not content with eating out the heart of our democracy, not content with enslaving American labor, now comes before Congress with an effrontery born of contempt and demands that we plunge into
the vortex of war and debt, that thereby they may be enabled to rob and
despoil the workers of a foreign land." But obviously the elite could not
manage this alone. They had solicited the national government to do their
bidding, while the "wealth producers of America are insolently commanded
by their despoilers to furnish mighty armies to subdue the wealth producers
of other lands, that plutocracy may have other fields to devastate." Imperialism was not so much the extension of national control as it was the expansion of economic interests into new fields under the umbrella of government
protection.

Castle's speech on commercial imperialism was one of the most thorough delivered by any western anti-imperialist, but he was certainly not the only one to hold such views. Congressman Jeremiah Botkin of Kansas explained that the present case of expansion was quite different from that which had come earlier in American history. "Climatic conditions are such" in the Philippines that a white American would "dare not undertake a permanent residence and ordinary labor" there. However, "a wealthy syndicate can secure large tracts of land on which to grow the products that constitute our chief imports from those islands, viz., sugar, tobacco, and hemp. Unfortunately the climate can not affect these syndicates. They are immunes." The military conquest of the archipelago was being plotted so that "the organized capital of this country and of Europe" could "exploit great enterprises in the Philippines, monopolize the valuable franchises, and lay under perpetual tribute to 'the bloodless spirit of wealth' the resources of that splendid archipelago." The large army that some proposed was designed to "enforce commercialism and imperialism" in the island possessions.[64]

Another western Populist, Freeman Knowles, questioned the justice of exporting the American system of exploitation and conflict. "What kind of 'blessings of law and liberty' is it that we are going to extend to the people of these islands?" he asked. "Is it the same kind which these same 'expansionists' are now extending to our own laboring classes in this country?" And if the Filipinos "claim enough of the products of their own labor to keep their families from starvation, will they be shot to death as our own laboring men were" in America's mining towns? He wondered aloud if a Filipino government would imprison men "without trial for advising their co-laborers to demand a fair share of the products of their own toil," as had happened in the United States. Was this "the kind of 'law and liberty' we are going to extend to the Filipinos?"[65] The extension of freedom was not possible anyplace under the control of American capitalists.

Western reformers had no desire to spread the reach of financiers and industrialists at the point of a gun, but they also believed that the proposed program of militarization would have dire consequences on the home front. Since at least the mid-1890s, top generals had called for a larger army, and the argument they increasingly employed pertained to the maintenance of domestic order. Even though the Indian wars were over, the army needed to be expanded, they said, and redeployed to bases near major urban centers.[66] The proponents of military reorganization were consistently thwarted in the years before 1899, but then the argument changed: soldiers were now needed to garrison the new possessions.

Many western Populists, Democrats, and Silver Republicans had been in Congress long enough to remember previous iterations of the Hull bill. Jerry Simpson had spent most of the 1890s in the House, and he reminded his colleagues that in the history of all nations in which "there is much concentrated wealth there comes an anxiety on the part of those who own the wealth of the country for a strong centralized government." For that reason, certain members of Congress had claimed for years "that our standing Army is too small; that we ought to have at least 100,000 men; that we ought to have a force sufficient to suppress domestic violence in this country." But now, he said, "here comes a new pretext, under cover, of course—the pretext that we want a large standing army now because we have got to hold the Philippine Islands." Simpson refused to consider it a legitimate excuse. Neither a brief colonial conflict nor the short-term demands of policing the islands would require a permanent expansion of the army, he said.[67]

The sentiments of western Populists and Democrats in the House regarding capitalist control of the army were nearly universal. "It is a significant fact," said Representative William Vincent, "that since the era of corporation rule set in and since our beneficent social system developed the tramp, the lock-out, and the strike, the Army has never been called out to suppress or hold in check the corporation, but always to suppress the striker." Despite his distaste for colonialism as well, he essentially believed "that the great corporate interests of the country have been and are now demanding a large standing army" for use domestically.[68] William Greene stated that Republicans wanted an expanded army "because the great corporations of the country, the accumulated wealth of the country, the capitalists, demand it to maintain order. Not order in the Philippines, but order here at home."[69] Democrat James Hamilton Lewis of Washington also suggested that "military force, drawn from portions of the country wholly foreign to the community in which they may be serving," would be employed against labor "to 'preserve order' by Winchesters and hush protests by bayonets!"[70] And so it was that war abroad would be used to destroy liberty in America.

Western reformers believed that the centralization and militarization that came with imperialism would necessarily pose an immense threat to American democracy, but the colonized people posed another kind of danger. Their imperialist counterparts were already well aware that support for annexation of the Pacific islands could leave them open to criticism. It was primarily with this fear in mind that Senator Perkins had written to the California legislature and asked for its advice. He certainly believed that annexation would involve many hazards, and he informed the state legislators:

[It] seems to me to be contrary to the spirit of our Constitution to acquire a territory on the Asiatic coast nine times as densely populated as California, whose inhabitants equal in numbers one seventh of the present population of the United States, and who are, moreover, a mixed people, consisting of Malays, Tagals, Chinese, Visayens, Sulus, and Negritos, that have no conception of a government by the people, and can only be controlled by force of arms.

The Filipinos, he argued, were an uncivilized lot who could never become Americans. And he went on to remind Californians of an old threat they knew only too well. "Our farmers cannot compete . . . against the cheap peon labor of these islands, where Chinese and Malays work for fifteen cents per day in silver. We labored for many years to pass the Chinese Restriction Act, and remove the blight of cheap servile contract labor from our land." Territorial expansion would undo all that, he feared.[71]

Perkins did not get his way. The California legislature informed him that if he were a true servant of the state, he would ratify the treaty.[72] But such a policy would have obvious consequences, and the Republicans' rivals were all too willing to exploit any apparent weakness. The Democratic senator from Utah, Joseph Rawlins, crudely asked if annexation of the Philippines was intended to "add a wholesome element to our population, that our sons may find wives and our daughters husbands?"[73] More commonly, the racial threat posed by the Filipinos was seen as economic in nature. Senator Allen suggested that they would threaten American labor, and perhaps this was the "sinister motive" behind the annexation scheme: "it may be that there are those who contemplate the rapid approach of the time when this debased population can be brought here and thrown in deadly contact with the laboring men of our country." Such an event would effectively put an end to Republican talk of tariff protection for the betterment of labor.[74]

The racial concerns expressed by westerners were closely linked to questions of constitutionality. Anti-imperialists saw no benefits in granting the "new possessions" statehood, but they simultaneously derided talk of colonial governance as un-American and unconstitutional. Imperialists pointed out that the Treaty of Paris left governance of the Philippines solely to the discretion of Congress, and some were eager to employ this plenary power to establish absolute dominion over the archipelago. Especially in the Senate, western opponents of expansion joined conservatives such as George Hoar of Massachusetts and Donelson Caffery of Louisiana in attacking this claim to absolute power. While some historians have emphasized the constitutional elements of this debate, the legal arguments made by both sides should be seen as a product of their positions on expansion and race rather than the other way around.[75]

According to western anti-imperialists (and most of their eastern counterparts, for that matter), race determined the proper boundaries of the American state. It was an argument as old as the republic, and it had reared its head most notably during the nation's last bout with "manifest destiny" in the late 1840s.[76] As Washington's Senator George Turner put it, the founders had provided for the addition of new states, "but the people who were to be protected by the great charter of our liberties at all times and any and every where beneath our flag were to be the American people—the great offshoot of the Anglo-Saxon race which had peopled the temperate zone of North America." Only these people were capable of full participation in the American state.[77] Like Turner, Senator Allen feared what would happen if the country were "overrun by a horde of alien peoples in no manner capable of using or enjoying the blessings and privileges of self-government, or of maintaining them when won by others, whose presence and influence would deteriorate or injure the nation, ultimately wrecking the Constitution and destroying our political institutions." Still, the Constitution would be ruined in any case if the people of the Philippines were denied government based on their consent. "We have no power, in my judgment, to hold the Filipinos as vassals," Allen said. "We have no right to deprive them, whatever they may be, of the right of self-government if they desire it."[78]

It is difficult for the modern reader to reconcile western anti-imperialists' views of racial inequality with their statements that self-government is the birthright of all, but such declarations were indeed plentiful. During the debate over Hawaiian annexation, Senator Stephen White had referred to the peoples of Asia as "semi-orang-outangs," and he was no more generous in 1899.[79] He now claimed that "the Philippines are tenanted by a very peculiar mass, a heterogeneous compound of inefficient oriental humanity." He did not care "whether these islanders are fit for free government. . . . If they are so fitted, they should be permitted to establish a free government; if they are not so fitted, they should not be brought into an alliance with us; we do not in that event want them." His tendency to describe the Filipinos as undesirable citizens did not prevent him from arguing that some of them were intelligent and capable and that they deserved the right to determine their own style of government. While "there may be a difference in this clime and that as to the method of the exercise of liberty," the "sensible American, deeply schooled in the walks of independence," understood that freedom was best for all of mankind.[80]

Allen had done nearly as much as White to paint the Filipinos as unfit for participation in American democracy, but he too claimed that they were due their freedom. Responding to Ohio senator Joseph Foraker's statement that the Declaration of Independence was nothing but a letter of complaint to Great Britain, Allen retorted, "It is as much the right of a Filipino to govern himself, if he is capable of doing so, as it is the right of an American citizen to do so. This doctrine is not confined to the people of the United States. It extends, according to the language, to all men, wherever found."[81]

Despite the apparent contradiction, these statements should at least be thought of as part of America's own contradictory traditions. The individual who put the phrase "all men are created equal" into the American lexicon—and, by most accounts, actually believed it—was the same one who held hundreds of men and women in bondage. Lincoln's particular fondness for the statement that governments derive "their just powers from the consent of the governed" did not speed his acceptance of universal manhood suffrage. Not infrequently, there has been a disparity between an individual's conception of justice and his or her belief in complete human equality, and the anti-imperialists were just another iteration of this contradiction.[82]

Despite the ambiguities in the anti-imperialists' statements on race, the legal and governmental implications were clear. But, as noted earlier, their rivals had effective counters. To those who pointed to the history of American expansion, Henry Teller responded by pointing out that previous treaties had contained specific provisions calling for the eventual statehood of the annexed regions and citizenship for the inhabitants. The Constitution had nothing to say on the matter, and the Treaty of Paris was silent as well.[83] Furthermore, the anti-imperialists admitted that annexation and whatever followed—even if unconstitutional—would not be rejected by the courts.[84] Imperialism could not be stopped except by political action.

A NEW WAR

As the final ratification vote approached, the situation in the Philippines changed dramatically. On the night of February 4–5, shots were fired by a sentry with the First Nebraska on the outskirts of Manila, followed by a full-scale battle. Aguinaldo and a number of his officers were absent at the time of the engagement—clearly indicating they had not planned an attack for that evening. The American commanders had no coordinated plan of attack to follow in the event of a disturbance, and the western volunteer regiments were flung against vital Filipino positions within a matter of hours. In the aftermath of the battle, Aguinaldo contacted Otis to seek a truce, but the American general responded that, "having begun," the fighting "must go on to the grim end." A new war had commenced in the Philippines.[85]

American media accounts of the fighting bore little resemblance to the facts, but neither did the official reports from Otis and Dewey to Washington. The first substantial report from Otis—one that was reprinted on the front page of nearly every newspaper by February 6—stated: "Insurgents in large force opened attack on our outer lines at 8.45 last evening. Renewed attack several times during night. At 4 o'clock this morning entire line engaged. All attacks repulsed." At later congressional hearings, much of that statement would be proved false. But for the time being, Otis's report was the most extensive official statement journalists could get their hands on, so they ran with it, embellishing as they went. Most papers described a fierce all-out assault by Aguinaldo's army. Among the ludicrous claims reported by the press—regardless of the newspaper's party affiliation—was that the Filipino force had charged the Americans armed with bows and arrows.[86]

The day of the treaty vote had already been set for February 6. It is difficult to state with any degree of certainty how the beginning of the war influenced that vote. Allen claimed it had no impact at all on his decision, and most senators concurred. Historians have tried to pin the outcome of the vote on either the president's use of spoils or Bryan's impact on his allies in the Senate. Of the two, Bryan was certainly in a weaker position to provide incentives.[87]

The final vote was 57–27—just one vote more than the required two-thirds majority. Heitfeld (Populist, Idaho), Pettigrew, Rawlins (Democrat, Utah), Roach (Democrat, North Dakota), and Turner were the only westerners to vote against the treaty. Those who voted with them were largely southern Democrats, along with two Republicans—George Hoar of Massachusetts and Eugene Hale of Maine. Allen and seven other western reformers voted for the treaty. Its ratification technically gave Congress greater authority over matters in the Philippines, but the outbreak of war left the initiative with McKinley.[88]

The start of a second war changed the tone of political combat. Conservatives had already linked patriotism with unquestioned loyalty to the administration, and such rhetoric had been prominent in 1898 and in the first month of 1899. During a speech by Nebraska congressman William Greene, a Republican yelled out, "Did you live here in 1860?" The heckler claimed that no true American who had witnessed the Civil War would question the executive in a time of crisis. Westerners responded by saying that the term *patriotism* was being misused by their opponents. Greene himself fired back at his Republican challengers, declaring, "[You] are now seeking to distract public attention from your evil deeds by pulling around you the flag, and shouting 'Patriotism!'"[89] Congressman William Vincent also mocked the imperialist definition of the term by suggesting that "patriotism under the old order of things, before the Declaration of Independence was expunged from the record, meant love of one's country." Now Republicans had changed it to mean "love for the other fellow's country."[90]

In the same way, western anti-imperialists' talk of "duty" or "obligation" challenged their opponents' claims with regard to a colonial duty or the "white man's burden." Instead, the westerners' emphasized their duty to the American people, the Constitution, and universal freedom. They had no great difficulty unsettling the definitions their rivals had employed as they advocated expansion. Senator White, for example, openly harangued those who claimed "that it is our duty to encircle the earth."[91] His colleague Joseph Rawlins admitted that imperialists always spoke of "some humane duty or moral obligation," but what did that really mean? The Filipinos had recently been allies, and both sides had rendered aid to the other in their respective wars against Spain. "Suppose we set off our obligations against theirs, balance the account, and let it go at that?"[92]

In the immediate aftermath of the battle over ratification, the defiant attitudes displayed by a number of westerners became more reserved. The tone of Republican attacks did not substantially change, but western Populists and their allies were more measured in their responses. Less than a week after news of the fighting reached Washington, Senator Allen sounded almost like one of McKinley's apologists. Whereas he had previously advocated the speediest possible withdrawal from the islands, he now said that "a duty is imposed upon us by our occupancy of the Philippine Islands that we can not escape." He affirmed the position that colonialism is wrong, but he also stated that he now agreed with "what I understand to be the policy of the President of the United States, to hold them [the islands] for such reasonable time that the influences and education of this Government may prepare them in some slight degree for the duties of an independent republican form of government."[93]

Earlier in the session, western Populists and their friends had few kind words for the regular army. Several members had opposed increases in the military because they believed the regular army consisted of men who were essentially failures, and the professional military only transformed them into unthinking automatons. According to Jerry Simpson, a man "who enlists in the standing Army is generally a person who can not get anything to do in any other way or in any other walk of life. . . . He is a hired fighter." Similarly, Curtis Castle considered regulars to be inherently unreliable citizens. "They are not anxious to fight at all; but if they must fight, they would as soon fight the citizens of the United States as anyone else. They become a part of the fighting machine and no longer think or act as individuals."[94] These statements were typical of the thinking of western reformers and were not merely bluster. In a private letter, Richard Pettigrew expressed his displeasure with the colonel of the First South Dakota Regiment—a man originally from the regular army—whom he considered unsuited to command a volunteer unit. Volunteers had "too much manhood and individuality" for a commander who was used to the discipline of the professional military, he said.[95] Likewise, John Shafroth and John Calhoun Bell had derided the regulars a year earlier, calling them unmotivated men who lacked self-reliance.[96]

Suddenly, the derision and scorn heaped upon the army were transformed into sympathy and support. It should be kept in mind that the first reports from the Philippines suggested that American forces had withstood a large-scale and unprovoked attack. And although the details that contributed to this shift in sentiment are important, the transition itself is quite noteworthy. Western anti-imperialists began to talk as if it were everyone's duty to rally behind the military establishment. For example, James Hamilton Lewis of Washington said, "We can only view the matter . . . in one light. These men who are there are American citizens; they are the sons of our brother men." For that reason, their actions were beyond question: "If they are wrong, they are innocently so; if they are right, they are justly so. There is no other position for the American House to take but to stand unanimously by the children of its own country."[97] While delivering a rather weak criticism of McKinley's policies, William Greene was nonetheless effusive in his praise for the obedient soldiers. "The American soldier must do what his officer commands him to do. . . . God bless the soldiers! They are doing their duty as brave, noble men, in obedience to the commands of their superiors. And I say that nobody on this side of the Chamber, or in this country, has anything to say against the men who are wearing the uniform of our country."[98]

The unanimity of praise for American soldiers would last for the remainder of the session, but a few continued to oppose the definitions of patriotism outlined by their rivals. One of the strongest statements was made by

South Dakota Populist Freeman Knowles, who felt the need to point out that he was a veteran of "every battle in which the Army of the Potomac was engaged from '62 to '65." He lashed out at those who celebrated the deaths of thousands of Filipinos, "whose only crime is a desire to govern themselves. What American citizen with a spark of self-respect, to say nothing of national pride or patriotism, can look upon this spectacle without hiding his head in shame?" he asked. "The Philippine people are struggling in the same cause and for the self-same rights that actuated our forefathers in the Revolution. Every denunciation . . . against Aguinaldo and his followers were simply echoes from the debates in the British Parliament against Washington and his army." Knowles predicted that American victory in the present conflict was already impossible. "Ten millions of people, with courage and manhood enough to fight for their freedom, in a tropical climate unendurable to the Caucasian race, are invincible to any and all force you can send against them." He depicted Aguinaldo and his people as embodying the kind of manly freedom Americans once possessed. "I am glad the Filipinos have the courage and manhood to fight for their liberty. If it was right for our forefathers to fight for their independence, it is right for the Filipinos to do the same." He concluded by suggesting that "the American people are not oppressors, but organized greed has the Administration by the throat." Despite the conservative command to worship the flag or follow the nation's leaders in silent obedience, Knowles praised classic American republican values—including those he saw among the Filipinos. At present, he believed the American faith in human freedom had been set aside to satisfy the needs of the economic elite.[99]

The Fifty-Fifth Congress adjourned on March 4, one month after fighting in the Philippines commenced. The debate over imperialism did not cease; it only intensified. The end of the treaty fight allowed the anti-imperialists to set aside their disagreements over methods and focus on opposing what they saw as McKinley's war of conquest. Of course, there was also another complexion to the debate over empire. Outside of Congress, governors, state legislators, and members of organized labor were weighing in on the expansion issue.

LOCAL POLITICS IN EARLY 1899

National political debates always exist alongside many local ones, and the regional context often adds meaning to the broader discussion. This had been

Charles S. Thomas. Courtesy of the Library of Congress

true with the silver issue, and so it was again with the question of expansion. In each state, local history, geography, and economics would play a part in shaping interpretations of the new policy.

Colorado's new governor, Charles S. Thomas, was certainly no Populist. In fact, he likely saw Populists as his chief political rivals. Shortly after taking office, he wrote privately (and with some satisfaction) that "populism has run its course." Yet he suggested that the new party had "compelled the recognition by the democracy of its ancient principles."[100] Thomas knew well of what he wrote. A few years after leaving office, he would return to his career as a successful corporate lawyer, including a stint as the attorney for the Anaconda mine in 1904, but he could show no such inclinations as governor.[101] During the campaign, he had won the backing of the Colorado State Federation of Labor by promising to support an eight-hour workday law for the mining industry.[102] When the election returns demonstrated clear support for him in typical Populist districts, Thomas surely understood his obligation.[103] As someone who was looking ahead to the senatorial election in 1901, he could not afford to alienate any of Colorado's reformers.

Upon assuming the governorship, Thomas's most pressing concern appeared to be labor relations with the mining interests. Although he and the legislature followed through on their promise to pass an eight-hour workday law, it would soon be challenged by a new entity. Rumors of consolidation among the mining and smelting corporations were proved true with the formation of the American Smelting and Refining Company (ASARCO) in the spring of 1899. It immediately challenged the law in court, and tensions rose as the law's June 15 implementation date approached. By June 15, ASARCO's smelters were shut down by strikes. The Colorado Supreme Court ruled the law unconstitutional in July, and the strike collapsed in mid-August; however, the state government's approach to the strike was important. Governor Thomas appointed a citizens' committee to resolve the strike, and when that failed, he called in the state's Board of Arbitration. The workers declared their willingness to submit to binding arbitration, but the company declined. Though the workers were frustrated by their defeat, Thomas's involvement suggested that labor's engagement in politics might yet bear fruit.[104]

Disputes between workers and capital were at the forefront of politics in Colorado, but the issue of imperialism had a significant presence in the background. The state senate approved a resolution that called for Teller and Wolcott to vote for the Treaty of Paris, but Populists and Democrats in the Colorado house initiated a two-hour debate over a resolution demanding the opposite. In a speech that one newspaper called (with a degree of condescension) one of the finest delivered by any woman in the legislature, Arapahoe Populist Mrs. H. G. R. Wright decried any policy that involved acquisition of the Philippines without the consent of the Filipinos. Other Populists and Democrats less charitably stated that the islands offered "no commerce, no trade, no manufactures, no nothing, except heathens and strife." Despite their efforts, the measure was voted down.[105]

The state executive also joined the fray. Governor Thomas, as perhaps the foremost anti-imperialist among state Democrats, was making speeches in opposition to the administration's presumed policies by at least February. He also focused a great deal of attention on the Colorado regiment's return from the Philippines, which he declared to be an unconstitutional use of the state militia. The men had enlisted for the duration of the war with Spain, and they were legally bound to be used only against foreign invasions or domestic rebellions.[106] In other statements, Governor Thomas attempted to draw connections between America's new overseas policies and the growing concentration of economic power. In response to a questionnaire he had received regarding the platform for the next national election, he stated, "Imperialism, both national and industrial, should be opposed, and the principle that the government exists by the consent of the governed should be applied to, and warfare waged against, the commercial and political oligarchy which is centralizing all industries, and repeating the policies and practices of despotisms abroad." Furthermore, in an antitrust message delivered to the legislature, Thomas suggested that the war was drawing attention away from concerns at home. Although most remembered 1898 as "the year of glory," it was "also the year of the trusts. The people have been diverted by the pomp and circumstances of war, during which period trusts, representing $950,000,000 of capital, real and fictitious, have been organized." In one case, imperialism was described as an extension of the systems of domination growing in America; in the other, war and nationalism were preventing desperately needed reforms. These interpretations resembled those developed by western reformers in Congress over the past year, and their use by a state politician demonstrates either that these ideas were being readily adopted or that the ideological basis for such conclusions was already established among western Populists and Democrats.[107]

In Nebraska, there were no strikes or industrial combinations to dominate the headlines as they did in Colorado. Governor William A. Poynter had to deal with a Republican legislature, and there was no real hope for major reform legislation. A few Republican-sponsored "reform" measures did pass and were signed into law—namely, a law to regulate the use of money in politics and another that limited the hours of railroad workers. In reality, both were weak measures. The penalty for committing bribery or exceeding campaign limitations was set at "not less than fifty dollars," while the other law merely limited railroad employees to a maximum of eighteen consecutive hours of work. The new laws were so noncontroversial that they passed the Nebraska senate without a dissenting vote.[108] Fate seemed to ordain that the legislature would win no great accomplishments. Even though the legislators quickly chose defeated gubernatorial candidate Monroe Hayward to replace William Allen in the Senate, Hayward died before taking office, and Poynter appointed Allen to resume his old seat.[109]

Instead of focusing on reform measures, the Nebraska legislature devoted a great deal of time to the discussion of events overseas, particularly those involving the state's regiment in the Philippines. One of these debates centered on Colonel John Stotsenburg, commander of the First Nebraska Regiment. In the months preceding the start of the conflagration, members of both houses had received letters from concerned parents and friends of men in the regiment, condemning the colonel for his harsh treatment of those under his command. Because of these reports of "unjust and unsoldierly treatment," Representative Fisher, a Republican from Dawes County, demanded on January 11 that the legislature call for Stotsenburg's immediate removal from command.[110] Debate of the resolution occurred on the following day.

After an abortive attempt by one fellow Republican to kill the proposal, a series of chaotic, nonpartisan, yet rather divisive engagements took place on the floor. A fusionist from Buffalo County, J. M. Easterling, offered to refer the resolution to committee to formally "investigate and report to this House."[111] Easterling argued that the legislature was stepping outside of its mandate, and the War Department could handle this issue on its own. Then, before a vote could be taken on the two main options, yet another Republican offered up an amendment designed to gut the original resolution.[112]

First the amendment was voted down, 54–44. Twenty-five fusionists and nineteen Republicans worked together to defeat it, with one member from each side abstaining. When Easterling's alternative was defeated in turn by forty Republicans and nineteen fusionists, the representative from Buffalo County felt compelled to explain his intentions. He declared that Fisher's resolution was a "criticism of the national administration," and he justified his rejection of such an act: "Owing to the critical situation in the Philippines, and the criticism of an officer without his having been heard, and a desire to support our president at this critical moment, and as a mark of my confidence in his prudence and loyalty, I vote 'No.'"[113] This reformer believed that questioning the authority of the War Department or the commander in chief was unacceptable at this time—and these statements were made during peacetime, more than three weeks before fighting began in the Philippines. The debate reflected the extent to which state Republicans had succeeded in cultivating a narrative of national unity amid crisis. Easterling was no Republican, but he accepted that narrative without question.[114]

William A. Poynter. Courtesy of the Nebraska State Historical Society

Remarkably, the legislature was not done discussing military matters. In late March 1899, nearly two months after the outbreak of war in the Philippines, both houses of the Nebraska legislature passed a resolution in support of the actions of the state's regiment. In its entirety, this resolution declared that the soldiers were "defending in the far-off Philippines the principles of our government and adding new glory to the flag." Not a single member voted against the resolution.[115]

Populist governor William Poynter could not bring himself to condone such a blanket statement. Although his veto message did not question the bravery of the volunteers, he did "regret that circumstances have compelled them to give their services and sacrifice their lives in a conflict at utter variance to the very fundamental principles of our government and contrary to the established policy of the nation for more than a century." The soldiers had enlisted in a fight for human liberty, but now they were forced to "engage in a conflict against a people who have been battling against the oppression of another nation for nearly 400 years." In conclusion, Poynter stated, "I cannot stultify myself and the calm judgment of the thinking people of this commonwealth by giving official approval to the statement that the war of conquest now carried on in the far away Philippines is in defense of the principles of our government and is adding new glory to our flag."[116]

Poynter's treatment of the resolution received mixed reviews. A writer for the *Omaha World-Herald* remembered that Poynter had repeatedly asked for legislation and funds to provide aid to the state's soldiers, but the legislature had repeatedly refused. The legislature would not lift a finger to help the soldiers but had no lack of worthless sentiment, the writer claimed. In addition to support from the local press, Poynter received several letters of support from private citizens. One came from a mother whose son was still serving in the Philippines and who felt that the governor's veto sent a powerful message to others. Since his public repudiation of the conflict, "other men and women have entered their protest against this unholy war. I hope and expect a storm to sweep across the land condemning the administration and make the powers that be call a halt and listen to the voice of the people."[117]

Republican newspapermen, by contrast, quickly attacked Poynter for opposing the will of the president. Republican journals tended not to explain the governor's reasoning, instead claiming that his veto was based "purely on political grounds, and indicates that our governor is more a politician that [sic] a statesman."[118] According to another paper, the governor "placed himself on the side of Aguinaldo and his band of bandits, who wished to walk over the American army and pillage the city of Manila." Claimed yet another, "As between a Filipino and our brave Nebraska boys the governor goes on record as in favor of the dirty Filipino. . . . It may be all right for a popocrat campaign argument, but as sure as there is a God in heaven the insult to our brave boys at Manila will be remembered by a good many people in the state at the ballot box in the coming election."[119] Members of the Grand Old Party of Nebraska now believed they had an issue they could win with.

In Washington, the legislature was no more productive and even less controversial. Nearly the entire session was devoted to a fight over the US Senate seat. The incumbent, Republican John L. Wilson, thought he would win reelection easily. Like recently elected Silver Republican George Turner, Wilson was from Spokane, and western Washington legislators demanded their share of representation in the Senate. However, working with the few Populists and Democrats left in the legislature, the coastal legislators blocked Wilson's victory. They eventually forced his withdrawal from the race in favor of Addison Foster, whom one author described as a "deservedly obscure partner in the St. Paul & Tacoma Lumber Company." The move essentially replaced an experienced political manipulator with a novice, but it represented a desire for greater patronage rather than an ideological shift.[120]

The legislature took no position on the growing debate over imperialism, but others in the state did. The Western Central Labor Union of Seattle devoted its entire February 1 meeting to the matter, and a week later (just days after the treaty was ratified) it passed resolutions in opposition to "the so-called 'expansion' theory of the National Administration." It should be noted that although the union had long been hostile to the idea of Asian immigration, its protest was not framed in such a manner. Instead, the union stated its opposition to "the United States setting the example of abrogating the right of self government." While members may have had their own interests in mind, they chose to emphasize what they claimed to be a universal right.[121]

Governor John Rankin Rogers—who, oddly enough, was about to print a pamphlet titled *The Inalienable Rights of Man*—had a different perspective on the subject.[122] When asked to explain his position, the governor declared, "I believe in progress and the manifest destiny of the American people to leave the impress of their directing force upon the political economy of the future." Rogers described the prospect of trade with Asia in remarkably rosy terms, and in another message he suggested that "our flour is even now replacing rice in China." For Washington State, and for the Puget Sound region in particular, an empire in Asia would lead to benefits that could not be ignored. Rogers's discussion of imperialism never touched on the rights of the Filipinos, merely the Americans' right to do as they would. His writing had often emphasized universal rights and freedoms, and because of that contradiction, it may have been easier for him to describe the inhabitants of Asia as a faceless mass rather than deal with the real issues he normally confronted directly. Instead of espousing ideals, he now spoke like a pragmatist.[123]

Of course, the alternative was not an easy course. In April one of the more prominent Democrats in the state, F. A. McDonald, gave a speech in which he sought to convince members of the state reform coalition to oppose the policy of imperialism. The war in the Philippines represented an attempt to "put us into the Eastern struggle to wrangle over territory like dogs over a bone," he said. He would gladly take back the life of one of the state's dead in exchange for "all the niggers in the Philippines." His audience of Populists, Democrats, and Silver Republicans was impressed. The editor of a Republican journal, however, called it a blunt expression of "the copperhead doctrine of the democracy of this state—the platform upon which it will go before the people in 1900." Certainly, opposition to empire came with some risks.[124]

In the time between the elections of 1898 and the end of the first month of the Philippine war, the archipelago's future came into its own as a subject of political debate. Previously, opinions on expansion had not conformed closely to party lines. However, an ideological and political divide began to take shape as it became increasingly clear in the last weeks of 1898 that the administration had taken aim at the Philippines. Nearly all western reformers united in opposition to an imperial policy and rule by force. Imperialism would extend the reach of American financiers and industrialists, they said, adding to their power while offering nothing to working people in the colonies or at home. In addition, the military establishment required to maintain the new empire would threaten the very foundations of democracy. The regular army was an undemocratic institution, they said, and its officers were only too willing to use their instruments of war to suppress domestic dissent.

Though they united to oppose colonialism, western reformers divided over the Treaty of Paris. Some believed that opposition to the treaty would force Americans to reconsider the course of empire. Others believed that the risks of a delayed peace were too great; rumors of foreign intervention continued to circulate, and tensions in the Philippines might lead to open conflict. It would be better to ratify the treaty and determine the fate of the colonies in Congress, they reasoned. Their votes, combined with those of the avid imperialists, approved the treaty just as the new conflict began. Once again, the reformers found themselves in the role of opposition party in wartime.

There were complicating factors that had the power to hinder the success of the anti-imperialist cause. The divergent philosophies held by antiimperialists of different regions and parties were—and would consistently prove to be—real obstacles to the formation of a unified opposition. Local factors made the cause less attractive to others, and their partisan enemies were once again able to draw on wartime nationalism to disparage their efforts. Furthermore, western reformers were losing power in much of the region, and they were in no position to push the wholesale transformations they had once promised. If they could not convince voters to support their vision of freedom at home and abroad in the contest of 1900, the whole purpose of their crusade would be defeated, likely forever.

7. SETTING THE STAGE FOR
THE CAMPAIGN

Senator Henry Moore Teller of Colorado was running short of allies in the nation's capital. Since his dramatic break with the Republicans in the summer of 1896, he had continued to lambaste McKinley and his old party for their subservience to financial interests. His western friends were still fond of him, but since the outbreak of the war with Spain, he had split with them to become one of the most consistent defenders of the administration's overseas policies. Early in 1900 he continued this course, at one point attacking the anti-imperialist Senator Bacon of Georgia. The problem with Bacon's most recent speech, according to Teller, was its assumption that "when the war is terminated, we propose to do something which is contrary to the Declaration of Independence." All the anti-imperialists had declared that expansion in the Pacific would be accompanied by colonial rule, meaning government without consent of the governed. Neither McKinley nor the majority of his expansionist supporters had declared any intent to rule in such a way, and Teller wanted to believe the administration would act in accordance with American principles. The so-called anti-imperialists were fighting against a hypothetical evil, he said. "They set up a condition which we hope will never exist, and then denounce that condition." He denied that any American would tolerate such a foreign concept as colonialism.[1]

Of course, his support for expansion was perceived to be a boon to the president. Among westerners, Teller had the longest and most distinguished record of anyone in public life, and when he rejected claims that America was acting the part of an imperial power, he bolstered the position of McKinley and his backers. As Richard Pettigrew lamented to a former colleague, "Teller is an Expansionist, and of course will be of no value to us in this campaign. . . . He is a dear splendid old fellow, but he does not agree with us on anything but silver."[2]

In fact, Pettigrew was wrong. Teller had always argued that expansion could take place without colonial oppression. Although he believed the nation had the legal power to hold colonies, he simultaneously contended that "we have no right to use it." At no point did he suggest that the people of the new possessions should be denied human rights.[3]

By the summer of 1900, the evidence was finally clear that the anti-imperialists had been right all along. In the preceding months, Republicans had passed an organic act for Puerto Rico, proposed resolutions declaring the Philippines to be a perpetual dependency, and even defended the rights of other empires to enforce their will around the globe. The senior senator from Colorado turned away in disgust. "The way to govern a people is to give them the right to govern themselves," Teller declared. "It will not do to say that the people of the Philippine Islands are incapable of self-government. They are capable of it. The people of Cuba are capable of it. The people of Porto [sic] Rico are capable of self-government." Though he admitted "they may not escape some trouble" as they developed democratic societies, he noted that American democracy was far from perfect. "In our early history we had a whisky revolution in Pennsylvania . . . and only a few years ago you had an army standing guard over the property of a railroad company for months in the city of Pittsburg. . . . You have now armed forces standing guard over property in the State of Idaho." Such examples did not prove that Americans were incapable of ruling themselves. "No nation in the world ever escaped these difficulties, and none ever will." Whatever the challenges, Teller denied that America could promote the cause of freedom by governing others without their consent.

From the close of the Fifty-Fifth Congress in March 1899 until the national conventions of 1900, events unfolded that kept the issues of imperialism, militarism, and economic centralization at the forefront of public attention. Both anti-imperialists and their rivals used that time to frame the terms of the upcoming contest. Imperialists pointed to strife, both overseas and closer to home, to justify the formation of a paternalistic federal government and validate its deployment of force. Although western reformers no longer held the balance of power in Congress, those who remained in the House and Senate were no less determined to voice their opposition to the war and the forces that drove conquest. In these efforts, western Populists, Democrats, and Silver Republicans in Congress were aided by local writers, activists, and organized laborers. In the run-up to the election of 1900, these dissidents pointed to both global events and nearby conflicts as the harbingers of a new age. As they saw it, the worldwide struggle for freedom was being waged against tremendous odds, but it could be won if enough Americans were ready to join the fight.

BOERS, BOXERS, AND MINERS

When war began in the Philippines in February 1899, Congress was already debating a military expansion bill. Just as many were busy decrying the dangers of militarism, McKinley wasted little time in justifying their warnings. In the last days of April 1899, a dispute over pay at the Bunker Hill mine in the Coeur d'Alene region of Idaho turned violent. Frustrated by obstinate managers who refused to pay the district's going wages, several hundred miners from throughout the county organized to attack the mill at Wardner. After an exchange of gunfire with company guards (which left two men dead), the miners dynamited the ore concentrator, a facility valued at $250,000. This violence proved to be a sudden spasm, and there was no escalation or threat of further conflict. Still, Governor Frank Steunenberg decided that the outbreak required a massive response. Labor clashes in the Coeur d'Alenes had been dealt with by federal troops before—in both 1892 and 1894—and this time the governor could rationalize their use to McKinley by pointing out that Idaho's National Guard regiment was currently in the Philippines. With little hesitation, the president complied with the governor's request. The first trainload of regulars arrived in northern Idaho on May 2, and Steunenberg officially proclaimed martial law for Shoshone County on May 3.[4]

As had been the case in 1892, the soldiers were used as the mine owners' police force, and they began rounding up suspected participants and placing them in boxcars or "bull pens"—open warehouses used as mass holding facilities. Along with actual suspects, many union men and labor sympathizers were arrested. Estimates of the total number taken into custody range from 700 to 1,000, roughly half of whom were held for months in the inadequate shelters that served as their prisons. Furthermore, the state (with direct support from the army under General Henry C. Merriam) instituted a mandatory work permit system. To obtain a permit, laborers had to openly renounce any allegiance to organized labor and forswear any interest in organizing in the future. Unlike previous federal interventions that had lasted between two and four months, martial law remained in effect for Shoshone County for nearly two years. Steunenberg—a Democrat elected on a fusion ticket—made it clear that he intended to use the regulars to destroy both the Shoshone County Populists and the local union, an affiliate of the Western Federation of Miners (WFM).

Republicans celebrated the actions of McKinley, Merriam, and even Steunenberg. The only dissenting voices among them suggested that the response had not gone far enough. One editor celebrated the news that the "anarchists and murderers" were now where they belonged when it was announced that the entire male population of Burke, Idaho, had been arrested.[5] A writer for one of Colorado's Republican papers suggested to readers that their own state should learn from the troubles in the Coeur d'Alenes. Laborers had been fooled by outside agitators, and the Colorado legislature should pass a law "making it a criminal offense for any of these outsiders . . . to come here and by their council and advice as 'organizers' or officers of organizations to egg on ignorant or inflammable men in our state."[6] Still others sought to associate the violence in Wardner with their political opponents. "The republican party is the party of law and order in Idaho and everywhere," said Bartlet Sinclair, a former aide to Steunenberg, when he declared his move from the Silver to the regular Republican Party. Those who took part were "either populists or democrats. . . . The dynamite methods are distinctively populistic." With no apparent sense of irony, he added that "Republicans, by training and belief, oppose violence."[7]

Western Populists, Democrats, and labor leaders countered that although they did not condone violence, the real "anarchists" were those who had imposed martial law, discarded habeas corpus, and replaced democratic government for rule at the point of a gun.[8] Gilbert Hitchcock, editor of the *Omaha World-Herald*, delivered biting polemics in opposition to military rule in Idaho. In the fall of 1899 he told Nebraskans not to forget that men were "imprisoned because they belonged to the miners' union" and—citing a popular but inaccurate rumor about the controlling interests of the Bunker Hill mine—that they were held captive "because the Standard Oil company wants that sort of thing done." In Hitchcock's opinion, this went beyond corporate favoritism; instead, he described it as an overt display of military force designed to cow organized labor.[9] Jason Lewis, an Omaha labor organizer, shared this analysis. "This man Merriam would make it a crime for laboring men to organize and ask for better wages," he declared to a Labor Day gathering. "This is a military man's idea of justice. The military, blinded by pomp and power, care nothing for liberty or justice."[10]

Those in the mining regions went even further in their characterization of the army's rule in Idaho. To a surprising extent, they tied the plight of the miners under arrest with that of the Filipinos fighting American control across the Pacific. One resident of Aspen, Colorado, used poetry to draw parallels between the two cases and, in the process, indict those who claimed these acts were necessary to preserve safety and freedom:

> Take down the Statue of Liberty
> And build one in its place
> With a tyrant on its pinnacle
> And a slave bound at its base.
> Erase your declaration
> That all the world may know
> We endorse the foul, despotic laws
> Of ill-famed Idaho
>
> Take down the Stars and Stripes,
> It should no longer wave
> As an emblem of liberty
> O'er despot, serf or slave:
> Transform your constitution,
> Suppress the eagle's scream
> 'Till the spirit of Glorious '76
> Prevails at Coeur d'Alenes.
>
> Since you have learned from cruel Spain
> The wisdom of stockades
> That relate more agony, woe,
> Than Weyler's bloody raids.
> Siberia blushed at our shame,
> Her victims sigh to know
> Their tyranny is mild compared
> To that in Idaho.
>
> You sowed the seeds of liberty
> On Cuban soil, 'tis true,
> But does that justify you in
> The course you now pursue?
> Well may Old Glory be despised
> In the far-off Philippines,
> While barbarity in the name of law
> Exists in Coeur d'Alenes.[11]

Whatever the poem's limits, the author drew an interesting parallel between oppression overseas and that at home, and he would not be the only one to do so. America had gone to war in 1898 ostensibly to ensure human freedom. Many Americans wanted to believe that their country provided an example of liberty that people the world over envied and wished to follow.[12] But the poet pointed out that their confidence was misplaced, for America had set aside its own guarantees of liberty to pursue policies of subjugation both at home and abroad.

The sharpest critics of military rule in the Coeur d'Alenes came, as expected, from inside the Western Federation of Miners. The organization had been born out of the often violent labor confrontations in the Rocky Mountain region (and the Coeur d'Alenes in particular), and its initial growth during the period of Davis Waite's administration in Colorado demonstrated the potential utility of political action. By the end of the decade, it was a substantial force throughout the region, and in many ways it had become the representative of Populist labor.[13]

Leaders of the WFM railed against the permit system, mass arrests, and coercion used against laborers, but they joined others in framing the campaign of intimidation as an act of militarism. *Miners' Magazine*—the WFM's official publication, which began circulation in 1900—declared, "The Krag-Jorgensen [rifle] is the law of the land, it is superior to all petitions, protests, legislatures, courts, and constitution; its report sounds the enslavement of the people, for it is forever trained upon them by the military men who are the servants of the privileged few who rule without mercy." Those who desired to strangle organized labor need only apply for aid from "Emperor McKinley," it claimed.[14]

While the conflict in Idaho dominated the pages of *Miners' Magazine* during its first year of existence, there was also substantial coverage of overseas imperialism, some of which merged foreign and domestic events in interesting ways.[15] The magazine's first issue included a satirical article by the "Sultan of Sulu," who declared the Filipino leaders' admiration for American efforts to protect the sanctity of the home but added, "My neighbors here in some of the other Philippine Islands had firesides and homes, but the American soldiers set them on fire, and burnt them to the ground." The "Sultan" also stated his intent to remain a Muslim, noting that the government had given him money for his promise of peace, but "they don't do it with the Christian Filipinos and just kill them off."[16] The next month, after reports began to circulate that the popular General Henry Lawton had been killed in action in the Philippines, a writer for the magazine wryly responded that if the general had "imitated Merriam and arrested the Filipinos and imprisoned them in a 'bull pen,' and then fought their wives," Lawton "would now be a live coward instead of a dead hero."[17]

Although they rarely linked the two directly, labor advocates often simultaneously attacked overseas imperialism and military rule in Idaho. By the time of the WFM convention in May 1900, there was near unanimity among members that both should be opposed. In his address to the delegates, James R. Sovereign—a supporter of the union, former grand master workman of the Knights of Labor, and Populist leader—warned of "the alarming tendency toward militarism in the United States" and the "increasing tendency by corporations to flood the country with Oriental labor to the ultimate annihilation of the American workman." It was suggested that both were intended to make labor servile to the demands of capital.[18]

The declaration of principles adopted by the convention consisted of an amalgam of anti-imperialist and anti-militarist declarations attached to the Omaha platform. It called for government ownership of the railroads, direct federal control of the currency, the "rehabilitation of silver as money," and the enactment of direct legislation laws. Despite the familiarity of these elements, much of the platform had a very different emphasis. The second plank opposed the annexation of territories "populated by other than the Caucasian race," and the eleventh supported the exclusion of all Asian immigrants. Although these provisions clearly reflected a traditional fear among western laborers and seemed to be based on a sense of racial difference, the third plank demanded that "civil government under our constitution be extended" to all the "insular possessions of the United States." This would have meant the complete incorporation of the people (and laborers) of the islands—presumably after the Philippines had been given up. The fourth and fifth planks attacked "arbitrary interference by the federal authorities in local affairs" and condemned proposals for an expanded national army. Their placement immediately after two anti-imperialist statements suggests a desire to link the condemnation of overseas conquest to the issue of undemocratic rule at home.[19]

The conflict in the Coeur d'Alenes was not the only one that placed imperialism and militarism at the forefront of public debate. In the fall of 1899 public attention was drawn to the war between Great Britain and two small settler-colonial republics in southern Africa. By that time, the American war in the Philippines was beginning to bog down, and Aguinaldo would soon order his units to disperse to conduct guerrilla operations.[20] By comparison, in late 1899 and for much of 1900, the South African War (also known as the Boer War) provided the media with epic battles between two unevenly matched foes. Popular sentiment in the United States largely favored the underdog Boers of the Transvaal and Orange Free State, and their early victories only added to their popularity. Anti-imperialists—from both the East and the West—soon declared their sympathy with the Boer cause. If Americans could sympathize with one anticolonial movement, it was rationalized, they could sympathize with another.[21]

For people today, the descendants of Dutch settlers hardly appear to be the archetypal heroes in an anti-imperialist narrative. The Boers themselves were imperialists who had conquered or displaced African peoples as they claimed sovereign possession of lands where they were relative newcomers. Yet the typical accounts of the conflict and the descriptions of the Boers that appeared in the American press ignored these facts. Native Africans were mentioned briefly, if at all, in the mainstream press, and it was claimed that they had worked out amicable relations with the Boers by this time. For most Americans, this was a white man's fight complicated by economic factors, not race. The diamond and gold mines of the Boer states had encouraged British immigration, and the demographic threat posed by this influx was partially responsible for increased tensions in the years before open hostilities began. The war, then, was portrayed as a conflict between a covetous great power and two small states fighting for freedom.[22]

Western reformers quickly joined the new cause. In early December 1899 Governor Poynter of Nebraska presided over a packed pro-Boer gathering in Omaha. In his keynote address he declared his own lack of sympathy for "the sickly sentimentalism being fostered in favor of the mother country, on account of Anglo-Saxon kinship." There was no special relationship between Britain and America, and any recent evidence of British friendship had only followed "indication[s] on the part of this government to depart from those great principles upon which this republic was founded." Others speakers discussed Britain's motives for war. Senator Allen, though unable to attend, had sent a letter that was read at the gathering. He claimed that "because of the discovery of diamond and gold mines of almost limitless value they [the Boer republics] are, under one pretext or another, through a spirit of greed, assailed by Great Britain." Allen's analysis typified the views presented at the meeting. Among the resolutions adopted was one that condemned England for its recent history of land grabbing. "As England sought to claim the gold fields of Venezuela by a dispute over a boundary line . . . so it does by a pretense against the laws of the Dutch republic seek to wrest from that people their liberty and independence, if necessary, in order to reach the gold fields of South Africa." After the meeting, some participants stayed behind to discuss the possibility of forming an anti-imperial organization to oppose both the war in South Africa and the one in the Philippines.[23]

In many ways, westerners described the struggle of the Boers as a fight similar to their own. An article in Miners' Magazine explained how this association was based on more than emotion. The story followed the career of John Hayes Hammond, a mining engineer and manager. In 1892 Hammond had served as an operative for the Mine Owners Association of the Coeur d'Alenes, and he had played a key role in the confrontation that led to the intervention of federal troops and the suppression of organized labor that year. By 1895, Hammond had relocated to South Africa, where he was in the employ of archimperialist Cecil Rhodes. Following the defeat of the Jameson raid—Rhodes's privately orchestrated and premature attempt to provoke hostilities between the British and the Boers—Hammond was arrested by authorities in the Transvaal for his role in the conspiracy. Although he was the focus of the article, the author suggested that Hammond was only one example. "The same stockholders in the South African Goldfields Company are stockholders in the mines of the United States and Canada." Their greed, and that of others like them, was at the core of all imperialism. Whether one was speaking of the miners of Idaho, the Boers of South Africa, or "the poor Filipinos who wrested their island homes from Spanish tyranny to find that a still greater tyrant had paid $20,000,000 for the privilege of shooting them down," it mattered not at all. All of them suffered so that "a few designing millionaires might increase their dividends." Global capitalism was the source of all these conflicts, and only its defeat could resolve them.[24]

Though they did so less dramatically, western congressmen also linked their own struggle with that of the Boers. In the House of Representatives, John Shafroth of Colorado claimed that the world's powers should be interested in stopping a conflict that was "shutting off more than one-third of the world's supply of gold."[25] While he suggested that this clearly damaged world markets, his description of the struggle in South Africa actually bore a close resemblance to the fight for corporate regulation in America. The Boers had looked forward "to the building of a great commonwealth" that required expensive internal improvements, but unfortunately, "most of these diamond fields and gold mines have passed into the hands of a few corporations, whose directors and officers nearly all are citizens of, or reside in other countries, and have no common interest . . . in building up a great republic in Africa." Instead of being used to build up their own states, the Boers saw "the only wealth the country possesses, being daily exhausted and shipped to foreign lands." Shafroth seemed to understand the Boers' frustration as "this vast wealth" was spent on "building magnificent structures in foreign cities and gorgeous palaces on the shores of the Mediterranean Sea," while the common Boer farmer "still lives in poverty, in his unpretentious cottage." The vivid imagery employed by Shafroth may have been more akin to the plight of western homesteaders than to any reality in South Africa, but it suggests his willingness to associate his struggle with that of the Boers.[26]

Another westerner viewed British colonialism in a different light but essentially agreed that the goal was economic oppression. Senator Richard Pettigrew contended that the British goal was to destroy the independence of labor in South Africa. He cited as evidence the latest speeches by British economist (and recent convert to anti-imperialism) J. A. Hobson, who claimed that "the mine owners in the Transvaal desired to overthrow the Republic so they could enact the same slave-labor laws in force at Kimberley [in British South Africa]; so that they could repeal the eight-hour law and compel the black laborers, at least, to work twelve hours a day; so that they could repeal the Sunday laws and run the mines seven days each week, as they do at Kimberley." Pettigrew argued that the brutal contract labor system employed in the British colonies necessarily degraded both those held to service and those still struggling to maintain their independence. The South Dakotan said British imperialism was rooted in the defense of corporate profits, as was its American counterpart.[27]

American popular opinion favored the Boers, but the national administration showed no interest in challenging the British. Many Boer supporters criticized McKinley for his unwillingness to show even the slightest sympathy for the South African republics, but most suggested that the United States was in no position to do so. Pettigrew rhetorically asked why the president said not a word "in behalf of liberty and humanity" before answering: "Simply because he is engaged in the same wretched business as that which is drenching the soil of Africa with the blood of martyrs. He is busy with an effort to rob the people of the Philippine Islands, and is slaughtering those who resist robbery because, forsooth, it will pay, because they are rich and are worth robbing, and because their island possessions will furnish a foothold for other robberies."[28]

Whatever his policy objectives, McKinley could not prevent others from taking sides. Western reformers conspicuously flocked to the Boer cause. When Boer representatives in America attempted to mobilize public support for their cause, western reformers became some of their strongest allies. By

May 1900, the most prominent members of the National Boer Relief Fund Association were senators, congressmen, and governors of western states. At that time, two of the six senators listed as members of the general committee were from the West (Pettigrew and Allen), as were three of the five governors (Thomas of Colorado, Poynter of Nebraska, and Rogers of Washington). Many realized this organizational effort could be used to further their own campaign against imperialism. In the summer of 1900 Boer envoys toured a number of states to drum up public interest, and they gladly added Omaha to their list of stops. The rally held in their honor was attended by William Jennings Bryan, and he used the event to refocus attention on matters closer to home by declaring that there must never be a day "when those fighting for liberty will look to the American nation in vain for sympathy and aid in their struggle." Whereas overt support for the Filipinos would be deemed traitorous, the Boers could be used as proxies.[29]

As much as western reformers used the South African War for their own purposes, it should not be assumed that they were interested only in political gain. Many of them had taken up anti-imperialism at an early point in the public discussion of expansion, so any extension of that viewpoint could not be considered disingenuous. For some, anti-imperialism was fundamental to their vision of human freedom. Franklin Pettigrew, the senator's twenty-something son, was so deeply impressed by his father's anti-imperialism that he adopted the cause as his own. In May 1900 Richard Pettigrew drafted a letter that Franklin carried with him to the Transvaal, where he intended to join the Boers in their fight. The senator wrote to Paul Kruger, president of the South African Republic, that his son was "prompted by a sentiment of devotion to the principles for which you contend," and he concluded by asking the Boer leader, "Will you look after him as you would your own son?" For the senator from South Dakota, the fight against empire was not merely rhetorical.[30]

By the summer of 1900, troubles in another region had reached a crisis phase. McKinley's policy in Asia, though never clearly outlined to the public, had always emphasized access to China. Interest in the Chinese market had long drawn the attention of all the world powers, and each had coerced the old empire into an unequal treaty. It was also widely known that all the great powers contemplated the day when China would be unable to maintain its sovereignty against foreign incursion, and each sought to position itself for such an eventuality. This contingency had always been in the minds of McKinley and his advisers, but the new secretary of state, John Hay, considered the partition of China contrary to American interests. In the closing months of 1899, the administration first formally expressed its desire to maintain an "Open Door" to China. Though hardly a new idea—in fact, this had been Britain's policy for most of the preceding century—this statement laid out America's policy objectives. The avenues of trade must be kept open, and the territorial integrity of China must remain intact.[31]

As foreign powers gained increasing influence over their government and their lives, the Chinese people channeled their frustrations into an antiforeign and anti-Christian movement. Known to English speakers as the Boxers, their influence grew rapidly in the last years of the 1890s. In some parts of China, they had already started to attack native Christians by mid-1899; however, because they initially abstained from assaults on foreign missionaries, they aroused little concern overseas. That would change in March 1900, when open rebellion broke out in the coastal province of Shandong. Within weeks, it had spread to the provinces surrounding Beijing. By the middle of June, foreign legations in the capital found themselves besieged, and soon Dowager Empress Cixi ordered China's armies to aid the Boxers.[32]

If the foreign ministers in China were to survive—along with their staffs and the missionaries who had crowded into the legations for protection— some kind of intervention would be required. Japan and the European powers began to hastily assemble forces, but with intervention came the danger of partition. McKinley reasoned that the United States could not demand maintenance of the Open Door policy from the sidelines. On June 16, shortly after Congress had adjourned, McKinley ordered a regiment (soon supplemented by additional units) to be sent from the Philippines to the coast of China. There, US soldiers would work in an informal alliance with the forces of the other imperial powers and battle their way inland to Beijing.[33]

From mid-June until at least mid-August 1900, this new conflict in China captured the headlines of the nation's press. Without exaggeration, one contemporary claimed, "Even the presidential campaign . . . occupies a subordinate place in the estimation of the American public." Whether this was true, it was an accurate reflection of the media's treatment of the conflict. The threat posed to American lives made the stories even more compelling. And, inevitably, these developments had implications for the upcoming electoral campaign.[34]

Those opposed to imperialism were suddenly in an awkward position. Despite generally negative descriptions of the Boxers as xenophobic and barbarous, some western anti-imperialists understood the source of Chinese anger, and many underscored the fact that the Europeans, Japanese, and

Americans had long harbored ill intentions toward the Middle Kingdom. Although the industrialized nations claimed to possess "no motive but that of the most unselfish philanthropy," one writer suggested that, "in reality we cared nothing at all as governments about Christianizing and civilizing the Chinese, but everything about the riches of spoliation which lay in the mysterious interior of their mighty empire."[35] Another editor agreed that China's wealth was the reason for foreign interest, and therefore "the partitioning of China is apparently close at hand." This author did not ascribe China's collapse to any weakness on its part. Instead, the Boxer turmoil merely represented a "breach" of Chinese insularity "created by the entering wedge of commercialism." China was in turmoil because of the disruptions created by its forced integration into the global economy, and this chaos now provided an opportunity to "bring the numerically greatest nation in the world under the foot of the trader."[36]

The anti-imperialists made their most favorable statements about the Boxers in the days before McKinley's decision to intervene. Shortly after that, as the media described the Boxer crisis as a serious issue with global implications, few depicted the Boxers as anything other than irrational and violent. Even the anti-imperialists made few declarations in opposition to intervention. To support the Boxers or to oppose a response was seen as disloyal.

Whether Populists and Democrats supported the Boxers was of little consequence to their rivals. Republicans were eager to associate Bryan and his allies with murderous hordes from Asia. Surely, one argued, "The matter of killing a few missionaries ought not to count" when compared with the savage plans of Aguinaldo, and Bryan's followers had already declared that attacks on the Filipino leader "and his brother cutthroats was an unspeakable crime." The same author asked, "How much worse is it in Tien Tsin [a city on the road to Beijing where a foreign cession was being besieged] than it was in northern Idaho some months ago" when the anarchist miners ruled the Coeur d'Alenes? According to their opponents, the Populists and Democrats always sympathized with those who represented disorder.[37]

Other Republicans chose to emphasize the opportunity presented by the outbreak of violence in China. The old Chinese civilization had become moribund, and although its people had thus far "resisted improvements and fought those who in a spirit of friendliness sought to aid her," they would now be commanded to change. The imperial powers, especially the United States, could guide the "almond-eyed and swarthy-skinned celestials," and suddenly "400,000,000 souls" would be awakened to the opportunities of the modern world.[38]

HARPER'S WEEKLY

A JOURNAL OF CIVILIZATION

VOL. XLIV.—No. 2370
Copyright, 1900, by HARPER & BROTHERS
(Harper Trust Company, Trustee)

NEW YORK, SATURDAY, JUNE 23, 1900

TEN CENTS A COPY
FOUR DOLLARS A YEAR

THE VANGUARD OF THE BOXERS

"The Vanguard of the Boxers," Harper's Weekly, *June 23, 1900. Copyright permission granted by Harpweek LLC*

CONGRESS AND THE DEBATE OVER COLONIALISM

While domestic conflicts and global affairs were used to shape political discourse, Congress had yet to determine America's relationship with its "new possessions." McKinley had made no declaration of policy by the beginning of 1900, but that could not continue for long. Pressing and intertwined issues pertaining to constitutionality, free governance, and trade could not be perpetually postponed.

The president and his allies in Congress—such as Senators Albert Beveridge and Henry Cabot Lodge—were still actively making their case that the war in the Philippines was necessary. In his annual message to Congress in December 1899, McKinley continued to stress that Aguinaldo and the other insurgent leaders had carefully plotted the attack of February 4. The insurgents represented a small minority, and it was up to the military to secure order. No proper civilian government could be installed "until order is restored," so all authority in the islands continued to rest with the commander in chief and his subordinates.[39]

Although McKinley's objectives remained hidden, freshman senator Beveridge took it upon himself to declare what the US attitude should be. The trade possibilities with Asia were too vital to simply abandon, and he saw the Philippines as a gateway to those markets. "Our largest trade henceforth must be with Asia. The Pacific is our ocean. More and more Europe will manufacture the most it needs, secure from its colonies the most it consumes. Where shall we turn for consumers of our surplus? Geography answers the question. China is our natural customer." For Beveridge, American profits and power were foremost, and he contended that "the power that rules the Pacific . . . is the power that rules the world. And, with the Philippines, that power is and will forever be the American Republic." For that reason, the United States must "hold it [the Philippines] fast and hold it forever."[40]

Despite Beveridge's suggestion that the United States should retain possession of the Philippines in perpetuity, the question of its status remained. Unsurprisingly, Beveridge and his ally Lodge considered the Filipinos totally unfit for American institutions. Beveridge claimed, "It is barely possible that 1,000 men in all the archipelago are capable of self-government in the Anglo-Saxon sense." According to the Indiana senator, this was a result of their racial qualities. In the same breath he called them mere "children" and said, "They are not of a self-governing race. They are Orientals, Malays." Lodge saw the situation in much the same light. "There never has been . . . the slightest indication of any desire for what we call freedom or representative government east of Constantinople," he said. "The form of government natural to the Asiatic has always been a despotism." This was the mandate of biology, Lodge claimed. The "theory, that you could make a Hottentot into a European if you only took possession of him in infancy. . . has been abandoned alike by science and history as grotesquely false." The claim that Filipinos, as a race, lacked the "capacity" to govern themselves would be one of the primary justifications of American occupation for the entire colonial period.[41]

Proponents of expansion were eager to legitimize conquest and colonial rule, and most of their explanations of national intentions were designed to link imperial ambitions with American ideals. In his message to Congress, McKinley clung to the narrative of self-defense regarding the war in the Philippines, even as evidence to the contrary mounted. Information from western volunteers made it clear that the Filipinos had not launched an all-out assault on the American positions surrounding Manila. The correspondence between Otis and the War Department also indicated that Aguinaldo had sought peace immediately after the outbreak of hostilities but had been spurned by Otis. Despite the renunciations of Senator Lodge, who joined the president in declaring, "They attacked us; we did not attack them," other senators such as Richard Pettigrew, George Turner, and John L. Rawlins (a Democrat from Utah) questioned that account and presented proof that Aguinaldo was a betrayed ally, that Otis had provoked the war, and that soldiers in the Philippines had committed atrocities.[42]

The Philippines remained foremost in everyone's minds, but soon a debate over a seemingly trivial issue—a tariff for Puerto Rico—would force the administration to reveal its intentions. Of all the islands claimed by the United States in recent years, Americans may have been most sympathetic to the inhabitants of Puerto Rico. They had not rebelled against American rule and had, in fact, welcomed the invasion force. A year later, in August 1899, one of the most powerful hurricanes ever recorded in the Atlantic barreled through the island, killing at least 2,500 and causing $20 million in damage. The inhabitants needed assistance, but no act had yet established the nature of the relationship between Puerto Rico and the United States, and the Treaty of Paris had left that determination solely with Congress. In his annual message in December, the president called for a direct aid bill but then added that it was "our plain duty" to establish free trade between the island and the mainland. He clearly did not foresee the fight that would ensue.[43]

The great oddity about the fight over the Puerto Rican tariff (also known as the Organic Act of 1900 or the Foraker Act, for the Ohio senator who proposed the original bill) was that the debate was not about the tariff itself or, for that matter, about only Puerto Rico. President McKinley had initially been opposed to any customs duties, in the hope that favorable legislation would encourage economic recovery on the island; however, he quickly reconsidered when anti-imperialists declared that Puerto Rico was an integral part of the United States and denied that Congress had the power to establish a tariff at all. They argued that the Constitution followed the flag, so the same legal freedoms that existed in territories like New Mexico existed in the island possessions. McKinley, and the vast majority who understood the logic of American overseas imperialism, contended that the colonies were not part of the United States; therefore, Congress held plenary power over customs, governance, and even the citizenship of residents. This principle needed to be demonstrated, especially before the same issue arose in the more controversial Philippines. As if to prove that it was merely symbolic, the proposed tariff for Puerto Rico was set at 85 percent below the standard rate. Although some claimed that this still constituted a protective tariff, the debate itself was really about colonialism and the limits of congressional power. For supporters and opponents alike, the tariff fight was about what could be done to the colonies, especially the ever-troubling Philippines.[44]

The greatest question pertained to the legal classification of the Puerto Ricans. The original bill presented by Foraker was somewhat contradictory, in that it included the low tariff and thus made it clear that Puerto Rico was not being integrated into the American body, yet it also granted citizenship to the inhabitants of the island. It simultaneously established a civilian administration but allowed few openings for Puerto Rican self-government. Teller pointed out the juxtaposition, in which the people would be integrated into the American system while the island and its government were not. If the Puerto Ricans were citizens, Teller asked, "are we not bound to extend to them all the rights and privileges of the people of the United States? Are we going to have a section of country where there are citizens, where they take the oath to obey the Constitution every time they hold office, and yet treat them as foreigners?" Foraker quickly amended the bill, and the residents of the island were relabeled "citizens of Puerto Rico" who were "as such entitled to the protection of the United States." This new construction, though still awkward, further established the line of division between colony and metropole.[45]

By drawing legal distinctions between American territory and the insular possessions, the Foraker bill was designed to create the legal basis for a system of colonialism. Although Teller had argued that even a democracy like the United States could possess colonies, he reiterated his claim that there was a difference between authority and propriety. In this case, he agreed that Puerto Rico could be governed differently from territories. Still, he wanted to "extend to them [the people of Puerto Rico] all the privileges which are consistent with their relations to this Government save that of citizenship." Unlike the statements of Beveridge and Lodge regarding the Filipinos, Teller had "no doubt of their [the Puerto Ricans'] ability to manage their own internal and domestic affairs practically without our supervision." Teller's vision differed markedly from that of the most aggressive expansionists, and he was finally forced to admit that his association with them had been a mistake.[46]

Teller accepted that Congress held plenary power over the acquired islands, but western anti-imperialists argued otherwise. Foremost among them was William V. Allen. He challenged Foraker in a number of exchanges on the floor of the Senate, forcing the friend of McKinley to repeatedly admit that—in his view—the Puerto Ricans had no guaranteed legal rights. In contrast, Allen claimed, "When we ratified the treaty of Paris, Puerto Rico became as much a part of the territory of the United States as New Mexico or Arizona." Rather than colonies, he considered the insular possessions to be the same as territories. The Constitution made no allowance for anything else. Furthermore, he did not consider the people of Puerto Rico so exceptionally different from others who had been integrated into the American body, so there was no reason for unrestrained colonial authority. The people of Florida and Louisiana were of much the same stock when they were annexed, he said. The people of Puerto Rico were also "substantially the same people who dwell in South America. There is much of the Mexican in their nature; much of the blood of all the people who dwell in Central and South America, in Venezuela, for instance. . . . Everyone of these South American countries has a republic." Even if they were not suited to American forms of self-rule, they were undoubtedly capable of governing themselves. Race did play a part in Allen's analysis, as it did for most anti-imperialists, but like others in Congress, he attacked the proposed bill as both unwarranted and unconstitutional.[47]

Western Republicans in Congress were virtually silent during the debate, as they had been for most of the controversies of the McKinley administration. One of the rare exceptions was Senator George Perkins of California. He had always been a skeptic of expansion, and for that reason he had asked his state legislature for its recommendation before the vote on the Treaty of Paris. Despite his own fears that it could allow the people of the Philippines easy entry into the United States, he had voted in favor of the treaty, as the state legislature had advised. Still, he only briefly succeeded in setting aside his anxieties.

Certainly, Perkins was not the only supporter of the administration who sensed the danger of expansion. His vocal support for the Foraker bill demonstrates the priorities of some western Republicans, and those from the Pacific coast especially. While others remained silent, Perkins was proud of his membership on the committee that assembled the bill in its final form. Despite the low tax rate it imposed, he suggested the tariff served a protective purpose, as well it must, for "more than one-third of the entire population [of Puerto Rico] is of the negro or mixed race," and perhaps as many as half of the population qualified as "poor." In particular, the mainland's sugar production was endangered by this cheap labor. While some idealists wanted to claim "the Constitution follows the flag," to Perkins, such statements were "merely claptrap and untrue."[48]

Perkins focused primarily on Puerto Rico in his discussion, but when the proposal was challenged, he made its real intent clear. South Carolina's anti-imperialist senator Ben Tillman attacked the bill on grounds similar to those presented by Senator Allen, claiming it was both unnecessary and unconstitutional. The Californian responded with a query: since Tillman supported free trade with a region where labor was valued at "15 to 20 cents a day," was he also "in favor of free trade with the Philippine Islands?" When Tillman said he was, Perkins was aghast. "Is it right for that cheap labor, that peon, contract labor, to come into competition with American labor?" he asked rhetorically.[49] Perkins understood that they were legislating to establish a principle. Even if the tariff rate between the United States and Puerto Rico was nominal, there was nothing to prevent the rate from being set higher when it came time to legislate for the Philippines.

By this time, Senator George Turner of Washington was one of only two non-Republicans representing the Pacific coast in either house of Congress. In many ways, he agreed with Perkins about the immigration and labor threats posed by the people of the Philippines to American industries and white workers; however, he also thought the bill made a mockery of American law. He attacked those imperialists who had been in favor of "admitting the labor and the products of the labor of the underpaid and underfed people of the Philippine Islands," but he thought the problem could not be counterbalanced by another violation of the Constitution. Republicans had "apparently awakened" to the danger, "which they are now trying to guard against." Imperialists were covering their weak spot, but it seemed to Turner

Senator George Turner. Courtesy of the Library of Congress

that they were simultaneously discarding the foundations of American law and justice.[50]

Although the debate was heated, the results were never in doubt. The final version of the bill was passed in the Senate on April 3 by a vote of 40–31. Of the westerners who had supported Bryan in 1896, only John P. Jones and William Stewart of Nevada voted in favor of the bill.[51] The House decision a week later was much the same. There, the bill passed 161–153, with no western Populist, Democrat, or Silver Republican support.[52] No western Republicans in either house of Congress voted against it. Members of the reform coalition, now united behind the cause of anti-imperialism, under-stood that a vote in favor would have sanctioned a system of colonial rule. It was impossible to oppose that policy and support the legal framework such a system would be based on. Western Republicans pulled together with the same understanding. Unequal colonialism—which would benefit Americans without altering their definition of citizenship or jeopardizing interests in the domestic economy—required such a law, and they happily approved it in a campaign year.

The bill's passage could not heal all the wounds created in the fight. Na-tionally, the bill became an object of scorn among Democrats and Repub-licans alike. While westerners in Congress divided along party lines, that was not the case for the rest of the House and Senate. Twenty House Re-publicans were critical of the original bill, yet all but six of them eventually voted in favor of it. In the Senate, even the imperialist Beveridge initially opposed the tariff in favor of free trade, but he too realized it was a fight he could not win. Republicans directed their vitriol at the bill in part because the president had promised free trade for humanitarian purposes. When McKinley changed course later, he did so in silence. Likewise, he never made a statement regarding the legal status of the Puerto Ricans. When Congress proposed the erection of tariff boundaries, even the nation's Republican press charged that the lawmakers were either defying the will of McKinley or mistreating the nation's new citizens.[53]

Even though their congressmen voted along party lines, some of the most emphatically imperialistic newspapers on the Pacific coast opposed the bill. The editor of the Evening Tribune of San Diego, California, consistently de-nied that McKinley had rethought his position and went on to call the tariff bill "the most radical measure of change in the policy of the United States since Abraham Lincoln's proclamation of emancipation." Though admitting that Southern California fruit producers might approve of a tariff to protect their own interests, the writer warned that "nine out of ten of our fruit growers will raise the thought . . . that we are unfairly handicapping these new citizens of our nation."[54] The pro-McKinley Oregonian also detested the measure, suggesting it was intended to benefit the "Protected Interests," and feared that "the Philippines [will get] the same treatment."[55] The Oregonian's writers also contended that American culture and institutions would civilize and invigorate Asia.[56] Tariffs and other boundaries created resentment rather than a sense of common interest or identity, and it was no way to cement the American position in any of the islands. In a similar tone, the editor of the staunchly Republican San Francisco Chronicle argued that the "general laws and the Constitution of the United States must cover the islands." The writer recognized the importance of trade but suggested that the purpose of this trade was to extend both the nation's "commercial identity" and the "spirit of American nationality."[57] After the bill passed, the *Chronicle* printed two full pages of an angry attack on the tariff. Although it again gave a nod to economic self-interest, nearly every paragraph that discussed the Filipinos or Puerto Ricans was littered with the word "citizen." As soon as possible, the author demanded, it was Congress's duty to "pass laws which will give such of the inhabitants of the Philippines as we have made citizens of the United States by annexation all the benefits and immunities of the Constitution."[58]

Republicans were caught in the whirlwind they had stirred up over the course of nearly two years. They claimed that Americans would bring freedom to the new possessions through a policy of "benevolent assimilation." They never mentioned whether citizenship accompanied the flag, nor did they devote many words to the limits of their benevolence. Only the most bellicose among them openly called for a true colonial policy, and much of that language had been employed only recently. Ultimately, members of the Republican press were guilty of taking the administration at its word. Yet the attacks on the administration were far from universal, and in fact, the Republican press in most of the western states rarely criticized the tariff or any other provision of the bill. The examples cited came from Oregon and California—the only two far western states that had voted for McKinley in 1896—and there was little threat of the party being dethroned in either state in 1900. There, Republicans could demand free trade to benefit their industries and the full, permanent integration of all the islands to guarantee long-term connections, while also fulfilling the moral imperative many expansionists employed to justify the policy.

In Nebraska and Colorado, the Republican press was largely dismissive of attacks on the proposal. Generally speaking, they did not discuss the issues of citizenship or governance for the people of Puerto Rico. Instead, they characterized the bill as an ordinary tariff measure and portrayed critics as partisan hacks. The *McCook Tribune*, for instance, declared that an analysis of the tariff "shows that it will be vastly more advantageous to Puerto Rico as well as to the United States than that which formerly existed in the island."[59] The formerly anti-imperialist *Omaha Daily Bee* also adopted this view. "The popocratic press must be very hard up for political capital when it has to fall back upon the Porto [sic] Rican muddle," claimed one writer for the paper. A tariff so low was hardly worth the protest.[60] Colorado's Republican press likewise categorized all opposition to the bill as a sign of the "desperate straits" the Democrats were in as they sought to "make a mountain out of this molehill" for the upcoming campaign.[61]

Farther west the emphasis was different. Writers for the *Seattle Post-Intelligencer* understood full well that the tariff was not about taxation. In a series of articles published in the weeks leading up to the vote, they attacked the Democrats who argued that the Constitution "follows the flag" to any acquired territory "no matter what the circumstances or the character of its people."[62] The purpose of this bill was to emphatically reject "the plea that our new possessions come immediately within the constitution, with explicit rights to statehood." The Democrats were trying to "put us in a dilemma where we should have had to confess that statehood must go ultimately to the Philippines or else that we must turn them over to Aguinaldo."[63] Analysis in the *Morning Olympian* was much the same. Although the paper initially supported a more inclusive relationship with Puerto Rico, its opinions soon shifted. Even Britain's free trade policies did not extend to its colonies, one writer explained. A month after the bill passed, another stated, "Wages paid in Puerto Rico should more closely approximate those paid on the mainland before the average islander should be permitted to come here in competition with the American wage-earner."[64]

Of course, some Washington newspapers were just as dismissive as those in Nebraska and Colorado, but it was not a coincidence that Washington Republicans saw the Foraker Act's significance in terms of citizenship and immigration.[65] Local papers described the state's location as a logical gateway to Asia, and the implications of that depiction were not lost on them. Interestingly, the act did not actually prohibit immigration from Puerto Rico, but because it denied the inhabitants American citizenship, it was presumed to de-incentivize immigration to the mainland. It also hypothetically allowed for immigration restriction in the future, something the Washington Republicans would play up in the campaign.

THE GOLD STANDARD ACT

As Congress was debating the Puerto Rican tariff, the McKinley administration made one more effort to secure new banking and monetary legislation. Their efforts in 1898 had led to humiliating defeat, but by the time the Fifty-Sixth Congress was installed, opponents in the Senate could no longer block their way. As had been the case with the Foraker Act, it was deemed desirable to pass such legislation before the upcoming election. Both laws demonstrated the administration's position on key issues, and both could be presented as "safe," in that they recognized and legalized the established order.[66]

The proposed reorganization, presented in a single bill, would make gold the currency of ultimate redemption, take $150 million in greenbacks out of circulation, authorize the secretary of the treasury to issue bonds if the greenback redemption fund dropped below a certain level, re-fund the national debt and postpone its final repayment, and allow national banks to issue bank notes equal to the value of federal bonds they owned. Though not a wholesale overhaul of the existing currency system, the changes in the bill were substantial.[67]

The reaction of the western reformers was overwhelmingly negative. They had waged the last national campaign against the gold standard, and they remained opposed to every element of the new bill. Allen, Turner, Teller, and others took turns accosting the sponsors of the bill, especially senators Nelson W. Aldrich of Rhode Island and William B. Allison of Iowa. There was not enough gold in the world to function as the global medium of exchange, they declared yet again. The destruction of greenbacks and the further marginalization of silver would contract the currency and leave producers at the mercy of creditors. Such a proposal was sure to produce national calamities. Senator Teller even suggested that a recent famine in India was a direct result of Britain's attempt to impose the gold standard on its colony.[68]

While they denigrated the gold standard, the bill's opponents in Congress focused their ire on the proposed entrenchment of a money and banking system even further removed from democratic influence. All remembered the bond issues of the Cleveland administration, and none looked forward to a repetition. Turner called the proposal a "most remarkable means to the accomplishment of the ends sought," as it essentially gave the secretary of the treasury policy-making power. Allen took the same principle even further, suggesting it was tantamount to handing "over the power of taxation" to the secretary. "When we say that the Secretary of the Treasury may issue Government bonds ad libitum, as he sees fit, as this bill provides, then the question of taxation to meet the interest upon those bonds is merely perfunctory, because the foundation for the taxation has been laid by the mere caprice of an executive officer, and the taxation can not be escaped."[69]

That kind of authority in the hands of a single bureaucrat was too much for them to accept. Teller pointed out that such centralization of power was especially dangerous because of the pressure likely to be applied on anyone in that position. A congressional investigation had just exposed letters from

A. B. Hepburn (vice president of National City Bank of New York, the predecessor of modern-day Citibank) to Secretary of the Treasury Lyman Gage in
which the banker expressed the hope that his institution could retain its position as a national depository and then emphasized the political contributions
made by the bank's director as evidence that it should do so. Obviously, said
the senior senator from Colorado, these examples highlighted the danger of
investing such power in a person holding an appointed position. Allen likewise stated that the Republicans were "debtors" to those he called "the gold
gamblers and the money sharks," and for that reason, control of the national
purse strings must never be taken from the national legislature.[70]

The greatest danger posed by the bill pertained to the position it gave
to national banks. Teller believed "that 75 per cent of all the loans made
in New York City by those banks are made to speculators and to operators,
and that it is a very common thing for the banks themselves to engage in
such operations." This gave the banks a direct interest in the outcomes of
certain markets, especially the commodities markets. Such institutions were
too deeply involved in profit-making activities to simultaneously wield power
over the money in circulation. At any moment they could disburse or withdraw their bank notes and inflate or deflate the currency as they wished.
These concerns were at the heart of the issue. As Representative Edwin Ridgely (a Kansas Populist) put it, "The real issue involved in this whole money
question is not between gold and silver alone; it is, in fact, a question of who
shall issue and control our money supply. Shall we by this legislation make
a gift of this great power and profit to the bank syndicate?" Properly, this
power must be held by the people and those chosen by them. "All money is
the creation of law. In a republic all laws emanate from the people; hence the
power to create and issue money is inherent and belongs to all the people."
Money, as Peffer had insisted at the beginning of the 1890s, was a tool to be
used for the public benefit. Instead, the proposed bill would allow private
enterprises to control something as fundamental as currency, and there were
few regulations in place to determine how they employed that power.[71]

In their analysis of the bill, Populists predicted it would only accelerate
the destruction of traditional American freedom. Allen considered it a har-
binger of the near future, when the nation would "raise up a great army of
industrial and agricultural serfs" to take the place of independent farmers
and laborers.[72] Ridgely declared, "We are approaching the rapid culmination
of the most tyrannical forms of capitalism." He believed world events were
demonstrating the guiding influence of capitalists, and this bill represented
only one form of their power. In the same speech, he noted:

[Armies are being] directed in their operations to support and extend the rights and interests of capital, even in the present wars waged under its orders against the Filipinos and the Boers; we hear the bold demand of capital claiming its right to conquer those people in order that it may appropriate nature's rich resources, using our armies to hold the people there in subjection, while capital works them at a few pennies per day, throwing their product of rice, tobacco, sugar, cotton, etc., on the market to force down wages of our home people.

The American people would not tolerate the continuous degradation of their lifestyles for long. The next step, and one that Ridgely seemed to look forward to, was socialism.[73]

This time, McKinley and his managers in Congress were more careful than they had been two years earlier. They secured the necessary votes well before the final determination, and both sides understood the inevitability of the bill's passage as soon as the dates were set. On March 6 the Senate passed the bill by a vote of 44-26. Seventeen senators took no part in the vote, including Edward Wolcott, James Kyle of South Dakota, and William Stewart of Nevada (former owner of the widely read *Silver Knight-Watchman*). All these men were now firmly in the McKinley camp. One week later, it was the House's turn. The vote was somewhat closer there—166-120, with sixty-six House members either absent or voting "present"—but the outcome was never in doubt.[74] McKinley had secured a substantial legislative victory.

The two sides had effectively laid the groundwork for the campaign of 1900 well before it was officially under way. Republicans entered the campaign by declaring their devotion to trickle-down prosperity in a united nation, one in which the divisions of class and race were perpetually muted by the acceptance of an orderly hierarchy. Empire secured the markets, while gold provided the monetary foundation for economic stability based on capital investment. In many ways, the events of the preceding four years had led to the recent culmination of their party's domestic and foreign policy initiatives. Over the course of 1899 and early 1900, challenges to their system had emerged, but in each case they responded by reinforcing its structure rather than abandoning it. These challenges provided opportunities to demonstrate and clarify their vision of American wealth and power.

The western reformers maintained a starkly different dream of what America should be. As the administration bolstered the gold standard, implemented a colonial policy, and informally allied the nation with America's oldest enemy, Democrats and Populists classified these developments as boons for special interests and threats to republican institutions. If political and economic freedom were to be saved—in America and around the world—the grip of powerful corporations and authoritarian government had to be loosened. They looked forward to the upcoming campaign as a chance to reverse the nation's present course, and they looked to Bryan to lead them in the contest against militaristic empire and arrogant wealth.

8. THE CONTEST OF 1900 AND THE DEFEAT OF REFORM

In the summer of 1900 William McKinley and William Jennings Bryan began their second campaign for the presidency against each other. The nominations of the two parties had been mere formalities, and in many ways, the previous campaign had never really ended. Bryan had only strengthened his position as the Democratic Party's leader since 1896, and McKinley had justified every action taken during his first term as though he were running against the same opponent. By midsummer, all that remained was for the two contenders to make their acceptance speeches, which would serve as the keynotes of their campaigns.

McKinley acknowledged the Republican Party's nomination in a speech on July 12. In it he boasted of his administration's successes, especially the recent passage of the Gold Standard Act. The second half of the address discussed the liberation of Cuba, the "beneficent government" that had recently been established for Puerto Rico, and the "obligations imposed by the triumph of our arms" in the Philippines, where the people who had been "misled into rebellion" had been dispersed, and conditions were improving. There were no longer any obstacles to the restoration of "peace and stable government" in the Philippines, but the real "obstructionists are here, not elsewhere." In his conclusion, the president had the audacity to declare that the same party that "broke the shackles of 4,000,000 slaves" was, under his own guidance, responsible for the "liberation of 10,000,000 of the human family from the yoke of imperialism."[1]

The president attempted to summarize his term, and he did so by combining discussions of American power with a distorted conception of American ideals. Whereas McKinley suggested that his policies had created prosperity and safety in the new American empire, his opponent chose to highlight the terrible consequences of those policies. Bryan would do so by emphasizing the one issue he considered the most dangerous and meaningful of them all.

In his acceptance speech, Bryan focused on the great foreign policy question of the day, but for the man known as the "Commoner" and those like him, this new empire was a reflection of ills at home. On August 8 a crowd of 40,000 people gathered in Military Park in Indianapolis to hear Bryan open with the declaration that "the contest of 1900 is a contest between democracy on one hand and plutocracy on the other." Through their actions over the last four years, Republicans had shown themselves to be "dominated by those influences which constantly substitute the worship of mammon for the protection of the rights of man." McKinley dared to suggest that the war in the Philippines had been for the benefit of the Filipinos; Bryan called it a war for corporate profit.[2]

From there, Bryan went on to describe the incongruence of imperialist policies with American principles. The war in the Philippines did not stem from a misunderstanding or the encouragement of disloyal Americans, as McKinley had suggested; it emanated from the principle of self-government espoused by the founders of the American nation. The right to govern oneself is not bound to any one group of people, and although Bryan acknowledged there may be differing "degrees of proficiency," he called it a poor "reflection upon the Creator to say he denied to any people the capacity for self-government." The nature of colonialism also gave lie to the talk of uplift, for education would only make the subject peoples more aware of their oppression and intensify their desire for freedom.

Bryan then laid out his own vision of what was possible. The Philippines should be guaranteed freedom and protected from outside interference, just as Cuba had been. This would set the stage for America's future greatness, when its moral authority would extend far beyond any influence it could attain as a colonial power. The United States could seize the opportunity to put its own house in order and be a republic in which "every citizen is a sovereign, but in which no one cares to wear a crown." At the same time, it could be "a republic, increasing in population, in wealth, in strength, and in universal brotherhood—a republic which shakes thrones and dissolves aristocracies by its silent example and gives light and inspiration to those who sit in darkness."

In the campaign of 1900, Bryan and his allies offered voters an alternative path for American development, one based on policies of moral influence abroad and the restraint of corporate power at home. Comparatively speaking, the differences between the two sides had been less dramatic in the "battle of standards" in 1896. Although the campaign rhetoric had spoken to certain concerns regarding egalitarianism in the republic, four years earlier, the Bryan campaign had not confronted many of the key facets of modern economic power. Conversely, the Democratic and Populist campaign at the dawn of the twentieth century was focused squarely on the rights and freedoms of people in a world dominated by aggregated wealth.

Though they faced many challenges—including an entrenched president and a divided anti-imperialist movement—the evidence suggests that the western reformers did not beat themselves in 1900. The ongoing war in the Philippines allowed western Republicans to shift the focus of the campaign to foreign policy, just as they had in 1898. This was crucial, because much of their economic message was just as weak as ever. They rarely refuted claims that corporate power was growing by the day, and they blandly denied the existence of any weaknesses in the new global market order they were establishing. They would prove victorious in 1900 by shunting aside talk of economic reform and equal rights and replacing it with a discussion of power, profit, and patriotism.

ANTI-IMPERIALISM IN THE EAST

Theoretically, given his opposition to expansion, Bryan should have been able to count on support in the eastern states, yet the most prominent eastern anti-imperialists had all railed against him and the western reform movement in 1896. The two sides differed on the importance of the tariff, on currency and banking matters, and, most fundamentally, on the states' role in the management of the economy and the equalization of wealth. One element that has hitherto been ignored, however, is their differing interpretations of imperialism. Based on the material presented in preceding chapters, it is clear that Populists and their western allies often described industrial and financial capitalists as the source of this new aggressive policy. Because of these views, they saw the fight against imperialism as a logical extension of their battle against "monopoly" at home, and they believed that neither of these contests could be won if the other were ignored. At best, the eastern anti-imperialists were ambivalent about such reform, and more commonly, they were openly hostile to the agendas of their ostensible allies.

It would be wrong to suggest that the eastern anti-imperialists believed that economic factors played no role in overseas imperialism; however, that role had a different kind of relevance for them. The conservatives who dominated the Anti-Imperialist League downplayed economic factors in general, but when they did address the subject, they approached it in the same kind of disjointed way they discussed inequality in industrial America. As was their style, they did not attribute wealth disparities or injustices to systemic problems, focusing instead on the failings of individuals.

The mugwumps and other conservatives who led the movement in the East frequently attributed the conquest of the Philippines to the inappropriate actions of individuals. For example, when Carl Schurz described the likelihood of imperial America's participation in future wars, he often emphasized the role played by "speculators." When he claimed the "greed of speculators working upon our Government will push us from one point to another," he was not condemning all the concentrated wealth of the United States or Europe. His focus on those individuals engaged in the indecorous business of speculation was reminiscent of his scorn for those who had profited from the "dishonest" money of the Civil War era. Unlike the Populists and their allies, he could not bring himself to condemn large numbers of industrialists or investors, nor would he suggest that imperialism and industrial inequality were inherently tied.[3]

Eastern anti-imperialists also commonly attributed expansion to "greed." Their use of the term further demonstrates the limits of their analysis. When western reformers spoke of greed, they commonly tied it to their understanding of a rapacious and unforgiving economic system. For members of the eastern elite, greed was a quality that an individual possessed, one suggestive of a personality flaw or a moral lapse; greedy persons were aberrations, not the norm. Anti-imperialist, industrialist, and liberal economist Edward Atkinson actually claimed that greed and commerce were antithetically opposed. Markets did not create greed or force people to covet wealth at the expense of others, they said. By placing the emphasis on morality and the failure of individuals, they avoided any attack on the system.[4]

In rare instances, conservatives appropriated more radical language, and some historians have used these cases to suggest that all anti-imperialists faulted the modern industrial economy. A biographer of prominent Anti-Imperialist League member Moorfield Storey felt the need to include a statement in which the old mugwump attributed imperialism to "the alliance between financial and political powers," despite admitting that such declarations were rare for him. The scholar who examined Mark Twain's attack on imperialism claimed that the great writer feared an "alliance between the trusts, the politicians and the military," but in the example he provides, Twain is merely critiquing those "money changers" who had "bought up half the country with soldier pensions"—not capitalists, but the politicians who used the corrupting influence of money for their own advantage. Another historian attributed similar attacks on corporate power to both Erving Winslow, the wealthy merchant who served as secretary of the original Anti-imperialist League (based in Boston), and George Boutwell, a conservative Republican who was president of the Boston organization and later the American Anti-Imperialist League (based in Chicago). The same writer willingly admitted that Winslow rarely used economic critiques and that his views were ill defined. In the case of Boutwell, although he was known to occasionally attack imperialism as the tool of the wealthy, these statements were exceptional. It was never a developed point in any of Boutwell's works, and he more often tried to distance himself from serious critiques of capitalism. In one speech that seems more in line with his general views, he told an audience, "I have no hostility to wealth, I have no great fear of trusts." He emphasized that he was no radical, even if he was forced to work with some who were.[5]

Despite their occasionally bombastic language, the two central tenets of the eastern anti-imperialists were expectedly moderate. The first emphasized the threat imperialism posed to intelligent representative government. Edwin Burritt Smith, secretary of the American Anti-Imperialist League, cited Lincoln's statement that "this government cannot endure permanently half slave and half free." If the United States was to become "the military base of the new despotism," then no one should be surprised if "the present ill-concealed impatience of constitutional restraints will grow until only the forms of representative government remain."[6] Carl Schurz agreed that it was a dangerous precedent to rule others without their consent, but to incorporate foreign peoples was no less risky. Even if the United States' interest was limited to territories closer to home, was it safe to grant citizenship to those with "the mixture of Spanish, French and negro blood on the West India Islands?" he asked.[7] Eastern conservatives also commonly lambasted imperialism as an immoral policy. Edward Atkinson, among others, noted the president's early declaration that the forced annexation of Cuba would amount to "criminal aggression." Surely, he suggested, the forced annexation of the Philippines was no less criminal.[8] Others, including Senator George Hoar, noted that many imperialists spoke of power, but "the words Right, Justice, Duty, Freedom were absent" from their remarks.[9]

Their second point of emphasis was the immorality and impropriety of colonial rule. The easterners' discussion of morality and rule based on consent of the governed was not fundamentally different from that of their western counterparts. All considered the conquest of the Philippines abhorrent, and all were troubled by the concentration of power around an imperial federal government. Most of the arguments levied by mugwumps and conservatives were also used by Populists and Democrats, and that is why some historians have incorrectly claimed that one derived their interpretation from the other. But the distinctions between them remained large. The conservative critique of empire was closely tied to the causes of conservative reform: minimal government, an informed electorate, and a moral code based on restraint. The rather mugwumpish solution to these ills involved a combination of public instruction and electoral influence. If politicians could not be convinced to conduct their affairs professionally, they would have to be replaced. Put simply, the conservatives called for personal accountability, not structural change. It was in this regard that the perspectives of Populists and Bryanite Democrats contrasted most sharply with those of the prestigious easterners.

Although their differing views of imperialism were insignificant obstacles to cooperation in a loose movement, the political rift and distrust between them made an effective coalition impossible. Even among conservatives there was dissension. Hoar and many other Republicans kept many members of the Anti-Imperialist League at arm's length, sure that their objective was nothing less than the destruction of their party.[10] Hoar was even less capable of viewing the westerners as allies, having long ago established himself as one of the fiercest opponents of the Populists and western Democrats in Congress.

The suspicion or partisanship of eastern anti-imperialists was not the only obstacle to cooperation. Leaders from the two regions viewed each other with a mutual distrust born of both substantial ideological differences and a history of clashes on the stump. A quick review of a few of the top names on the Anti-Imperialist League's membership list reveals some of the source of this distrust. Republican George S. Boutwell, president of the league from its formation until his death in 1905, had been treasury secretary under Grant, and it was at his urging that Congress had passed the Coinage Act of 1873 (the "crime of '73" to many in the West). Former senator and secretary of state John Sherman was one of the capital's archconservatives for more than a generation, and he had helped Boutwell formulate that currency bill and push it swiftly through Congress. The mugwumps had earned their ill repute among westerners more recently. During the 1896 campaign, Carl Schurz had been more active in his opposition to Bryan than in any other contest since leading the mugwump revolt in 1884. In the same campaign, E. L. Godkin informed readers of the *Nation* that it was perfectly acceptable for businessmen to coerce labor into opposing the Democratic candidate. Industrialist and free-trade economist Edward Atkinson, one of the league's chief pamphleteers, was so well known for the anti-silver articles he published in 1896 that three years later, one Populist paper still identified him as "the great juggler of figures for the Republican party."[11]

This distrust manifested itself in clear ways. Eastern anti-imperialists were hesitant to contact western leaders, and western politicians likewise feared the political consequences of an open alliance with their political opponents. The case of Andrew Carnegie and William Jennings Bryan best illustrates this latter point. Carnegie was one of the few eastern anti-imperialists of consequence who was in direct correspondence with Bryan early on, and although the Nebraskan tried to maintain the lines of communication between them, he simultaneously sought to keep their connection out of the public eye. In December 1898 the two had a private meeting in New York that left the industrialist so impressed he decided to publish an article endorsing Bryan's presumed presidential run in 1900. Bryan was forewarned of Carnegie's intentions by a friend who strongly advised "against permitting public endorsement of you by promoter of [H]omestead riots." Bryan hesitated and then took the safest course available. "I have not discussed [the] interview publicly," he told Carnegie, "and prefer that you do not." He denied being a candidate for any office and then pointed to the necessary limits of their relationship. "You and I agree in opposing militarism and imperialism, but when these questions are settled we may find ourselves upon opposite sides as heretofore." He understood he had little to gain and much to lose from an alliance with the steel magnate. After ratification of the Treaty of Paris, their correspondence declined precipitously.[12]

As 1900 commenced, it was apparent that Bryan would again take the Democratic nomination. Their distaste for McKinley should have made all anti-imperialists eager to support a viable alternative, but unlike Carnegie, most conservatives from the East could not bring themselves to initiate a direct correspondence with Bryan. Instead, Elwood Corser, a Minneapolis banker and Silver Republican, took on the role of intermediary. It may have been through his business connections that Corser found himself in correspondence with Edwin Burritt Smith, the Chicago banker who was secretary of the American Anti-Imperialist League. Corser's efforts to establish communication were largely in vain. In February, Smith informed Corser that Bryan's best course would be to make the next campaign about imperialism and civil service reform—to appeal to mugwumps specifically. Smith even suggested that the platform "will be especially effective if this is coupled with the charge that the controlling motive for the acquisition of the Spanish islands is spoils"—in other words, if imperialism was equated with corruption. Most notably, for Bryan to win over the "many conservative men who opposed his candidacy in 1896," the next Democratic platform had to be "as free from objection as possible."[13]

Smith's letter was a portent of the kind of relationship many of the conservative anti-imperialists envisioned: they would instruct, and the western reformers would follow.[14] They demanded the abandonment of the issues that had so effectively won the West four years earlier and their replacement with "sound" issues. But Bryan was in no mood to listen. The conservatives were only one of many groups demanding his attention, and all claimed the right to dictate his agenda. If he was going to follow anyone, it would not be his erstwhile enemies.

With their own conflicted feelings toward Bryan and no reason to believe he would take the course they advised, many anti-imperialists wanted to explore the possibility of a third party. A separate ticket thrown together at the last minute would have no chance of victory, but some believed it could do to McKinley what the Gold Democrats had done to Bryan in 1896: provide an outlet for those unwilling to commit political apostasy. On January 6, 1900, leading anti-imperialists—including Senator Richard Pettigrew—met at the Plaza Hotel in New York to discuss the third-party option, but little came of it. They agreed to postpone the decision on a third ticket while maintaining a nonpartisan approach. Of course, this did not end talk of such an option.[15]

Proponents of the third ticket organized behind the scenes. Carl Schurz began serious discussions on the subject with Moorfield Storey and Edwin Burritt Smith in March. They all played a part in organizing a "Liberty Congress," a gathering of anti-imperialists to be held in Indianapolis after the two major party conventions. If the Democrats did not offer an attractive alternative to McKinley, the meeting could be transformed into a nominating convention, or it could be used to set the stage for a separate convention to be held shortly thereafter. Up to the very last moment, the conservative anti-imperialists looked for a way out of what they saw as a Faustian bargain.[16]

POPULISM AND THE COMING CAMPAIGN

Whatever the eastern conservatives thought of Bryan, their opinion apparently concerned him little. He was more anxious about securing his position in the West and laying out the guiding principles of the campaign, both of which were done with little reference to the eastern conservatives. Bryan had some reason for concern. In many of the western states, the coalition of Populists, Democrats, and Silver Republicans had either failed to materialize or suffered defeats in 1898. There had always been some Populists who opposed fusion agreements unless their party could dictate the terms of cooperation. The coalition had been difficult to pull off even when victory seemed certain. Now that the prospects of success had dimmed, Populists had to work to unify the movement.

The antifusion "middle-of-the-road" faction made itself heard in 1898. Founding members of the party such as Davis Waite in Colorado and Henry Loucks of South Dakota openly supported the Republicans that year, and both decried the supposed domination of their organizations by the Democrats. Expressions of such fears could be heard with increasing frequency in many places, even among those who maintained their Populist loyalties. In 1898 one Populist legislator in Nebraska complained that internal contests were "already fixed from the primaries up. . . . [N]o matter whether straight pop, fusion, or straight democratic, it is all the same outfit nominated by the democratic club in Omaha."[17] Some who remained in the Nebraska Farmers' Alliance also sounded the call for the mid-roaders. Twice in 1898 the alliance called for those "who are opposed to fusion with either wing of plutocracy" to meet and organize.[18] The story was much the same in Washington State. Governor John Rankin Rogers had fought with the mid-roaders over appointments in 1897, and his willingness to appoint Democrats to key posts led many in that wing of the party to denounce their titular leader. By 1898, Rogers was forced to turn to the Democrats for aid during the fusion conventions.[19]

There were, however, indications that the mid-roaders' actual numbers were less than their noisy demonstrations would suggest. They held a lightly attended convention in Cincinnati in 1898, where they renounced free silver and nominated Wharton Barker for president and Ignatius Donnelly for vice president. The small number of attendees (well under a hundred were present) and the peculiarity of setting nominations two years in advance of an election suggested a sense of desperation.[20] It was much the same in Nebraska in 1898, where calls for conventions by the Farmers' Alliance went largely unanswered, even though in the same year the mainstream Populist state convention attracted more than a thousand delegates.[21] Elsewhere, there is little evidence that Waite's defection hurt the fusion ticket in Colorado in 1898. Even in South Dakota, after Loucks returned to the Republican fold,

Populist governor Andrew Lee managed to win reelection. This is not to say that the mid-roaders were insignificant, but rather that the destruction of the state Populist parties cannot be attributed primarily to them.

More than a few in the Populist ranks looked forward to the next major party shake-up. Many, including Pettigrew, believed that the conflicting elements within the parties—especially the Democrats—were unstable and could be contained only by a new organization. As the editor of the *Ellensburg Dawn* pointed out in 1899, "There are Bryan Democrats and Anti-Bryan Democrats, Expansion and Anti-Expansion Democrats, Silver Democrats and Gold Democrats." Such divisions need not exist within a single party, and the writer called for "the different reform parties to drop their present names and all unite into one new grand party." Such talk did not die down until late 1899, with no solution in sight.[22]

Washington's leading Populist, Governor Rogers, took an alternative path to counter local Populist dysfunction. He had suggested to some correspondents in 1898 that a new party could be formed in the future and the mid-roaders' frustrations overcome, but he soon shifted to another tactic. He told Senator Turner, "We in Washington are engaged in the formation of a new party" at the national level, but "the battle of 1900 will largely be fought under the democratic name." Rogers had helped the single-tax faction of the Democrats in the 1898 convention in order to build a base of support outside his own party. His frustration with the mid-roaders and his projections about the upcoming campaign led him to officially join the Democrats in April 1900.[23]

Few who still held office followed the example of Rogers. Instead, most party leaders sought an alternative means of securing the Populist vote. Pettigrew and Senator Marion Butler, chair of the party's central committee, advocated holding an early convention. Pettigrew believed they "should come bravely to the front, add to the Chicago platform those things which time has made necessary, re-assert the doctrines then asserted, and begin the fight, waiting for nobody." The Democrats, however, did not favor a long campaign because they did not have the money to fund one.[24] Still, fusion Populists could hold an early convention, name Bryan and their own choice for vice president, and push the Democrats to accept it as a fait accompli. As Pettigrew would tell Bryan in April, any mistake "will recruit the ranks of the Cincinnati [middle-of-the-road] wing of the Populist party," and if the Democrats refused to follow the Populist lead, "serious consequences might follow."[25]

Bryan was unsure about a Populist candidate for vice president, but he had already taken steps to shore up his support among Populists. Perhaps the most important of these was the broad platform he openly advocated even before the year began. To take a step back, it is important to remember that both Bryan's contemporaries and modern historians have frequently labeled his 1896 campaign a shallow emasculation of the Populist vision.[26] But a coordinated drive for more sophisticated reform was simply not possible at that early date. The Democrats and Silver Republicans that made up so much of Bryan's base of support remained divided on tariff and tax concerns, and few were willing to go as far as the most radical Populists in their attacks on monopoly and wealth. Bryan emerged as a leader who could pull these groups together, but a simplistic campaign was a necessary product of the coalition.

The situation was quite different in 1900. After his defeat in 1896, Bryan continued to give speeches in favor of free silver, but over time, he added a more sophisticated view of wealth and power.[27] The increasing rapidity of mergers forced those who supported silver in 1896 to take notice, and Bryan soon joined the Populists in their attack on trusts. Many leaders of the western reform coalition attended a major conference in Chicago on the trust problem in September 1899, where Bryan gave one of the featured addresses. Unlike more conservative reformers, he declared, "I do not divide monopolies in private hands into good monopolies and bad monopolies. There is no good monopoly in private hands." To those who claimed that efficient monopolies provided goods at lower prices, he stated his opposition to "settling every question upon the dollar argument."[28] Bryan stated that it was the people's right to control the market, and they must ultimately make the decisions. His argument fit well with the views of the antimonopoly Populists.

Added to the topics of imperialism and trusts was the issue of 1896: free silver. Easterners had repeatedly called for silver to be kept out of the 1900 campaign, and in all likelihood, even Bryan probably hoped to de-emphasize it. At the beginning of the year, before he was regularly bombarded with letters from easterners, Bryan had expressed to Pettigrew his fear that the Populist nomination of a known silver advocate for the vice presidency would "intensify the silver issue a little too much."[29] Even so, it was not to Bryan's advantage to discard that old issue altogether. He was so thoroughly associated with the cause of currency and banking reform that suggesting it could be dropped would only give easterners an excuse to challenge his leadership.[30] Bryan also wanted to use silver to demonstrate his commitment to Populist-style reform. When one supporter asked him to abandon silver for the two new issues, Bryan responded negatively. He denied that it would be beneficial to support one or two issues when all three represented valid critiques of the present administration's policies. Bryan claimed, "The people who oppose the gold standard also oppose the trusts and imperialism and there are *nine* who oppose all three to *one* who favors the gold standard and yet opposes the trusts or imperialism." He then castigated the conservatives who had "left the party and did what they could to defeat the ticket. . . . Now they want to drive away the Populists and silver republicans who came to us when the gold democrats deserted."[31] Bryan's support for free silver would continue to cement the bonds of the fusion coalition.

The statements and the correspondence of western reform leaders show that they accepted Bryan's premise that change on all fronts was necessary.[32] Bryan did not lead them to reform, but he viewed the unfolding of events in the same light as many Populists, Democrats, and Silver Republicans from the West. He still had not fully adopted the ideology of the Populists, but his actions and words allowed many to see him as one of their own. Even the cynical and calculating Pettigrew told a friend, "I think he [Bryan] is as good a Populist as any of us."[33] Although the most dedicated mid-roaders may have disagreed, Bryan and other members of the reform coalition developed a national platform with their western political base in mind.

CONVENTIONS AND CAMPAIGNS

The first of the conventions, that of the Populists, took place in the spring. The fusionists began their meeting in Sioux Falls, South Dakota, on May 9, the same day the mid-roaders met in Cincinnati. The platform adopted was a lengthy indictment of the ills that still challenged American producers, but it focused largely on the issues that nearly all the western reformers had already come to emphasize. The first section was devoted to finance, and it denounced the recently passed Gold Standard Act, pledged the party to ceaseless "agitation until this great financial conspiracy is blotted from the statute-books," and called for silver and greenbacks to replace national bank notes. The second section attacked land monopoly and trusts, and in response to this "overshadowing evil of the age," it stated, "The one remedy for the trusts is that the ownership and control be assumed and exercised by the people." The third major section was devoted to the evils of imperialism and militarism, which were policies "at war with the Declaration of Independence, the Constitution, and the plain precepts of humanity," and the platform demanded that the war in the Philippines be halted and the people guaranteed their independence.[34]

The only disagreement in Sioux Falls was that between Senator Allen and his allies, who favored a conference committee with the Democrats to select a nominee for vice president, and leaders such as Butler and Pettigrew, who preferred to name their own vice presidential candidate. The latter were clearly hoping to deprive mid-roaders of the claim that the Populist Party merely followed the orders of Bryan and the Democrats. In a brief but heated contest, one delegate shouted that easterners wanted to control the nomination and that the real opponents of a Populist nomination came from "the Tory end of the country" who wanted "a moderate man—a veneered man." Those who wanted to select their own nominee won out, and Silver Republican Charles Towne of Minnesota was named to the ticket alongside Bryan. It was an odd show of independence, but many believed it was vital for the party.[35]

The Democrats' convention in Kansas City opened on July 4. Although Bryan was not in attendance (following the tradition for favored candidates), the selection of a city so close to his home was an indication of his certain nomination. Obviously, the anniversary of the nation's independence held special meaning as well, especially for a campaign that would place anti-imperialism at the center of the debate. But July 4 was also the eighth anniversary of the Populists' Omaha convention and their proclamation of a "Second Declaration of Independence," inaugurating a new campaign to throw off the financial domination of Europe and the East.[36] Supporters of Bryan courted parallels between the two conventions. The portrayal of the convention in the *Rocky Mountain News* was based on a full recognition of the connotations the date invoked. The front page of the paper included a large split image, with Jefferson on one side holding up the Declaration of Independence and Bryan on the other holding up "The New Declaration of Independence"—the presumed planks that would be adopted by the Democratic convention.[37] A writer for the paper also made it clear that Bryan was a true follower of the Jeffersonian tradition. When Jefferson assumed the presidency, he "rescued the youthful nation from the centralizing tendencies of the Federal party, and gave to the republic a system of governmental principles which have ever been the light of the people in their contests against the aggression of organized and concentrated wealth and power." At the dawn of a new century:

> [A] power more insidious, more dangerous, more arrogant even than the despotism against which the men of 1776 rebelled, has gained a foothold in the republic, and is seeking to enthrone itself in the national govern-

ment. It is the power of plutocracy that is seeking to elevate the dollar above the man, to create an empire within the forms of a republic, and to fasten upon the people a system of finance that will forever enslave the industrial classes and condemn the laboring poor to a life of continuous servitude.

Just as the founders had fought against the British plan to enslave the colonists, those who met in Kansas City opposed the "schemes of plutocracy and the money power."[38]

Unlike that of their allies, the Democrats' platform opened with a flourish by reaffirming their "faith in that immortal proclamation of the inalienable rights of man." Nearly half the document covered the issues of imperialism and militarism, and it specifically attacked colonial rule in Puerto Rico, the American military occupation of Cuba, and the "unnecessary war" in the Philippines. The platform favored an immediate declaration of policy that guaranteed the Philippines independence. It also condemned the "greedy commercialism" the Republicans used to justify overseas conquest. Although it proclaimed support for extension of "the Republic's influence among the nations," that influence "should not be extended by force and violence, but through the persuasive power of a high and honorable example." The second section of the platform pledged the party to "an unceasing warfare in nation, State, and city against private monopoly in every form." A mere two paragraphs were devoted to the currency dispute, although the statement included a complete reiteration of the demand for free silver at the ratio of sixteen to one and condemned the recently passed law that ceded federal authority over the currency to private corporations. Additional planks supported the direct election of senators, opposed "government by injunction" and favored the arbitration of labor disputes, and called for the creation of a federal Department of Labor.[39]

The Democratic platform offered much that could appeal to Populists, but the convention also snubbed Bryan's western allies. Bryan thought highly of Charles Towne, but the Democrats had no interest in nominating a member of another party. Instead, they selected Adlai Stevenson, the Illinois bimetallist who had already served as vice president in the second Cleveland administration. Stevenson was sound enough on the issues that mattered to Bryan, and his loyalty to the Democratic Party in both 1892 and 1896 made him acceptable to eastern and western wings of the party. If the nomination of Stevenson represented an olive branch to the eastern wing of the Democratic Party, it was a slap in the face to the Populists. No one wanted to replicate the confusion of 1896, when Bryan shared the ticket with two vice presidential candidates. Bryan would not ask Stevenson to quit the race, and despite Populist opposition, Towne was forced to withdraw.[40]

The Bryan campaign was constantly hamstrung by the need to maintain a delicate balancing act. Even so, the addition of anti-imperialism to an otherwise Populist platform forced anti-imperialist conservatives to take Bryan seriously. It encouraged many eastern Democrats to return to the party, and Bryan's effective acceptance speech may have helped kill the conservative-led movement for a third party. Schurz, one of the leading advocates of a separate ticket, attempted to tamp down some of the enthusiasm Bryan created, but even he was forced to admit that, "as to Imperialism, he cannot do better than he has done in his speech."[41] Bryan's address was delivered just before the opening of the Liberty Congress, and once he demonstrated his commitment to the issue, it proved difficult to rally support for a second anti-imperialist ticket.[42] Schurz, Storey, and Smith continued to discuss other options, but nothing of substance ever materialized. All three eventually supported Bryan, although others in the Anti-Imperialist League proved unwilling to do the same.[43]

The Republican gathering in Philadelphia on June 19 had an orderly feel, unlike the other affairs that bookended the national convention season. At least some controversy had stirred the Populist and Democratic assemblies, but there would be none among the Republicans. The aggressive expansionist Henry Cabot Lodge was named permanent chair of the proceedings, and he would soon be joined on the stage by his friend Theodore Roosevelt. Despite the mild protests of McKinley and Hanna in the weeks preceding the convention (and his own public denials), the governor of New York had made himself the favorite for the vice presidential nomination, taking the place of the deceased Garret Hobart. The eagerness that accompanied the selection of the self-proclaimed war hero and evangelist of empire suggested the delegates' mood better than any formal declaration could.[44]

The party's platform opened with some revisionist history. It stated that four years earlier, when the Democrats had offered no solution to the economic crisis other than free silver, the Republican Party had promised to save the nation's economy with "a protective tariff and a law making gold the standard of value." Next, it congratulated the administration for leading the nation to victory in "a war for liberty and human rights." Ten million had been "given 'a new birth of freedom,'" and the American people had inherited a new global responsibility. These words would be echoed in McKinley's acceptance speech a month later. The platform included vague antitrust and pro-labor planks and warnings that business could be conducted only if public confidence in the government were maintained. A few additional words were used to praise the president's program regarding Cuba, Hawaii, Puerto Rico, and the Philippines without any explanation of his policy. On the whole, the document was as self-laudatory as it was vague, and it contained no substantial statement about plans for the future. All controversies, including the ongoing war in the Philippines, were avoided.[45]

The Republicans appeared to be playing a double game. The antitrust plank seemed out of place for a party that had Mark Hanna as chair of its national committee. Weeks later, the party chief gained national attention when he declared, "There is not a trust in the United States."[46] The convention also downplayed imperialism while making conspicuous use of the most vociferous advocates of expansion. McKinley undoubtedly viewed the issue as a weak spot and wanted to emphasize conservative economic values and the safety guaranteed by the maintenance of his own administration, but not all his supporters agreed to follow that script. All in all, it was flexible platform for a national campaign, and it is hardly surprising that local contests took on a complexion all their own.

THE STATE CONVENTIONS AND FUSION

The campaign in each western state contained its own unique features; however, unlike two years earlier, there was a national campaign in 1900 that made certain issues central in them all. As it had been for a decade, economic "progress" was once again a topic of political debate. But unlike national elections in the recent past, there was now a foreign policy component as well. This sometimes overshadowed the discourse of progress and prosperity, but at other times it was integrated into that debate.

Fusion arrangements were once again made in Nebraska, Colorado, Washington, and elsewhere in the West, accompanied by the usual difficulties. Bryan pushed for two rounds of conventions in Nebraska, the first taking place in March to select delegates to the national conventions and create party platforms. Bryan wanted to use these platforms to reiterate his points of emphasis in advance of the meeting in Kansas City. The state Democrats used their platform to attack trusts and the gold standard while also pointing to the injustice of colonialism. The Populists had even less to say about money and trusts and devoted nearly their whole platform to imperialism and militarism.[47]

Nebraska's fusionist nominating conventions reconvened in Lincoln just days after the conclusion of the Kansas City convention. Bryan, Towne, and even James B. Weaver were in attendance, encouraging unity at every step. Such efforts were necessary. The large Populist convention attracted more than 1,200 delegates, and even the widely respected Senator Allen had a difficult time maintaining order. Despite the struggles, the governor's vocal stands on imperialism and trusts put him in a strong position, and this time, Poynter won the gubernatorial nomination of the fusion parties with little opposition. The Democrats were disappointed to be left with only the nomination for state attorney general, but according to their representatives, the Populists were unwilling to give up more. With little further disagreement, the ticket was agreed to on July 12.[48]

The relative harmony in Nebraska was absent in its neighbor to the west. In Colorado, the silver consensus appeared to be in jeopardy, as many Silver Republicans rejoined the party of McKinley. Some Populists, including former Democrat Thomas Patterson, had tried and failed to bring members of the party into the Democratic camp, while the state's Democratic leaders were increasingly opposed to sharing offices.[49] When the conventions met in mid-September, Governor Thomas declared fusion to be dead at the first sign of difficulty. Both Henry Teller and writers for the *Denver Post* later attested that the majority of delegates felt differently. In an unprecedented move, Teller and Patterson were given the opportunity to address the Democrats and plead for renewal of the coalition. But before the delegates could vote fusion up or down, the Democratic conference committee took the opportunity to reconsider. Shortly thereafter, an agreement was reached.[50]

Under the arrangement, most state offices went to the Populists and Silver Republicans, while John Shafroth and John C. Bell were renominated for their House seats. Democrats claimed the nomination for governor, selecting James Orman, the former mayor of Pueblo. Despite their arrogance, the Democrats still desperately needed fusion. Their state platform was mild, and Orman's record of moderation hardly added to their appeal. Their bland candidate and platform illustrated their own anomalous position. Only fusion made the Colorado Democrats something more than the old party of laissez-faire. The state convention of the Populists made statements against both overseas imperialism and the "Wardner [Idaho] outrages," and they also supported an amendment to the state constitution that would allow for an eight-hour workday law. To this platform they added candidates with known records of labor advocacy. Their first selection for lieutenant governor was rejected by their fusion partners due to claims that he was a proponent of violence; their alternative selection, president David C. Coates of the Colorado State Federation of Labor, was accepted. Even though Democrats received the nomination for the highest state office, they understood that there was no chance of victory on their own so long as the votes of militant organized workers remained decisive.[51]

Perhaps the strangest situation of all was in Washington. There, Governor John Rankin Rogers had succeeded in alienating at least some portion of both major fusion parties, but he retained high political ambitions. He had fought mid-roaders among the Populists shortly after his election. Since then, he had cooperated with the single-taxers among the Democrats in 1898, only to openly blame them for the defeats suffered that year. He would announce his conversion to the Democratic Party in early 1900, but few Populists mourned the loss. While most of Rogers's disputes had been factional and not due to differences in ideology, he was also out of place in this regard. Unlike most other Washington fusionists, he favored retention of the Philippines and argued that it would provide new markets in Asia, thus making Seattle one of the greatest ports in the country. He also felt that popular support for the war with Spain and anger over the deaths of Americans in the Philippines made anti-imperialism a risky proposition. As was the case with many western governors, Rogers was widely regarded as a senatorial aspirant, so his foreign policy statements cannot be seen as just the offhand comments of a local politician.[52]

All of Washington's reform parties had agreed to participate in a single convention to make nominations, with a two-thirds majority vote required for the winning candidate. The delegates were apportioned so that the Populists and Democrats were evenly represented, while the Silver Republicans had roughly one-third the delegates of the other two parties. These arrangements were agreed to well in advance of the convention, and some assumed the amalgamated convention would provide an opportunity for the anti-Rogers forces to unite. Instead, the exact opposite was true. One by one, the alternatives to Rogers were discredited or outmaneuvered. Rogers's friends at the *Seattle Times* had dredged up lurid and personal stories about one rival in the weeks leading up to the gathering, and Turner's deft maneuvering at the convention strengthened Rogers's position. While the anti-Rogers delegates were left divided and looking for alternatives, those who were more amenable to the governor came together after some initial hesitation. Following the first rounds of balloting, votes began to shift to Rogers. He emerged victorious after eight rounds, but his victory did not heal any wounds.[53]

Rogers had survived the convention, but the divisions were obvious.

The platform adopted was a blatantly anti-expansionist document that condemned "the twin relics of barbarism—imperialism and militarism—whether in the form of trusts at home or greed of conquest abroad." Rogers remained an outlier. To emphasize their hostility to Rogers, a rump convention of his opponents left with a declaration that Senator Turner and Governor Rogers had bribed delegates and promised offices in exchange for votes, and they publicly condemned the "cajoling and bull-dozing" on the convention floor. It was hardly the image of unity the fusion parties had hoped to project going into the campaign.[54]

The Republicans in each state came together much more quickly. There had been conflicts between silver or antimonopoly factions and dedicated conservatives earlier in the decade, but now was not the time for that. The substantial victories won by many western Republican parties in 1898 gave them confidence that they could achieve unity rather than strife. All of them followed the script laid out by the Republican convention in Philadelphia. In Washington State, the Republican platform praised prosperity, which it claimed resulted directly from Democratic defeat. It added praise for the gold standard and American rule in the Philippines, where the inhabitants were "rapidly learning to appreciate and accept that kind of liberty which is known and understood only by the American people." Washington's ticket of archconservatives was led by gubernatorial candidate John M. Frink, one of the wealthiest men in King County. The Nebraska Republicans openly mocked fusionist fears of "imaginary evils threatening our country" and endorsed the gold standard for the first time in recent memory. Imperialism and militarism were described as un-American, but the platform denied that McKinley's policies qualified as such. For governor, they nominated a German American banker from Hastings, Charles Dietrich. In Colorado, Wolcott was again the dominant figure, but he understood that the party was in an especially vulnerable position. As late as 1898, he had argued that only the Republican Party could reintroduce the bimetallic standard. He was hardly alone in his support for silver; the head of the new state ticket, Frank Goudy, had been one of the bolters in 1896. Now the national convention had declared that silver would destroy the economy, but instead of dealing with the change, Colorado Republicans simply ignored the currency question altogether. More so than other Republicans in the West, they chose to ride the coattails of McKinley and Roosevelt back into office.[55]

THE "FULL DINNER PAIL" AND THE
ECONOMIC DEBATE

Typical descriptions of the campaign of 1900 have emphasized the return
of prosperity rather than the impact of imperialism or foreign policy—essentially following the narrative employed by McKinley and Hanna in their bid
to secure the president's reelection. Although some of these histories have
mentioned the inherent difficulty of distinguishing between votes for prosperity and those motivated by foreign policy, most accounts essentially accept
the idea that the economy made McKinley and his supporters invincible.[56]

The standard interpretation misses some key points, especially with regard to the situation in the West. First, the argument that prosperity made
all other factors moot is based on the belief that those who had advocated
reform in 1896 rapidly abandoned their cause after economic conditions
improved. According to this version of events, Bryan's support in the West
dried up because farmers (in particular) had more interest in the value of
their crops in the short term than in the structural changes that would have
guaranteed them security in the long term. Second, perhaps the most notable weakness of this economic determinism is its inability to explain the
motives of historical actors. Other elections of the 1890s were not so directly
linked to the state of the economy, and there is no reason to assume the
contest of 1900 was any different.

The economic debate of 1900 was not a mere rerun of that which had occurred in 1896. In a reversal of that situation, Republicans held the highest
national office but fewer state and local positions in the West. They sought
to attribute prosperity to their party, but there were certain difficulties associated with doing so. Although many historians and others who have
studied the period agree that an increase in global gold production helped
bring about economic recovery, western Republicans were hesitant to make
the same argument.[57] Bryan and the reformers of 1896 had argued that the
money supply was inadequate. To essentially agree with their contention
would have been heretical for any good partisan.

Instead, Republicans argued that their party's success was itself the har-
binger of economic growth. The "policy" they advocated, then, involved a
defense of the existing corporate order and the administration that effectively
symbolized prosperity. Along these lines, a writer for the *Omaha Daily Bee*
suggested that the cause of the last economic calamity had been the threat of
silver itself and that prosperity was a product of Bryan's defeat.[58] The state secretary of Washington's Republican Party likewise declared, "When President

McKinley was elected the whole country was immediately revived from the effect of democratic maladministration," and prosperity was the inevitable result.[59] Identical statements were made by Republicans throughout the West.[60]

The Republican focus on the impact of the electoral victory obviously fit the needs of the campaign, but there were additional reasons for it. First, except for a slight revision of the tariff and the war revenue measure, McKinley had been unable to push through any economic legislation until the third month of 1900. Of far greater significance, few western Republicans had the stomach to discuss the past—a time when a great many of them had supported silver or other economic reforms—or the future—about which the president said remarkably little. In 1896 some western Republicans had scrambled to find articles written by gold advocates to bolster their campaign, while others contended that silver currency was attainable only under their rule; four years later, they did not bother to justify any domestic policy at all. In the local press, the gold standard was not described as the positive good or the exemplar of economic morality it had been in 1896; instead, it represented an element of the status quo that could not be upset if good times were to continue.[61]

Following this model, the partisan press consistently delivered direct arguments in opposition to change. "If the Republican policy has brought prosperity, which it surely has, how could an opposite policy, intended to upset the Republican policy, bring other than the reverse?" asked one Nebraska paper. Security could be maintained if the fusionists would "lay aside partisanship for a moment and give these facts and figures sober and dispassionate thought."[62] Another paper claimed that, although many in 1896 had believed silver would bring prosperity, "the majority, remembering the history of the republican party, were willing to trust it with the duty and they have not been disappointed."[63]

The partisan talk of widespread prosperity must also be considered in the context of the 1890s. Populists and the reformers who followed in their footsteps had not merely promised to increase the quantity of money in voters' pockets. Instead, they had demanded democratic control of the economy, which they believed was necessary to provide long-term security for farmers and laborers while counteracting the ever-growing influence of corporations in the political sphere. McKinley and his backers provided no current or future domestic policy that responded to these demands. Bryan and the rest of the western reform coalition advocated an alternative form of development, and the need for that program would have been as apparent as ever. This was reinforced by growing public concern over the trust issue.

The public had a keen awareness of the rising tendency toward the combination of corporations; similarly, the public recognized the ability of such
combinations to control the agents of government. One event in Nebraska
highlighted the extent of their influence. During his brief tenure as Nebraska
attorney general, Constantine J. Smyth made good use of his state's antitrust
laws in cases against a secret ring of grain dealers and against the "starch
trust," which had reportedly purchased a factory just to shut it down.[64] But
in late 1899, before tackling these foes, Smyth brought suit against one of
the largest corporations in America, Standard Oil.[65] The case initially caused
little controversy until February 1900, when Senator John Thurston raced
back from his duties in Congress to act as the representative of the Rockefel-
lers. Thurston was immediately attacked by the state's Populists and Democrats, and the story even received some coverage in neighboring states. The
Denver Post ran a front-page cartoon depicting the senator carrying bags of
money from both the state and Standard Oil, and even the conservative
Omaha Daily Bee borrowed the image to lampoon Thurston.[66] This event
thoroughly demonstrated the influence of trusts, and Thurston was forced
to declare that he would not be a candidate for reelection.[67]

Remarkably, even after this controversy, Republicans throughout the
West denied that trusts were a serious issue. Edward Rosewater, owner and
editor of the *Omaha Bee*, was one of the few to declare that trusts needed to
be regulated, but he simultaneously declared, "You cannot destroy these corporate concerns" without damaging the overall economy.[68] Most denied that
trusts were a problem, and more than a few agreed with Hanna that they did
not exist at all. Shortly after Hanna made that remark, the editor of the *Colorado Springs Gazette* called Bryan's attacks on trusts hollow because "there
is no such thing in the United States as a private monopoly." Elsewhere
the paper praised the benefits of massive corporate combinations in terms
designed to eliminate any sense of menace.[69] A writer for the *Morning Olympian* asked, "What does Mr. Bryan mean by trusts?" If he meant a monopoly
that "destroys all competition," then "how many such trusts are there, what
are they and where are the evidences of their appaling [sic] growth?" Surely
their number was "insignificant compared with the combination of capital
that are perfectly legitimate," and there were no "evidences of calamity" that
could interrupt Republican prosperity.[70] Still another paper claimed that
even "suspicion that a corporation is obtaining exhorbitant [sic] profits at
once brings competition into the field," so monopolies could never survive
for long.[71]

This was the fundamental problem with the Republican argument in

1900. In their most basic descriptions of the American economy, western Republicans still had little to offer. They had no real explanation of the improved national economy, their plans for future prosperity were tied to an unquestioned allegiance to the status quo, and they proposed no plans for any impending restrictions on the powers of concentrated wealth. It had even become the standard party line to suggest that monopolies and trusts existed only in fiction. Their statements on political economy offered nothing to appeal to the Populists' converts.

While Republicans offered uncertain economic messages, Democrats and Populists continued the attacks that had brought them success during the 1890s. While Republicans downplayed the impact of gold discoveries and inflated currency on economic growth, western reformers suggested that any economic improvement was due to the increase in the supply of money. Charles Towne, the vice presidential pick of the Populists, reminded one audience that "McKinley's own letter of acceptance four years ago declares that we had money enough," but by now "we have in the country not far from five hundred millions of dollars more, six dollars a head more, than we had four years ago."[72] Fusion newspapers of all sizes also mocked Republicans for downplaying this fact.[73] Better times were the result of the "higher prices of farm products resulting from more money in circulation," and what the people wanted was "prosperity that will stay with them during years of peace at home and plenty abroad."[74] The Republicans offered nothing to limit the ravaging effects of global market swings, and western reformers brought that point home.

But there was reason to doubt the rosy picture the Republicans were trying to paint. There is evidence that a real economic slowdown had begun by the summer of 1899 and continued through the end of 1900.[75] One newspaper noted with alarm the reported 947 business failures in May—the largest on record for that month—"as compared with 581 last year and 917 in the 'calamitous' year of 1896."[76] Critics of the administration also pointed to reports that bankers and industrialists had become pessimistic about the short-term prospects of the economy.[77] Though the downturn was not nearly as severe as the Panic of 1893, and it would not substantially alter the prices of the West's commodities, it suggested that all was not well.

Other indicators contributed to make prosperity seem illusory. Republicans were fond of saying that huge quantities of farm mortgages had been paid off in the preceding four years, but Bryan pointed to statistics from Nebraska showing that many of them had been "paid" through foreclosure.[78] Information on farm mortgages and tenancy published by the Census Bureau in 1910 (the bureau had dramatically scaled back its work on these subjects in 1900) demonstrates that Bryan was not exaggerating. In 1890, when the Populist movement made its first foray into politics, 39 percent of Nebraska farmers held mortgages, nearly 25 percent were tenants, and the remainder owned their land outright. By 1900, the rate with mortgages had dropped to less than 29 percent, and 37 percent of the state's farmers now worked lands owned by someone else.[79] The trend was even more significant in central Nebraska, the core region of Populist power in the state.[80]

Of course, some of the figures cited did not encompass the main thrust of the reformers' economic argument. For them, the real issue was not full employment or industrial productivity but popular control of the economy and the distribution of wealth. The growing imbalance in wealth—and the power that accompanied it—made all the Republican talk of a "full dinner pail" seem hollow. Senator Allen went into the countryside and reminded the people that farmers had held nearly half the nation's wealth in 1860, whereas today they held only 18 percent.[81] A writer for a rural Washington paper told readers, "The modicum of prosperity we have is artificial. . . . [T]he only prosperity there is goes to the syndicates, carpetbaggers and sub-sidy hunters."[82]

The editor of Nebraska's most prominent Populist paper, the Independent, used a recent personal example to summarize the real purpose of the move-ment. Just the previous Sunday, he had heard a local minister declare, "I would rather trust the one per cent who own one-half of the property of the United States than the fifty percent of the poorest classes." Such senti-ments, similar to those the author attributed to McKinley and his support-ers, represented "plutocracy pure and simple. . . . It is the most dangerous sentiment ever expressed on American soil." It was incomprehensible that people like Rockefeller, who had "stolen the hard earned wealth of hundreds of men by the vilest means ever employed by man," were more trustworthy than the "thirty-five or forty millions" who had actually created the wealth. Ultimately, the author declared, the fight was not about whether farmers or laborers had enough for themselves now; it was about who would hold the reins of government and shape the nation's economic future.[83]

The debate over domestic economics was only one portion of the broader debate, and perhaps not even the most important part. Republicans in the West had followed the national script and beaten the drum of "prosperity," but they had been challenged. They shunted aside the question of trusts and monopolies rather than addressing it. In many regards, their statements were the most honest assessments of the party's economic philosophy in years, but certainly western Republicans could not count on honesty alone to win over voters. Reformers continued to shift the emphasis to popular control and the kind of restraint of power necessary in a democratic country, and they refuted the suggestion that any temporary improvement in the economy should be allowed to forestall that kind of change. Still, their claims carried more weight when accompanied by examples that demonstrated the antirepublican tendencies of the administration.

IMPERIALISM AND MILITARISM IN THE CAMPAIGN OF 1900

The use of American power overseas was a central point of contention between the two sides. Additionally, both Republicans and reformers used the issues that accompanied the war and the acquisition of empire to appeal to different aspects of American identity. Western reformers used imperialism to reinforce their points about concentrated wealth and power. They had always believed that the government was too distant from its people, that it ruled for the benefit of the few, and that it helped the great business combinations crush resistance to their power. The reformers described an imperial America as the antithesis of the republican ideal, and they focused their campaign on the free white laborers whose positions would be threatened in a militarized, aristocratic, and racially diverse society. Western Republicans, too, sought an adjunct to their domestic platform, but they saw the conflict primarily as a means of smoothing over strife at home. Patriotism and nationalism were the keys to their campaign.

Shortly after Dewey's victory in May 1898, politicians and the media had made projections about the great wealth the United States would obtain through Pacific trade. As imperialism emerged as a subject of debate, the tone of these forecasts took a progressively more partisan tone. By 1900, Republicans attempted to turn all evidence of increased foreign trade into propaganda, and their opinion columns were laced with figures designed to demonstrate that trade was central to future economic growth. In no state was this more true than in Washington. There, even the smallest local papers reported that "our exports to Asia and Oceanica [sic] are gaining with greater proportionate rapidity than to any other part of the world," and they claimed that such growth was likely to continue. An eastern Washington weekly added, "If we can place three ounces of flour a day in each family in Hong Kong and Shanghai, it will raise the price of Washington wheat to seventy-five cents per bushel."[84] Local Nebraska newspapers began to print identical campaign supplements designed to convey the same message. One showed a grinning Uncle Sam holding a piece of paper with the words "Agricultural Exports" at the top. It listed a nearly 50 percent increase in exports between 1895 and 1900, which caused Uncle Sam to remark, "It sort o' looks as if I'd have to expand."[85] Another supplement included a map showing the historical growth of the United States surrounded by small articles on the subject of expansion. Most of the articles were about the necessity of foreign trade and, in particular, the importance of the Philippines to that trade. One suggested that the "commerce of half of the world's population, of which Manila may be made the great commercial center, now amounts to more than $2,000,000,000 per annum," and nearly all that money "is expended for the class of goods for which the people of this country are now seeking a market."[86]

For a party that was struggling to find an appealing economic message, the talk of trade was vital. However, by the time of the campaign, these statements had become much less frequent than they had been a year or even two years earlier. Perhaps the best explanation for that change has to do with the arguments of Bryan and his followers. The Democratic platform had, after all, condemned the Republicans for justifying their conquests in the name of "greedy commercialism." Although this charge had always been thrown at the imperialists, it became increasingly effective in the wake of the Puerto Rican tariff bill. The controversy over the tariff caused many to doubt that American rule could be simultaneously profit seeking and benevolent.[87]

Whether Republicans continued to deploy the argument or not, western reformers attacked them for ever making it. The reformers ridiculed their rivals for emphasizing wealth over human rights, and such statements took a number of forms. In one case, a Colorado editor simply tacked the headline "McKinley Prosperity in Province of Luzon" onto an article about a bloody battle that had just taken place in the Philippines.[88] Another pointed to a most unfortunate contrast: "While our soldier boys, though poor, are bleeding for their country, the wealthy monopolists are bleeding their country."[89]

These simple swipes at imperialism dotted the pages of reform papers, but many critics also drew direct links between aggregated capital and imperial policies. In a letter to the editor, one supporter of reform noted, "Nearly all imperialists are trust defenders, and all trust defenders are single gold standard advocates." This was not a coincidence, for certainly, "Imperialism cannot long endure without substantial financial backing and wealth cannot long be concentrated without imperialistic support."[90] Populists suggested that this view had already been proved true in Idaho. "Having denied the right of self-government to millions in the Philippines and Porto [sic] Rico and even the right to labor in one of the states of the union," what would prevent a reelected McKinley from extending "his imperial power over larger sections of these states?"[91]

Many anti-imperialist arguments brought the imperial threat home for readers, and the most sophisticated developed rather complex critiques of global capitalism. In an interesting example, the editor of the *Independent* explained the limited utility of the new emphasis on foreign trade. If the quantity theory of money was correct, and those who advocated foreign trade justified it with the hope of increasing the gold and silver currency of America, then the unequal trade necessitated by this policy would eventually bankrupt the other nations of the world. Trade could be profitable into the future only if America succeeded in getting its trading partners into a cycle of perpetual debt, although this too would lead to "the impoverishment of foreign nations after a while." Fundamentally, the author declared, the talk of "overproduction," which imperialists had employed to explain both economic decline and the sudden need for overseas markets, was bogus. The solution to America's economic problems would be found at home, not abroad.[92]

Still others considered overseas colonialism a policy designed to exploit the poor of both the United States and the world. Thomas Patterson's *Rocky Mountain News* pointed out that the war in the Philippines cost $10 million per month. If the country devoted that much money to internal improvements, such as irrigation of the arid West, domestic producers could reap the benefits. Within just a few years, the improved land could provide new homes for 5 million to 10 million people in the West. This would never happen, of course, because the "financial influences represented by the present national administration do not want the far West to grow too fast." They preferred for the region to remain economically and politically dependent, just like those colonies being conquered on the other side of the world.[93]

The reformers also perceived another more tangible threat to the freedom of white American breadwinners. In September, McKinley's newly appointed judge for the District Court of the Territory of Hawaii made statements with far-reaching implications. After presiding over the naturalization of Reymond Reyes, Judge Morris Estee observed that the naturalization proceedings were unnecessary because, by virtue of annexation, the people of Guam were already American citizens. Two weeks later, he overruled the actions of a local customs agent who had denied entry to Ah Sing, a Chinese sailor working on an American ship. Hawaii was an America port, Estee stated, and could not be treated as legally different from any point along the mainland.[94] The judge had no intention of creating a stir, but in the coming weeks, both sides wantonly misinterpreted his words to suit their own political arguments.

When news of Estee's remarks reached the mainland, reformers, especially those along the Pacific coast, reacted with alarm. Labor organizers and western reformers held rallies of workingmen to protest "the recent decision of Federal Judge Estee, in which he holds that the Chinese exclusion act and the alien contract law cannot be enforced as against Chinamen and contract laborers coming into the United States from the new island possessions."[95] In Washington, the editor of the Aberdeen Herald published a number of articles linking the immigration threat to the policy of imperialism. "If we pursue the policy as laid down by McKinley, [to] subjugate and retain the Philippines, there can and will be absolutely no way by which we can prevent the millions of cheap laborers of those islands from coming to the United States." The immigration of a mere 10 percent of the poor workers of the Philippines "would crush out every white laborer on the Pacific coast," he warned.[96] The news from Hawaii only magnified the reformers' depiction of an Asian immigration threat.[97]

Republicans responded with dubious claims of their own. Some declared that Estee's statements about citizenship had nothing to do with the Philippines. Others argued (incorrectly) that, "of the Philippines, Chinese, Malays or what not, not a mother's son of them can immigrate to this country unless specifically permitted to by congress." Still others suggested that it did not matter because a Filipino "could no more reach the United States and become a factor in its economic life than he could go to Mars." They provided enough of a response to tamp down some of the public excitement, but the issue would be raised by their opponents throughout the campaign.[98]

While fending off talk of the "yellow peril," Republican discussion of race and empire became necessarily complicated.[99] During the campaign, the bombastic rhetoric of racial greatness or the "white man's burden" was largely set aside. Instead, Republicans denied that their enterprise was truly a colonial project; in fact, quite the opposite was true, they said, as America had destroyed empires. Because of the administration's efforts, "millions of men have been freed from a cruel tyranny." They also sought to enhance their image as benevolent protectors of the downtrodden by changing public perceptions of the Filipinos. In both editorials and supplemental materials, they cast Aguinaldo as an ambitious dictator who was interested only in plundering the islands for his own benefit. The people, too, were portrayed as tribal and diverse, and this diversity was described as an obstacle to national unity. In most cases, the conflict in the Philippines was characterized by its supporters as a war to protect the many peoples of the archipelago against the Tagalogs—the ethnic group to which Aguinaldo belonged. According to this view, Bryan was calling for the end of Spanish and American domination, but the next "imperial" rulers of the Philippines would be Aguinaldo and his cronies.[100] This interpretation provided by the administration and its backers was both misleading and portentous. The war raged throughout the islands, not merely in the regions populated by the Tagalog ethnic group.[101] But by arguing that the Filipinos were incapable of governing themselves because of their diversity, they made independence seem impossible within the next several generations. Again, the white right to rule was not explicitly emphasized during the campaign. Instead, the Republicans simply claimed that Americans were responsible for controlling a region that would descend into despotism without their guiding hand.

Just as white supremacy provided no direct enhancement to the arguments of western imperialists, neither did Rooseveltian conceptions of "rugged" manhood. The Republican vice presidential candidate actually toured the West as McKinley's surrogate in September and October, but his reception was somewhat mixed. His speech in the mining town of Victor, Colorado, was followed by a small riot that left Roosevelt running for cover. He had entered town as usual, flanked by men in Rough Rider costumes, and attempted to follow a fairly regular script. But the rowdy miners of Victor would have none of it. When Roosevelt derided the Democrats for their corruption, he was met with the cry, "What about the rotten beef?"—a reference to the "embalmed beef" requisitioned by corrupt or incompetent officials of the War Department in 1898, a story that Roosevelt had first brought to national attention. The New York governor responded that the men in the audience had nothing to fear, for they "will never get near enough to be hit with a bullet." When the men then cheered for Bryan, he asked aloud, "Why not cheer for Aguinaldo also?" First he had placed his own manly experience above those of the miners, and then he proceeded to question their patriotism. Moments later, any remaining order completely dissolved. Roosevelt and his entourage of faux Rough Riders were forced to fight their way back to the train. If the miners of Victor did not reject the concept of aggressive manhood, they at least rejected its apostle.[102]

Perhaps the miners knew that in Roosevelt's version of militarized manhood, they had only a minimal place. Over the summer, several western newspapers noted that Roosevelt's early writings had scorned western cowboys who drank alcohol and participated in needless gunfights. But, he said, no matter their defects, "they are much better fellows and pleasanter companions than the small farmers or agricultural laborers, nor are the mechanics of a great city to be mentioned in the same breath."[103] Despite Roosevelt's advocacy of a kind of rugged manhood, his message was only for the increasingly refined upper and professional classes. These men would lead the industrial masses, and the farmers and laborers would dutifully follow. Although he did not believe in a rigid class society, his acceptance of "natural" hierarchies led him to favor paternalism over genuine equality.[104]

Any discussion of "manhood" in the western campaign was not what Roosevelt or Lodge might have desired. But neither of them was the presidential candidate of the Republican Party—fifty-seven-year-old William McKinley was. Their Democratic rival was a forty-year-old known for his whirlwind tours and energetic style, whereas their own candidate was known for his caution and maturity, and he had waged the previous campaign as close to his home as possible. This persona also fit with the narrative McKinley demanded: America was to be portrayed as a kindly protector rather than an aggressive conqueror.

Democrats and Populists continued to emphasize a very different kind of manhood. They argued that free men and concentrated wealth could not coexist and that the battle against trusts was the battle to save American manhood.[105] But their campaign against militarism would soon hit a snag. At the heart of their critique of militarism was fear that an army of unthinking drones could be unleashed on workers or political opponents. The regular army, they frequently said, was made up not of independent men but of those who had failed at all other avocations. After induction, what little independence remained was driven out of them through the usual rigors of life in a rigid hierarchal order. As one critic put it, "The worst part about making a soldier of a man is not that a soldier kills brown men or white men, [but] that the soldier loses his own soul."[106] Nebraska's governor soon found himself in an awkward position due to comments like this.

Throughout September and October, Governor Poynter toured the state, emphasizing the dangers associated with militarism and imperialism. But as the campaign entered its last month, Republicans claimed Poynter had made slanderous remarks about the American soldiery. Some accused him of calling members of the regular army "hired butchers," while others said he referred to them as "$15-a-month hirelings." Poynter attempted to refute the story, but it proved too difficult to stop. The actual evidence provided by his rivals was of dubious quality—the Republicans' gubernatorial nominee, Charles Dietrich, was the primary witness who attested to the story's veracity—but the regional and national media printed the story with little hesitation. Roosevelt was touring Nebraska just as the rumors began to take off, and he repeated the story at nearly every stop. In Omaha he suggested there was no difference between regular soldiers and the volunteers who had signed up for the war with Spain, noting, "The mould is fresh on the graves of these 'hirelings' who lay in the Philippines," where many of the First Nebraska Volunteers had died.[107]

Poynter's alleged remarks did not introduce the issue of patriotism into the campaign; the loyalty of those opposed to the wartime president had been questioned since 1898, and the attacks had only escalated after the outbreak of the second war. Western Republicans were more than happy to substitute the debate over political economy with the language of patriotic nationalism. While they continued to pay lip service to prosperity, just as McKinley wanted, they eagerly shifted the focus of the campaign. They adopted this rhetoric in all its guises, but the easiest to use and, simultaneously, the most powerful allowed them to represent themselves as the true friends of the soldiers. The reformers often walked a fine line in their own speeches and remarks, and they were sometimes forced to transition between praising the soldiers' bravery and lambasting the ongoing operations as an affront to humanity. Republicans were delighted with the situation. A writer for the *Omaha Daily Bee* suggested, "There are two sides to the question of assaulting the soldiers who are in the Philippines," and the "fathers, brothers, and friends of those in the army and those who have died fighting against the insurgents do not take kindly to having them called murderers and supporters through force of bayonets of an unholy cause."[108] A reporter in eastern Washington also pointed out how quickly one Democratic speaker had "lost prestige with his audience when he referred to the brave boys in the Philippines as being there on 'a mission of murder and looting, and insulting men, women, and children.'"[109] The soldiers were in the Philippines "defending the American flag, American honor and American prestige," said a Colorado editor. "They have the right to demand that we shall rally to their support."[110] The Republicans successfully depicted their party as the defenders of the nation's men in uniform.

Republicans further argued that support for the anti-imperialists actually kept the war going. The administration was merely trying to secure the peace, but "in the Philippines this is retarded by the position of the democratic party."[111] One of the Republicans' campaign supplements titled

"Does It Fit?" Judge, October 27, 1900. Copyright permission granted by Harpweek LLC

"Bryan's Avowed Aid and Comfort to Aguinaldo" was distributed by several Nebraska newspapers, and its content was just as damning as the name suggested.[112] Once again, supporters of the president said that American men in combat "have a right to denounce as traitors those who for the advancement of selfish party and personal interests are making their task harder, who are encouraging their enemies, and are helping the attack upon that flag," which all true Americans must defend.[113] They remorselessly attacked "the Byranism that still encourages the Tagal to ply the bolo or lurk in the swamps to ambush American soldiers, who, according to Bryan, are loafers walking about in idleness."[114] Their rivals had no proper response to such allegations.

To the charge of treason, the Republicans added historical context. In Washington, Congressman Cushman told audiences, "There was a certain party 40 years ago that maligned and attacked Abraham Lincoln, just as there is a certain party today which is attacking and maligning William McKinley. Then it was the southern half of our own continent that was in insurrection, now it is the Philippines."[115] The Democrats had been the party of treason in 1861, they contended, and that legacy continued to the present time. When the Chicago Inter-Ocean ran an article that compared Bryan with the infamous copperhead Democrat Clement Vallandigham, it was picked up throughout the West.[116] The editor of the Morning Olympian liked the piece so much that he provided his own commentary on the parallels between the two men. It was no surprise that the "notorious copperhead's thoughts are echoed in all of Mr. Bryan's recent speeches . . . for Mr. Bryan now, like Vallandigham in 1863, advocates surrender to rebels." In the meantime, Bryan was "now encouraging rebels, just as Vallandigham and his party did then."[117]

Accusations of copperheadism and other reminders of the Civil War era were especially prominent in Nebraska, where that war's veterans and their descendants made up a large portion of the population. Of course, Poynter's words were used to recall the memories of the great conflict. "In 1861–5 the Knights of the Golden Circle and their copperhead allies called the union soldiers 'Lincoln hirelings,'" recounted one editor, "but it is now left to Governor Poynter to refer to the soldier boys in the Philippines in his speeches as '$15-a-month hirelings.'"[118] In that same vein, Roosevelt targeted veterans and their descendants in the speeches he gave as he toured the state: "You, my comrades, remember when you were called Lincoln's hirelings."[119] Others propagated the notion that both wars were products of partisan discord. One former Confederate told a local paper that the war in the Philippines would have ended quickly if not for the anti-imperialists, just as the Civil War "would not have lasted three months but for the northern Democratic encouragement."[120] An Omaha minister put it more powerfully when he wrote that the Democrats had "lied as they always have about our presidents from Lincoln to McKinley, then when the outbursts of war came, ran to their holes as they did in 1861 and left the republican party to clear up the mess. . . . If Aguinaldo had not been encouraged, just as Jeff Davis was, the war would have been settled."[121]

Articles and speeches that charged the Democrats with treason were often aimed directly at disgruntled Populists and Silver Republicans. In fact, the Republicans propped up the mid-roaders throughout the campaign.[122] Of even greater interest to Republicans were the former Populist and Silver Republican leaders who had turned on their own movement. Many had been cast aside after the creation of lasting fusion arrangements, while others were drawn to the Republicans because of their aggressive foreign policy. Now these former Populists claimed their old friends had been deceived and had taken up a cause that was both disloyal and contrary to national interests. The former Silver Republican senator from Montana, Lee Mantle, stated, "The paramount issue today is the issue of maintain[ing] the honor and dignity of the nation and the supremacy of its flag." Bryan called for the country to "abandon our advanced position, throw down our arms, cravenly hoist the white flag and admit to the world that we are incapable of solving the problems which confront us." Former Kansas Populist William Peffer agreed, calling the platform of the reformers a "brazen assault on the honor of the republic," which amounted to "little less than treason." In a speech he delivered in Denver, Senator William Stewart of Nevada declared, "This campaign had a parallel in the campaign of '64," though he branded contemporary Democrats worse than those of the previous generation. "Mr. McClellan was not as treasonable as Mr. Bryan is," he concluded.[123]

Although the Republicans frequently talked of loyalty to the soldiers, their real focus was on the broader public's unquestioned obedience to the administration. Opposition to the president was both damaging and disloyal, and the death of soldiers represented the collateral damage. By contrast, people could show their loyalty and love of country by following the course laid out by McKinley. Of all the campaign literature used in the western states, few pieces better exemplified this attitude than a bit of serial fiction titled the "Dear Boy Letters." These letters were supposed to represent the advice of a respectable Republican father to his young, emotional son who was infatuated with the words of Bryan. In one, the father points out that America has gained respect around the world because of its defeat of Spain and its responsible dealings in Asia. National power is significant, he admits, but it is even more important that the world has learned that Americans always "fight, not merely for money, but for ideas, for liberty, and for the deliverance of the oppressed of other lands and races." The father ends by telling his son to "be honest, be true, be Christian, and BE AN AMERICAN."[124] In a later edition of the serial, the father tells his son that, even though he could not enlist in 1898 due to poor health, "I want you to realize that you can serve your country as truly when you cast an honest ballot as if you were a soldier in the field." Even though "your country did not seem to need you as a soldier," the son can serve his country by following the Republican Party. And after the ballots were cast, he could "sleep sweetly that night, with a sense of duty faithfully done."[125]

The goal of the Republicans was to project a need for nationalist unity in time of war. As they did so, they understood that their opponents were casting them as dangerous militarists and aggressive expansionists. Even when they appealed to a milder form of nationalism, they feared their rhetoric might drive off immigrants and others disinterested in a nationalist project. German immigrants and German Americans, for example, were widely believed to have a distaste for overseas expansion, and their concerns had to be addressed. In the case of Nebraska, Germans were the largest immigrant group, and most German-language papers in the state openly opposed imperialist or militarist policies.[126] Some western Republicans attempted to dismiss claims about German American suspicion by declaring that the "Germans who have the ballot in this country are American citizens, and they will vote as they please."[127] However, the large number of articles directed specifically at German voters suggests a fear of alienation. Most of the editorials and campaign supplements warned Germans not to be fooled by Bryan's anti-imperialism—free silver was his real objective.[128] Still, Republican apprehensions were not easily assuaged.

In Nebraska, the Republicans decided to address the issue by granting the gubernatorial nomination to Charles Dietrich, a banker from Hastings whom the party labeled as German American.[129] Dietrich proved to be an awful choice—in part because of a past that was best left forgotten, but also because his "beer and sauerkraut" campaign repelled both prohibitionists and those Germans who considered him a phony.[130] His selection represented a deployment of nationalism that was designed to attract members of the state's ethnic communities. By presenting himself as both German American and a defender of the nation's soldiers, Dietrich showed that one could retain an ethnic identity and still act as a "proper" American.[131] Theodore Roosevelt made a similar argument while campaigning in the state:

"In the big war we had Sherman and Sheridan. Who cared that one was of New England and the other of Irish stock? Or Siegel, who was of German stock; or Farragut, whose father came from Majorca?" Ethnic background did not matter, as long as one "was an American in heart and purpose."[132] By Roosevelt's reckoning, "Americanism" was a quality that immigrants could attain, so long as they were willing to serve the nation or follow its leaders without question.

The Republicans were quite successful at emphasizing a militarized version of patriotic nationalism. Populists and other reformers still occasionally made reference to the kind of civic nationalism or republican patriotism they had appealed to for much of the decade, but much less frequently. Now when they compared their struggle with that of the nation's founders, it was often a defensive response. Their frequent reactions to the appellations of "copperhead" and "traitor" also suggest that these remarks were taken seriously. One Colorado editor lamented that the Republicans could not explain their foreign policy "without going into a frenzy and howling 'Copperhead,' 'traitor,' and similar 'argument' which constitutes most of their campaign stock-in-trade this year."[133] A Washington Democrat explained the logic used by the administration's defenders: "All persons who oppose the McKinley policy in the Philippines are guilty of giving aid and comfort to the enemy, and are therefore traitors. No traitor should be allowed to vote. Consequently, the right to vote should be limited to persons who intend to vote for Mr. McKinley."[134]

Conscious of the power of such labels, some Democrats and Populists threw them back at their opponents. In Colorado, the accusation of "traitor" was just as likely to be made against Republican Senator Wolcott as it was against Bryan. In a front-page cartoon in the *Rocky Mountain News*, Bryan was depicted as a gladiator who defended silver against a semihuman figure labeled "Money Trust." But lurking behind Bryan was Wolcott, knife in hand, ready to betray the defender of silver when the moment was right.[135] The editor of Nebraska's leading Populist paper took a different tack. Under the headline "High Treason," the author consciously replicated the Republicans' language and accused them of statements worse than "Vallandingham [sic] ever made during the civil war." Many of the old leaders of the Republican Party were working with conspirators who planned "to overthrow this government and establish a monarchy in its place," and "these republican leaders are traitors," claimed the editor. "They have made a secret alliance by which the upholders of monarchy in the old world shall assist the believers in that form of government in this country."[136] The editor had hit upon a

key point central to the debates of the 1890s. When Populists and allied reformers had accused their opponents of cooperation with the money power
or plutocracy, they had in fact been accusing them of treason. But with the
outbreak of war overseas, the rhetoric of patriotism had largely been appropriated by their opponents.[137]

Rather than following the national party's line, John Rankin Rogers refused to condemn the war and instead favored expansion. By midsummer,
however, he had toned down his statements on the issue, which Republicans
attributed to pressure from the Bryan campaign.[138] Rogers did not renounce
his earlier position, but he decided to split the difference. In his speech at
the largest fusion rally in Washington during the campaign, he stated that
he intended to emphasize local matters. "I will say, however, that I believe
in commercial expansion in the fullest sense." Puget Sound was to be "the
future commercial emporium of the world," and Washingtonians could not
deny that destiny. At the same time, he denied that expansion required "imperialism" or rule by force of arms. He made no reference to the Philippines
or any present conflict, and his statements could be read as support for
whatever the listener chose to believe. McKinley himself had denied that his
policies were imperialistic, and if Rogers refused to say whether he defined
them as such, there was little reason to believe the governor specifically condemned the ongoing war. Undoubtedly, that is exactly what he wanted.[139]

RESULTS OF THE CONTEST

Bryan's defeat in the election of 1900 was perhaps a disappointment but
probably not a genuine surprise. In 1896 he had failed to win any state in the
Midwest or Northeast. The addition of anti-imperialism and antitrust planks
to the platform swayed some voters in those regions, but the electoral map in
the East looked very much like it had four years earlier, and that fact alone
made his victory in the presidential contest impossible.[140]

Far more devastating than his defeat was the decimation of his base of
support in the West. Among the states he had carried in 1896, Bryan lost
Kansas, the Dakotas, Wyoming, Utah, Washington, and his home state of
Nebraska. The Populists, Democrats, and Silver Republicans who had been
swept into office in the West in 1896 were nearly swept out again. In Nebraska, Bryan's earlier majority of nearly 12,000 votes was turned into a
defeat by 8,000. The gubernatorial contest was closer, but Dietrich's narrow
victory—by roughly 800 ballots—was certainly attributable to a local cam-

paign that repulsed traditional Republican voters. The reformers fared better in Colorado, where Bryan won by more than 30,000 and Orman secured the governorship with a somewhat smaller total.[141]

Strangest of all were the results in Washington State. Bryan had claimed a 12,000-vote majority in 1896; four years later, he was defeated by the same margin. Despite Bryan's defeat, Governor Rogers managed a surprising re-election. During his four years in office, Rogers had alienated mid-road Populists, single-tax Democrats, and finally even mainstream Populists when he abandoned their party altogether. Compared with his Republican rival, he had little national or local organizational support. Despite all these factors running against him, he outpaced Bryan's totals by more than 7,000 votes (out of 107,000 cast). When one considers how rare ticket splitting was at this time, the difference is even more impressive.[142]

The defeat of reform in the West was nearly complete. Republicans claimed governorships, legislative majorities, and most of the congressional delegations from the Plains and the coast. Only in the states of the mining West were the results different. Much as they had in Colorado, Democrats won victories in Montana and Idaho with the aid of Populists. Organized labor applied pressure through the Populists, forcing Idaho Democrats to officially renounce the administration of their own governor. But because of the Democrats' relative strength in the mining states compared with else-where in the West, fusion arrangements had always faced serious obstacles. Even though Populists joined winning coalitions in the region in 1900, these victories painted no bright picture for the party's future.[143]

Bryan's explanation of the defeat was published the next month in the *North American Review*. Despite being imbalanced in places and overly sim-plistic in others, his account made a few substantive points worthy of note. He observed that there had been no national shift in votes toward McKinley; instead, McKinley had taken the West, while Bryan had improved in the East. In accounting for his poorer showing in this election than four years earlier, Bryan pointed to the substantial Republican campaign chest, the war in the Philippines, and "better times." He acknowledged that many voters had likely been influenced by the ongoing war and the argument "that it is not safe to swap horses while crossing a stream," but he concluded that "prosperity" had won the day for the president.[144]

Bryan's acceptance of the Republicans' campaign rhetoric is too simplistic an explanation of what happened either nationally or in the West. Bryan be-lieved that farmers were especially susceptible to the "prosperity" campaign, but one historian's examination of the Nebraska vote demonstrated that—for the first time in several years—cultural factors were a stronger indicator of voting behavior than economic factors in 1900. Farmers were influenced at least as much by their ethnic background as by their pocketbooks.[145] In Colorado, the single most important determinant was vocation. Miners provided solid support for Bryan and Orman, while farmers and ranchers were less interested.[146] The miners' view of events in Idaho and the subsequent rejection of militarization likely played a more substantial role than the faint hope that silver could be remonetized.

Rogers's victory may be the most telling of all. In Washington State, the governor outpaced Bryan by 5 to 10 percent of the vote in nearly every county, whether urban or rural, eastern or western. Though his victory is difficult to pin on any single factor, his acceptance of the American empire and his willing participation as the state's leading booster surely made a difference. Voters who had identified with the Populists and Silver Republicans earlier in the 1890s supported McKinley in 1900, but no small number of them remained loyal to Rogers. Although many did so in support of empire or to back the nation's soldiers in a time of conflict, the results also suggest that some continued to hope for reform.[147]

Perhaps the anti-imperialists never really stood a chance of winning—not because Americans overwhelmingly supported empire, but because of the challenges they faced. The intellectual and personal divide between the eastern mugwumps and conservatives and the western reformers was too wide to bridge. In their home region, Populists and Democrats contrasted their vision of an egalitarian democracy with their opponents' desire for an empire held together by an orderly hierarchy. Yet the very depth of their critique left them exposed. They attacked the administration and, worse yet, were labeled enemies of the nation's soldiers. It was impossible to avoid charges of treason when they claimed that those who held up the flag were part of some nefarious scheme to crush the republic and extinguish the rights of others. They called for common Americans to see themselves as laborers and free men, while their opponents demanded that they identify only with their nation. Crude patriotism won the day.

The defeat of both Populism and anti-imperialism in 1900 was no small matter. The campaign had been waged on many fronts, and it had more fully demonstrated the complexity of American life and the nation's place in the world than the celebrated contest of just four years earlier. Political economy, an overseas war, and questions of American identity had been discussed in detail, even if those debates had not been resolved as neatly as the electoral contest. But now, the most substantial late-nineteenth-century movement for economic justice was all but dead. And McKinley's vision of harmonious empire would receive its trial run at the opening of the twentieth century.

CONCLUSION

The Populist movement was unique in American history. Rarely have so many Americans joined together to call for sweeping political and economic transformations. Their proposals—whether they would have achieved their intended results or not—would have surely reshaped the course of national development. Despite being unable to supplant either of the two existing major parties at the national level, they won offices throughout the West and translated their agenda into action. After just four years in existence, they were playing an outsized role in shaping regional and national debates, and they forced both the Republican and Democratic Parties to adapt. Though unable to help William Jennings Bryan attain the presidency in 1896, they appeared poised to be a potent political force, especially in the West.

In the months following Bryan's defeat, Populists increasingly applied their analysis of wealth and power to the realm of foreign affairs. The inaction of successive conservative administrations despite bloody atrocities in Cuba convinced western Populists and their allies that the wealthy of the world supported colonial exploitation. McKinley's demands for the annexation of Hawaii and colonial rule in the Philippines and Puerto Rico seemed to confirm their suspicions. They attacked expansion as a tool of financiers and industrialists. Empire would provide new peoples to be manipulated and new resources to be pillaged. Centralized authority, now detached from the consent of the governed, would prove to be as suppressive at home as it was abroad. Empire would also fuel endless conflicts with subject peoples and with great powers, which could stir up nationalistic sentiment and distract from the need for change at home.

Ultimately, the Populists' attack on the administration would play a part in their undoing. Before 1898, McKinley's Republican Party had been on the decline throughout the West. The Populists had succeeded in changing the political discourse from matters of culture and recent history to concerns about economic and political power. Then, in the campaigns of 1898 and 1900, Republicans in the West triumphantly came back into power. They did so by stressing national unity and by painting their opponents as prophets of strife and traitors to their nation. In 1898 they claimed that the threat of renewed war (including the possibility of intervention by the great powers) required all to reject the opponents of the president. Two years later, the Republican campaign—both nationally and in the West—would prove more nationalist than imperialist. They said little about the new American empire, but when they did discuss it, they stressed secure prosperity through the forceful control of international markets. Far worse, Republicans claimed, the rhetoric of Populists and Democrats only encouraged the enemies of America. Republicans were successful at labeling their partisan rivals, and no response was adequate to refute the persistent charge of treason. The Republican "redemption" of much of the West in 1900 only added to the party's dominant position at the beginning of the new century.

Populism was extinguished shortly thereafter. In most of the West, the party's decline was precipitous. The Pacific coast Populists essentially disappeared after 1900. The movement in Washington State dissolved, and the newly minted Democrat John Rankin Rogers died just over a year after his reelection.[1] Among the Plains states, Populist parties continued for a few years, but with such reduced membership that they became irrelevant almost immediately. In Nebraska, the Populists remained a bit stronger, and they were able to name the fusion gubernatorial candidate in 1902 and influence the selection in 1904, although neither one would win. Many joined the Democrats and made elections more competitive than they had been prior to the 1890s, but this only reduced the Republican margin of victory.[2]

The situation proved no better in the Mountain West. There, strong Democratic parties tried to discard their junior partners. In Colorado, state Democrats put an end to fusion in 1902, hoping to take the labor vote for themselves. Instead, pro-corporate Republican James H. Peabody won the governorship, and he set about destroying organized labor in the state. Labor unrest in 1903 led Peabody to call out the Colorado National Guard, and under the leadership of former mine manager and onetime Rough Rider Sherman Bell, the state militia was used to crush local chapters of the Western Federation of Miners. Strikebreakers received official escorts, union leaders were arrested without cause, and many WFM members were forcibly transported beyond the state line. The WFM never fully recovered in Colorado, and the Populists died with them.[3] Theodore Roosevelt, now in the White House, looked on with approval.[4]

Following their defeats, many of the Populists' chief demands were shunted aside and ignored by future generations. Although some of their proposals for more direct democratic channels were acknowledged, their calls for a transformed national economy went unanswered. The reformers who would take prominent places in state and national governments in the decades that followed were committed to limiting the influence of centralized economic power, but few among them showed an interest in destroying it. Fewer still demanded reform and questioned the desirability of an all-powerful bureaucratic state. Never again would so many governorships and seats in the Senate be held by individuals who seriously questioned something as fundamental as the foundations of property rights or the propriety of a private financial services sector. The death of Populism was truly a significant moment in the history of American political development.

The connection between nationalism and populism (that is, any grassroots movement for reform) is very real, although, as this study suggests, scholars have not always correctly identified it. Although the Populists of the 1890s were no more nationalistic or xenophobic than their neighbors, they were every bit as vulnerable to patriotic appeals. At the same time, the success of their movement made some otherwise cautious conservatives willing to adopt policies that would have been inconceivable a decade earlier. If working people were going to be brought together in solidarity, conservatives preferred that it be based on nationalism rather than a shared distrust of the upper class.

Other simultaneous manifestations of these two trends would differ in important ways, but nationalism and populism continued to be linked in the generations that followed. The 1910s saw the rise of both left-leaning progressives and socialists alongside the ultranationalists who would eventually call for "100 percent Americanism" in war and peace. The Depression of the 1930s brought waves of labor radicalism and quasi-fascism, manifested in the likes of Father Coughlin and, later, in the right wing of the America First movement. The social movements of the late 1960s ran parallel to the rise of George Wallace, the return of Richard Nixon, and the formation of the New Right. Although it can be argued, especially in the last case, that the emergence of one led directly to a reaction by the other side, there is a commonality connecting all these moments. In each, serious social disruptions left Americans looking for answers, with no easy choices ahead. They could push for substantive structural changes that would remake the nation into something quite different. Alternatively, they could embrace what they already knew and shun the more difficult path.[5]

Most careful observers see that we are approaching a similar juncture at present. Social tensions caused by globalization, the concentration of wealth, and movements to restore or disrupt the existing racial order have once again emerged on both sides of the ideological divide. Shall Americans blame their problems on immigrants, "violent" minorities, or others who disrespect the traditional social order? Or will Americans demand a fairer economy, one in which giant institutions are restrained and held to account for their actions? The former is certainly easier than the latter, if significantly less constructive. America will undoubtedly be pulled down one path or the other, but which one has yet to be determined. Voters, activists, and (perhaps) political leaders must ultimately decide.

NOTES

INTRODUCTION

1. *Congressional Record*, 55th Cong., 3rd sess., January 26, 1899, appendix, 90-94. Unless otherwise stated, all such quoted material was read or spoken aloud while Congress was in session.

2. Richard Hofstadter, *The Age of Reform: From Bryan to F.D.R.* (New York: Vintage Books, 1955), 88-93; Richard Hofstadter, "Cuba, the Philippines, and Manifest Destiny," in *The Paranoid Style in American Politics, and Other Essays* (1952; reprint, Cambridge, MA: Harvard University Press, 1996), 145-187.

3. For a few examples of their depiction of Populist involvement, see Walter LaFeber, *New Empire: An Interpretation of American Expansion, 1860-1898* (Ithaca, NY: Cornell University Press, 1963), 201, 205, 414-416; William Appleman Williams, *The Roots of Modern American Empire: A Study of the Growth and Shaping of Social Consciousness in a Marketplace Society* (New York: Random House, 1969), 34-36, 362-365, 370-375.

4. Kristin L. Hoganson, *Fighting for American Manhood: How Gender Politics Provoked the Spanish-American and Philippine-American Wars* (New Haven, CT: Yale University Press, 1998), 28-30, 50, 57, 63, 81, 103-104, 118; Paul T. McCartney, *Power and Progress: American National Identity, the War of 1898, and the Rise of American Imperialism* (Baton Rouge: Louisiana State University Press, 2006), 122-125, 238, 256.

5. Robert L. Beisner, *Twelve against Empire: The Anti-Imperialists, 1898-1900* (New York: McGraw-Hill, 1968); E. Berkeley Tompkins, *Anti-Imperialism in the United States: The Great Debate, 1890-1900* (Philadelphia: University of Pennsylvania Press, 1970); Daniel B. Schirmer, *Republic or Empire: American Resistance to the Philippine War* (Cambridge, MA: Schenkman, 1972); Michael Patrick Cullinane, *Liberty and American Anti-Imperialism, 1898-1909* (New York: Palgrave Macmillan, 2012). For earlier works on the subject, see Maria C. Lanzar, "The Anti-Imperialist League," *Philippine Social Science Review* 3, 1 (1930): 7-41; Fred H. Harrington, "The Anti-Imperialist

Movement in the United States, 1898–1900," *Mississippi Valley Historical Review* 22, 2 (1935): 211–230.

6. Schirmer, *Republic or Empire*, 149–150, 161–169, 175–176, 205–206; Cullinane, *Liberty and American Anti-Imperialism*, 43–46, 55–56; Jim Zwick, "The Anti-Imperialist Movement, 1898–1921," in *Whose America? The War of 1898 and the Battles to Define the Nation*, ed. Virginia M. Bouvier (Westport, CT: Praeger, 2001), 171–192, especially 172, 176.

7. Robert Beisner, "1898 and 1968: The Anti-Imperialists and the Doves," *Political Science Quarterly* 85, 2 (1970): 192.

8. Amy Kaplan, *The Anarchy of Empire in the Making of U.S. Culture* (Cambridge, MA: Harvard University Press, 2002); Paul A. Kramer, *The Blood of Government: Race, Empire, the United States, & the Philippines* (Chapel Hill: University of North Carolina Press, 2006); Alfred W. McCoy, *Policing America's Empire: The United States, the Philippines, and the Rise of the Surveillance State* (Madison: University of Wisconsin Press, 2009); Alfred W. McCoy and Francisco A. Scarano, eds., *Colonial Crucible: Empire in the Making of the Modern American State* (Madison: University of Wisconsin Press, 2009).

9. Thomas A. Bailey, "Was the Presidential Election of 1900 a Mandate on Imperialism?" *Mississippi Valley Historical Review* 24, 1 (1937): 43–52.

10. Göran Rystad, *Ambiguous Imperialism: American Foreign Policy and Domestic Politics at the Turn of the Century* (Lund, Sweden: Esselte Studium, 1975), especially 294. For works that cite either Bailey or Rystad or both, see Stuart Creighton Miller, *"Benevolent Assimilation": The American Conquest of the Philippines, 1899–1903* (New Haven, CT: Yale University Press, 1982); David M. Pletcher, *The Diplomacy of Involvement: American Economic Expansion across the Pacific, 1784–1900* (Columbia: University of Missouri Press, 2001), especially 304–305; Noel Jacob Kent, *America in 1900* (New York: M. E. Sharpe, 2002); Michael Kazin, *A Godly Hero: The Life of William Jennings Bryan* (New York: Anchor Books, 2006).

11. As I demonstrate later, there was little link between the short-term performance of the economy and electoral results in the 1890s. See J. Rogers Hollingsworth, *The Whirligig of Politics: The Democracy of Cleveland and Bryan* (Chicago: University of Chicago Press, 1963), 1–10; R. Hal Williams, *Realigning America: McKinley, Bryan, and the Remarkable Election of 1896* (Lawrence: University Press of Kansas, 2010), 4–23; Lawrence Goodwyn, *Democratic Promise: The Populist Moment in America* (New York: Oxford University Press, 1976), 544.

12. There are many studies that describe Populist parties that maintained relevance in the western states after 1896, and they all include somewhat muddled explanations of the debate over empire. See Walter T. K. Nugent, *The Tolerant Populists: Kansas Populism and Nativism* (Chicago: University of Chicago Press, 1963); O. Gene Clanton, *Kansas Populism: Ideas and Men* (Lawrence: University Press of Kansas, 1969); James Edward Wright, *The Politics of Populism: Dissent in Colorado* (New Haven, CT: Yale University Press, 1974); Robert W. Cherny, *Populism, Progressivism, and the*

Transformation of Nebraska Politics, 1885–1915 (Lincoln: University of Nebraska Press, 1981); Thomas W. Riddle, *The Old Radicalism: John R. Rogers and the Populist Movement in Washington* (New York: Garland, 1991); R. Alton Lee, *Principle over Party: The Farmers' Alliance and Populism in South Dakota* (Pierre: South Dakota State Historical Society Press, 2011). Clanton also contributed a work on Populism at the national level and one on Populists in Congress; see O. Gene Clanton, *Populism: The Humane Preference in America, 1890–1900* (Boston: Twayne, 1991), and *Congressional Populism and the Crisis of the 1890s* (Lawrence: University Press of Kansas, 1998). However, when it comes to imperialism, both these works say more about the influence of morality on the Populist perspective than they do about the full Populist interpretation of imperialism.

CHAPTER 1. WESTERN POPULIST IDEOLOGY AND WORLDVIEW

1. "Labor and Labor Saving Machinery," *Advocate* (Topeka, KS), April 11, 1894, 4–5. See also Norman Pollack, *The Just Polity: Populism, Law, and Human Welfare* (Chicago: University of Illinois Press, 1987), 145–147.

2. John Rankin Rogers to Anna Goodyear, October 18, 1898, John Rankin Rogers Papers, Washington State Archives, Olympia. On Rogers's beliefs regarding Spencer and individualism, see Karel Bicha, "Peculiar Populist: An Assessment of John Rankin Rogers," *Pacific Northwest Quarterly* 65, 3 (1974): 110–117.

3. On the composition of the party and changes over the decade, see James Edward Wright, *The Politics of Populism: Dissent in Colorado* (New Haven, CT: Yale University Press, 1974), 126–158; Robert W. Cherny, *Populism, Progressivism, and the Transformation of Nebraska Politics, 1885–1915* (Lincoln: University of Nebraska Press, 1981), 53–73, 89–108; Peter H. Argersinger, *The Limits of Agrarian Radicalism: Western Populism and American Politics* (Lawrence: University Press of Kansas, 1995), 4–6, 23.

4. Richard Hofstadter, *The Age of Reform: From Bryan to F.D.R.* (New York: Vintage Books, 1955); Lawrence Goodwyn, *Democratic Promise: The Populist Moment in America* (New York: Oxford University Press, 1976). See also David S. Brown, *Richard Hofstadter: An Intellectual Biography* (Chicago: University of Chicago Press, 2006), 100–119; James Turner, "Understanding the Populists," *Journal of American History* 67, 2 (1980): 354–373.

5. For works that view Populism as republican, producerist, or premodern, see Goodwyn, *Democratic Promise*; Steven Hahn, *The Roots of Southern Populism: Yeoman Farmers and the Transformation of the Georgia Upcountry, 1850–1890* (New York: Oxford University Press, 1983); Barton C. Shaw, *The Wool-Hat Boys: Georgia's Populist Party* (Baton Rouge: Louisiana State University Press, 1984); Worth Robert Miller, *Oklahoma Populism: A History of the People's Party in the Oklahoma Territory* (Norman: University of Oklahoma Press, 1987); Thomas W. Riddle, *The Old Radicalism: John R. Rogers and the Populist Movement in Washington* (New York: Garland, 1991). For those

that attribute the Populist downfall to their premodern beliefs, see Christopher Lasch, *The True and Only Heaven: Progress and Its Critics* (New York: W. W. Norton, 1991), 168–225; James Kloppenberg, *The Virtues of Liberalism* (New York: Oxford University Press, 1998), 67. For those that argue instead that the Populists were "modern" and essentially liberal, see Pollack, *Just Polity*, especially 11–13; Norman Pollack, *The Humane Economy: Populism, Capitalism, and Democracy* (New Brunswick, NJ: Rutgers University Press, 1990); Charles Postel, *The Populist Vision* (New York: Oxford University Press, 2007), especially 3–22, 142.

6. On market connections in the postbellum period, see William Cronon, *Nature's Metropolis: Chicago and the Great West* (New York: W. W. Norton, 1991); David Blanke, *Sowing the American Dream: How Consumer Culture Took Root in the Rural Midwest* (Athens: Ohio University Press, 2000); Postel, *Populist Vision*, especially 27–32, 45–54, 103–133. The organization of new trading centers was afoot in the South as well, throwing into doubt any credible discussion of political revolt emanating from "island communities." For the older image, see Robert H. Wiebe, *The Search for Order, 1877–1920* (New York: Hill & Wang, 1967). On the South, see Edward Ayers, *Promise of the New South: Life after Reconstruction*, 2nd ed. (New York: Oxford University Press, 2007), especially 55–80.

7. There is a great deal of literature on this subject. See, for example, Peter Berkowitz, *The Making of Modern Liberalism* (Princeton, NJ: Princeton University Press, 1999); Richard C. Sinopoli, *The Foundations of American Citizenship: Liberalism, the Constitution, and Civic Virtue* (New York: Oxford University Press, 1992); Joyce Appleby, *Liberalism and Republicanism in the Historical Imagination* (Cambridge, MA: Harvard University Press, 1992); Richard Dagger, *Civic Virtues: Rights, Citizenship, and Republican Liberalism* (New York: Oxford University Press, 1997).

8. Kloppenberg, *Virtues of Liberalism*, 59–70. For an earlier attempt to reconcile Populist republicanism with individualistic liberalism, see Bruce Palmer, *"Man over Money": The Southern Populist Critique of American Capitalism* (Chapel Hill: University of North Carolina Press, 1980). For one historian whose work on late-nineteenth-century labor republicanism matches the sort presented here, see Andrew Neather, "Labor Republicanism, Race, and Popular Patriotism in the Era of Empire," in *Bonds of Affection: Americans Define Their Patriotism*, ed. John Bodnar (Princeton, NJ: Princeton University Press, 1996), 82–101; Andrew Neather, "Popular Republicanism, Americanism, and the Roots of Anti-Communism, 1890–1925" (Ph.D. diss., Duke University, 1993).

9. On antimonopolism and Republican policies, see Robert W. Larson, *Populism in the Mountain West* (Albuquerque: University of New Mexico Press, 1986); Cherny, *Populism, Progressivism*, 1–12, 32–52.

10. William A. McKeighan, "Wealth as a Political Power," *Farmers' Alliance* (Lincoln, NE), March 1, 1890; see also Pollack, *Just Polity*, 179–180.

11. "A Message to the People of Aspen and Vicinity," *Aspen (CO) Union Era*, January 7, 1892, 1.

12. Pollack, *Just Polity*, 5.

13. James B. Weaver, *A Call to Action: The Great Uprising, Its Source and Causes* (Des Moines: Iowa Printing Company, 1892), 153–155.

14. "Corrupt Foot-Prints," *Aspen Union Era*, October 22, 1891, 5.

15. On "infant industries" and tariffs, see Richard Franklin Bensel, *The Political Economy of American Industrialization: 1877–1900* (New York: Cambridge University Press, 2000), 460, 477. Bensel provides some of the most interesting explanations of Gilded Age tariff policies in this work.

16. "The Steel Rail Trust," *Aspen Union Era*, November 26, 1891, 1.

17. William A. Peffer, *The Farmer's Side: His Trouble and Their Remedy* (New York: D. Appleton, 1891), 133.

18. Weaver, *Call to Action*, 248, 29.

19. Peffer, *Farmer's Side*, 176–177. Weaver made an even more thorough attack on the courts in *Call to Action*, 102–110, 132–133.

20. Weaver, *Call to Action*, 391–392.

21. Peffer, *Farmer's Side*, 62–63. See similar comments on the coal industry in "Western News Notes," *Aspen Union Era*, February 4, 1892, 4.

22. Weaver, *Call to Action*, 265–266, 5.

23. "Message to the People of Aspen and Vicinity," 1.

24. Postel, *Populist Vision*, especially 103–133.

25. Peffer, *Farmer's Side*, 170.

26. *Advocate*, December 16, 1891, 6.

27. "Co-operation vs. Capitalism," *Free Press*, date and location unknown, reprinted in *Aspen Union Era*, June 23, 1892, 4.

28. John Rankin Rogers, *Politics: An Argument in Favor of the Inalienable Rights of Man* (Seattle: Allen, 1894), 21.

29. John Rankin Rogers to D. C. Ashmun, January 18, 1900, John Rankin Rogers Papers, Washington State Archives.

30. John Rankin Rogers, *Life* (San Francisco: Whitaker & Ray, 1899), 57.

31. Peffer, *Farmer's Side*, 51–52.

32. Untitled article from *Coming Crisis* (Pueblo, CO), date unknown, reprinted in *Aspen Union Era*, July 7, 1892, 4.

33. Rogers, *Politics*, 37.

34. Ibid., 31–38.

35. Weaver, *Call to Action*, 136, 282–283, 286–287, 293.

36. G. C. Rohde, "Mesa Ditch Problem and the Land Question," *Aspen Union Era*, January 7, 1892, 2.

37. According to Weaver, state regulation had been the preferred method of controlling railroads and other corporations, but the courts essentially destroyed that alternative. See Weaver, *Call to Action*, 82–86, 94–98, 110–135. For an interesting take on legal and political battles over local regulation, see Gerald Berk, *Alternative Tracks: The Constitution of American Industrial Order, 1865–1917* (Baltimore: Johns Hopkins University Press, 1994).

38. Weaver, *Call to Action*, 419; "The Strike," *Advocate*, July 25, 1894, 7.

39. Peffer, *Farmer's Side*, 172-173.

40. Quoted in Jeffrey Ostler, *Prairie Populism: The Fate of Agrarian Radicalism in Kansas, Nebraska, and Iowa, 1880-1896* (Lawrence: University Press of Kansas, 1993), 102-103, 105. For comments from Colorado and the rest of the West, see "President Smith's Annual Address," *Aspen Union Era*, October 29, 1891, 4; Goodwyn, *Democratic Promise*, 166-168.

41. "The Rise of Plutocracy in America," *Advocate*, August 31, 1892, 6.

42. "Prepare to Meet Thy Fate!" *Aspen Union Era*, August 4, 1892, 4. For nearly identical remarks from Populists in the wake of American Railway Union strike of 1893, see "Resolution of Condemnation," *Advocate*, July 25, 1894, 10.

43. Rogers, *Politics*, 8.

44. On the financial situation in the 1890s, see Richard Timberlake, *Monetary Policy in the United States: An Intellectual and Institutional History* (Chicago: University of Chicago Press, 1993), 84-171; Marshall Gramm and Phil Gramm, "The Free Silver Movement in America: A Reinterpretation," *Journal of Economic History* 64, 4 (2004): 1108-1129.

45. Bensel, *Political Economy*, 355-456.

46. For the impact of greenback ideology on Populism, see Goodwyn, *Democratic Promise*, 14-16, 82-83, 140, 241; Ostler, *Prairie Populism*, 78; Postel, *Populist Vision*, 150-153.

47. Peffer, *Farmer's Side*, 42, 99, 192.

48. Ibid., 196-197, 206-210.

49. The term *money power* originated in the Jacksonian era, and its precise meaning changed over time. On the early use of the term, see Lawrence Frederick Kohl, *The Politics of Individualism: Parties and the American Character in the Jacksonian Era* (New York: Oxford University Press, 1989), 25, 41-42, 53-55; Gerald Leonard, *The Invention of Party Politics: Federalism, Popular Sovereignty, and Constitutional Development in Jacksonian Illinois* (Chapel Hill: University of North Carolina Press, 2002), 54.

50. "The Farmers' Alliance," *McCook Tribune* (NE), December 5, 1890, 7.

51. "Mr. Sovereign's Letter," *Cherry County Independent* (Valentine, NE), March 5, 1896, 1. Sovereign was also a member of the Populist Party, as he noted in the article.

52. Quoted in Hofstadter, *Age of Reform*, 74.

53. See Hofstadter, *Age of Reform*, 70-81, for his explanation of the use conspiracy; Brown, *Richard Hofstadter*, 100-119. For others who claimed to see parallels between Populism and fascism (both before and after Hofstadter), see Victor C. Ferkiss, "Populist Influences on American Fascism," *Western Political Quarterly* 10, 2 (1957): 350-373; David Peal, "The Politics of Populism: Germany and the American South in the 1890s," *Comparative Studies in Society and History* 31, 2 (1989): 340-362.

54. The most thorough repudiation of Populist prejudice is Walter T. K. Nugent's *The Tolerant Populists: Kansas Populism and Nativism* (Chicago: University of Chicago Press, 1963). However, Nugent did not confront the actual conspiratorial material

itself; instead, he set it aside as unrepresentative of real Populist thought. For a work that deals directly with *Age of Reform*, see Norman Pollack, "Hofstadter on Populism: A Critique of 'The Age of Reform,'" *Journal of Southern History* 26, 4 (1960): 478–500.

55. The only book that deals directly with the money power conspiracy is Walter T. K. Nugent's *Money and American Society, 1865–1880* (New York: Free Press, 1968). But it is devoted more to proving that the nineteenth-century conspiracy theory was wrong than to addressing the actual content or concerns that appeared in the tracts.

56. Jeffrey Ostler, "The Rhetoric of Conspiracy and the Formation of Kansas Populism," *Agricultural History* 69, 1 (1995): 1–27; Ostler, *Prairie Populism*, 77–80, 100–101, 124, 131–132. Similarly, Hofstadter hinted that the Populists were not alone when it came to conspiratorial belief, but he still felt the need to call conspiracy language the stuff of "cranks and political fakirs." Hofstadter, *Age of Reform*, 72.

57. In his acclaimed book on Populist ideology, Charles Postel largely ignored conspiratorial language and never referenced the money power theory specifically. He may have even misread one of the major texts on the subject. He claimed that Sarah Emery's *Seven Financial Conspiracies* showed a "preoccupation with the 'Crime of '73' and the silver question" and offered little for greenback theorists. Postel, *Populist Vision*, 151. As I explain later, Emery demonstrated a clear preference for greenback currency, and in only one chapter did she discuss the demonetization of silver. See also Ostler, "Rhetoric of Conspiracy," 5–9.

58. "The Glorious Fourth!" *National Labor Tribune* (Pittsburgh), July 6, 1878, 2. The description of the influence of Ernest Seyd is almost identical to what appeared later in the work of Sarah Emery and others.

59. Mark Wahlgren Summers, *Party Games: Getting, Keeping, and Using Power in Gilded Age Politics* (Chapel Hill: University of North Carolina Press, 2004), 260.

60. *Congressional Record*, 45th Cong., 2nd sess., December 11, 1877, 124–125.

61. Hofstadter considered it one of the more important works on the subject, and Ostler noted that Kansans during the 1890s specifically mentioned Emery's pamphlet. See Hofstadter, *Age of Reform*, 75–76; Ostler, "Rhetoric of Conspiracy."

62. Henry George, *Progress and Poverty: An Inquiry into the Cause of Industrial Depressions and of Increase of Want with Increase of Wealth* (Garden City, NY: Doubleday, Page, 1879), 3–12.

63. Sarah E. V. Emery, *Seven Financial Conspiracies Which Have Enslaved the American People*, rev. ed. (1887; Lansing MI: Robert Smith, 1894), 9–10.

64. As a reflection of their own views of society, both the Alliance and the Knights excluded bankers, lawyers, and other so-called nonproductive classes from membership. See Robert E. Weir, *Beyond Labor's Veil: The Culture of the Knights of Labor* (University Park: Pennsylvania State University Press, 1996), 11; John D. Hicks, *The Populist Revolt: A History of the Farmers' Alliance and the People's Party*, 3rd ed. (Lincoln: University of Nebraska Press, 1961), 112.

65. Emery, *Seven Financial Conspiracies*, 10.

66. Ibid., 13–15.

67. Ibid., 15–16.

68. Ibid., 17–19, 21.

69. Ibid., 25, 33, 38–43, 47–48.

70. Ibid., 51–52. According to Walter T. K. Nugent, the supposed story in *Banker's Magazine* does not exist. See Nugent, *Money and American Society*, 167; see also Ostler, "Rhetoric of Conspiracy," 8 n. 19. For Hooper's original remarks, see *Congressional Globe*, 42nd Cong., 2nd sess., April 9, 1872, 2304–2305. Hooper's own language does not suggest much consideration of the demonetization of silver; he spoke of the discoveries of precious metals in the West, including both gold and silver, without remarking that these discoveries had changed the market ratios of exchange.

71. Emery, *Seven Financial Conspiracies*, 57–58. For contemporary works that mention the *Hazzard Circular*, see Oscar F. Lumry, *National Suicide and Its Prevention* (Chicago: George F. Cram, 1886), 30–31, 51; George W. Bell, *The New Crisis* (Des Moines, IA: Moses Hull, 1887), 171–174.

72. Ostler, "Rhetoric of Conspiracy," 5 n. 13.

73. Rogers, *Politics*, 16; Weaver, *Call to Action*, 19–21, 316–321. Weaver may not have used a conspiratorial work directly, or it is just as likely that he attempted to hide the influence of such a tract. In the case of his reference to Seyd, for example, he cites a speech made by Senator John W. Daniel of Virginia, and the senator was clearly reading directly from a conspiratorial pamphlet when he claimed to be referencing the *Bankers' Magazine* article.

74. The advertisement for the "Hazard [sic] Circular" appeared in most editions of the weekly paper printed from March 3 through May 26, 1892. Regarding the rumors surrounding Emery's work, see "Despotism," *Aspen Union Era*, July 21, 1892, 4.

75. Information on Patterson's efforts can be found in Gordon Clark, *Shylock: As Banker, Bondholder, Corruptionist, Conspirator* (Washington, DC: American Bimetallic League, 1894), 89.

76. W. Scott Morgan, *History of the Wheel and Alliance and the Impending Revolution* (Fort Scott, KS: J. H. Rice & Sons, 1889).

77. Weaver, *Call to Action*, 19–21.

78. Rogers, *Politics*, 23–24, 40.

79. Peffer, *Farmer's Side*, 162–163, 259.

80. For an overview of the major concepts employed in the world systems model, see Immanuel Wallerstein, *World-Systems Analysis: An Introduction* (Durham, NC: Duke University Press, 2004), especially 1–41.

81. For examples of the literature describing the West as a colonial or "peripheral" region, see William G. Robbins, *Colony and Empire: The Capitalist Transformation of the American West* (Lawrence: University Press of Kansas, 1994); Elizabeth Sanders, *Roots of Reform: Farmers, Workers, and the American State, 1877–1917* (Chicago: University of Chicago Press, 1999). See also William G. Robbins, "The 'Plundered Province' Thesis and the Recent Historiography of the American West," *Pacific Historical Review* 55, 4 (1986): 577–597. For an early work that describes Populists' frustration

with their own semicolonial status, see Leon W. Fuller, "The Populist Regime in Colorado" (Ph.D. diss., University of Wisconsin, 1933).

82. Peffer, *Farmer's Side*, 167.

83. William V. Allen, "Western Feeling toward the East," *North American Review* 162 (1896): 588–593.

84. "Silver Linings for Clouds," *Omaha (NE) Daily Bee*, July 26, 1893, 1.

85. "Good Silver Talk," *Aspen (CO) Daily Leader*, September 3, 1892, 8.

86. "A European Receivership," *Chicago Express*, reprinted in *Daily Camera* (Boulder, CO), July 13, 1894, 3. For more on the *Chicago Express*, see Postel, *Populist Vision*, 73, 97, 144.

87. "Supply and Demand," *Goodland Republic* (KS), April 8, 1892.

88. In particular, certain liberal mugwumps had lost faith in democratic government; among them were E. L. Godkin, Charles Francis Adams Jr., and Francis Parkman. See Alexander Keyssar, *The Right to Vote: The Contested History of Democracy in the United States* (New York: Basic Books, 2000), 119–127; John G. Sproat, *The Best Men: Liberal Reformers in the Gilded Age* (New York: Oxford University Press, 1968), especially 250–257.

89. Hofstadter, *Age of Reform*, 71.

90. On the meaning of the Populists' use of patriotic or nationalist language, see Pollack, *Just Polity*, 28–29; Robert C. McMath Jr., *American Populism: A Social History, 1877–1898* (New York: Hill & Wang, 1992), 72–73; Nina Silber, *Romance of Reunion: Northerners and the South, 1865–1900* (Chapel Hill: University of North Carolina Press, 1993), 99–100. Although they put far too much emphasis on Populist "xenophobia," see also Joseph Gerteis and Alyssa Goolsby, "Nationalism in America: The Case of the Populist Movement," *Theory and Society* 34, 2 (2005): 197–225. Neather describes a similar form of patriotic republicanism in "Labor Republicanism," 82–101. However, he may be wrong when he suggests that laborers' patriotic rhetoric made it impossible for them to level criticism against American imperialist ventures. His statement suggests that labor's conception of patriotism was no different from that of those who called for unquestioned patriotism. Some tried to develop alternative models, although it seems clear that a majority did not accept them.

91. Summers, *Party Games*, especially 19–53.

92. "The Warrior Becomes Facetious," *Advocate*, October 30, 1895, 6.

93. Weaver, *Call to Action*, 354.

94. "Lewelling and Harris," *Advocate*, October 31, 1894, 1.

95. *Aspen Union Era*, October 15, 1891, 6.

96. Rebecca Edwards, *Angels in the Machinery: Gender in American Party Politics from the Civil War to the Progressive Era* (New York: Oxford University Press, 1997), 91–110; Silber, *Romance of Reunion*, 99. For a similar example, see Neather, "Labor Republicanism," 86.

97. For attempts by the urban middle and upper classes to refashion manhood or manliness, see Gail Bederman, *Manliness and Civilization: A Cultural History of Gender*

and Race in the United States, 1880–1917 (Chicago: University of Chicago Press, 1995), especially 1–44, 170–240; Kristin L. Hoganson, *Fighting for American Manhood: How Gender Politics Provoked the Spanish-American and Philippine-American Wars* (New Haven, CT: Yale University Press, 1998), especially 8–12, 143–145, 151–153; Philip Deloria, *Playing Indian* (New Haven, CT: Yale University Press, 1998), 95–127; Jocelyn Wills, "Respectable Mediocrity: The Everyday Life of an Ordinary American Striver, 1876–1890," *Journal of Social History* 37, 2 (2003): 323–349.

98. Despite the fact that most members of organized labor were no longer financially independent, they continued to use the language of independence by putting a new emphasis on the breadwinner role. See Robyn Muncy, "Trustbusting and White Manhood in America, 1898–1914," *American Studies* 38, 3 (1997): 21–42; Weir, *Beyond Labor's Veil*, 19–69. On farmers and manhood, see Michael Lewis Goldberg, *An Army of Women: Gender and Politics in Gilded Age Kansas* (Baltimore: Johns Hopkins University Press, 1997), 148–160.

99. Edwards, *Angels in the Machinery*, 94–95.

100. "The Purple of Royalty," *Coming Crisis*, date unknown, reprinted in *Aspen Union Era*, June 23, 1892, 3.

101. "Duty," *Aspen Union Era*, October 1, 1891, 4.

102. "A Populist Address," *Aspen (CO) Daily Times*, January 9, 1894, 2.

103. "Orations of Labor Day," *Leadville (CO) Daily and Evening Chronicle*, September 5, 1893, 1.

104. "Old Issues Dead," *Aspen Union Era*, October 22, 1891, 4.

105. James M. Beeby, *Revolt of the Tar Heels: The North Carolina Populist Movement, 1890–1901* (Jackson: University Press of Mississippi, 2008), 45–46.

106. Kevin P. Murphy, *Political Manhood: Red Bloods, Mollycoddles, & the Politics of Progressive Era Reform* (New York: Columbia University Press, 2008), 17. Very similar remarks, used by members of the old parties against nonpartisans or others, appear in Summers, *Party Games*, 23, 34.

107. On Roosevelt's conception of manliness, see Bederman, *Manliness and Civilization*, 170–216; Hoganson, *Fighting for American Manhood*, 26–28, 121–124, 153–154.

108. On the eastern middle-class view of women's suffrage, see Bederman, *Manliness and Civilization*, 13, 170–171, 175, 186; Hoganson, *Fighting for American Manhood*, 26–37.

109. Postel, *Populist Vision*, 72–87, 90. For the contradictory gender views that developed in many of the alliances, see Goldberg, *Army of Women*, 130–148.

110. Postel, *Populist Vision*, 86–88, 91. For a description of both the strengths and limits of arguments based on women's moral authority, see Peggy Pascoe, *Relations of Rescue: The Search for Female Moral Authority in the American West, 1874–1939* (New York: Oxford University Press, 1990), especially 32–69.

111. Rebecca J. Mead, *How the Vote Was Won: Woman Suffrage in the Western United States, 1868–1914* (New York: New York University Press, 2004), 53–72.

CHAPTER 2. THE LOCAL CONTEXT

1. John D. Hicks, *The Populist Revolt: A History of the Farmers' Alliance and the People's Party*, 3rd ed. (Lincoln: University of Nebraska Press, 1961), 231, 439–444; *Omaha (NE) Daily Bee*, July 5, 1892, 1–2.

2. Many historians have attributed the decline of Populism to fusion, differing only on the extent to which they view it as destructive. Most, including Hicks, place the blame jointly on fusion politics and improved economic conditions. See Hicks, *Populist Revolt*, 380–402; Lawrence Goodwyn, *Democratic Promise: The Populist Moment in America* (New York: Oxford University Press, 1976), 493–555; Robert C. McMath Jr., *American Populism: A Social History, 1877–1898* (New York: Hill & Wang, 1992), 199–206; Charles Postel, *Populist Vision* (New York: Oxford University Press, 2007), 269–275; Stanley L. Jones, *The Presidential Election of 1896* (Madison: University of Wisconsin Press, 1964), especially 244–262.

3. For the material presented in this and the following paragraphs, see Richard White, *"It's Your Misfortune and None of My Own": A New History of the American West* (Norman: University of Oklahoma Press, 1991), 125–127, 142–147, 183–210, 246–258, 298–326; Nell Irvin Painter, *Standing at Armageddon: A Grassroots History of the Progressive Era* (1987; reprint, New York: W. W. Norton, 2008), 90; Eric Foner, *Reconstruction: America's Unfinished Revolution, 1863–1877*, rev. ed. (New York: Perennial Classics, 2002), 462–475; Heather Cox Richardson, *West from Appomattox: The Reconstruction of America after the Civil War* (New Haven, CT: Yale University Press, 2007), 31–37, 74–76; Gerald Berk, *Alternative Tracks: The Constitution of American Industrial Order, 1865–1917* (Baltimore: Johns Hopkins University Press, 1994), 27–37; Richard White, *Railroaded: The Transcontinentals and the Making of Modern America* (New York: W. W. Norton, 2011), 9–16, 26–36, 106–125.

4. For the political lay of the land in Nebraska, Colorado, and Washington, covered in this and the following paragraphs, see Robert W. Cherny, *Populism, Progressivism, and the Transformation of Nebraska Politics, 1885–1915* (Lincoln: University of Nebraska Press, 1981), 1–31; Jeffrey Ostler, *Prairie Populism: The Fate of Agrarian Radicalism in Kansas, Nebraska, and Iowa, 1880–1896* (Lawrence: University Press of Kansas, 1993), 72–77; James Edward Wright, *The Politics of Populism: Dissent in Colorado* (New Haven, CT: Yale University Press, 1974), 11–84; Thomas W. Riddle, *The Old Radicalism: John R. Rogers and the Populist Movement in Washington* (New York: Garland, 1991), 61–78. On the GAR, see Stuart McConnell, *Glorious Contentment: The Grand Army of the Republic, 1865–1900* (Chapel Hill: University of North Carolina Press, 1992), especially 65; on its social role, see Elizabeth Jameson, *All that Glitters: Class, Conflict, and Community in Cripple Creek* (Chicago: University of Illinois Press, 1998), 92–95, 188–189.

5. Burton W. Folsom Jr., *No More Free Markets or Free Beer: The Progressive Era in Nebraska, 1900–1924* (New York: Lexington Books, 1999), 1–12; Wright, *Politics of Populism*, 62–74, 79, 108–110; David Brundage, *The Making of Western Labor Radi-*

calism: Denver's Organized Workers, 1878-1905 (Chicago: University of Illinois Press, 1994), 47-66, 76-81, 88-91; John P. Enyeart, *The Quest for "Just and Pure Law": Rocky Mountain Workers and American Social Democracy, 1870-1924* (Stanford, CA: Stanford University Press, 2009), 25-28, 41-84; *Guide to U.S. Elections*, 6th ed. (Washington, DC: CQ Press, 2010), 1078; Riddle, *Old Radicalism*, 79-81, 89-92; Thomas W. Riddle, "Populism in the Palouse: Old Ideals and New Realities," *Pacific Northwest Quarterly* 65, 3 (1974): 97-109.

6. Ostler, *Prairie Populism*, 75-76, 87-89, 91-95, 99-103, 113-115, 118-125; Cherny, *Populism, Progressivism*, 33-35.

7. Leon W. Fuller, "The Populist Regime in Colorado" (Ph.D. diss., University of Wisconsin, 1933), 43-44; Wright, *Politics of Populism*, 117-125; Robert W. Larson, *Populism in the Mountain West* (Albuquerque: University of New Mexico Press, 1986), 25-32.

8. For the election results, see Michael J. Dubin, *United States Gubernatorial Elections, 1861-1911: The Official Results by State and County* (Jefferson, NC: McFarland, 2010), 77-78.

9. Cherny, *Populism, Progressivism*, 32-37; Dubin, *Gubernatorial Elections*, 358-359; *Guide to U.S. Elections*, 1088.

10. Riddle, *Old Radicalism*, 79-81, 89-115; Riddle, "Populism in the Palouse," 97-109; Carlos Schwantes, *Radical Heritage: Labor, Socialism, and Reform in Washington and British Columbia, 1885-1917* (Seattle: University of Washington Press, 1979), 52-53; Robert E. Ficken, *Washington State: The Inaugural Decade, 1889-1899* (Pullman: Washington State University Press, 2007), 95-96.

11. Hicks, *Populist Revolt*, 207-215, 223-230; McMath, *American Populism*, 139-146, 160-163.

12. *Congressional Record*, 52nd Cong., 1st sess., April 20, 1892, 3846; Elmer Ellis, *Henry Moore Teller: Defender of the West* (Caldwell, ID: Caxton Printers, 1941), 188-208, 210-211; Sybil Downing and Robert E. Smith, *Tom Patterson: Colorado Crusader for Change* (Niwot: University of Colorado Press, 1995), 68-69.

13. Downing and Smith, *Tom Patterson*, 70-71; Richard E. Welch, *The Presidencies of Grover Cleveland* (Lawrence: University Press of Kansas, 1988), 102-106.

14. Hicks, *Populist Revolt*, 231-237, 439-444; McMath, *American Populism*, 166-170; Nina Silber, *Romance of Reunion:Northerners and the South, 1865-1900* (Chapel Hill: University of North Carolina Press, 1993), 99-100; *Omaha Daily Bee*, July 5, 1892, 1-2.

15. For this and the following discussion of the old parties, see Fuller, "Populist Regime," 50-57; Wright, *Politics of Populism*, 139-144; Downing and Smith, *Tom Patterson*, 72-75; Ellis, *Henry Moore Teller*, 211; Albert Watkins, *History of Nebraska, from the Earliest Explorations to the Present Time*, vol. 3. (Lincoln, NE: Western Publishing and Engraving, 1913), 242-244; Cherny, *Populism, Progressivism*, 39-42; "Shall We Have Unlimited Silver Coinage? . . . Part I," *Omaha Daily Bee*, January 27, 1892, 5; "Shall We Have Unlimited Free Silver Coinage? . . . Part II," *Omaha Daily Bee*,

February 3, 1892, 5; "Shall We Have Unlimited Silver Coinage? . . . Part III," *Omaha Daily Bee*, February 11, 1892, 5; Riddle, *Old Radicalism*, 121–126; Ficken, *Washington State*, 96–97.

16. Gordon Clark, *Shylock: As Banker, Bondholder, Corruptionist, Conspirator* (Washington, DC: American Bimetallic League, 1894), 88–89.

17. "The Situation," *Rocky Mountain News* (Denver, CO), October 26, 1892, 4.

18. "Populists Line Up," *Rocky Mountain News*, October 16, 1892, 5.

19. John Rankin Rogers, *The Irrepressible Conflict, or an American System of Money: A Compilation of Facts Leading to a Knowledge of the Money Question* (Puyallup, WA: Rogers, 1892); Riddle, *Old Radicalism*, 127–129.

20. O. G. Chase, "New Idea Income Tax—No. 15," *Aberdeen (WA) Herald*, August 18, 1892, 2. On Chase's candidacy for the Populists, see "People's Party Convention," *Aberdeen Herald*, July 28, 1892, 2; *Aberdeen Herald*, August 18, 1892, 3. See also "Red Hot Discussion," *Morning Olympian* (WA), September 17, 1892, 4.

21. Quoted in "Shall We Have Unlimited Free Silver Coinage? . . . Part II," 5. See also "Shall We Have Unlimited Silver Coinage? . . . Part III," 5.

22. "Logic of Judge Crounse," *Omaha Daily Bee*, September 28, 1892. Although the *Bee* appears to have garbled the quote, another reference to it can be found in Watkins, *History of Nebraska*, 244. Watkins notes that Edward Rosewater's *Bee* had previously depicted the candidate, Van Wyck, favorably, but the editor took offense at his remark. Watkins does not explain the matter further, but it is worth noting that Rosewater was a Jewish immigrant.

23. Dubin, *Gubernatorial Elections*, 78–79, 199, 359–360, 597; *Guide to U.S. Elections*, 1091–1095; Hicks, *Populist Revolt*, 238–273.

24. During the early years of statehood, this was a fairly typical outcome in Washington State. See Riddle, *Old Radicalism*, 136–137; Ficken, *Washington State*, 85–88.

25. Cherny, *Populism, Progressivism*, 37; Watkins, *History of Nebraska*, 231–237; *Laws, Joint Resolutions, and Memorials of the Legislature of the State of Nebraska, at the Twenty-Second Session* (Omaha, NE: Festner, 1891), 63–64, 214–216, 238–260, 361–362.

26. On Allen, see O. Gene Clanton, *Populism: The Humane Preference in America, 1890–1900* (Boston: Twayne, 1991), especially 103; O. Gene Clanton, *Congressional Populism and the Crisis of the 1890s* (Lawrence: University Press of Kansas, 1998), especially 11, 26, 35, 43, 52–53; David Wayne Hoelscher, "Genuine Populist: William V. Allen in the United States Senate, 1893–1901" (M.A. thesis, University of Nebraska at Omaha, 2003).

27. Watkins, *History of Nebraska*, 244–253; Cherny, *Populism, Progressivism*, 42–43; *Laws, Joint Resolutions, and Memorials Passed by the Legislative Assembly of the State of Nebraska, Twenty-Third Session* (Lincoln, NE: State Journal Company, 1893), 164–348, 403–404.

28. Fuller, "Populist Regime," 96–114; Wright, *Politics of Populism*, 162–166.

29. Welch, *Presidencies of Grover Cleveland*, 115–117; R. Hal Williams, *Realigning*

America: McKinley, Bryan, and the Remarkable Election of 1896 (Lawrence: University Press of Kansas, 2010), 25–28; Milton Friedman and Anna Jacobson Schwartz, *A Monetary History of the United States, 1867–1963* (1963; reprint, Princeton, NJ: Princeton University Press, 1993), 108–111.

30. Welch, *Presidencies of Grover Cleveland*, 116–118; Williams, *Realigning America*, 29–32. The desirability of repeal is still a matter of debate for some academics. For differing perspectives, see Friedman and Schwartz, *Monetary History*, 111; Richard Franklin Bensel, *The Political Economy of American Industrialization, 1877–1900* (New York: Cambridge University Press, 2000), 238.

31. Fuller, "Populist Regime," 132–135.

32. Henry M. Teller, "Traitorous," *Rocky Mountain News*, June 9, 1893, 1.

33. Clanton, *Congressional Populism*, 52–53, 60–61.

34. *Congressional Record*, 53rd Cong., 1st sess., October 7, 1893, 2260–2270.

35. Ibid., September 28, 1893, 1870–1873; ibid., October 2, 1893, 2004–2005. White sent Teller a letter and a news clipping that purported to demonstrate Seyd's whereabouts at the time. See Stephen M. White to H. M. Teller, October 15, 1893, box 1, FF 10, and box 5, FF 68, Henry M. Teller Papers, Colorado State Historical Society, Denver.

36. For material in this and the following paragraph, see Paolo E. Coletta, *William Jennings Bryan: Political Evangelist, 1860–1908* (Lincoln: University of Nebraska Press, 1964), 66–68, 72–73, 79–86; Louis W. Koenig, *Bryan: A Political Biography of William Jennings Bryan* (New York: G. P. Putnam's Sons, 1971), 72–73, 80–86, 97–100, 117–129; Michael Kazin, *A Godly Hero: The Life of William Jennings Bryan* (New York: Anchor Books, 2006), 26, 32, 34–40.

37. *Congressional Record*, 53rd Cong., 1st sess., August 16, 1893, 400–411.

38. Williams, *Realigning America*, 33–35; J. Rogers Hollingsworth, *The Whirligig of Politics: The Democracy of Cleveland and Bryan* (Chicago: University of Chicago Press, 1963), 17–18.

39. Welch, *Presidencies of Grover Cleveland*, 125–127.

40. Jameson, *All that Glitters*, 54–60. On the criticism of Waite, see Downing and Smith, *Tom Patterson*, 84–85.

41. Wright, *Politics of Populism*, 183–194.

42. Cherny, *Populism, Progressivism*, 44–45; Hicks, *Populist Revolt*, 328; Watkins, *History of Nebraska*, 256–260.

43. Riddle, *Old Radicalism*, 160–164; Ficken, *Washington State*, 185.

44. Several authors have suggested that the Populists were due to make gains in 1894 but their own ideas or voters' logical preference for Republican policies prevented it. For a few examples, see Richard Hofstadter, *The Age of Reform: From Bryan to F.D.R.* (New York: Vintage Books, 1955), 100–101; Robert H. Wiebe, *The Search for Order, 1877–1920* (New York: Hill & Wang, 1967), 90; Williams, *Realigning America*, 29, 37–44.

45. Dubin, *Gubernatorial Elections*, 79–80, 361–362; *Guide to U.S. Elections*, 1096–

1100; Wright, *Politics of Populism*, 195–197; Cherny, *Populism, Progressivism*, 46; Riddle, *Old Radicalism*, 168–169; Ficken, *Washington State*, 185.

46. *Laws, Joint Resolutions, and Memorials Passed by the Legislative Assembly of the State of Nebraska, Twenty-Fourth Session* (Omaha, NE: Omaha Printing Co., 1895), 57–62, 318–324; *Laws Passed at the Tenth Session of the General Assembly of the State of Colorado* (Denver: Smith-Brooks, 1895), 252.

47. "Capital Gossip," *Tacoma (WA) Daily News*, January 17, 1895, 1; *Session Laws of the State of Washington, Session of 1895* (Olympia, WA: O. C. White, 1895), 122–124; Riddle, *Old Radicalism*, 174–177.

48. "Thrilling Thurston," *McCook (NE) Tribune*, October 26, 1894, 1; "Thurston's Speech," *Columbus (NE) Journal*, October 31, 1894, 3; Cherny, *Populism, Progressivism*, 47.

49. "Open Insult," *Rocky Mountain News*, January 17, 1895, 1, 5; "Senator Wolcott," *Rocky Mountain News*, January 17, 1895, 4; Stephen J. Leonard and Thomas J. Noel, *Denver: Mining Camp to Metropolis* (Niwot: University Press of Colorado, 1990), 78.

50. "A Wilson Petition," *Tacoma Daily News*, January 18, 1895, 3; "Ankeny Is Ahead," *Tacoma Daily News*, January 23, 1895, 1; Ficken, *Washington State*, 185–186.

51. For several of those who attribute the movement's collapse to fusion, see note 2 above. On the importance of the monetary issue to Populism, see Postel, *Populist Vision*, 150–153; Bruce Palmer, *"Man over Money": The Southern Populist Critique of American Capitalism* (Chapel Hill: University of North Carolina Press, 1980), 81–82; Larson, *Populism in the Mountain West*, 147–159; Bensel, *Political Economy*, 134–138; Robert F. Durden, *The Climax of Populism: The Election of 1896* (Lexington: University of Kentucky Press, 1965), 7.

52. Jones, *Presidential Election of 1896*, 91, 95, 97–98.

53. Williams, *Realigning America*, 60–63; Jones, *Presidential Election of 1896*, 161–173.

54. On the situation leading up to the convention and the disposition of the delegates, see Richard Franklin Bensel, *Passion and Preferences: William Jennings Bryan and the 1896 Democratic National Convention* (New York: Cambridge University Press, 2008), 24–87.

55. For an interesting analysis of Bryan's use of the speech, see ibid., 222–247. For the speech itself, see William Jennings Bryan, *The First Battle: A Story of the Campaign of 1896* (Chicago: W. B. Conkey, 1896), 199–206.

56. It is worth repeating that the divide in the convention was sectional, not between radicals and conservatives, as some have claimed. See Durden, *Climax of Populism*, 22–31; James L. Hunt, *Marion Butler and American Populism* (Chapel Hill: University of North Carolina Press, 2003), 95–100; Jones, *Presidential Election of 1896*, 254.

57. Durden, *Climax of Populism*, 13–20, 31, 34–43; Hunt, *Marion Butler*, 95–97, 102–106, 123; Downing and Smith, *Tom Patterson*, 90. Allen's remarks during the

convention also show that he did not favor the total abandonment of other issues, as has been suggested. See "Allen Is Chairman," *Omaha (NE) World-Herald*, July 24, 1896, 6. For the claim that Allen had "no qualms" about dropping every other element of the platform, see Goodwyn, *Democratic Promise*, 426–427.

58. Jones, *Presidential Election of 1896*, 212–229, 244–275.

59. Durden, *Climax of Populism*, 73–74, 78–81; Watkins, *History of Nebraska*, 263–264; Riddle, *Old Radicalism*, 205–217.

60. Wright, *Politics of Populism*, 209–213.

61. Although many of these remarks could be found in the editorial pages of newspapers, antisilver statements more frequently appeared in the campaign supplements prepared by the national Republican campaign. For examples of antisilver declarations by Republicans, see "The M'Kinley Letter," *Columbus Journal*, September 16, 1896; "Would Not Benefit," *Islander* (Friday Harbor, WA), October 15, 1896, 3; "The Mortgaged Farm," *McCook Tribune*, August 28, 1896; "The Mortgaged Farm," *Islander*, September 24, 1896; "The Money Question," *Omaha Daily Bee*, August 1, 1896; "Wheat and Silver," *Pullman (WA) Herald*, October 10, 1896, 4; "From Bryan's Home," *Columbus Journal*, September 30, 1896; "Playing for a Big Stake," *Omaha Daily Bee*, October 17, 1896, 11.

62. "Queries for Bryan," *Columbus Journal*, September 9, 1896; "Free Silver Not Bimetallism," *McCook Tribune*, August 28, 1896.

63. "A Financial Calendar," *Colorado Springs Gazette*, September 27, 1896, 4; "Mr. Wolcott's Great Speech," *Colorado Springs Gazette*, October 1, 1896, 2. For another piece in favor of international agreement, see "Real vs. Sham Bimetallism," *Colorado Springs Gazette*, August 2, 1896, 4.

64. "Senator Wilson's Views," *Morning Olympian* (Portland, OR), July 20, 1896, 2. See also "Bimetallism in England," *Morning Olympian*, September 28, 1896, 2; "International Bimetallism," *Morning Olympian*, October 1, 1896, 2.

65. Speech, undated, box 4, FF 54, Teller Papers.

66. "Mr. McKinley's Speeches," *Yakima (WA) Herald*, August 20, 1896, 1, reprinted from the *American* (Philadelphia), date unknown.

67. For the votes, see Dubin, *Gubernatorial Elections*, 80–81, 122–123, 201–202, 349, 362–363, 495, 597–598; Edgar Eugene Robinson, *The Presidential Vote, 1896–1932* (1947; New York: Octagon Books, 1970), 46–53; *Guide to U.S. Elections*, 1101–1104. In the three states under examination here, the vote for Bryan was Colorado, 85 percent; Nebraska, 51.5 percent; and Washington, 55.2 percent.

68. For some of the major works dealing with the entrenched politics of these regions, see Ostler, *Prairie Populism*; Paul Kleppner, *The Cross of Culture: A Social Analysis of Midwestern Politics, 1850–1900* (New York: Free Press, 1970); Richard Jensen, *The Winning of the Midwest: Social and Political Conflict, 1888–1896* (Chicago: University of Chicago Press, 1971); Samuel McSeveney, *The Politics of Depression: Political Behavior in the Northeast, 1893–1896* (New York: Oxford University Press, 1972). On Bryan's

tour of the Midwest and East, see Coletta, *William Jennings Bryan*, 161–189; Kazin, *Godly Hero*, 67–78.

69. Coletta, *William Jennings Bryan*, 213–214; Koenig, *Bryan*, 259–260; Kazin, *Godly Hero*, 83–86.

70. On Marion Butler, see Durden, *Climax of Populism*, 156. For examples of this sentiment, see H. D. C., "Washington Letter," *Frontier County (NE) Faber*, November 26, 1896; *Gibbon (NE) Reporter*, June 10, 1897; "Voice of the People," *Independent* (Lincoln, NE), September 23, 1897, 2; "Plans for a New Party," *Fort Collins (CO) Courier*, March 18, 1897, 6, reprinted from *Times-Herald* (Chicago), date unknown; *Dawn* (Ellensburg, WA), November 18, December 23, 1898. In early 1898 former senator William Peffer was one of those who called for the formation of a new party of Populists, Silver Republicans, and Bryanite Democrats. See "Passing of the Populist Party," *Topeka (KS) Weekly Capital*, January 7, 1898, 8; "People Must Unite," *Aspen (CO) Daily Times*, January 14, 1898, 2. For a brief introduction to the southern Populists' struggle in 1896 and after, see C. Vann Woodward, *Tom Watson: Agrarian Rebel* (1938; reprint, New York: Oxford University Press, 1963), 302–353; Sheldon Hackney, *Populism to Progressivism in Alabama* (Princeton, NJ: Princeton University Press, 1969), 100–108; Connie L. Lester, *Up from the Mudsills of Hell: The Farmers' Alliance, Populism, and Progressive Agriculture in Tennessee, 1870–1915* (Athens: University Press of Georgia, 2006), 203–207; Hunt, *Marion Butler*, 107–123.

71. Nothing closely resembling the reforms advocated by the Populists, Farmers' Alliance, or organized labor was passed in the 1897 legislature, and there is no indication that much of an attempt was made to do so. See *Laws Passed at the Eleventh Session of the General Assembly of the State of Colorado* (Denver: Smith-Brooks, 1897), 286–296. For comments on the legislature, see "The Legislative Outlook," *Denver Post*, March 5, 1897, 4; "In Special Session," *Colorado Springs Gazette*, April 7, 1897, 1.

72. Riddle, *Old Radicalism*, 231–238. On Rogers, see "George Turner at Colfax," *Spokesman-Review* (Spokane, WA), July 5, 1894; Claudius O. Johnson, "George Turner, Part I: The Background of a Statesman," *Pacific Northwest Quarterly* 34, 3 (1943): 243–269.

73. For an overtly negative interpretation of the legislature, see Carroll H. Wooddy, "Populism in Washington: A Study of the Legislature of 1897," *Washington Historical Quarterly* 21, 2 (1930): 103–119. For better accounts, see Riddle, *Old Radicalism*, 234–239; Schwantes, *Radical Heritage*, 64.

74. For a general overview of the session, see James F. Pederson and Kenneth D. Wald, *Shall the People Rule: A History of the Democratic Party in Nebraska Politics* (Lincoln, NE: Jacob North, 1972), 134; Cherny, *Populism, Progressivism*, 80–81. On the antitrust laws (which other historians have largely ignored), see *Laws, Joint Resolutions, and Memorials of the Legislature of the State of Nebraska, at the Twenty-Fifth Session* (Lincoln, NE: State Journal Company, 1897), 461–462, 347–352, 352–354. The last of these laws included a provision that explicitly prevented its use against organized labor.

75. *House Journal of the Legislature of the State of Nebraska, Twenty-Fifth Regular Session* (Lincoln, NE: State Journal Company, 1897), 165–166. Addison Sheldon would go on to earn a Ph.D. and become one of the state's most prominent early historians.

76. A similar resolution appeared in the Washington State senate. See *Senate Journal of the Fifth Legislature of the State of Washington* (Olympia, WA: O. C. White, 1897), 235–236.

CHAPTER 3. THE MONEY POWER AND THE WAR OF 1898

1. *Congressional Record*, 55th Cong., 2nd sess., February 9, 1898, 1574–1577.

2. The fourteen western reformers in the Senate consisted of four Populists, five Silver Republicans, three Democrats, and two members of Nevada's Silver Party. In the House, they numbered sixteen Populists, three Silver Republicans, five Democrats, and one member of the Silver Party. Also, there were twelve Republican senators and ten Republican House members from the western states. See *Guide to U.S. Elections*, 6th ed. (Washington, DC: CQ Press, 2010).

3. J. Rogers Hollingsworth, *The Whirligig of Politics: The Democracy of Cleveland and Bryan* (Chicago: University of Chicago Press, 1963), 120–121.

4. *Statement of Hon. Lyman J. Gage, Secretary of the Treasury, before the Committee on Banking and Currency, in Explanation of the Bill H.R. 5181* (Washington, DC: Government Printing Office, 1897), 5.

5. *Speeches and Addresses of William McKinley* (New York: Doubleday & McClure, 1900), 2–16.

6. "Mr. Gage's Financial Views," *Omaha (NE) Daily Bee*, February 2, 1897, 4. See also "Wolcott Not Supported," *Rocky Mountain News* (Denver), February 6, 1897, 4; "What Does He Now Say?" *Seattle Weekly Times*, February 18, 1897, 4.

7. *Statement of Gage.*

8. "Mr. Gage's Currency Bill," *Omaha Daily Bee*, December 17, 1897, 4.

9. "The Issue Now Clear," *Yakima (WA) Herald*, February 10, 1898, 2.

10. *Congressional Record*, 55th Cong., 2nd sess., January 7, 1898, 418–423.

11. *Statement of Gage*, 6.

12. *Congressional Record*, 55th Cong., 2nd sess., January 5, 1898, 311. Nebraska's entire Populist House delegation entered its criticism of the administration's bond proposal, along with its defenses of greenback currency, into the appendix of the *Congressional Record*. See *Congressional Record*, 55th Cong., 2nd sess., appendix, 48–50, 127–128, 130–131, 131–135. James H. Lewis of Washington also introduced a concurrent resolution against "the retirement of greenbacks and issuance instead of gold-bearing bonds." See *Congressional Record*, 55th Cong., 2nd sess., February 5, 1898, 1486.

13. *Congressional Record*, 55th Cong., 2nd sess., January 7, 1898, 423–427.

14. Richard F. Pettigrew to F. T. Dubois, January 23, 1898, Richard F. Pettigrew Collection, microfilm edition, reel 20, Pettigrew Museum, Sioux Falls, SD.

15. The "whoop and holler" quote is from Robert Wiebe, and though not specific to the Populists, it was based on his interpretation of the demand for war by irrational (and rural) Americans. See Robert H. Wiebe, *The Search for Order, 1877–1920* (New York: Hill & Wang, 1967), 241. For another famous historian's interpretation of Americans' irrationality regarding the Cuban situation, see Richard Hofstadter, *The Age of Reform: From Bryan to F.D.R.* (New York: Vintage Books, 1955), 88–93; Richard Hofstadter, "Cuba, the Philippines, and Manifest Destiny," in *The Paranoid Style in American Politics, and Other Essays* (1952; reprint, Cambridge, MA: Harvard University Press, 1996), 145–187.

16. James B. Weaver, *A Call to Action: The Great Uprising, Its Source and Causes* (Des Moines: Iowa Printing Company, 1892), 280, 339–340; "A Kansas Cyclone," *Freeman* (Indianapolis), March 17, 1894, 6; "Watson Speaks at Lincoln," *Omaha (NE) World-Herald*, September 17, 1896, 5.

17. "In Most Vigorous Terms," *San Francisco Chronicle*, August 3, 1893, 1; "Closing of Indian Mint," *Silverite-Plaindealer* (Ouray, CO), March 20, 1896, 4; "England's Infamy," *Leader* (Loveland, CO), August 4, 1893, 7.

18. For some examples, see Worth Robert Miller, ed., *Populist Cartoons: An Illustrated History of the Third Party Movement of the 1890s* (Kirksville, MO: Truman State University Press, 2011), 143–148.

19. *Congressional Record*, 54th Cong., 1st sess., December 3, 1895, 25, December 4, 1895, 36–37.

20. Ibid., February 20, 1896, 1971–1972.

21. Louis A. Pérez Jr., *Cuba between Empires, 1878–1902* (Pittsburgh: University of Pittsburgh Press, 1983), 41, 43. For examples of the early coverage, see "Revolution Now in Cuba," *Daily Camera* (Boulder, CO), February 26, 1895, 1; *Herald Democrat* (Leadville, CO), February 27, 1895, 1; *Leadville (CO) Daily and Evening Chronicle*, February 27, 1895, 2; *Castle Rock (CO) Journal*, March 6, 1895, 3; *Silver Cliff (CO) Rustler*, March 6, 1895, 3.

22. "The Cruel Spaniard," *Herald Democrat* (Leadville, CO), August 24, 1895, 1; "Butcheries in Cuba," *Petersburg (NE) Index*, April 9, 1896.

23. John Lawrence Tone, *War and Genocide in Cuba, 1895–1898* (Chapel Hill: University of North Carolina Press, 2006), 193.

24. "Million Lives," *Spokane (WA) Daily Chronicle*, November 29, 1897, 7. On the population of Cuba, see *Report on the Census of Cuba, 1899* (Washington, DC: Government Printing Office, 1900), 72. This report estimates that 200,000 Cubans died in the conflict.

25. For the contention that xenophobia and pent-up frustrations led to the war, see Hofstadter, *Age of Reform*, 88–93; Hofstadter, "Cuba, the Philippines, and Manifest Destiny," 145–187. For the stereotypical accounts of the media, see Joseph E. Wisan, *The Cuban Crisis as Reflected in the New York Press (1895–1898)* (New York:

Columbia University Press, 1934); George W. Auxier, "Middle Western Newspapers and the Spanish American War, 1895-1898," *Mississippi Valley Historical Review* 26, 4 (1940): 523-534. Among those who argue that the war was intended to strengthen American economic power or international standing are Walter LaFeber, *New Empire: An Interpretation of American Expansion, 1860-1898* (Ithaca, NY: Cornell University Press, 1963), 400-406; William Appleman Williams, *The Roots of Modern American Empire: A Study of the Growth and Shaping of Social Consciousness in a Marketplace Society* (New York: Random House, 1969), 408-453; and Thomas Schoonover, *Uncle Sam's War of 1898 and the Origins of Globalization* (Lexington: University Press of Kentucky, 2003). Ernest May takes a middle-ground position in partial agreement with both common explanations of the war. See Ernest R. May, *Imperial Democracy: The Emergence of America as a Great Power* (1961; reprint, New York: Harper & Row, 1973).

26. Tone, *War and Genocide in Cuba*, 193-224.

27. "A National Disgrace," *Aspen (CO) Daily Times*, April 7, 1897, 2.

28. "Cuba and the Republican Platform," *Omaha (NE) World-Herald*, May 21, 1897, 4.

29. *Omaha World-Herald*, May 27, 1897, 4.

30. "Said by Mr. Harvey," *Pagosa (CO) Springs News*, September 6, 1895, 3.

31. *Aberdeen (WA) Herald*, February 11, 1897, 1. Similar remarks appeared in the December 23, 1897, edition.

32. *Aspen (CO) Tribune*, December 22, 1896, 2.

33. *Ouray (CO) Herald*, May 17, 1897, 2.

34. *Silverton (CO) Standard*, April 3, 1897, 10, reprinted from *Durango (CO) Wage Earner*, date unknown.

35. "The President and Cuba," *New York Times*, December 3, 1897. The patrols to stop filibustering expeditions from the United States to Cuba had been ongoing since the Cleveland administration. The patrols led to a tremendous amount of negative publicity for the government, but their effectiveness is a matter of some debate. See Tone, *War and Genocide in Cuba*, 82-86; Pérez, *Cuba between Empires*, 114-115.

36. *Congressional Record*, 55th Cong., 2nd sess., December 8, 1897, 39-40.

37. For one of the few secondary sources that notes the importance of Spain's bonds (if only in passing), see Philip S. Foner, *The Spanish-Cuban-American War and the Birth of American Imperialism, 1895-1902*, vol. 1 (New York: Monthly Review Press, 1972), 254-255.

38. "Prediction of Peace," *New York Times*, April 1, 1898; "Progress of Cuba's Rebellion," *Omaha Daily Bee*, July 2, 1895, 1.

39. Sarah E. V. Emery, *Seven Financial Conspiracies Which Have Enslaved the American People*, rev. ed. (Lansing, MI: Robert Smith, 1894). See also Gordon Clark, *Shylock: As Banker, Bondholder, Corruptionist, Conspirator* (Washington, DC: American Bimetallic League, 1894).

40. *Congressional Record*, 55th Cong., 2nd sess., January 20, 1898, 802-804.

41. Ibid., January 19, 1898, 763–764.

42. Ernest May notes the bonds and the reactions of the bondholders, but they are almost mentioned in passing, and he makes little reference to any perceived significance by Americans. See May, *Imperial Democracy*, 119, 123.

43. On the increasing volume of stories about the Spanish bonds, see Paul S. Holbo, "The Convergence of Moods and the Cuban-Bond 'Conspiracy' of 1898," *Journal of American History* 55, 1 (1968): 58–68. Frank Cannon claimed he read the story in a newspaper that usually took a pro-administration, anti-Cuba position. For the resolution, see *Congressional Record*, 55th Cong., 2nd sess., February 8, 1898, 1543; for the remarks, see ibid., February 9, 1898, 1574–1577.

44. *Congressional Record*, 55th Cong., 2nd sess., March 24, 1898, 3162–3165; H. Wayne Morgan, *William McKinley and His America* (Syracuse, NY: Syracuse University Press, 1963), 210.

45. *Congressional Record*, 55th Cong., 2nd sess., April 5, 1898, 3545–3546.

46. Ibid., March 31, 1898, 3433–3434.

47. Ibid., April 4, 1898, 3497–3499. For similar remarks by Senator Clarence Clark, a Wyoming Republican, see ibid., April 16, 1898, 3966–3968. On the Republican shift following the *Maine* report, see John Offner, *An Unwanted War: The Diplomacy of the United States and Spain over Cuba, 1895–1898* (Chapel Hill: University of North Carolina Press, 1992), 127–128, 150–154.

48. *Congressional Record*, 55th Cong., 2nd sess., April 11, 1898, 3699–3702; Lewis L. Gould, *The Presidency of William McKinley* (Lawrence: University Press of Kansas, 1980), 84–86; David F. Trask, *The War with Spain in 1898* (Lincoln: University of Nebraska Press, 1981), 52–54.

49. *Congressional Record*, 55th Cong., 2nd sess., April 11, 1898, 3702–3703.

50. Ibid., April 12, 1898, appendix, 279–281.

51. Morgan, *William McKinley*, 408–409.

52. "Spain's Impossible Demands," *New York Times*, October 20, 1898; "The Question of Spanish Bonds," *New York Times*, November 9, 1898.

53. *Congressional Record*, 55th Cong., 2nd sess., April 16, 1898, 3944–3945.

54. Ibid., April 19, 1898, 4069.

55. Ibid., March 31, 1898, 3433–3434.

56. Ibid., April 19, 1898, 4069.

57. According to historian Philip Foner, members of the Cuban junta were negotiating with a syndicate of major American bankers to secure the purchase of Cuban independence. See Foner, *Spanish-Cuban-American War*, 220–222.

58. "New Plan of Sugar Trust," *Omaha Daily Bee*, June 22, 1897, 5; "Cockran for Cuba's Liberty," *Omaha Daily Bee*, November 28, 1896, 1.

59. Holbo, "Convergence of Moods," 54–72.

60. *Congressional Record*, 55th Cong., 2nd sess., March 31, 1898, 3410–3413.

61. Ibid., April 16, 1898, 3954; Morgan, *William McKinley*, 378; Trask, *War with Spain*, 55–58. For the motivation behind Teller's amendment, see Holbo, "Conver-

gence of Moods," 68–69; Pérez, *Cuba between Empires*, 186; Duane A. Smith, *Henry Teller: Colorado's Grand Old Man* (Boulder: University Press of Colorado, 2002), 217.

62. There was much talk of sectional and political reconciliation at the time. See Nina Silber, *The Romance of Reunion: Northerners and the South, 1865–1900* (Chapel Hill: University of North Carolina Press, 1993), 178–185; David W. Blight, *Race and Reunion: The Civil War in American Memory* (Cambridge, MA: Harvard University Press, 2001), 346–354.

63. *Congressional Record*, 55th Cong., 2nd sess., April 27, 1898, 4296–4299.

64. Ibid., April 29, 1898, appendix, 358–360.

65. Ibid., May 25, 1898, 5178–5182; ibid., June 3, 1898, 5449–5450, 5452–5453.

66. Ibid., April 29, 1898, appendix, 358–360.

67. Ibid., April 29, 1898, 4437.

68. Ibid., May 3, 1898, 4538–4539.

69. Ibid., April 29, 1898, 4434–4436.

70. Ibid., April 28, 1898, 4395–4400.

71. Emery, *Seven Financial Conspiracies*, especially 11–26; Clark, *Shylock*, especially 29–52.

72. *Congressional Record*, 55th Cong., 2nd sess., April 28, 1898, 4407–4409.

73. Emery, *Seven Financial Conspiracies*, 18–24.

74. *Congressional Record*, 55th Cong., 2nd sess., April 27, 1898, 4323–4326.

75. The silver seigniorage consisted of the difference between the value of a dollar of silver and the actual amount of silver in a coined dollar. The Treasury had built up large reserves when the price of silver plummeted in the 1890s. See Richard Franklin Bensel, *The Political Economy of American Industrialization: 1877–1900* (New York: Cambridge University Press, 2000), 413.

76. *Congressional Record*, 55th Cong., 2nd sess., April 27, 1898, 4308–4309.

77. Ibid., May 25, 1898, 5178–5182.

78. Ibid., May 27, 1898, 5272–5278.

79. Ibid., June 3, 1898, 5454–5458. For Wolcott's role in the bimetallic commission, see Morgan, *William McKinley*, 282–285.

80. *Congressional Record*, 55th Cong., 2nd sess., April 28, 1898, appendix, 709–714, 349–352; White's remarks are in ibid., May 26, 1898, appendix, 502–507.

81. Ibid., April 29, 1898, appendix, 416–418; ibid., May 26, 1898, appendix, 502–507.

82. Ibid., April 28, 1898, 4395–4400; ibid., appendix, 349–352.

83. Ibid., May 20, 1898, 5080–5083.

84. Ibid., June 1, 1898, 5396.

85. Ibid., June 4, 1898, 5518.

86. Ibid., June 1, 1898, 5396–5397; ibid., June 4, 1898, 5517–5518.

87. Ibid., June 4, 1898, 5531–5533.

88. War Revenue Bill of 1898, *United States Statutes at Large* XXX (1899): 448–470.

89. *Congressional Record*, 55th Cong., 2nd sess., June 9, 1898, 5727; ibid., June 10,

1898, 5749; Thomas A. Clinch, *Urban Populism and Free Silver in Montana: A Narrative of Ideology in Political Action* (Missoula: University of Montana Press, 1970), 162; R. Alton Lee, *Principle over Party: The Farmers' Alliance and Populism in South Dakota, 1880–1900* (Pierre: South Dakota State Historical Society Press, 2011), 139–143.

CHAPTER 4. HAWAIIAN ANNEXATION AND THE BEGINNING
OF THE DEBATE OVER EMPIRE

1. *Congressional Record*, 55th Cong., 2nd sess., May 4, 1898, 4600.

2. Lewis L. Gould, *The Presidency of William McKinley* (Lawrence: University Press of Kansas, 1980), 98.

3. *Congressional Record*, 55th Cong., 2nd sess., April 29, 1898, appendix, 416–418.

4. Newlands and Stewart were clearly competition with each other by 1898, and the rivalry only intensified. See Russell R. Elliot, *Servant of Power: A Political Biography of William M. Stewart* (Reno: University of Nevada Press, 1983), especially 195–215.

5. "Pettigrew's Indian Policy," *Aberdeen (SD) Weekly News*, April 7, 1892, 2; "On Behalf of the Indians," *New Haven (CT) Register*, February 15, 1892, 2; Richard F. Pettigrew, *Triumphant Plutocracy: The Story of American Public Life from 1870s to 1920* (New York: Academy Press, 1921), 288–289; Judith A. Boughter, *Betraying the Omaha Nation, 1790–1916* (Norman: University of Oklahoma Press, 1998), 149–152; *Congressional Record*, 53rd Cong., 2nd sess., July 19, 1894, 7679–7682.

6. Noenoe K. Silva, *Aloha Betrayed: Native Hawaiian Resistance to American Colonialism* (Durham, NC: Duke University Press, 2004), 24–122, 129–130, 167; Eric Love, *Race over Empire: Racism and U.S. Imperialism, 1865–1900* (Chapel Hill: University of North Carolina Press, 2004), 73–114; E. Berkeley Tompkins, *Anti-Imperialism in the United States: The Great Debate, 1890–1900* (Philadelphia: University of Pennsylvania Press, 1970), 27–62; William Michael Morgan, *Pacific Gibraltar: US-Japanese Rivalry over the Annexation of Hawaii, 1885–1898* (Annapolis, MD: Naval Institute Press, 2011).

7. *Congressional Record*, 53rd Cong., 2nd sess., February 21, 1894, appendix, 470–486.

8. Ibid., July 2, 1894, 7069–7070. For another example of his opposition to actions he considered precursors to annexation, see Love, *Race over Empire*, 121–124.

9. *Congressional Record*, 53rd Cong., 2nd sess., May 24, 1894, 5193, and May 29, 1894, 5434–5435.

10. *Congressional Record*, 53rd Cong., 3rd sess., January 25, 1895, 1329.

11. *Congressional Record*, 53rd Cong., 2nd sess., January 29, 1894, 1578–1579.

12. Tompkins, *Anti-Imperialism in the United States*, 61.

13. Gould, *Presidency of William McKinley*, 48–49. For more on the increasingly common view of Japan as a threat, see Morgan, *Pacific Gibraltar*, 188–197.

14. *Congressional Record*, 55th Cong., 2nd sess., February 3, 1898, 1394, and February 7, 1898, 1495–1496.

15. Richard Pettigrew to Toru Hoshi, undated (but likely January 1898), Richard F. Pettigrew Collection, microfilm edition, reel 20, Pettigrew Museum, Sioux Falls, SD. Through Hoshi, the government of Japan repeatedly denied any interest in acquiring the islands. On the Japanese response, see David F. Trask, *The War with Spain in 1898* (Lincoln: University of Nebraska Press, 1981), 388.

16. *Congressional Record*, 55th Cong., 2nd sess., December 17, 1897, 240, and January 24, 1898, 908; Richard Pettigrew to Fred T. Dubois, January 29, 1898, and Richard Pettigrew to Joseph O. Carter, undated (but likely January 1898), Pettigrew Collection, reel 20; Merze Tate, *The United States and the Hawaiian Kingdom: A Political History* (New Haven, CT: Yale University Press, 1965), 322.

17. On the petitions, see Silva, *Aloha Betrayed*, 145–163. The exact fate of the petition given to Senator Pettigrew remains a mystery.

18. There is near consensus that the "necessity of war" argument carried some weight in the summer of 1898. See Tompkins, *Anti-Imperialism in the United States*, 103–108; Love, *Race over Empire*, 148–158; Morgan, *Pacific Gibraltar*, 225–230. Thomas Osborne saw this argument as a red herring, but the simple truth is, regardless of facts, it was mentioned repeatedly by members whose opinion of annexation had changed. See Thomas J. Osborne, *"Empire Can Wait": American Opposition to Hawaiian Annexation, 1893–1898* (Kent, OH: Kent State University Press, 1981), 121–126.

19. *Congressional Record*, 53rd Cong., 3rd sess., March 2, 1895, 3082–3084. On Lodge and Hawaii, see Morgan, *Pacific Gibraltar*, 172–177.

20. Morgan's statements in this and the following paragraph are from "Senator Morgan's Views," *New York Times*, February 3, 1898, 1.

21. *Congressional Record*, 53rd Cong., 3rd sess., January 22, 1895, 1210–1211.

22. For claims that the Sino-Japanese War led to widespread recognition of Japan as a great power, see S. C. M. Paine, *The Sino-Japanese War of 1894–1895: Perceptions, Power, and Primacy* (New York: Cambridge University Press, 2003).

23. *Congressional Record*, 53rd Cong., 3rd sess., January 21, 1895, 1172, and March 2, 1895, 3107–3108. On a perceived Japanese threat, see Morgan, *Pacific Gibraltar*, 188–197; Gould, *Presidency of William McKinley*, 48–49; Love, *Race over Empire*, 114–148.

24. *Congressional Record*, 55th Cong., 2nd sess., June 14, 1898, 5910–5913.

25. Ibid., 5927.

26. Ibid., 5911–5913, 5927.

27. Ibid., June 13, 1898, 5828–5831. Congressman Marion De Vries, a California Democrat, demonstrated a similar perspective in his entry in ibid., June 14, 1898, appendix, 655–666.

28. Ibid., June 27, 1898, 6366–6370.

29. For Teller's opinions in this and the following paragraphs, see ibid., June 25, 1898, 6346–6348. For more of his opinions about the history of expansion and Jefferson in particular, see ibid., June 27, 1898, 6367, 6372, and July 1, 1898, 6586–6587.

30. *Congressional Record*, 53rd Cong., 2nd sess., January 29, 1894, 1578–1579.

31. See Carl Schurz, *Speeches, Correspondence and Political Papers of Carl Schurz*, ed. Frederic Bancroft (New York: G. P. Putnam's Sons, 1913), 5:191–214.

32. Nearly all westerners who spoke in opposition to Hawaiian annexation included references to the other colonies their rivals proposed to take next. For Shafroth's and White's comments, see *Congressional Record*, 55th Cong., 2nd sess., June 14, 1898, appendix, 633–637, and July 6, 1898, appendix, 603–619, respectively.

33. Among those that pointed to American possession of Pearl Harbor were Senators William V. Allen, Stephen White, and William Roach (a North Dakota Democrat) and Congressman John Shafroth. For Allen, see *Congressional Record*, 55th Cong., 2nd sess., July 6, 1898, 6702–6707; for White, see ibid., appendix, 603–619; for Roach, see ibid., June 27, 1898, 6357–6363; for Shafroth, see ibid., June 14, 1898, appendix, 633–637.

34. *Congressional Record*, 55th Cong., 2nd sess., June 23, 1898, 6258–6268.

35. Ibid., June 27, 1898, 6357–6363.

36. Ibid., July 6, 1898, 6702–6707.

37. Ibid., appendix, 603–619.

38. Ibid.

39. Ibid., June 14, 1898, appendix, 633–637.

40. Ibid., June 13, 1898, 5832–5835.

41. Ibid., July 4, 1898, 6634–6637, 6639–6651.

42. Ibid., June 21, 1898, appendix, 590–603.

43. Ibid., June 23, 1898, 6258–6268.

44. Ibid., June 13, 1898, 5832–5835.

45. Ibid. On anti-expansionists and their alternative deployment of masculine language, see Kristin Hoganson, *Fighting for American Manhood: How Gender Politics Provoked the Spanish-American and Philippine-American Wars* (New Haven, CT: Yale University Press, 1998), 167–172, 193–196.

46. *Congressional Record*, 55th Cong., 2nd sess., June 27, 1898, 6369–6370.

47. Ibid., June 14, 1898, appendix, 633–637.

48. For Bell's remarks in this and the following paragraph, see ibid., June 13, 1898, 5832–5835.

49. For Roach's remarks, see ibid., June 27, 1898, 6357–6363. For Allen's remarks, see ibid., July 6, 1898, 6702–6707.

50. Ibid., June 14, 1898, appendix, 633–637; June 27, 1898, 6357–6363; June 13, 1898, 5832–5835; July 6, 1898, 6693–6702.

51. Ibid., July 6, 1898, 6702–6707.

52. Richard Pettigrew to L. C. Campbell, January 31, 1898, Pettigrew Collection, reel 20.

53. For Pettigrew's remarks on Japanese civilization and Hawaiians, see *Congressional Record*, 55th Cong., 2nd sess., June 22, 1898, 6229–6232, and July 6, 1898, 6693–6702.

54. The following paragraphs covering Pettigrew's speech are based on ibid., June 22, 1898, 6229-6232.

55. Ibid., July 4, 1898, 6634-6637, 6639-6651.

56. This paragraph and the one that follows are based on ibid., July 6, 1898, 6702-6707.

57. This paragraph and the one that follows are based on ibid., June 13, 1898, 5832-5835.

58. For Asian laborers in America, see Tomas Almaguer, *Racial Fault Lines: The Historical Origins of White Supremacy in California* (Berkeley: University of California Press, 1994), especially 153-204; Cletus E. Daniel, *Bitter Harvest: A History of California Farmworkers, 1870-1941* (Ithaca, NY: Cornell University Press, 1981), 27-74; Matthew Frye Jacobson, *Barbarian Virtues: The United States Encounters Foreign Peoples at Home and Abroad, 1876-1917* (New York: Hill & Wang, 2000), 74-88; Roger Daniels, *Guarding the Golden Door: American Immigration Policy and Immigrants since 1882* (New York: Hill & Wang, 2004), 3-26.

59. Congressman Charles Hartman of Montana had remarks placed in the *Congressional Record* that attributed the push for annexation to the money power, but there is no evidence the speech was ever delivered. See *Congressional Record*, 55th Cong., 2nd sess., June 11, 1898, appendix, 540-545.

60. Ibid., June 15, 1898, 6019.

61. Robert L. Beisner, *Twelve against Empire: The Anti-Imperialists, 1898-1900* (New York: McGraw-Hill, 1968), 148-150.

62. *Congressional Record*, 55th Cong., 2nd sess., July 6, 1898, 6693-6702.

63. Ibid., 6712.

CHAPTER 5. PATRIOTISM AND THE ELECTIONS OF 1898

1. Richard F. Pettigrew to H. L. Loucks, January 29, February 16, March 1, 1898, Richard F. Pettigrew Collection, microfilm edition, reel 20, Pettigrew Museum, Sioux Falls, SD. On Loucks's return to Republican Party, see R. Alton Lee, *Principle over Party: The Farmers' Alliance and Populism in South Dakota* (Pierre: South Dakota State Historical Society Press, 2011), 154.

2. Richard F. Pettigrew to U. S. G. Cherry, January 28, 1898, and Richard F. Pettigrew to L. C. Campbell, January 31, 1898, Pettigrew Collection, reel 20.

3. Richard F. Pettigrew to Thomas H. Ayres, January 21, 1898, ibid.; Richard F. Pettigrew to S. A. Cochran, June 2, 1898, and Richard F. Pettigrew to C. B. Kennedy, June 8, 1898, ibid., reel 21. The last two letters suggest that Pettigrew's goal was not just to create a single state party dedicated to reform. He seems to have believed that the same situation was playing out nationally.

4. Richard F. Pettigrew to Everitt Smith, January 20, 1898, ibid., reel 20.

5. Richard F. Pettigrew to U. S. G. Cherry, April 2 and 11, 1898, ibid.

6. Although he tried to remain confident about the state campaign, he told a confidant that he expected victory "unless the war upsets our calculations." See Richard F. Pettigrew to Alfred N. Coe, June 8, 1898, ibid., reel 21.

7. He sent a similar message to another regular correspondent on the same day. See Richard F. Pettigrew to U. S. Cherry and Richard F. Pettigrew to Andrew E. Lee, June 20, 1898, ibid.

8. Richard F. Pettigrew to Andrew E. Lee, June 27, 1898, ibid.

9. "Appeal for a Silver Union," *Omaha (NE) Daily Bee*, February 16, 1898, 7.

10. "The Issue Now Clear," *Yakima (WA) Herald*, February 10, 1898, 2.

11. *Congressional Record*, 55th Cong., 2nd sess., January 7, 1898, 418–423.

12. "Republican Mockery," *New Castle (CO) Nonpareil*, February 24, 1898, 4, reprinted from *Denver Times*, date unknown.

13. "Colorado Springs Patriots," *Durango (CO) Wage Earner*, March 31, 1898, 1.

14. *Congressional Record*, 55th Cong., 2nd sess., May 26, 1898, 5210–5215.

15. Ibid., April 28, 1898, 4375. For similar comments from Jerry Simpson, see ibid., 4395–4400.

16. Ibid., April 29, 1898, appendix, 358–360.

17. Ibid., 4437.

18. "Criticism," *Yakima (WA) Herald*, April 28, 1898, 4.

19. *Rocky Mountain News* (Denver), May 9, 1898, 5.

20. *Omaha (NE) World-Herald*, May 5, 1898, 4.

21. *Omaha Daily Bee*, April 28, 1898, 4, and May 18, 1898, 4.

22. From the *Omaha Daily Bee*, see "No Call for a Bond Issue," April 29, 1898, 4; "Not a Popular Loan," May 4, 1898, 4; "The Plea for a Bond Issue," May 8, 1898, 12. The *Bee* was, on certain rare occasions, an unorthodox Republican paper. A more strictly partisan paper presented the bill in much the same way, stating, "Although these bonds will only pay three per cent interest, the big financiers are so certain that they will soon command a premium that they will gladly take them all." See *Red Cloud (NE) Chief*, June 17, 1898, 1. Another thoroughly partisan paper, the *Spokane (WA) Chronicle*, made no reference at all to the war revenue bill in its opinion pages, and its overall coverage was minimal.

23. *Congressional Record*, 55th Cong., 2nd sess., June 14, 1898, 5910–5913.

24. Ibid., 5927.

25. Ibid., June 11, 1898, appendix, 535–537. There is no evidence the speech was read aloud in Congress.

26. Ibid., June 15, 1898, 5989–5990.

27. *Morning Oregonian* (Portland), June 24, 1898, 4.

28. Both can be found in the *Yakima Herald*, June 16, 1898, 4. "Stand by the President" was taken from the *Cincinnati Enquirer*, date unknown.

29. Paolo E. Coletta, *William Jennings Bryan: Political Evangelist, 1860–1908* (Lin-

coln: University of Nebraska Press, 1964), 223–224; Gerald F. Linderman, *The Mirror of War: American Society and the Spanish-American War* (Ann Arbor: University of Michigan Press, 1974), 60–64.

30. Coletta, *William Jennings Bryan*, 226.

31. David F. Trask, *The War with Spain in 1898* (Lincoln: University of Nebraska Press, 1981), 382–387; Brian McAllister Linn, *The Philippine War, 1899–1902* (Lawrence: University Press of Kansas, 2000), 6–15; Stuart Creighton Miller, *"Benevolent Assimilation": The American Conquest of the Philippines, 1899–1903* (New Haven, CT: Yale University Press, 1982), 42–44.

32. William V. Allen to William Jennings Bryan, May 18, 1898, and Jeremiah Botkin to William Jennings Bryan, May 18, 1898, William Jennings Bryan Papers, box 21, Manuscript Division, Library of Congress, Washington, DC. These warnings and others like them were also mentioned in Bryan's biographies. See Coletta, *William Jennings Bryan*, 223; Louis W. Koenig, *Bryan: A Political Biography of William Jennings Bryan* (New York: G. P. Putnam's Sons, 1971), 273–274; Michael Kazin, *A Godly Hero: The Life of William Jennings Bryan* (New York: Anchor Books, 2006), 87.

33. Richard F. Pettigrew to Charles A. Towne, April 26, 1898, Pettigrew Collection, reel 21.

34. For one of the first of these letters, see Richard F. Pettigrew to Jonas Lien, May 20, 1898, ibid. For more on Lien, see Dana R. Bailey, *History of Mennehaha County, South Dakota* (Sioux Falls, SD: Brown & Saenger, 1899), 602–605.

35. Geoffrey R. Hunt, *Colorado's Volunteer Infantry in the Philippine Wars, 1898–1899* (Albuquerque: University of New Mexico Press, 2006), 49. Johnson also authored the regiment's official history. See Arthur C. Johnson, *Official History of the Operation of the First Colorado Infantry, U.S.V., in the Campaign in the Philippine Islands* (San Francisco: Hicks-Judd, 1899).

36. For a description of Ballaine and his involvement with the regiment, see William L. Luhn, *Official History of the Operations of the First Washington Infantry, U.S.V., in the Campaign in the Philippine Islands* (San Francisco: Hicks-Judd, 1899), 4, 114.

37. *Independent* (Lincoln, NE), May 19, 1898, 3. Eager wrote the official regimental history, which contains a brief biographical section. See Frank Eager, *History of the Operations of the First Nebraska Infantry, U.S.V., in the Campaign in the Philippine Islands* (San Francisco: Hicks-Judd, 1899), 49.

38. Linn, *Philippine War*, 6–15; Miller, *Benevolent Assimilation*, 42–44.

39. H. Wayne Morgan, *William McKinley and His America* (Syracuse, NY: Syracuse University Press, 1963), 387–389, 402–411; Lewis L. Gould, *The Presidency of William McKinley* (Lawrence: University Press of Kansas, 1980), 113–119, 131–135.

40. "What of the Philippines?" *Morning Oregonian*, May 9, 1898, 4; "Out of the Rut," *Morning Oregonian*, May 12, 1898, 4; "Our Permanent Advantage," *Morning Oregonian*, May 14, 1898, 4.

41. "George Washington's Advice," *Seattle Post-Intelligencer*, June 5, 1898, 4.

42. For coverage in the *Omaha Daily Bee*, see "Occupation of Philippines," May

4, 1898, 4; "Threatening Conditions in Europe," May 12, 1898, 4; "World Power a Costly Luxury," May 18, 1898, 4.

43. For coverage by two of the most important reform papers in Nebraska, see "Lest We Forget," *Independent*, May 5, 1898, 4; "Cost of Killing," *Independent*, May 26, 1898, 4; "Empire Can Wait," *Omaha World-Herald*, June 12, 1898, 4.

44. "Shadow of Coming Events," *Spokesman-Review* (Spokane, WA), May 19, 1898, 4. For a sample of others, see "We May Need Them," *Durango Wage Earner*, June 9, 1898, 2; "The Philippine Islands," *Aspen (CO) Daily Times*, July 16, 1898, 3; The Future of America," *Rocky Mountain News*, May 16, 1898, 4; "New National Policy," *Rocky Mountain News*, May 6, 1898, 4; "Shadow of Coming Events," *Spokesman-Review*, May 19, 1898, 4.

45. On Populism and boosterism, see Charles Postel, *The Populist Vision* (New York: Oxford University Press, 2007), 25–44.

46. "Platform and Policy," *Independent*, July 14, 1898, 3; "True Populist Policy," *Independent*, July 21, 1898, 3.

47. "What Shall We Do with the Philippines?" *Denver Post*, May 6, 1898, 5. See also "The Imperial Idea in Colorado," *Greely (CO) Tribune*, July 14, 1898, 4.

48. Linn, *Philippine War*, 13–15; Miller, *Benevolent Assimilation*, 40–42.

49. William Jennings Bryan, "First Speech against Imperialism," in *Republic or Empire? The Philippine Question*, ed. William Jennings Bryan (Chicago: Independence Company, 1899), 10–13.

50. Michael Patrick Cullinane, *Liberty and American Anti-Imperialism, 1898–1909* (New York: Palgrave Macmillan, 2012), 18–20; E. Berkeley Tompkins, *Anti-Imperialism in the United States: The Great Debate, 1890–1920* (Philadelphia: University of Pennsylvania Press, 1970), 120–126.

51. Trask, *War with Spain*, 411–422; Miller, *Benevolent Assimilation*, 43–46; Linn, *Philippine War*, 23–25.

52. *Session Laws of the State of Washington: Session of 1897* (Olympia, WA: O. C. White, 1897), 92, 225–226.

53. Melvyn Dubovsky, "The Origins of Western Working Class Radicalism, 1890–1905," *Labor History* 7, 2 (1966): 139–144; David Brundage, *The Making of Western Labor Radicalism: Denver's Organized Workers, 1878–1905* (Chicago: University of Illinois Press, 1994), 122–123; John P. Enyeart, *The Quest for "Just and Pure Law": Rocky Mountain Workers and American Social Democracy, 1870–1924* (Stanford, CA: Stanford University Press, 2009), 112–113.

54. Morgan, *William McKinley*, 285.

55. For an interesting discussion of the decision and its impact, see Gerald Berk, *Alternative Tracks: The Constitution of American Industrial Order, 1865–1917* (Baltimore: Johns Hopkins University Press, 1994), 156–158.

56. *Congressional Record*, 55th Cong., 2nd sess., March 4, 1898, 2460–2463.

57. "The Maximum Rate Decision," *Independent*, March 10, 1898, 4.

58. See "Maximum Rate Case," *Independent*, March 10, 1898, 1; "Beaten by the

Board," *Independent*, March 17, 1898, 1; "Regulation a Failure," *Independent*, April 7, 1898, 1.

59. "Gov. Pingree's Effort," *Grand Forks (ND) Daily Herald*, July 16, 1897, 2; *Omaha Daily Bee*, December 23, 1897, 2; "Pingree Pleased," *Idaho Statesman* (Boise), March 1, 1898, 2; *Aberdeen (SD) Daily News*, March 11, 1898, 2.

60. "Republican Party's Peril," *New York Times*, February 3, 1898.

61. "Poynter for Governor," *Omaha Daily Bee*, August 3, 1898, 1, 4; Robert W. Cherny, *Populism, Progressivism, and the Transformation of Nebraska Politics, 1885–1915* (Lincoln: University of Nebraska Press, 1981), 77–80.

62. US Works Progress Administration, *Nebraska Party Platforms, 1858–1940* (Lincoln, NE, 1940), 232–237, 239–241.

63. Thomas Riddle, *The Old Radicalism: John R. Rogers and the Populist Movement in Washington* (New York: Garland, 1991), 251–253; Winston B. Thorson, "Washington State Nominating Conventions," *Pacific Northwest Quarterly* 35, 2 (1944): 106–107; "Agreement Reached," *Tacoma (WA) Daily News*, September 8, 1898, 1; "Populists Give Way," *Tacoma Daily News*, September 9, 1898, 1; John C. Putnam, *Class and Gender Politics in Progressive-Era Seattle* (Reno: University of Nevada Press, 2008), 89–90.

64. "Political Fight at Colorado Springs Begins in a Tragedy," *Denver Times*, September 7, 1898, 1; "There Is Blood on the Wolcott Banner," *Rocky Mountain News*, September 8, 1898, 1; "Teller Seems to Be on Top," *Denver Post*, September 1, 1898, 3; "Broad Shows His Hand against Teller," *Denver Post*, September 6, 1898, 1.

65. "A Trinity of Conventions," *Denver Post*, September 9, 1898, 1; *Rocky Mountain News*, September 11, 1898, 1, 3–6, 12; James Edward Wright, *The Politics of Populism: Dissent in Colorado* (New Haven, CT: Yale University Press, 1974), 216–218. On Charles S. Thomas's complicated views of labor, see Wright, *Politics of Populism*, 217; Brundage, *Making of Western Labor Radicalism*, 102, 140–141.

66. "Populists Called to Order," *Omaha World-Herald*, August 3, 1898, 2.

67. "Thurston on War Issues," *Omaha Daily Bee*, August 9, 1898, 1. Just a week after the fusion conventions, the Republican convention also chose to make no statement regarding the acquisition of territories. See US Works Progress Administration, *Nebraska Party Platforms*, 238–239.

68. See William L. Greene's comments in *Congressional Record*, 55th Cong., 3rd sess., January 24, 1899, 1006–1012.

69. On Rogers's views, see John Rankin Rogers to W. R. Hearst, June 20, 1898, and "A Proclamation by the Governor," August 27, 1898, John Rankin Rogers Papers, Washington State Archives, Olympia; Riddle, *Old Radicalism*, 250.

70. "Denver Democrats on the So-Called Policy of Imperialism," *Denver Post*, July 7, 1898, 3; "The Imperial Idea in Colorado," *Greeley (CO) Tribune*, July 14, 1898, 4.

71. For just a few examples, see "Not a Campaign Issue," *Seattle Daily Times*, August 20, 1898, 4; "Col. Lewis' Arraignment of the Men in Authority," *Seattle Daily Times*, September 3, 1898, 4; "Success! Success!" *Seattle Daily Times*, September 8,

1898, 2; "The Campaign Is Opened," *Yakima Herald*, October 6, 1898, 1; "Issues of the Day," *Spokesman-Review*, October 18, 1898, 5; "Against a Vicious Policy," *Omaha World-Herald*, October 22, 1898, 1; "Murder of Soldiers," *Independent*, September 1, 1898, 4; "Democrats for Congress," *Western News-Democrat* (Valentine, NE), October 27, 1898, 3; "Inside Story of a Military Wrong," *Rocky Mountain News*, October 20, 1898, 8.

72. "Currency the Issue," *Aberdeen (WA) Herald*, October 6, 1898, 4.

73. "Rothschild and Hanna," *Western News-Democrat*, October 6, 1898, 2.

74. "Senator Turner Speaks to an Enthusiastic Audience," *Spokesman-Review*, November 8, 1898, 1.

75. "Will He Stay in the Race?" *Denver Post*, September 23, 1898, 1, 3; "Guggenheim Quits," *Colorado Springs Gazette*, October 8, 1898, 1; "No More Pretense," *Greely Tribune*, October 27, 1898, 4. For those who argued that McKinley and silver could be reconciled, see "Charles A. Wilkin's Friendship for Silver," *Fairplay (CO) Flume*, October 28, 1898, 2; *Fort Collins (CO) Courier*, November 3, 1898, 4; "An Honest Campaign," *Colorado Springs Gazette*, October 24, 1898, 4. See also Wright, *Politics of Populism*, 216–217.

76. The historians of Washington State have been particularly wedded to the idea that "prosperity" destroyed Populism. See Riddle, *Old Radicalism*, 231–232; Robert E. Ficken, *Washington State: The Inaugural Decade, 1889–1899* (Pullman: Washington State University Press, 2007), 215–230; Putnam, *Class and Gender Politics*, 25. For others, see John D. Hicks, *The Populist Revolt: A History of the Farmers' Alliance and the People's Party*, 3rd ed. (Lincoln: University of Nebraska Press, 1961), 388–389; Robert F. Durden, *The Climax of Populism: The Election of 1896* (Lexington: University of Kentucky Press, 1965), 163.

77. For one very good example, see the Republican campaign speeches presented in "Rousing Republican Rally," *Omaha Daily Bee*, November 3, 1898, 1.

78. *Pullman (WA) Herald*, November 5, 1898, 10. In a similar speech, a Republican legislative candidate said that although the party might not have a direct hand in creating better crop prices, "There's a just God who rules in high Heaven. He created a famine in India, and figure it any way you want to, there's always good times when the Republican Party is in power." See "Mayor Humes' Speech," *Seattle Daily Times*, August 23, 1898, 8.

79. "Vote for Prosperity," *Omaha Daily Bee*, October 27, 1898, 6.

80. "Rally in the Third Ward," *Omaha Daily Bee*, November 5, 1898, 4.

81. *Speeches and Addresses of William McKinley: From March 1, 1897 to May 30, 1900* (New York: Doubleday & McClure, 1900), 100–106; Gould, *Presidency of William McKinley*, 134–137; Morgan, *William McKinley*, 406–408. For descriptions of McKinley's speeches throughout the tour, see Eric Love, *Race over Empire: Racism and U.S. Imperialism, 1865–1900* (Chapel Hill: University of North Carolina Press, 2004), 176–177; Morgan, *William McKinley*, 397–399; George F. Hoar, *Autobiography of Seventy Years*, vol. 2 (New York: Charles Scribner's Sons, 1903), 309–311; Tompkins,

Anti-Imperialism in the United States, 171–172; Ernest R. May, *Imperial Democracy: The Emergence of America as a Great Power* (New York: Harper & Row, 1973), 254–262.

82. *Speeches and Addresses of McKinley,* 100–106, 94–95.

83. "Opening Peace Negotiations," *Omaha Daily Bee,* October 1, 1898, 6; "Peace Negotiations," *Evening Star* (Washington, DC), October 21, 1898, 1; "The Powers May Object," *Times* (Washington, DC), November 3, 1898, 1; "Would Help Spain," *San Francisco Call,* November 8, 1898, 5.

84. May, *Imperial Democracy,* 169–172.

85. Frank D. Eager, "From Far Away Manila," *Independent,* August 25, 1898, 3. For a similar message from roughly the same time, see "Washington Letter," *Aberdeen Herald,* July 14, 1898, 8.

86. "Sagasta's Little Bluff," *Evening Times* (Washington, DC), September 22, 1898, 1.

87. Thomas J. McCormick, *China Market: America's Quest for Informal Empire* (Chicago: Quadrangle Books, 1967), 54–60; S. C. M. Paine, *The Sino-Japanese War of 1894–1895: Perceptions, Power, and Primacy* (New York: Cambridge University Press, 2003), 247–294.

88. Trask, *War with Spain,* 426, 442–443, 445–446; McCormick, *China Market,* 110; May, *Imperial Democracy,* 196–239. In addition, intervention by either Britain or France would have been incredibly unlikely at the time because, from September until mid-November, these two countries were on the verge of war over the possession of a small trading fort at Fashoda. See John A. Corry, *1898: Prelude to a Century* (New York: Fordham University Press, 1998), 262–285.

89. *Columbus (NE) Journal,* October 26, 1898, 2.

90. *McCook (NE) Tribune,* November 4, 1898, 4. Similar, if vague, comments about the need to rally around the president during this time of crisis were also made on the stump. One speaker said that to "desert Mr. McKinley now" would be like deserting a general "on the field of battle." See "Rally in the Third Ward," *Omaha Daily Bee,* November 5, 1898, 4.

91. "The Duty of Patriots," *Nebraska Advertiser* (Nemaha, NE), October 28, 1898, 8.

92. Untitled article, *McCook Tribune,* October 21, 1898, 4, reprinted from *Red Cloud Argus,* date unknown.

93. "Let Every Citizen Do His Duty," *Omaha Daily Bee,* November 8, 1898, 6.

94. "Support the Administration," *Spokane Daily Chronicle,* October 11, 1898, 4.

95. "Today the Verdict," *Morning Olympian,* November 8, 1898, 2. For similar statements, see "Spain's Interest in Our Election," *Spokane Daily Chronicle,* October 31, 1898, 4; "It is National," *Spokane Daily Chronicle,* November 7, 1898, 4; "Stand by Him!" *Seattle Post-Intelligencer,* November 2, 1898, 4.

96. "Not a Campaign Issue," *Seattle Daily Times,* October 6, 1898, 4; "Has Become a Degenerate," *Seattle Daily Times,* November 3, 1898, 4.

97. "Lewis Calls Soldiers 'Tasseled Sapheads,'" *Daily Ledger* (Tacoma, WA), October 24, 1898, 4.

98. "Turner Repeating His Abuse," *Daily Ledger*, October 29, 1898, 5 (emphasis in original).

99. "Lieu Landers Win the Fight," *Pullman Herald*, November 5, 1898, 10. For similar comments about Lewis and Turner, see "In Poor Business," *Seattle Post-Intelligencer*, October 30, 1898, 4.

100. "The Keynote of the Campaign," *McCook Tribune*, September 30, 1898, 10.

101. "Uncle Jake in the Civil War," *Omaha Daily Bee*, September 13, 1898, 3; "Uncle Jake's Great Record," *Omaha Daily Bee*, October 18, 1898, 3; "100 Questions for the Popocratic Speakers to Answer," *Nebraska Advertiser*, October 21, 1898, 8.

102. Frederick C. Luebke, *Immigrants and Politics: The Germans of Nebraska, 1880–1900* (Lincoln: University of Nebraska Press, 1969), 123, 125, 134; Cherny, *Populism, Progressivism*, 35.

103. "Cheyenne Cheers Thurston," *Omaha Daily Bee*, October 25, 1898, 1.

104. On the claim that Lewis was never in the military, see "The Same Old Sixpence," *Spokane Daily Chronicle*, November 3, 1898, 4; "Lewis Is Caught in His Own Trap," *Pullman Herald*, November 5, 1898, 9. A copy of the official dispatch confirming his position was printed in the *Seattle Daily Times*, November 3, 1898, 1.

105. "W. V. Allen as Private," *Independent*, September 1, 1898, 1.

106. J. Rogers Hollingsworth, *The Whirligig of Politics: The Democracy of Cleveland and Bryan* (Chicago: University of Chicago Press, 1963), 141–143; Robert Saldin, *War, the American State, and Politics since 1898* (New York: Cambridge University Press, 2011), 54–58.

107. For the gubernatorial results, see *House Journal of the Legislature of the State of Nebraska, Twenty-Sixth Regular Session* (Lincoln, NE: Jacob North, 1900), 104–107.

108. For congressional election results in this and following paragraphs, see *Guide to U.S. Elections*, 6th ed. (Washington, DC: CQ Press, 2010), 1104, 1106–1109. For state results, see Riddle, *Old Radicalism*, 251–266; Cherny, *Populism, Progressivism*, 90–94; O. Gene Clanton, *Kansas Populism: Ideas and Men* (Lawrence: University Press of Kansas, 1969), 213–215; Lee, *Principle over Party*, 153–160.

109. Wright, *Politics of Populism*, 217–218; Russell R. Elliott, *Servant of Power: A Political Biography of Senator William M. Stewart* (Reno: University of Nevada Press, 1983), 191–215; William Joseph Gaboury, *Dissension in the Rockies: A History of Idaho Populism* (New York: Garland, 1988), 308–323; Thomas A. Clinch, *Urban Populism and Free Silver in Montana: A Narrative of Ideology in Political Action* (Missoula: University of Montana Press, 1970), 156–159.

110. Richard F. Pettigrew to Jonas Lien, November 30, 1898, Pettigrew Collection, reel 22. For a similar analysis of the election, see Richard F. Pettigrew to Victoria Connor, no date (but likely November 1898), ibid.

111. "Chairman J. H. Schively Comments on the Great Republican Victory," *Seattle Post-Intelligencer*, November 10, 1898, 5. Similar comments appeared in the *Tacoma Daily Ledger*, November 9, 1898, 4.

112. C. R. Tuttle, "What Did It?" *Seattle Daily Times*, November 12, 1898, 4; *Seattle Times*, November 14, 1898, 4.

113. *Omaha Daily Bee*, November 11, 1898, 6; "The Legislature Is Republican," *Nebraska Advertiser*, November 11, 1898; "A Lesson for Democrats," *Omaha Daily Bee*, November 14, 1898, 4.

114. "The Coming Issue," *Independent*, November 17, 1898, 1. The *Independent* had practically stopped covering the issue of imperialism during the campaign, but that policy was reversed immediately following the election. See "Imperialism," *Independent*, November 10, 1898, 4.

CHAPTER 6. IMPERIALISM COMES TO THE FOREFRONT

1. *Congressional Record*, 55th Cong., 3rd sess., February 6, 1899, 1480–1484.

2. Regarding the population of the Philippines in 1898, both literature from that era and modern secondary works cite widely differing numbers, ranging from 7 million to 10 million. For more, see Ken De Bevoise, *Agents of Apocalypse: Epidemic Disease in the Colonial Philippines* (Princeton, NJ: Princeton University Press, 1995), 6–13.

3. David F. Trask, *The War with Spain in 1898* (Lincoln: University of Nebraska Press, 1981), 445–466.

4. A reprint of his message appears in *Congressional Record*, 55th Cong., 3rd sess., January 11, 1899, 572–573.

5. Lewis L. Gould, *The Presidency of William McKinley* (Lawrence: University Press of Kansas, 1980), 148; Stuart Creighton Miller, *"Benevolent Assimilation":The American Conquest of the Philippines, 1899–1903* (New Haven, CT: Yale University Press, 1982), 52. For Aguinaldo's formal response to the proclamation, see *Correspondence Relating to the War with Spain, Including the Insurrection in the Philippine Islands and the China Relief Expedition*, 2 vols. (Washington, DC: Government Printing Office, 1902), 2:912–913.

6. E. Berkeley Tompkins, *Anti-Imperialism in the United States: The Great Debate, 1890–1920* (Philadelphia: University of Pennsylvania Press, 1970), 126–127; Michael Patrick Cullinane, *Liberty and American Anti-Imperialism, 1898–1909* (New York: Palgrave Macmillan, 2012), 22–25.

7. Jonas Lien to Richard F. Pettigrew, October 8, 1898, Richard F. Pettigrew Collection, microfilm edition, reel 31, Pettigrew Museum, Sioux Falls, SD.

8. Richard F. Pettigrew to Jonas Lien, November 30, 1898, ibid., reel 22.

9. See Robert Beisner, *Twelve against Empire: The Anti-Imperialists of 1898–1900* (New York: McGraw-Hill, 1968), 153; Daniel B. Schirmer, *Republic or Empire: American Resistance to the Philippine War* (Cambridge, MA: Schenkman, 1972), 114.

10. According to Robert Beisner, George Hoar realized that McKinley was aware of this option, but Hoar believed that if the treaty could be rejected, the opposition would have "sufficient momentum to defeat the pact a second time." See Beisner,

Twelve against Empire, 153. See also H. Wayne Morgan, *William McKinley and His America* (Syracuse, NY: Syracuse University Press, 1963), 408; Gould, *Presidency of William McKinley*, 143; Miller, *Benevolent Assimilation*, 27.

11. William Jennings Bryan to Adjutant General, December 10, 1898, and Adjutant General to William Jennings Bryan, December 12, 1898, William Jennings Bryan Papers, box 22, Manuscript Division, Library of Congress, Washington, DC; Paolo E. Coletta, *William Jennings Bryan: Political Evangelist, 1860–1908* (Lincoln: University of Nebraska Press, 1964), 232; Louis W. Koenig, *Bryan: A Political Biography of William Jennings Bryan* (New York: G. P. Putnam's Sons, 1971), 287–288.

12. For a description of Bryan's views, see "Bryan Says Ratify Treaty," *Evening Star* (Washington, DC), January 9, 1899, 5; Paolo E. Coletta, "Bryan, McKinley, and the Treaty of Paris," *Pacific Historical Review* 26, 2 (1957): 131–146; Coletta, *William Jennings Bryan*, 233–237; Koenig, *Bryan*, 290–294.

13. For examples of historians with skeptical views of Bryan's motives, see Beisner, *Twelve against Empire*, vi; Tompkins, *Anti-Imperialism in the United States*, 179–180, 188–190; Schirmer, *Republic or Empire*, 108, 110; Cullinane, *Liberty and American Anti-Imperialism*, 42–43. See also Andrew Carnegie, *Autobiography of Andrew Carnegie* (Boston: Houghton Mifflin, 1920), 364–365.

14. Geoge F. Hoar, *Autobiography of Seventy Years*, vol. 2 (New York: Charles Scribner's Sons, 1903), 322–323. See also Beisner, *Twelve against Empire*, 155–158; 180–181; Tompkins, *Anti-Imperialism in the United States*, 188–191; Cullinane, *Liberty and American Anti-Imperialism*, 42–43.

15. William Jennings Bryan to Andrew Carnegie, December 24, 1898, Bryan Papers, box 22.

16. William Jennings Bryan to Andrew Carnegie, January 13 and 11, 1899, ibid.

17. See Robert Beisner, "1898 and 1968: The Anti-Imperialists and the Doves," *Political Science Quarterly* 85, 2 (1970): 193. Nearly the only work that actually accepts Bryan's fear of renewed war is Merle Eugene Curti, *Bryan and World Peace* (1931; reprint, New York: Octagon Books, 1969), 131–132. The subject is also addressed (dismissively) in Tompkins, *Anti-Imperialism in the United States*, 188–189.

18. For evidence that such rhetoric continued after the campaign, see *Tacoma (WA) Daily Ledger*, November 14, 1898, 1; "Will Not Please Europe," *Pullman (WA) Herald*, December 3, 1898, 3; "It Pains the Continent," *Red Cloud (NE) Chief*, December 2, 1898, 2.

19. "At the National Capital," *Red Cloud Chief*, January 13, 1899, 1. For similar statements, see "Anti-American Prejudice," *Colorado Springs Gazette*, January 28, 1899, 4.

20. *Morning Oregonian* (Portland), January 27, 1899, 4. See also *Morning Oregonian*, January 26, 1899, 4, and February 3, 1899, 4.

21. "Senate Expected to Railroad Peace Treaty," *Denver Post*, January 1, 1899, 2. See also "Hand of Germany Again Showing," *Denver Post*, November 17, 1898, 1.

22. Richard F. Pettigrew, *Triumphant Plutocracy: The Story of American Public Life*

from 1870s to 1920 (New York: Academy Press, 1921), 273–274. For references to Pettigrew's account, see Tompkins, *Anti-Imperialism in the United States*, 189–190; Schirmer, *Republic or Empire*, 108–110.

23. Pettigrew's account of a later anti-imperialist meeting has been characterized as seriously flawed. See Göran Rystad, *Ambiguous Imperialism: American Foreign Policy and Domestic Politics at the Turn of the Century* (Lund, Sweden: Esselte Studium, 1975), 169. Pettigrew claimed that Hoar tried to convince him to vote for the treaty and then fight for Philippine independence afterward. Pettigrew suggested that Hoar voted against the treaty only when it was certain to pass. See Pettigrew, *Triumphant Plutocracy*, 206–207.

24. *Congressional Record*, 55th Cong., 3rd sess., December 6, 1898, 20.

25. Tompkins, *Anti-Imperialism in the United States*, 178–179, 194; Eric Love, *Race over Empire: Racism and U.S. Imperialism, 1865–1900* (Chapel Hill: University of North Carolina Press, 2004), 186–188, 190, 194.

26. On the desire of certain imperialists to acquire Cuba, despite the Teller amendment, see Louis A. Pérez Jr., *Cuba between Empires, 1878–1902* (Pittsburgh: University of Pittsburgh Press, 1983), especially 270–281.

27. *Congressional Record*, 55th Cong., 3rd sess., January 11, 1899, 562, February 4, 1899, 1445, February 11, 1899, 1731–1732.

28. As just one example, Populist senator William Harris of Kansas offered a resolution disavowing any claim to permanent sovereignty over the Philippines and guaranteeing the islands' independence in the near term. See *Congressional Record*, 55th Cong., 3rd sess., February 3, 1899, 1416. Like all the others, his was unsuccessful.

29. For context, see Jerry M. Cooper, *The Army and Civil Disorder: Federal Military Intervention in Labor Disputes, 1877–1900* (Westport, CT: Greenwood Press, 1980), 217–218; Clayton D. Laurie and Ronald H. Cole, *The Role of Federal Military Forces in Domestic Disorders, 1877–1945* (Washington, DC: Government Printing Office, 1997), 152. On the Hull bill as proposed in 1899, see Graham A. Cosmas, "Military Reform after the Spanish-American War: The Army Reorganization Fight of 1898–1899," *Military Affairs* 35, 1 (1971): 12–18.

30. *The Journal of the Senate during the Thirty-Third Session of the Legislature of the State of California, 1899* (Sacramento: A. J. Johnston, 1899), 9–11; George E. Mowry, *The California Progressives* (Chicago: Quadrangle Books, 1963), 16.

31. *Congressional Record*, 55th Cong., 3rd sess., January 30, 1899, 1242–1243.

32. Ibid., January 26, 1899, 1108–1113.

33. Ibid., February 11, 1899, 1735–1736.

34. Ibid., January 30, 1899, 1278–1279.

35. Ibid., February 4, 1899, 1450–1451.

36. Ibid., January 26, 1899, 1108–1113.

37. Ibid., December 20, 1898, 325–330.

38. Ibid., February 4, 1899, 1450–1451.

39. Morgan, *William McKinley*, 404–412; Gould, *Presidency of William McKinley*, 140–142.

40. Michael H. Hunt, *Ideology and U.S. Foreign Policy*, rev. ed. (New Haven, CT: Yale University Press, 2009), 30–45; Paul T. McCartney, *Power and Progress: American National Identity, the War of 1898, and the Rise of American Imperialism* (Baton Rouge: Louisiana State University Press, 2006), especially 199–223. On the use of paternalism in another case, see Mary A. Renda, *Taking Haiti: Military Occupation and the Culture of U.S. Imperialism, 1915–1940* (Chapel Hill: University of North Carolina Press, 2001), especially 13–29.

41. *Congressional Record*, 55th Cong., 3rd sess., February 14, 1899, 1830–1832.

42. Ibid., January 26, 1899, 1108–1113.

43. Ibid., December 20, 1898, 325–330.

44. Ibid., February 14, 1899, 1830–1832.

45. Ibid., January 26, 1899, 1108–1113.

46. Ibid., February 4, 1899, 1450–1451.

47. For a brief history of American settler colonialism and republican freedoms, see Aziz Rana, *Two Faces of American Freedom* (Cambridge, MA: Harvard University Press, 2010).

48. The subject is most thoroughly explained in Walter LaFeber, *New Empire: An Interpretation of American Expansion, 1860–1898* (Ithaca, NY: Cornell University Press, 1963), especially 412–417 (quote from 416); and William Appleman Williams, *The Roots of Modern American Empire: A Study of the Growth and Shaping of Social Consciousness in a Marketplace Society* (New York: Random House, 1969), especially 432–445.

49. LaFeber, *New Empire*, 47, 105, 408–417; Williams, *Roots of Modern American Empire*, 246–248, 254–263. On this interpretation of the American empire of the 1890s and early 1900s, see also Thomas J. McCormick, *China Market: America's Quest for Informal Empire, 1893–1901* (Chicago: Quadrangle Books, 1967); Lloyd C. Gardner, *Imperial America: American Foreign Policy since 1898* (New York: Harcourt Brace Jovanovich, 1976); Thomas Schoonover, *Uncle Sam's War of 1898 and the Origins of Globalization* (Lexington: University Press of Kentucky, 2003).

50. Both LaFeber and Williams often use Democrats, mugwumps, and Populists as examples to demonstrate the growth of a consensus on the issues of trade. See LaFeber, *New Empire*, 201, 205, 414–416; Williams, *Roots of Modern American Empire*, 34, 36, 362–365, 370–375. See also William Appleman Williams, *The Tragedy of American Diplomacy*, rev. ed. (New York: Dell, 1962), 22–26, 37–39. On the politics of the tariff and trade, see Richard Franklin Bensel, *The Political Economy of American Industrialization: 1877–1900* (New York: Cambridge University Press, 2000), 457–509.

51. *Congressional Record*, 55th Cong., 2nd sess., June 21, 1898, appendix, 599–600.

52. Richard F. Pettigrew to H. P. Pettigrew, June 8, 1898, Pettigrew Collection, reel 21.

53. *Congressional Record*, 55th Cong., 3rd sess., January 23, 1899, 921-928, 930-931.

54. Ibid., January 24, 1899, 1001-1006.

55. Ibid., 1006-1012.

56. Ibid., 55th Cong., 2nd sess., April 1, 1898, 3465-3467. One recent author noted Simpson's talk of a more powerful navy but totally ignored the limits he wanted to put on it. See McCartney, *Power and Progress*, 112.

57. For Shafroth and Bell, see *Congressional Record*, 55th Cong., 2nd sess., April 6, 1898, 3636-3637, April 7, 1898, 3689.

58. *Congressional Record*, 55th Cong., 3rd sess., January 11, 1899, 562.

59. Ibid., January 25, 1899, 1054-1056. For similar remarks by Curtis Castle, see ibid., January 26, 1899, appendix, 90-94.

60. Ibid., January 26, 1899, appendix, 229-230.

61. Ibid., 90-94.

62. Ibid., January 24, 1899, 1006-1012.

63. The quotes from Castle in this and the following paragraph are from ibid., January 26, 1899, appendix, 90-94.

64. Ibid., January 30, 1899, 1263-1266.

65. Ibid., January 25, 1899, 1054-1056.

66. Cooper, *Army and Civil Disorder*, 217-218; Laurie and Cole, *Role of Federal Military Forces*, 152.

67. *Congressional Record*, 55th Cong., 3rd sess., January 24, 1899, 1001-1006.

68. Ibid., January 26, 1899, 1126-1128.

69. Ibid., January 24, 1899, 1006-1012.

70. Ibid., January 31, 1899, appendix, 122-128.

71. *Journal of the Senate of California, 1899*, 9-11.

72. Ibid., 24-25, 30, 126; *The Journal of the Assembly during the Thirty-Third Session of the Legislature of the State of California, 1899* (Sacramento: A. J. Johnston, 1899), 9, 43; "Mr. Nelson on Expansion," *New York Times*, January 21, 1899, 4.

73. *Congressional Record*, 55th Cong., 3rd sess., February 1, 1899, 1343-1348.

74. Ibid., February 6, 1899, 1480-1484.

75. Cullinane, *Liberty and American Anti-Imperialism*, 29-50.

76. On the history of these views, see Hunt, *Ideology and U.S. Foreign Policy*, 46-101; Reginald Horsman, *Race and Manifest Destiny: The Origins of American Racial Anglo-Saxonism* (Cambridge, MA: Harvard University Press, 1981), especially 72-73, 154-155, 242-243, 262-263.

77. *Congressional Record*, 55th Cong., 3rd sess., January 19, 1899, 783-789.

78. Ibid., February 6, 1899, 1480-1484.

79. Ibid., 55th Cong., 2nd sess., July 6, 1898, appendix, 603-619.

80. Ibid., 55th Cong., 3rd sess., January 23, 1899, 921-928, February 27, 1899, 2445-2446.

81. Ibid., February 6, 1899, 1480-1484.

82. Paul Finkelman, *Slavery and the Founders: Race and Liberty in the Age of Jefferson* (Armonk, NY: M. E. Sharpe, 1996), 133, 140; Henry Louis Gates Jr., ed., *Lincoln on Race and Slavery* (Princeton, NJ: Princeton University Press, 2009), especially 177–180, 279-280. For an older interpretation of anti-imperialist racism, see Christopher Lasch, "The Anti-Imperialists, the Philippines, and the Inequality of Man," *Journal of Southern History* 24, 3 (1958): 319-331.

83. *Congressional Record*, 55th Cong., 3rd sess., December 20, 1898, 325-330.

84. Senator George Turner noted this, and he specifically cited a speech by George Vest in which the Missouri senator admitted the same. See ibid., January 19, 1899, 783-789.

85. Miller, *Benevolent Assimilation*, 60-63; Brian McAllister Linn, *The Philippine War, 1899-1902* (Lawrence: University Press of Kansas, 2000), 46-49.

86. *Correspondence Relating to the War with Spain*, 2:893-894; "Filipinos Attack the Americans," *Omaha World-Herald*, February 6, 1899, 1; "Troops Fighting at Manila," *Omaha Daily Bee*, February 6, 1899, 1; "Aguinaldo's Troops Attack Americans Defending Manila," *San Francisco Call*, February 5, 1899, 1; "Aguinaldo's Horde Repulsed with Great Slaughter," *Salt Lake (UT) Herald*, February 6, 1899, 1.

87. *Congressional Record*, 55th Cong., 3rd sess., February 6, 1899, 1480-1484; Beisner, *Twelve against Empire*, 155-158; Tompkins, *Anti-Imperialism in the United States*, 188-195; Schirmer, *Republic or Empire*, 108-120, 134-135; Miller, *Benevolent Assimilation*, 27-30; Cullinane, *Liberty and American Anti-Imperialism*, 41-49; Pettigrew, *Triumphant Plutocracy*, 272-274.

88. *Journal of the Executive Proceedings of the Senate*, 55th Cong., February 6, 1899, 1284. Senators Cannon (Silver Republican, Utah) and White (Democrat, California) were paired and did not vote on the treaty. Cannon was on record supporting the treaty, while White was opposed.

89. *Congressional Record*, 55th Cong., 3rd sess., January 24, 1899, 1006-1012.

90. Ibid., January 26, 1899, 1126-1128.

91. Ibid., January 23, 1899, 926.

92. Ibid., February 1, 1899, 1347.

93. Ibid., February 11, 1899, 1737-1738.

94. Ibid., January 26, 1899, appendix, 90-94.

95. Richard Pettigrew to Lee Stover, January 28, 1899, Pettigrew Collection, reel 22.

96. *Congressional Record*, 55th Cong., 2nd sess., April 6, 1898, 3636-3637, April 7, 1898, 3689-3690.

97. Ibid., 55th Cong., 3rd sess., February 14, 1899, 1863.

98. Ibid., February 25, 1899, 2408.

99. Ibid., February 27, 1899, 2474.

100. Charles S. Thomas to T. F. O'Mahoney, April 9, 1899, Charles S. Thomas Papers, Colorado State Archives, Denver.

101. Sewell Thomas, *Silhouettes of Charles S. Thomas: Colorado Governor and United States Senator* (Caldwell, ID: Caxton Printers, 1959), 75.

102. John P. Enyeart, The Quest for "Just and Pure Law": Rocky Mountain Workers and American Social Democracy, 1870–1924 (Stanford, CA: Stanford University Press, 2009), 113–114; D. C. Coates, "Thomas Is with Us," Rocky Mountain Sun (Aspen, CO), October 8, 1898, 1.

103. Comparing the elections of 1898 and 1894—when Thomas was the Democratic candidate for governor—the vote for Thomas in 1898 corresponded more closely to the vote for radical Davis Waite in 1894 than to his own totals in the earlier contest. James Edward Wright, The Politics of Populism: Dissent in Colorado (New Haven, CT: Yale University Press, 1974), 217.

104. Enyeart, Quest for "Just and Pure Law," 113–114; William E. Forbath, Law and the Shaping of the American Labor Movement (Cambridge, MA: Harvard University Press, 1989), 46–48; Senate Journal of the General Assembly of the State of Colorado, Twelfth Session (Denver: Smith-Brooks, 1899), 124, 516–523; David Brundage, The Making of Western Labor Radicalism: Denver's Organized Workers, 1878–1905 (Chicago: University of Illinois Press, 1994), 140–141; Duane A. Smith, Rocky Mountain Boom Town: A History of Durango, Colorado (Boulder: University Press of Colorado, 1992), 78–79; Wright, Politics of Populism, 233–235. On the provisions of the law, see Laws Passed at the Twelfth Session of the General Assembly of the State of Colorado (Denver: Smith-Brooks, 1899), 232.

105. Senate Journal of Colorado, Twelfth Session, 190, 202–203, 216, 246; "Hangings and the Philippines," Denver Post, January 30, 1899, 3; "No Emblems on Ballots," Rocky Mountain News, January 31, 1899, 5; "Their Minds Wandered," Aspen (CO) Tribune, January 31, 1899, 1.

106. "Tribute to Washington," Rocky Mountain News, February 20, 1899, 3; "Volunteers Illegally Detained in Philippines," Rocky Mountain News, April 18, 1899, 8; "Work Done for Three Years," Rocky Mountain News, April 20, 1899, 8.

107. Charles S. Thomas to W. S. McComas, April 13, 1899, Thomas Papers; Senate Journal of Colorado, Twelfth Session, 520.

108. For the votes and provisions of the laws, see House Journal of the Legislature of the State of Nebraska, Twenty-Sixth Regular Session (Lincoln, NE: Jacob North, 1900), 645, 819; Senate Journal of the Legislature of the State of Nebraska, Twenty-Sixth Regular Session (Lincoln, NE: Jacob North, 1900), 985, 988; Laws, Joint Resolutions, and Memorials Passed by the Legislative Assembly of the State of Nebraska, Twenty-Sixth Session (Lincoln, NE: Jacob North, 1900), 147–161, 330–331.

109. Paolo E. Coletta, "A Tempest in a Teapot? Governor Poynter's Appointment of William V. Allen to the United States Senate," Nebraska History 38 (June 1957): 155–163.

110. House Journal of Nebraska, Twenty-Sixth Regular Session, 267–268.

111. Ibid., 275. It should be pointed out that the exact party affiliation of reform members is difficult to determine because all official records list them as "fusionist."

112. Ibid., 276.

113. Ibid., 276–278.

114. Ibid., 1198–1199. The senate struggled in its initial attempts to expunge the record; see *Senate Journal of Nebraska, Twenty-Sixth Regular Session*, 820, 836–837, 989.

115. US Works Progress Administration, *Messages and Proclamations of the Governors of Nebraska, 1854–1941*, vol. 2, *1887–1909* (sponsored by the University of Nebraska, 1942), 437; *Senate Journal of Nebraska, Twenty-Sixth Regular Session*, 618; *House Journal of Nebraska, Twenty-Sixth Regular Session*, 1091.

116. US Works Progress Administration, *Messages and Proclamations*, 437.

117. "A Good Veto," *Omaha World-Herald*, April 3, 1899, 4; Almira Scott to William A. Poynter, undated, William A. Poynter Papers, Nebraska State Historical Society, Lincoln.

18. *Albion (NE) Weekly News*, April 7, 1899.

119. "Poynter and His Two Vetoes," *Omaha Daily Bee*, April 10, 1899, 4, reprinted from the *Pierce Call* and the *Aurora Republican*, dates unknown. The page from the *Bee* included twelve reprinted responses by Nebraska's Republican papers. Poynter's veto also gained some national attention. See "Holding Nebraska in Check," *Evening Star* (Washington, DC), April 3, 1899, 6; "A Bad 'Poynter,'" *Times* (Washington, DC), April 4, 1899, 4; "Governor Poynter and Our Soldiers," *Sun* (New York, NY), April 4, 1899, 6; "Practical Rebuke to Imperialism," *Watchman and Southron* (Sumter, SC), April 5, 1899, 6. It remained a significant story in Nebraska's papers for weeks afterward. For example, see "Who Was Patriotic," *Custer County Republican* (Broken Bow, NE), June 15, 1898, 4.

120. Robert E. Ficken, *Washington State: The Inaugural Decade, 1889–1899* (Pullman: Washington State University Press, 2007), 259–260; Don Brazier, *History of the Washington Legislature, 1854–1963* (Olympia,: Washington State Senate, 2000), 54–55.

121. Minutebook of the Western Central Labor Union, February 1 and 8, 1899, Western Central Labor Union, King County Labor Council Records, box 35, Special Collections, University of Washington, Seattle. For an example of its discussion of Asian exclusion, see ibid., November 2, 1898.

122. John Rankin Rogers, *The Inalienable Rights of Man* (Olympia, WA, 1900).

123. John Rankin Rogers to William H. Snell, March 8, 1899, and John Rankin Rogers to *New York Journal*, April 11, 1899, John Rankin Rogers Papers, Washington State Archives, Olympia.

124. "The Jeffersonians" and "Should Get Together," *Morning Olympian*, April 15, 1899, 2, 3.

CHAPTER 7. SETTING THE STAGE FOR THE CAMPAIGN

1. *Congressional Record*, 56th Cong., 1st sess., January 30, 1900, 1314–1316.

2. Richard F. Pettigrew to F. T. Dubois, no date (but likely March 8, 1900), Richard F. Pettigrew Collection, microfilm edition, reel 23, Pettigrew Museum, Sioux Falls, SD.

3. For this and the following paragraph, see *Congressional Record*, 56th Cong., 1st sess., June 4, 1900, 6510-6515.

4. For the conflicts in the Coeur d'Alenes and their context, see Jerry M. Cooper, *The Army and Civil Disorder: Federal Military Intervention in Labor Disputes, 1877–1900* (Westport, CT: Greenwood Press, 1980), 165-209; Clayton D. Laurie and Ronald H. Cole, *The Role of Federal Military Forces in Domestic Disorders, 1877–1945* (Washington, DC: Government Printing Office, 1997), 153-178; Katherine G. Aiken, *Idaho's Bunker Hill: The Rise and Fall of a Great Mining Company, 1885–1981* (Norman: University of Oklahoma Press, 2005), 10-14, 21-37.

5. *Adams County News* (Ritzville, WA), May 10, 1899, 3.

6. *Aspen (CO) Daily Times*, June 24, 1899, 3.

7. "Who the Rioters Were," *Colfax (WA) Gazette*, July 20, 1900, 3.

8. In June 1899 the Colorado Federation of Labor declared General Merriam to be "an anarchist for his action in the Coeur d'Alenes." See "Call for Winchesters," *Longmont (CO) Ledger*, June 9, 1899, 1.

9. "Holcomb and Harvey Speak," *Omaha (NE) World-Herald*, October 25, 1899, 3; "Lest We Forget," *Omaha World-Herald*, October 29, 1899, 4; "Why an Increased Standing Army?" *Omaha World-Herald*, November 19, 1899, 4. The United States Industrial Commission must have heard of the rumors, because it specifically reported that the Bunker Hill mine was not controlled by Standard Oil. See *Report of the Industrial Commission on the Relations and Conditions of Capital and Labor Employed in the Mining Industry*, vol. 12 (Washington, DC: Government Printing Office, 1901), lxxxv.

10. "Labor Day Incidents in Omaha," *Omaha World-Herald*, September 10, 1899, 32.

11. John E. Sullivan, "Labor's Appeal to Uncle Sam," *Aspen Daily Times*, August 19, 1899, 4.

12. On the vision of American freedom as an example for others and the internal conflict between liberty and power, see Michael H. Hunt, *Ideology and U.S. Foreign Policy*, rev. ed. (New Haven, CT: Yale University Press, 2009), especially 19-45; Paul T. McCartney, *Power and Progress: American National Identity, the War of 1898, and the Rise of American Imperialism* (Baton Rouge: Louisiana State University Press, 2006), especially 25-44.

13. Melvyn Dubovsky, "The Origins of Western Working Class Radicalism, 1890-1905," *Labor History* 7, 2 (1966): 139-144; John P. Enyeart, *The Quest for "Just and Pure Law": Rocky Mountain Workers and American Social Democracy, 1870-1924* (Stanford, CA: Stanford University Press, 2009), 112-113.

14. See "Another Outrage," *Miners' Magazine*, February 1900, 2-3, "Congressional Investigation," *Miners' Magazine*, March 1900, 7-8, "Fired from Ambush," *Miners' Magazine*, June 1900, 14-15.

15. For a small sampling of articles on imperialism in *Miners' Magazine*, see "General Lawton's Death," January 1900, 1; February 1900, 35-36; April 1900, 36; "The Philippine Problem," July 1900, 20-23; "The Philippine Problem," August 1900,

27–28; "Altgeld's Speech," August 1900, 28–33; "Dangers of Militarism," September 1900, 9–10; "The Philippine Problem," September 1900, 23–27.

16. *Miners' Magazine*, December 1899, 40–41.

17. "General Lawton's Death," *Miners' Magazine*, January 1900, 1.

18. "Grievances Go to the Poles [sic]," *Rocky Mountain News* (Denver, CO), May 19, 1900, 10.

19. "Declaration of Principles Adopted by the Western Federation of Miners May 18, 1900," *Miners' Magazine*, May 1900, 16.

20. For information on the end of the conventional campaign, see Stuart Creighton Miller, *"Benevolent Assimilation": The American Conquest of the Philippines, 1899–1903* (New Haven, CT: Yale University Press, 1982), 70–99; Brian McAllister Linn, *The Philippine War, 1899–1902* (Lawrence: University Press of Kansas, 2000), 88–159.

21. On the popularity of the Boers and the anti-imperialists' use of the South African war, see Richard Mulanax, *The Boer War in American Politics and Diplomacy* (Lanham, MD: University Press of America, 1994), 108–111, 117–118; William N. Tilchin, "The United States and the Boer War," in *The International Impact of the Boer War,* ed. Keith Wilson (New York: Palgrave, 2001), 113–114.

22. Mulanax, *Boer War,* 126. For a brief analysis of the theories of causation both from the time of the conflict and by later historians, see Bill Nasson, *The South African War, 1899–1902* (New York: Oxford University Press, 1999), 19–42.

23. "Long Live the Republic," *Omaha World-Herald,* December 12, 1899, 1; "Bombard Governor Poynter," *Omaha Daily Bee,* December 12, 1899, 1, 3; William V. Allen to William A. Poynter, December 11, 1899, William A. Poynter Papers, Nebraska State Historical Society, Lincoln.

24. "War the Handmaid of Monopoly," *Miners' Magazine,* February 1900, 5–10.

25. *Congressional Record,* 56th Cong., 1st sess., February 1, 1900, 1401–1404.

26. Ibid., February 7, 1900, 1622–1625.

27. For Pettigrew's quotes in this and the following paragraph, see ibid., April 12 and 14, 1900, 4095–4096, 4159–4166.

28. On Anglo-American diplomacy during the conflict, see Mulanax, *Boer War,* chap. 5; Tilchin, "United States and the Boer War," 107–122.

29. "Western Hearts Cheer for the Boer," *Omaha World-Herald,* June 10, 1900, 3. For information on the contact between the Boer representatives and western governors, see George W. Van Siclen to William A. Poynter, February 20 and May 10, 1900, Poynter Papers; George W. Van Siclen to John R. Rogers, March 10 and May 14, 1900, Charles D. Pierce to John R. Rogers, July 28, 1900, John Rankin Rogers Papers, Washington State Archives, Olympia. Rogers came to regret his decision to join the association. See John R. Rogers to George W. Van Siclen, June 7, 1900, ibid.

30. Richard F. Pettigrew to George W. Van Sicklen [sic], May 16, 1900, and Richard F. Pettigrew to Paul Kruger, May 19, 1900, Pettigrew Collection, reel 24.

31. For a discussion of the Open Door policy and the administration's views on China in 1899–1900, see Thomas J. McCormick, *China Market: America's Quest for*

Informal Empire, 1893-1901 (Chicago: Quadrangle Books, 1967), 127-175; Marilyn Blatt Young, *The Rhetoric of Empire: American China Policy, 1895-1901* (Cambridge, MA: Harvard University Press, 1968), 115-197; H. Wayne Morgan, *William McKinley and His America* (Syracuse, NY: Syracuse University Press, 1963), 466-473; Lewlis L. Gould, *The Presidency of William McKinley* (Lawrence: University Press of Kansas, 1980), 220-224.

32. For an account based largely on the perspective of Europeans and Americans in China, see David J. Silbey, *The Boxer Rebellion and the Great Game in China* (New York: Hill & Wang, 2012). For a discussion of events from the Chinese perspective, see Joseph Esherick, *The Origins of the Boxer Uprising* (Berkeley: University of California Press, 1987).

33. *Correspondence Relating to the War with Spain, Including the Insurrection in the Philippine Islands and the China Relief Expedition*, vol. 1 (Washington, DC: Government Printing Office, 1902), 412.

34. Allen S. Will, *World Crisis in China, 1900* (Baltimore: John Murphy, 1900), vii.

35. "The Bitter Fruit of International Rapacity," *Denver Post*, July 15, 1900, 4.

36. *Yakima (WA) Herald*, June 14, 1900, 2.

37. "The Democratic Chinese Plank," *Salt Lake (UT) Tribune*, date unknown, reprinted in *Aspen Weekly Times*, June 30, 1900, 3. For similar perspectives, see "A Glorious Issue for the Democrats," *Ouray (CO) Herald*, June 14, 1900, 4; *Colfax (WA) Gazette*, June 22, 1900, 4.

38. "To Awaken China," *Adams County News* (Ritzville, WA), June 27, 1900, 2.

39. James D. Richardson, ed., *A Compilation of the Messages and Papers of the Presidents, 1789-1908*, vol. 10 (Washington, DC: Bureau of National Literature and Art, 1908), 166-174.

40. *Congressional Record*, 56th Cong., 1st sess., January 9, 1900, 704-712.

41. Ibid.; ibid., March 7, 1900, 2617-2627. For historical works dealing with perceptions of Filipino "capacity," see Glenn Anthony May, *Social Engineering in the Philippines: The Aims, Execution, and Impact of American Colonial Policy, 1900-1913* (Westport, CT: Greenwood Press, 1980), 9-12, 76-126; Paul A. Kramer, *The Blood of Government: Race, Empire, the United States & the Philippines* (Chapel Hill: University of North Carolina Press, 2006), especially 159-227; Warwick Anderson, *Colonial Pathologies: American Tropical Medicine, Race, and Hygiene in the Philippines* (Durham, NC: Duke University Press, 2006).

42. For just a few examples, see *Congressional Record*, 56th Cong., 1st sess., December 14, 1899, 378-379; January 8, 1900, 669-670; January 22, 1900, 1038-1043; March 12, 1900, 2763-2772.

43. Julian Go, *American Empire and the Politics of Meaning: Elite Political Cultures in the Philippines and Puerto Rico during U.S. Colonialism* (Durham, NC: Duke University Press, 2008), 55-56, 142; Bartholomew H. Sparrow, *The Insular Cases and the Emergence of American Empire* (Lawrence: University Press of Kansas, 2006), 75-77; Gould, *Presidency of William McKinley*, 208-209; Morgan, *William McKinley*, 463-

464; Göran Rystad, *Ambiguous Imperialism: American Foreign Policy and Domestic Politics at the Turn of the Century* (Lund, Sweden: Esselte Studium, 1975), 69–70.

44. Gould, *Presidency of William McKinley*, 208–212; Morgan, *William McKinley*, 464–465.

45. José A. Cabranes, "Citizenship and the American Empire: Notes on the Legislative History of the United States Citizenship of Puerto Ricans," *University of Pennsylvania Law Review* 127, 2 (1978): 427–433; *Congressional Record*, 56th Cong., 1st sess., March 2, 1900, 2471–2473.

46. *Congressional Record*, 56th Cong., 1st sess., March 14, 1900, 2873–2876.

47. Ibid., March 2, 1900, 2474; March 15, 1900, 2924–2926; March 30, 1900, 3517–3521.

48. Ibid., April 2, 1900, 3636–3639.

49. Ibid., March 23, 1900, 3209–3213.

50. Ibid., March 13, 1900, 2812–2820, 2176–2882.

51. Ibid., April 3, 1900, 3697–3698.

52. Ibid., April 11, 1900, 4071.

53. Rystad, *Ambiguous Imperialism*, 73–81.

54. "The Puerto Rico Tariff," *Evening Tribune* (San Diego, CA), March 1, 1900, 2; *Evening Tribune*, March 7, 1900, 2; "Puerto Rico's Tariff," *Evening Tribune*, March 16, 1900, 2.

55. "A Discouraging Beginning," *Morning Oregonian* (Portland), April 9, 1900, 4.

56. "Two Views of Oriental Development," *Morning Oregonian*, April 7, 1900.

57. "Nationalizing Our Islands," *San Francisco Chronicle*, April 9, 1900, 4.

58. "The Duty of Congress toward the Inhabitants of the Philippine and Porto Rico Islands," *San Francisco Chronicle*, April 30, 1900, 6–7.

59. *McCook (NE) Tribune*, March 2, 1900, 4.

60. "Puerto Rican Twaddle," *Omaha Daily Bee*, March 26, 1900, 4.

61. "Where the Puerto Rico Bill Is At," *Ouray Herald*, April 12, 1900, 2; "The Law for Puerto Rico," *Wray (CO) Rattler*, April 14, 1900, 2; *Akron (CO) Weekly Pioneer Press*, April 20, 1900, 1.

62. "Republicans Fall into Line," *Seattle Post-Intelligencer*, March 22, 1900, 4. See also "Relapse and Recovery," *Seattle Post-Intelligencer*, March 31, 1900, 4.

63. "Puerto Rico Bill a Law," *Seattle Post-Intelligencer*, April 12, 1900, 4.

64. *Morning Olympian*, February 17, 1900, 2; April 14, 1900, 2; May 15, 1900, 2. It should also be noted that even those papers that did not explicitly link the tariff and immigration emphasized the need to establish the constitutional principle. See "Kindness for Puerto Rico," *Spokane (WA) Daily Chronicle*, April 4, 1900; "Puerto Rico and Alaska," *Spokane Daily Chronicle*, April 10, 1900, 4; *San Juan Islander*, March 15, 1900, 2.

65. "A Partisan Howl," *Morning Olympian*, March 22, 1900, 2; "Must Have a New Issue," *Colfax Gazette*, March 30, 1900, 4; "Where Is the Bad Faith?" *Colfax Gazette*, April 13, 1900, 4.

66. Morgan, *William McKinley*, 482–484; Gould, *Presidency of William McKinley*, 169–171.

67. Gold Standard Act of 1900, *United States Statutes at Large* XXXI (1900): 45–50; James Livingston, *Origins of the Federal Reserve: Money, Class, and Corporate Capitalism, 1890–1913* (Ithaca, NY: Cornell University Press, 1986), 122–125.

68. See especially *Congressional Record*, 56th Cong., 1st sess., January 18, 1900, 941–950; March 3, 1900, 2509–2514.

69. Ibid., February 7, 1900, 1603–1610, 1616–1621.

70. Ibid., January 18, 1900, 941–950; February 7, 1900, 1616–1621; "Secretary Gage and National City Bank," *New York Times*, January 14, 1900.

71. *Congressional Record*, 56th Cong., 1st sess., December 14, 1899, 423–425; January 31, 1900, 1341–1344.

72. Ibid., February 8, 1900, 1639–1641.

73. Ibid., December 14, 1899, 423–425.

74. Ibid., March 6, 1900, 2589–2590; March 13, 1900, 2863.

CHAPTER 8. THE CONTEST OF 1900 AND THE DEFEAT OF REFORM

1. Walter LaFeber, "Election of 1900," in *History of American Presidential Elections*, vol. 3, ed. Arthur M. Schlesinger Jr. (New York: McGraw-Hill, 1971), 1939–1942.

2. For Bryan's speech, see ibid., 1943–1956.

3. For Schurz's discussion of "speculators" and the mugwumps' understanding of them, see Carl Schurz, *Speeches, Correspondence and Political Papers of Carl Schurz*, ed. Frederic Bancroft (New York: G. P. Putnam's Sons, 1913), 6:17, 93; David M. Tucker, *Mugwumps: Public Moralists of the Gilded Age* (Columbia: University of Missouri Press, 1998), 15–25.

4. Judy Arlene Hilkey, *Character Is Capital: Success Manuals and Manhood in Gilded Age America* (Chapel Hill: University of North Carolina Press, 1997), 88; Tucker, *Mugwumps*, 24. For more on the mugwumps and their views of industrialization, see Tucker, *Mugwumps*, 15–25, 121–122; John G. Sproat, *The Best Men: Liberal Reformers in the Gilded Age* (New York: Oxford University Press, 1968), 205–242; Richard Hofstadter, *The Age of Reform: From Bryan to F.D.R.* (New York: Vintage Books, 1955), 137–141.

5. Ann L. Leger, "Moorfield Storey: An Intellectual Biography" (Ph.D. diss., University of Iowa, 1968), 281; Jim Zwick, ed., *Mark Twain's Weapons of Satire: Anti-Imperialist Writings on the Philippine-American War* (Syracuse, NY: Syracuse University Press, 1992), 74–80; Richard E. Welch, *Response to Imperialism: The United States and the Philippine-American War, 1899–1902* (Chapel Hill: University of North Carolina Press, 1979), 44–47; George S. Boutwell, *Bryan or Imperialism: Address by the Hon. George S. Boutwell* (Boston: New England Anti-Imperialist League, 1900), 11.

6. Edwin Burritt Smith, *Essays and Addresses* (Chicago: A. C. McClurg, 1909), 257–258.

7. Schurz, *Speeches, Correspondence and Political Papers*, 13–14. Schurz had employed these arguments since the 1870s, when, as a member of the Senate, he opposed the annexation of Santo Domingo. See Robert L. Beisner, *Twelve against Empire: The Anti-Imperialists, 1898–1900* (New York: McGraw-Hill, 1968), 22–34.

8. Edward Atkinson, *Criminal Aggression: By Whom Committed?* (Brookline, MA, 1899); Schurz, *Speeches, Correspondence and Political Papers*, 24; Smith, *Essays and Addresses*, 243–253.

9. Richard E. Welch, *George Frisbie Hoar and the Half-Breed Republicans* (Cambridge, MA: Harvard University Press, 1971), 260.

10. Ibid., 225–226, 229, 242.

11. Walter T. K. Nugent, *Money and American Society, 1865–1880* (New York: Free Press, 1968), 158–171; Paolo E. Coletta, *William Jennings Bryan: Political Evangelist, 1860–1908* (Lincoln: University of Nebraska Press, 1964), 185; Hans L. Trefousse, *Carl Schurz: A Biography* (Knoxville: University of Tennessee Press, 1982), 277–279; *Dawn* (Ellensburg, WA), May 12, 1899, 2.

12. A. Brisbane to William Jennings Bryan, December 23, 1898, William Jennings Bryan to A. Brisbane, no date, William Jennings Bryan to Andrew Carnegie, December 24, 1898, William Jennings Bryan Papers, box 22, Manuscript Division, Library of Congress, Washington, DC; Louis W. Koenig, *Bryan: A Political Biography of William Jennings Bryan* (New York: G. P. Putnam's Sons, 1971), 289.

13. Edwin Burritt Smith to Elwood S. Corser, February 26, 1900, Bryan Papers, box 24; Göran Rystad, *Ambiguous Imperialism: American Foreign Policy and Domestic Politics at the Turn of the Century* (Lund, Sweden: Esselte Studium, 1975), 174.

14. Nearly all the letters from conservative anti-imperialists presumed the right to set the Democratic platform. See David Starr Jordan to William Jennings Bryan, February 7, 1900, Edwin Burritt Smith to William Jennings Bryan, June 30, 1900, W. A. Croffut to William Jennings Bryan, July 7, 1900, Bryan Papers, box 24. See also Elwood S. Corser to James K. Jones, February 27, 1900, Elwood S. Corser to William Jennings Bryan, March 6 and April 12, 1900, ibid.

15. A certainly inaccurate account of the meeting is contained in Richard F. Pettigrew, *Triumphant Plutocracy: The Story of American Public Life from 1870s to 1920* (New York: Academy Press, 1921), 275–276, 323–328. Pettigrew claimed that a separate ticket was agreed to and Carnegie offered to fund it. This account is largely accepted in the following: E. Berkeley Tompkins, *Anti-Imperialism in the United States: The Great Debate, 1890–1920* (Philadelphia: University of Pennsylvania Press, 1970), 217; Daniel B. Schirmer, *Republic or Empire: American Resistance to the Philippine War* (Cambridge, MA: Schenkman, 1972), 188–189. For better explanations, see Rystad, *Ambiguous Imperialism*, 168–169. For Pettigrew's correspondence with third-ticket advocates—none of which supports his claims—see Richard F. Pettigrew to Carl Schurz, February 1, 1900, Richard F. Pettigrew to Edwin Burritt Smith, January 23 and 29 and February 6, 1900, Richard F. Pettigrew to Irving [sic] Winslow, March 7, 1900, all in Richard F. Pettigrew Collection, microfilm edition, reel 23, Pettigrew Museum,

Sioux Falls, SD; Richard F. Pettigrew to Edwin Burritt Smith, April 25, 1900, Richard F. Pettigrew to Irving [sic] Winslow, May 4, 1900, Richard F. Pettigrew to Carl Schurz, May 22, 1900, all in ibid., reel 24.

16. For a sample of the discussion of a third party among Schurz, Story, and Smith, see Carl Schurz to Edwin Burritt Smith, March 11, 19, and 26, 1900, Moorfield Storey to Carl Schurz, March 14, 1900, Carl Schurz to Moorfield Storey, March 20, 1900, Edwin Burritt Smith to Carl Schurz, March 17 and 24, 1900, all in Carl Schurz Papers, microfilm edition, reel 67, Manuscript Division, Library of Congress, Washington, DC. Schurz also corresponded (somewhat reluctantly) with Erving Winslow, who persistently warned against the third-party option. See Erving Winslow to Carl Schurz, March 21, 22, and 27, 1900, Carl Schurz to Erving Winslow, March 28, 1900, ibid.

17. "Platform and Policy," *Independent* (Lincoln, NE), July 14, 1898, 3.

18. Jane Taylor Nelsen, ed., *A Prairie Populist: The Memoirs of Luna Kellie* (Iowa City: University of Iowa Press, 1992), 175.

19. Thomas W. Riddle, *The Old Radicalism: John R. Rogers and the Populist Movement in Washington* (New York: Garland, 1991), 237–242, 250–253.

20. John D. Hicks, *The Populist Revolt: A History of the Farmers' Alliance and the People's Party*, 3rd ed. (Lincoln: University of Nebraska Press, 1961), 383–387.

21. The vote totals for temporary chair and, later, for governor indicate that just over 1,000 attended as delegates. See "Poynter for Governor," *Omaha (NE) Daily Bee*, August 3, 1898, 1; "Populists Called to Order," *Omaha (NE) World-Herald*, August 3, 1898, 2.

22. See Richard F. Pettigrew to H. L. Loucks, January 29 and March 1, 1898, Pettigrew Collection reel 20; Richard F. Pettigrew to S. A. Cochran, June 2, 1898, ibid., reel 21; *Dawn*, May 12, 1899; "Washington Letter," *Frontier County Faber* (Stockville, NE), November 26, 1896; J. M. Snyder, "Voice of the People," *Independent*, September 23, 1897, 1.

23. John R. Rogers to W. H. Plummer, March 29, 1898, John R. Rogers to Maurice A. Langhorne, March 20, 1899, John R. Rogers to George Turner, February 16, 1898, John Rankin Rogers Papers, Washington State Archives, Olympia; Riddle, *Old Radicalism*, 252–253, 270.

24. Richard F. Pettigrew to Thomas Ayres, no date (but likely December 1900), Richard F. Pettigrew to Howard Taylor, December 13, 1899, Richard F. Pettigrew to Charles A. Towne, January 1, 1900, Pettigrew Collection, reel 22.

25. Richard F. Pettigrew to William J. Bryan, April 9, 1900, ibid., reel 23.

26. For a few examples, see Hofstadter, *Age of Reform*, 106–108; Robert C. McMath Jr., *American Populism: A Social History, 1877–1898* (New York: Hill & Wang, 1992), 202–206; Lawrence Goodwin, *Democratic Promise: The Populist Moment in America* (New York: Oxford University Press, 1976), 426–555.

27. Koenig, *Bryan*, 296–298.

28. See *Chicago Conference on Trusts: Speeches, Debates, Resolutions, List of the Del-*

egates, Committees, etc. (Chicago: Civic Foundation of Chicago, 1900), especially 496–514.

29. Richard F. Pettigrew to Charles A. Towne, January 23, 1900, Pettigrew Collection, reel 23.

30. Blanton Duncan to William Jennings Bryan, April 21, 1899, Bryan Papers, box 22; Charles A. Towne to William Jennings Bryan, December 15, 1899, ibid., box 23.

31. William Jennings Bryan to Merrill, April 26, 1900, ibid., box 24 (emphasis in original).

32. William Jennings Bryan, "The Next Democratic Platform," *Aberdeen (WA) Herald*, May 4, 1899, 1, reprinted from *National Watchman*, date unknown; "Washington Letter," *Aberdeen Herald*, May 25, 1899, 4; William H. Harvey, *Coin on Money, Trusts, and Imperialism* (Chicago: Thomas Knapp, 1899); Richard Pettigrew to James Conzett, January 5, 1900, Pettigrew Collection, reel 22.

33. Richard Pettigrew to Walter Price, January 29, 1900, Pettigrew Collection, reel 23.

34. LaFeber, "Election of 1900," 1928–1931.

35. Koenig, *Bryan*, 313–314; Hicks, *Populist Revolt*, 398–399. For more on the convention and especially the nomination, see "Trouble Ahead for Populists," *San Francisco Call*, May 9, 1900, 3; "Populists at Sioux Falls Cheer the Name of Bryan," *San Francisco Call*, May 10, 1900, 2; "Standard Bearers Chosen by the Two Populist Conventions," *San Francisco Call*, May 11, 1900, 1. Pettigrew was deeply involved in the nomination process, and he demanded an independent nomination specifically to forestall the growth of the mid-roaders. See Richard F. Pettigrew to Charles A. Towne, April 18, 24, and 27, May 1 and 16, 1900, Richard F. Pettigrew to George H. Shibley, April 25, 1900, Pettigrew Collection, reel 24.

36. Material on the convention in this and the following paragraphs comes from Coletta, *William Jennings Bryan*, 257–261; Koenig, *Bryan*, 320–324; Michael Kazin, *A Godly Hero: The Life of William Jennings Bryan* (New York: Anchor Books, 2006), 99–100.

37. *Rocky Mountain News* (Denver, CO), July 4, 1900, 1.

38. "The Day and Its Suggestions," *Rocky Mountain News*, July 4, 1900, 4.

39. LaFeber, "Election of 1900," 1919–1924.

40. Coletta, *William Jennings Bryan*, 266–268. On Populist objections, see W. J. Waite to William A. Poynter, July 17, 1900, William A. Poynter Papers, Nebraska State Historical Society, Lincoln; Richard F. Pettigrew to William Jennings Bryan, May 1 and June 9, 1900, Pettigrew Collection, reel 24.

41. Moorfield Storey to Carl Schurz, August 10, 1900, Carl Schurz to Moorfield Storey, August 11, 1900, Schurz Papers, reel 68.

42. See Trefousse, *Carl Schurz*, 285–288; Tompkins, *Anti-Imperialism in the United States*, 229–232; Edwin Burritt Smith to Carl Schurz, August 11, 1900, Schurz Papers, reel 68.

43. On the Liberty Congress, see Edwin Burritt Smith to Carl Schurz, August 18, 1900, Moorfield Storey to Carl Schurz, August 18, 1900, Schurz Papers, reel 68. On their lingering hopes for a third ticket, see Carl Schurz to Moorfield Storey, August 20 and 25, 1900, Moorfield Storey to Carl Schurz, August 27, 1900, ibid.; Carl Schurz to Moorfield Storey, September 1, 1900, ibid., reel 69. See also Beisner, *Twelve against Empire*, 127-130, 182; Schirmer, *Republic or Empire*, 200-203; Rystad, *Ambiguous Imperialism*, 251-255.

44. For this and the paragraphs that follow, see H. Wayne Morgan, *William McKinley and His America* (Syracuse, NY: Syracuse University Press, 1963), 489-498; Lewis L. Gould, *The Presidency of William McKinley* (Lawrence: University Press of Kansas, 1980), 213-219.

45. LaFeber, "Election of 1900," 1924-1928.

46. Gould, *Presidency of William McKinley*, 225.

47. US Works Progress Administration, *Nebraska Party Platforms, 1858-1940* (Lincoln, NE, 1940), 254-259.

48. Robert. W. Cherny, *Populism, Progressivism, and the Transformation of Nebraska Politics, 1885-1915* (Lincoln: University of Nebraska Press, 1981), 78; "Convention Advance Guard," *Omaha World-Herald*, July 10, 1900, 1; "Fusion Conventions Today," *Omaha World-Herald*, July 11, 1900, 7; "Complete Fusion Effected at Lincoln," *Omaha World-Herald*, July 12, 1900, 1; "Three Meetings Work for Fusion," *Omaha World-Herald*, July 12, 1900, 5; "Poynter Named by Acclamation," *Omaha World-Herald*, July 13, 1900, 1-2.

49. Thomas M. Patterson to William Jennings Bryan, June 9, 1899, Bryan Papers, box 23; Charles S. Thomas to William Jennings Bryan, May 16, 1900, ibid., box 24; Alva Adams to William Jennings Bryan, July 17, 1900, ibid., box 25.

50. For this and the following paragraph, see Elmer Ellis, *Henry Moore Teller: Defender of the West* (Caldwell, ID: Caxton Printers, 1941), 331-332; Henry M. Teller to Tom Dawson, September 13, 1900, Henry M. Teller Papers, box 3, ff. 37, History Colorado Center, Denver; "The Greatest Silver Orators in Colorado Swayed the Democratic Convention," *Denver Post*, September 12, 1900, 1, 3; "Fusion Ticket Completed but Must Be Changed," *Denver Post*, September 13, 1900, 1, 3.

51. See "Platforms of Silver Voters," *Rocky Mountain News*, September 12, 1900, 12.

52. Riddle, *Old Radicalism*, 231-269. For Rogers's views on expansion, see "Rogers on Expansion," *Morning Olympian* (WA), July 6, 1899, 3; John Rankin Rogers to William H. Snell, March 8, 1899, John Rankin Rogers to *New York Journal*, April 11, 1899, Rogers Papers.

53. For this and the following paragraphs, see Riddle, *Old Radicalism*, 274-279; Richard Evans Fisch, "A History of the Democratic Party in the State of Washington, 1854-1956" (Ph.D. diss., University of Oregon, 1975), 100-103; Winston B. Thorson, "Washington State Nominating Conventions," *Pacific Northwest Quarterly* 35, 2 (1944): 108-111; "Rogers Is the Nominee," *Morning Olympian*, August 30, 1900,

1; "Gov. John R. Rogers Is Renominated," *Seattle Daily Times*, August 30, 1900, 1, 7. Early reports from one Republican paper are especially demonstrative of expectations heading into the convention. See "Rogers Defeated," *Morning Olympian*, August 28, 1900, 3; "Fusionists Are at Sea," *Morning Olympian*, August 29, 1900, 1, 4.

54. See "The Fusion Platform," *Seattle Daily Times*, August 30, 1900, 7.

55. Fisch, "History of the Democratic Party," 104; "Wilson and M'Graw Smash the Old Southwest Combination," *Seattle Daily Times*, August 15, 1900, 1–2; "The State Platform," *Morning Olympian*, September 2, 1900, 4; Frederick C. Luebke, *Immigrants and Politics: The Germans of Nebraska, 1880–1900* (Lincoln: University of Nebraska Press, 1969), 169; US Works Progress Administration, *Nebraska Party Platforms*, 262–264; "The M'Kinley Republican State Ticket," *Denver Post*, September 18, 1900, 1; "Old Gang Whoops It up for Wolcott," *Rocky Mountain News*, September 18, 1900, 12; "Silver Is Ignored," *Rocky Mountain News*, September 19, 1900, 2.

56. Thomas A. Bailey, "Was the Presidential Election of 1900 a Mandate on Imperialism?" *Mississippi Valley Historical Review* 24, 1 (1937): 43–52; Rystad, *Ambiguous Imperialism*, especially 294; Welch, *Response to Imperialism*, 70–71; Stuart Creighton Miller, *"Benevolent Assimilation": The American Conquest of the Philippines, 1899–1903* (New Haven, CT: Yale University Press, 1982), 148; David M. Pletcher, *The Diplomacy of Involvement: American Economic Expansion across the Pacific, 1784–1900* (Columbia: University of Missouri Press, 2001), especially 304–305.

57. On the contention that gold production improved economic conditions, see Hicks, *Populist Revolt*, 388–389; Milton Friedman and Anna Jacobson Schwartz, *A Monetary History of the United States, 1867–1960* (1963; reprint, Princeton, NJ: Princeton University Press, 1993), 8, 137.

58. "Is There Gold Enough," *Omaha Daily Bee*, August 3, 1900, 6.

59. "Arrasmith at Seattle," *Colfax (WA) Gazette*, September 28, 1900, 6.

60. For other examples, see *Montezuma Journal* (Cortez, CO), October 12, 1900, 2; "The Prosperity Issue," *Aspen (CO) Daily Times*, October 20, 1900, 2, reprinted from *Colorado Springs Gazette*, date unknown.

61. See *Norfolk (NE) Weekly News*, August 30, 1900, 6. For similar pieces, see *Red Cloud (NE) Chief*, August 24, 1900, 4; "The Matter of Chief Interest," *Omaha Daily Bee*, August 16, 1900, 6; "Financial Element in Bryanism," *Omaha Daily Bee*, September 19, 1900, 6; "False Prophet Bryan," *Colfax Gazette*, August 10, 1900, 4; "Open Mills, Not Open Mints," *San Juan Islander* (Friday Harbor, WA), October 25, 1900, 2; *Glenwood (CO) Post*, September 1, 1900, 4.

62. "Bright Outlook," *Nebraska Advertiser* (Nemaha, NE), August 24, 1900, 4.

63. *Norfolk Weekly News*, July 19, 1900, 6.

64. "Arrests the Grain Trust," *Omaha World-Herald*, August 7, 1900, 3; "Smyth Sues Starch Company," *Omaha Daily Bee*, September 20, 1900, 3.

65. "Fight Is on Now," *Omaha World-Herald*, August 12, 1899, 1.

66. *Omaha Daily Bee*, April 25, 1900, 7, reprinted from *Denver Post*, February 9, 1900, 1.

67. "Will Defend Standard Oil," *Omaha Daily Bee*, February 7, 1900, 1; "Standard Oil Case Continued," *Columbus (NE) Journal*, February 14, 1900, 1; "To Argue for the Trust," *Western News Democrat* (Valentine, NE), February 15, 1900, 3.

68. "Report of the Rosewater-Hitchcock Debate," *Omaha Daily Bee*, October 21, 1900, 19–20.

69. "What Is a Trust?" *Colorado Springs Gazette*, September 27, 1900, 4. The paper had already run articles praising the benefits of massive corporate combinations, and it continued to do so for the remainder of the campaign. See "The Trusts and the People," *Colorado Springs Gazette*, July 20, 1900, 9; "Pennsylvanian Says Trusts Will Remain," *Colorado Springs Gazette*, September 1, 1900, 5.

70. "Rubbish About Trusts," *Morning Olympian*, September 29, 1900, 2.

71. "Competing with the Trusts," *San Juan Islander*, September 20, 1900, 2.

72. "Address of Charles A. Towne to the Voters of Seattle," *Seattle Daily Times*, September 17, 1900, 11–12.

73. "Political Hypocrisy Will Fail This Time," *Seattle Daily Times*, August 14, 1900, 6.

74. "The 'Prosperity Argument,'" *Omaha World-Herald*, September 15, 1900, 4.

75. Friedman and Schwartz, *Monetary History*, 136, 148.

76. *Aberdeen Herald*, August 16, 1900, 4.

77. "The Bubble of Trust Prosperity," *Denver Post*, August 21, 1900, 4.

78. "From Sunrise to Sunset Bryan Talked to Farmers," *Rocky Mountain News*, November 6, 1900, 5.

79. These percentages were mathematically derived from information found in US Department of the Interior, *Thirteenth Census of the United States, Taken in the Year 1910*, vol. 7, *Agriculture 1909 and 1910, Reports by States with Statistics for Counties* (Washington, DC: Government Printing Office, 1913), 19–20.

80. For a comparison of 1890 and 1900, see US Department of the Interior, *Report on the Statistics of Agriculture in the United States at the Eleventh Census: 1890* (Washington, DC: Government Printing Office, 1895), 162–163; US Department of the Interior, *Twelfth Census of the United States, Taken in the Year 1900*, vol. 5, *Agriculture*, pt. 1, *Farms, Livestock, and Animal Products* (Washington, DC: Government Printing Office, 1902), 102–103.

81. "Evils of Republican Rule," *Omaha World-Herald*, October 18, 1900, 5.

82. *Yakima (WA) Herald*, November 1, 1900, 2.

83. "That One Per Cent," *Independent*, October 25, 1900, 4.

84. "Oriental Trade Growing," *San Juan Islander*, September 27, 1900, 4; *Colfax Gazette*, November 2, 1900, 6. For similar reports, see *Adams County News* (Ritzville, WA), August 8, 1900, 2; "News of the States," *Colfax Gazette*, October 12, 1900, 1; "Growth of Commerce," *Morning Olympian*, October 16, 1900, 4; *Pullman (WA) Herald*, November 3, 1900, 4.

85. This supplement, which also included a statement on trade expansion from California senator George Perkins, was printed in many of Nebraska's small-town

Republican newspapers. See *McCook Tribune*, October 12, 1900; *Columbus Journal*, October 3, 1900; *North Platte Semi-Weekly Tribune*, October 23, 1900; *Custer County Republican*, October 18, 1900; *Red Cloud Chief*, October 19, 1900.

86. "Our Commercial and Territorial Expansion," *North Platte (NE) Semi-Weekly Tribune*, November 2, 1900, and *Custer County Republican* (Broken Bow, NE), November 1, 1900.

87. For example, the editor of the *Tacoma (WA) Daily Ledger* wrote a substantial number of opinion pieces in March and early April that were very optimistic about the prospects of trade with Asia. By the time of the campaign, these had nearly disappeared. See "Pacific States Should Be Represented," March 4, 1900, 4; "Our Markets Are in the Orient," March 7, 1900, 4; "Study Trade Conditions in the Orient," March 21, 1900, 4; "Developing Oriental Trade," March 26, 1900, 4; "Senator Foster and the Chinese Trade," April 10, 1900, 4; "To Increase Oriental Trade," April 12, 1900, 4.

88. "McKinley Prosperity in the Province of Luzon," *Daily Journal* (Telluride, CO), October 26, 1900, 1.

89. *Valentine (NE) Democrat*, July 19, 1900, 4.

90. S. Arion Lewis, "Imperialism and the Money Question," *Omaha World-Herald*, August 24, 1900, 7.

91. "Shall Liberty Endure," *Independent*, October 18, 1900, 4. For a similar work, see *Yakima Herald*, October 11, 1900, 2.

92. "Imperialist Argument," *Independent*, October 18, 1900, 4.

93. "The West and Imperialism," *Rocky Mountain News*, August 10, 1900, 4.

94. For the best accounts of the actual court decisions, see "Guam Men Americans?" *Hawaiian Star* (Honolulu), September 7, 1900, 5; "A Chinese Sailor Not an Immigrant," *Honolulu Republican*, September 20, 1900, 3. The latter article includes the full text of Estee's ruling.

95. "Mass Meeting at Armory," *Seattle Daily Times*, October 26, 1900, 7.

96. "A Sign of the Times," *Aberdeen Herald*, October 25, 1900, 4 (also reprinted in the *Omaha World-Herald* as "Cheap Labor Threatens America," November 4, 1900, 4); "Filipinos Are Citizens," *Aberdeen Herald*, November 1, 1900, 1; "Here Is the Danger," *Aberdeen Herald*, November 1, 1900, 4.

97. LaFeber, "Presidential Election of 1900," 1920. For other examples of reaction and anti-Asian sentiment on the campaign trail, see "Yakima's Yellow Peril," *Yakima Herald*, October 25, 1900, 1; "Estee Hits Them Again," *Seattle Daily Times*, October 29, 1900, 1–2; "Turner at Ballard," *Seattle Daily Times*, October 13, 1900, 5; "Favor Letting Chinese In," *Omaha World-Herald*, September 12, 1900, 8; "Labor Faces Grave Issue," *Omaha World-Herald*, October 12, 1900, 5; "Threatens Labor," *Omaha World-Herald*, October 15, 1900, 1.

98. For articles by imperialists designed to allay the fear of Asian immigration, see "Japanese Immigration," *Tacoma Daily Ledger*, October 29, 1900, 4; "A Criminal Cunard," *Seattle Post-Intelligencer*, October 24, 1900, 4; "Sharp, but Scurvy Trickery,"

Tacoma Daily Ledger, November 3, 1900, 4; "Dred Scott Decision Revived," *Seattle Post-Intelligencer*, November 6, 1900, 4. See also "A Decision by Estee," *Morning Olympian*, November 4, 1900, 1.

99. The racial component of imperialism has gained greater attention, but it has often been described in fairly one-dimensional terms. See Rubin Francis Weston, *Racism in U.S. Imperialism: The Influence of Racial Assumptions on American Foreign Policy, 1893–1946* (Columbia: University of South Carolina Press, 1972); Eric Love, *Race over Empire: Racism and U.S. Imperialism, 1865–1900* (Chapel Hill: University of North Carolina Press, 2004). For more sophisticated works on the subject, see Matthew Frye Jacobson, *Barbarian Virtues: The United States Encounters Foreign Peoples at Home and Abroad, 1876–1917* (New York: Hill & Wang, 2000); Mary A. Renda, *Taking Haiti: Military Occupation and the Culture of U.S. Imperialism, 1915–1940* (Chapel Hill: University of North Carolina Press, 2001).

100. For the supplements, see "American Occupation of the Philippines," in *Adams County News* (Ritzville, WA), August 22, 1900; *San Juan Islander*, August 23, 1900; "Issues Discussed by Men of All Parties," in *Columbus Journal*, September 26, 1900; *North Platte Semi-Weekly Tribune*, September 28, 1900; *Colfax Gazette*, October 12, 1900. Much of the material in these supplements came from reports of the First Philippine Commission. On the use of the commission's findings, see Paul A. Kramer, *The Blood of Government: Race, Empire, the United States, & the Philippines* (Chapel Hill: University of North Carolina Press, 2006), 112–124; Miller, *Benevolent Assimilation*, 132–133. For similar statements, see "Cost of the War," *Tacoma Daily Ledger*, October 17, 1900, 4; "Turner's Campaign Speech," *Tacoma Daily Ledger*, October 23, 1900, 4.

101. Resil B. Mojares, *The War against the Americans: Resistance and Collaboration in Cebu, 1899–1906* (Quezon City, Philippines: Ateneo de Manila University Press, 1999). A number of other works described the motivations of Filipino participants quite differently from the Philippine Commission or the American imperialist press. See, for example, Teodoro A. Agoncillo, *Malolos: The Crisis of the Republic* (Quezon City: University of the Philippines, 1960); Reynaldo Ileto, *Pasyon and Revolution: Popular Movements in the Philippines* (Quezon City, Philippines: Ateneo de Manila University Press, 1979); Glenn Anthony May, *Battle for Batangas: A Philippine Province at War* (New Haven, CT: Yale University Press, 1991).

102. The byline analyses offered by Colorado newspapers usually attributed the disturbance to the presence of controversial Senator Edward Wolcott onstage with Roosevelt. The actual accounts, however, made it appear that Roosevelt himself was the target of the rioters. For the description that most closely matches the former, see "Inflamed by Wolcott," *Denver Post*, September 27, 1900, 1. For other versions, see "Wolcott Incites a Riot at Victor," *Rocky Mountain News*, September 27, 1900, 1; "Afraid of Free Speech," *Colorado Springs Gazette*, September 27, 1900, 1.

103. "Roosevelt versus Roosevelt," *Omaha World-Herald*, September 29, 1900, 12; "Teddy's Late Discovery," *Valentine (NE) Democrat*, October 25, 1900, 4.

104. The best description of Roosevelt's views of race, class, and mastery appears in Gail Bederman, *Manliness and Civilization: A Cultural History of Gender and Race in the United States, 1880–1917* (Chicago: University of Chicago Press, 1995), 170–216. See also Kristin L. Hoganson, *Fighting for American Manhood: How Gender Politics Provoked the Spanish-American and Philippine-American Wars* (New Haven, CT: Yale University Press, 1998), 26–28, 121–124, 153–154.

105. See, for example, "Women Declare for William J. Bryan," *Castle Rock (CO) Journal*, October 19, 1900, 5; "McKinley Republicanism Severely Arraigned," *Silverite-Plaindealer* (Ouray, CO), September 21, 1900, 1; "Intellectual Lackeys," *Valentine Democrat*, September 13, 1900, 4; "Where Do I Come In?" *Valentine Democrat*, November 1, 1900, 4.

106. "Imperial Government and Its Logical Results," *Littleton (CO) Independent*, October 26, 1900, 4.

107. Roosevelt's remarks are from "Hands Poynter Hot Shot," *Omaha Daily Bee*, October 5, 1900, 1, 7. See also "Roosevelt Accusation Denounced by Poynter," *Omaha World-Herald*, October 3, 1900, 1; "Savage Denies 'Teddy's' Story," *Omaha World-Herald*, October 6, 1900, 1; "Poynter and the Hired Soldiers," *Norfolk Weekly News*, October 18, 1900, 4; "Citizens Tell of Speech," *Omaha World-Herald*, October 17, 1900, 5; "Enthusiasm Grows Daily," *Omaha Daily Bee*, October 24, 1900, 7; "Answers Governor Poynter," *Minneapolis Journal*, October 5, 1900, 1; *Aberdeen (SD) News*, October 8, 1900, 2; Miller, *Benevolent Assimilation*, 141.

108. *Omaha Daily Bee*, October 24, 1900, 6.

109. *Pullman Herald*, October 27, 1900, 5.

110. "The Flag as a Campaign Issue," *Colorado Springs Gazette*, September 30, 1900, 12.

111. *Omaha Daily Bee*, October 24, 1900, 6.

112. *Columbus Journal*, September 12, 1900; *North Platte Semi-Weekly Tribune*, September 14, 1900.

113. "The Flag as a Campaign Issue," *Colorado Springs Gazette*, September 30, 1900, 12.

114. "Democracy's Borrowed Livery," *Tacoma Daily Ledger*, October 12, 1900, 4. For others with similar statements, see "As to the American Flag," *Tacoma Daily Ledger*, November 1, 1900, 4; Alma L. Parker, "Simon Grey's Family," *Columbus Journal*, October 24, 1900; *Custer County Republican*, October 25, 1900; *Pullman Herald*, October 27, 1900, 5; "An Old Soldier Pleased," *San Juan Prospector* (Del Norte, CO), September 22, 1900.

115. "The Campaign Opened," *Pullman Herald*, September 29, 1900, 1.

116. "The New Copperheadism," *Fort Collins (CO) Weekly Courier*, September 20, 1900, and *Longmont (CO) Ledger*, September 21, 1900, 3.

117. "Bryan and Vallandigham, *Morning Olympian*, September 7, 1900, 2.

118. *St. Edward (NE) Sun*, September 28, 1900. For similar remarks, see "Poynter and the 'Hired Soldiers,'" *Norfolk Weekly News*, October 18, 1900, 4.

119. "Hands Poynter a Hot Shot," *Omaha Daily Bee*, October 5, 1900, 7. Similar remarks appeared in "Roosevelt," *Kearney (NE) Daily Hub*, October 2, 1900, 2.

120. "Caused the Rebellion," *Kearney Daily Hub*, September 24, 1900.

121. *Norfolk Weekly News*, October 18, 1900, 4.

122. In the weeks leading up to the election, Republican newspapers rather suspiciously published accounts of the Populists' glowing reputation in the days before they became contaminated by fusion, and some even reported on recent mid-road meetings. See *Custer County Republican*, July 19, 1900, 4, and August 16, 1900, 4; "The Mid-Roaders Meet," *McCook (NE) Tribune*, October 12, 1900, 4; "Treachery of Rogers," *Colfax Gazette*, November 2, 1900, 6.

123. From the *Colorado Springs Gazette*, see: "Mantle Returns," August 10, 1900, 1; "Mr. Mantle's Enlightenment," August 11, 1900, 4; "Mr. Stewart on Bryan," September 30, 1900, 1; "Is It Patriotism or Treason?" August 18, 1900, 4.

124. "Dear Boy Letters—No. 4," *North Platte Semi-Weekly Tribune*, September 14, 1900, and *Columbus Journal*, September 12, 1900.

125. "Dear Boy Letters—No. 9," *Columbus Journal*, October 17, 1900; *Custer County Republican*, October 18, 1900; *Red Cloud Chief*, October 19, 1900; and *North Platte Semi-Weekly Tribune*, October 23, 1900. Some of the "Dear Boy Letters" appeared in newspapers in Washington State, Colorado, and other locations, but in most places, these campaign supplements were not consistently preserved. See "Dear Boy Letters—No. 5," *Colfax Gazette*, September 28, 1900; "'Dear Boy' Letter," *Wet Mountain Tribune* (Westcliffe, CO), September 22, 1900; "Dear Boy Letters—No. 10," *American Citizen* (Kansas City, KS), October 26, 1900.

126. Luebke, *Immigrants and Politics*, 170–171.

127. *Adams County News*, October 3, 1900, 2.

128. "More German Opinion," *Omaha Daily Bee*, October 11, 1900, 6; "German-American for Gold Standard," *Columbus Journal*, October 17, 1900; *Custer County Republican*, October 18, 1900; and *North Platte Semi-Weekly Tribune*, October 23, 1900; "Prominent German Hopes for Bryan's Defeat," *Columbus Journal*, October 24, 1900, and *Custer County Republican*, October 25, 1900; "The Expert Patriot and Statesman," *Colfax Gazette*, August 24, 1900, 4; "Germans Standing Firm," *San Juan Islander*, September 27, 1900, 4; "The German Vote," *Aspen Daily Times*, September 22, 1900, 2; *Fort Collins Weekly Courier*, August 30, 1900, 2; *Daily Journal* (Telluride, CO), July 24, 1900, 2.

129. See especially Luebke, *Immigrants and Politics*, 173.

130. Dietrich was accused of a wide range of crimes and misdeeds—the most sordid from his early days in Deadwood, South Dakota. See Luebke, *Immigrants and Politics*, 173–176. For Republican refutations of the charges (which often examined the rumors in some detail), see "Resorting to Falsehood," *McCook Tribune*, October 19, 1900, 5, and *Custer County Republican*, October 25, 1900, 4; "Slanders Are Rebuked," *Omaha Daily Bee*, October 31, 1900, 3; "Campaign Lies Disproved," *Omaha Daily*

Bee, September 10, 1900, 7; "Free Speech Plenty," *Custer County Republican*, October 11, 1900, 7.

131. For Dietrich's defense of soldiers, see "Poynter and the 'Hired Soldiers,'" *Norfolk Weekly News*, October 18, 1900, 4; "Enthusiasm Grows Daily," *Omaha Daily Bee*, October 24, 1900, 7.

132. "Hands Poynter a Hot Shot," *Omaha Daily Bee*, October 5, 1900, 1, 7.

133. *Basalt (CO) Journal*, August 4, 1900, 2.

134. *Aberdeen Herald*, September 20, 1900, 2.

135. This cartoon, titled "Assassin in the Rear," depicted Wolcott in a way that greatly resembled anti-imperialist cartoons in the Republican press. See *Rocky Mountain News*, October 17, 1900, 1; Miller, *Benevolent Assimilation*. For other examples of this attack on Wolcott, see "Gov. Thomas Roasts Wolcott," *Aspen Democrat*, September 13, 1900, 1; "Named Candidates for Legislature," *Denver Post*, September 30, 1900, 3; *Durango (CO) Wage Earner*, October 18, 1900, 1.

136. "High Treason," *Independent*, August 30, 1900, 4.

137. For another interesting conspiratorial piece that examined the use of "traitor," see "Grand Democratic Party," *Aberdeen Herald*, August 30, 1900, 1.

138. See, for example, *Pullman Herald*, October 13, 4; *Colfax Gazette*, October 26, 1900, 4; "As to the American Flag," *Tacoma Daily Ledger*, November 1, 1900, 4.

139. "The Rally at the Armory," *Seattle Daily Times*, September 13, 1900, 8.

140. Coletta, *William Jennings Bryan*, 277–279; Koenig, *Bryan*, 344–345; Kazin, *Godly Hero*, 107–108. For presidential vote totals here and in the following paragraphs, see Edgar Eugene Robinson, *The Presidential Vote, 1896–1932* (1947; reprint, New York: Octagon Books, 1970), especially 46–53.

141. Cherny, *Populism, Progressivism*, 77–79, 94–96; James E. Wright, *The Politics of Populism: Dissent in Colorado* (New Haven, CT: Yale University Press, 1974), 217–225. For gubernatorial vote totals in this and the following paragraphs, see Michael J. Dubin, *United States Gubernatorial Elections, 1861–1911: The Official Results by State and County* (Jefferson, NC: McFarland, 2010).

142. Riddle, *Old Radicalism*, 280–281; Robert D. Saltvig, "The Progressive Movement in Washington" (Ph.D. diss., University of Washington, 1966), 29–31, 66–73.

143. On the congressional races, see *Guide to U.S. Elections*, 6th ed. (Washington, DC: CQ Press, 2010), 1111–1114.

144. William Jennings Bryan, "The Election of 1900," *North American Review* 171 (December 1900): 788–801.

145. Cherny, *Populism, Progressivism*, 100–103.

146. Wright, *Politics of Populism*, 222–224.

147. On the votes, see Dubin, *Gubernatorial Elections*, 598; Robinson, *Presidential Vote*, 364–367.

CONCLUSION

1. On the end of Populism and its legacy in Washington, see Thomas W. Riddle, *The Old Radicalism: John R. Rogers and the Populist Movement in Washington* (New York: Garland, 1991), 280–287.

2. Robert. W. Cherny, *Populism, Progressivism, and the Transformation of Nebraska Politics, 1885–1915* (Lincoln: University of Nebraska Press, 1981), 74–108.

3. James Edward Wright, *The Politics of Populism: Dissent in Colorado* (New Haven, CT: Yale University Press, 1974), 219–225; Elizabeth Jameson, *All that Glitters: Class, Conflict, and Community in Cripple Creek* (Chicago: University of Illinois Press, 1998), 199–225; George G. Suggs Jr., *Colorado's War on Militant Unionism: James H. Peabody and the Western Federation of Miners* (1972; reprint, Norman: University of Oklahoma Press, 1991).

4. George E. Mowry, *The Era of Theodore Roosevelt, 1900–1912* (New York: Harper & Brothers, 1958), 140–141; Michael McGerr, *A Fierce Discontent: The Rise and Fall of the Progressive Movement* (New York: Free Press, 2003), 139–140.

5. On other "populist" movements, see Michael Kazin, *The Populist Persuasion: An American History*, rev. ed. (Ithaca, NY: Cornell University Press, 1998). Kazin does not define populism as being on the Left or the Right, and essentially, he discusses the two themes of nationalism-xenophobia and egalitarian populism using a different lexicon but from a similar perspective.

BIBLIOGRAPHY

MANUSCRIPT COLLECTIONS

Bryan, William Jennings, Papers. Manuscript Division, Library of Congress, Washington, DC.

Pettigrew, Richard F., Collection. Microfilm edition. Pettigrew Museum, Sioux Falls, SD.

Poynter, William A., Papers. Nebraska State Historical Society, Lincoln.

Rogers, John Rankin, Papers. Washington State Archives, Olympia.

Schurz, Carl, Papers. Microfilm edition. Manuscript Division, Library of Congress, Washington, DC.

Shafroth Family Papers. Western History/Genealogy Department, Denver Public Library, Denver, CO.

Teller, Henry Moore, Manuscript Collection. Stephen H. Hart Library, History Colorado Center, Denver.

Thomas, Charles S., Papers. Colorado State Archives, Denver.

Western Central Labor Union, King County Labor Council Records. Special Collections, University of Washington, Seattle.

BOOKS, ARTICLES, PAMPHLETS, AND DISSERTATIONS

Agoncillo, Teodoro A. *Malolos: The Crisis of the Republic*. Quezon City: University of the Philippines, 1960.

Aiken, Katherine G. *Idaho's Bunker Hill: The Rise and Fall of a Great Mining Company, 1885–1981*. Norman: University of Oklahoma Press, 2005.

Allen, William V. "Western Feeling toward the East." *North American Review* 162 (1896): 588–593.

Almaguer, Tomas. *Racial Fault Lines: The Historical Origins of White Supremacy in California*. Berkeley: University of California Press, 1994.

311

Anderson, Warwick. *Colonial Pathologies: American Tropical Medicine, Race, and Hygiene in the Philippines*. Durham, NC: Duke University Press, 2006.

Appleby, Joyce. *Liberalism and Republicanism in the Historical Imagination*. Cambridge, MA: Harvard University Press, 1992.

Argersinger, Peter H. *The Limits of Agrarian Radicalism: Western Populism and American Politics*. Lawrence: University Press of Kansas, 1995.

Atkinson, Edward. *Criminal Aggression: By Whom Committed?* Brookline, MA, 1899.

Auxier, George W. "Middle Western Newspapers and the Spanish American War, 1895–1898." *Mississippi Valley Historical Review* 26, 4 (1940): 523–534.

Ayers, Edward. *Promise of the New South: Life after Reconstruction*. 2nd ed. New York: Oxford University Press, 2007.

Bailey, Dana R. *History of Mennehaha County, South Dakota*. Sioux Falls, SD: Brown & Saenger, 1899.

Bailey, Thomas A. "Was the Presidential Election of 1900 a Mandate on Imperialism?" *Mississippi Valley Historical Review* 24, 1 (1937): 43–52.

Bederman, Gail. *Manliness and Civilization: A Cultural History of Gender and Race in the United States, 1880–1917*. Chicago: University of Chicago Press, 1995.

Beeby, James M. *Revolt of the Tar Heels: The North Carolina Populist Movement, 1890–1901*. Jackson: University Press of Mississippi, 2008.

Beisner, Robert L. "1898 and 1968: The Anti-Imperialists and the Doves." *Political Science Quarterly* 85, 2 (1970): 187–216.

———. *Twelve against Empire: The Anti-Imperialists, 1898–1900*. New York: McGraw-Hill, 1968.

Bell, George W. *The New Crisis*. Des Moines, IA: Moses Hull, 1887.

Bensel, Richard Franklin. *Passion and Preferences: William Jennings Bryan and the 1896 Democratic National Convention*. New York: Cambridge University Press, 2008.

———. *The Political Economy of American Industrialization: 1877–1900*. New York: Cambridge University Press, 2000.

Berk, Gerald. *Alternative Tracks: The Constitution of American Industrial Order, 1865–1917*. Baltimore: Johns Hopkins University Press, 1994.

Berkowitz, Peter. *The Making of Modern Liberalism*. Princeton, NJ: Princeton University Press, 1999.

Bicha, Karel. "Peculiar Populist: An Assessment of John Rankin Rogers." *Pacific Northwest Quarterly* 65, 3 (1974): 110–117.

Blanke, David. *Sowing the American Dream: How Consumer Culture Took Root in the Rural Midwest*. Athens: Ohio University Press, 2000.

Blight, David W. *Race and Reunion: The Civil War in American Memory*. Cambridge, MA: Harvard University Press, 2001.

Bodnar, John, ed. *Bonds of Affection: Americans Define Their Patriotism*. Princeton, NJ: Princeton University Press, 1996.

Boughter, Judith A. *Betraying the Omaha Nation, 1790–1916*. Norman: University of Oklahoma Press, 1998.

Boutwell, George S. *Bryan or Imperialism: Address by the Hon. George S. Boutwell*. Boston: New England Anti-Imperialist League, 1900.

Bouvier, Virginia M., ed. *Whose America? The War of 1898 and the Battles to Define the Nation*. Westport, CT: Praeger, 2001.

Brazier, Don. *History of the Washington Legislature, 1854–1963*. Olympia: Washington State Senate, 2000.

Brown, David S. *Richard Hofstadter: An Intellectual Biography*. Chicago: University of Chicago Press, 2006.

Brundage, David. *The Making of Western Labor Radicalism: Denver's Organized Workers, 1878–1905*. Chicago: University of Illinois Press, 1994.

Bryan, William Jennings. "The Election of 1900." *North American Review* 171 (December 1900): 788–801.

———. *The First Battle: A Story of the Campaign of 1896*. Chicago: W. B. Conkey, 1896.

———, ed. *Republic or Empire? The Philippine Question*. Chicago: Independence Company, 1899.

Cabranes, José A. "Citizenship and the American Empire: Notes on the Legislative History of the United States Citizenship of Puerto Ricans." *University of Pennsylvania Law Review* 127, 2 (1978): 391–492.

Carnegie, Andrew. *Autobiography of Andrew Carnegie*. Boston: Houghton Mifflin, 1920.

Cherny, Robert W. *Populism, Progressivism, and the Transformation of Nebraska Politics, 1885–1915*. Lincoln: University of Nebraska Press, 1981.

Chicago Conference on Trusts: Speeches, Debates, Resolutions, List of the Delegates, Committees, etc. Chicago: Civic Foundation of Chicago, 1900.

Clanton, O. Gene. *Congressional Populism and the Crisis of the 1890s*. Lawrence: University Press of Kansas, 1998.

———. *Kansas Populism: Ideas and Men*. Lawrence: University Press of Kansas, 1969.

———. *Populism: The Humane Preference in America, 1890–1900*. Boston: Twayne, 1991.

Clark, Gordon. *Shylock: As Banker, Bondholder, Corruptionist, Conspirator*. Washington, DC: American Bimetallic League, 1894.

Clinch, Thomas A. *Urban Populism and Free Silver in Montana: A Narrative of Ideology in Political Action*. Missoula: University of Montana Press, 1970.

Coletta, Paolo E. "Bryan, McKinley, and the Treaty of Paris." *Pacific Historical Review* 26, 2 (1957): 131–146.

———. "A Tempest in a Teapot? Governor Poynter's Appointment of William V. Allen to the United States Senate." *Nebraska History* 38 (June 1957): 155–163.

———. *William Jennings Bryan: Political Evangelist, 1860–1908*. Lincoln: University of Nebraska Press, 1964.

Cooper, Jerry M. *The Army and Civil Disorder: Federal Military Intervention in Labor Disputes, 1877–1900*. Westport, CT: Greenwood Press, 1980.

Correspondence Relating to the War with Spain, Including the Insurrection in the Philippine Islands and the China Relief Expedition. 2 vols. Washington, DC: Government Printing Office, 1902.

Corry, John A. *1898: Prelude to a Century*. New York: Fordham University Press, 1998.

Cosmas, Graham A. "Military Reform after the Spanish-American War: The Army Reorganization Fight of 1898–1899." *Military Affairs* 35, 1 (1971): 12–18.

Cronon, William. *Nature's Metropolis: Chicago and the Great West*. New York: W. W. Norton, 1991.

Cullinane, Michael Patrick. *Liberty and American Anti-Imperialism, 1898–1909*. New York: Palgrave Macmillan, 2012.

Curti, Merle Eugene. *Bryan and World Peace*. 1931. Reprint, New York: Octagon Books, 1969.

Dagger, Richard. *Civic Virtues: Rights, Citizenship, and Republican Liberalism*. New York: Oxford University Press, 1997.

Daniel, Cletus E. *Bitter Harvest: A History of California Farmworkers, 1870–1941*. Ithaca, NY: Cornell University Press, 1981.

Daniels, Roger. *Guarding the Golden Door: American Immigration Policy and Immigrants since 1882*. New York: Hill & Wang, 2004.

De Bevoise, Ken. *Agents of Apocalypse: Epidemic Disease in the Colonial Philippines*. Princeton, NJ: Princeton University Press, 1995.

Deloria, Philip. *Playing Indian*. New Haven, CT: Yale University Press, 1998.

Downing, Sybil, and Robert E. Smith. *Tom Patterson: Colorado Crusader for Change*. Niwot: University of Colorado Press, 1995.

Dubin, Michael J. *United States Gubernatorial Elections, 1861–1911: The Official Results by State and County*. Jefferson, NC: McFarland, 2010.

Dubovsky, Melvyn. "The Origins of Western Working Class Radicalism, 1890–1905." *Labor History* 7, 2 (1966): 131–154.

Durden, Robert F. *The Climax of Populism: The Election of 1896*. Lexington: University of Kentucky Press, 1965.

Eager, Frank. *History of the Operations of the First Nebraska Infantry, U.S.V., in the Campaign in the Philippine Islands*. San Francisco: Hicks-Judd, 1899.

Edwards, Rebecca. *Angels in the Machinery: Gender in American Party Politics from the Civil War to the Progressive Era*. New York: Oxford University Press, 1997.

Elliott, Russell R. *Servant of Power: A Political Biography of Senator William M. Stewart*. Reno: University of Nevada Press, 1983.

Ellis, Elmer. *Henry Moore Teller: Defender of the West*. Caldwell, ID: Caxton Printers, 1941.

Emery, Sarah E. V. *Imperialism in America: Its Rise and Progress*. Rev. ed. Lansing, MI: D. A. Reynolds, 1893.

———. *Seven Financial Conspiracies Which Have Enslaved the American People*. Rev. ed. Lansing, MI: Robert Smith, 1894.

Enyeart, John P. *The Quest for "Just and Pure Law": Rocky Mountain Workers and American Social Democracy, 1870–1924*. Stanford, CA: Stanford University Press, 2009.

Esherick, Joseph. *The Origins of the Boxer Uprising*. Berkeley: University of California Press, 1987.

Ferkiss, Victor C. "Populist Influences on American Fascism." *Western Political Quarterly* 10, 2 (1957): 350–373.

Ficken, Robert E. *Washington State: The Inaugural Decade, 1889–1899*. Pullman: Washington State University Press, 2007.

Finkelman, Paul. *Slavery and the Founders: Race and Liberty in the Age of Jefferson*. Armonk, NY: M. E. Sharpe, 1996.

Fisch, Richard Evans. "A History of the Democratic Party in the State of Washington, 1854–1956." Ph.D. diss., University of Oregon, 1975.

Folsom, Burton W., Jr. *No More Free Markets or Free Beer: The Progressive Era in Nebraska, 1900–1924*. New York: Lexington Books, 1999.

Foner, Eric. *Reconstruction: America's Unfinished Revolution, 1863–1877*. Rev. ed. New York: Perennial Classics, 2002.

Foner, Philip S. *The Spanish-Cuban-American War and the Birth of American Imperialism, 1895–1902*. Vol. 1. New York: Monthly Review Press, 1972.

Forbath, William E. *Law and the Shaping of the American Labor Movement*. Cambridge, MA: Harvard University Press, 1989.

Friedman, Milton, and Anna Jacobson Schwartz. *A Monetary History of the United States, 1867–1963*. 1963. Reprint, Princeton, NJ: Princeton University Press, 1993.

Fuller, Leon W. "The Populist Regime in Colorado." Ph.D. diss., University of Wisconsin, 1933.

Gaboury, William Joseph. *Dissension in the Rockies: A History of Idaho Populism*. New York: Garland, 1988.

Gardner, Lloyd C. *Imperial America: American Foreign Policy since 1898*. New York: Harcourt Brace Jovanovich, 1976.

Gates, Henry Louis, Jr., ed. *Lincoln on Race and Slavery*. Princeton, NJ: Princeton University Press, 2009.

George, Henry. *Progress and Poverty: An Inquiry into the Cause of Industrial Depressions and of Increase of Want with Increase of Wealth*. Garden City, NY: Doubleday, Page, 1879.

Gerteis, Joseph, and Alyssa Goolsby. "Nationalism in America: The Case of the Populist Movement." *Theory and Society* 34, 2 (2005): 197–225.

Go, Julian. *American Empire and the Politics of Meaning: Elite Political Cultures in the Philippines and Puerto Rico during U.S. Colonialism*. Durham, NC: Duke University Press, 2008.

Goldberg, Michael Lewis. *An Army of Women: Gender and Politics in Gilded Age Kansas*. Baltimore: Johns Hopkins University Press, 1997.

Goodwyn, Lawrence. *Democratic Promise: The Populist Moment in America*. New York: Oxford University Press, 1976.

Gould, Lewis L. *The Presidency of William McKinley*. Lawrence: University Press of Kansas, 1980.

Gramm, Marshall, and Phil Gramm. "The Free Silver Movement in America: A Reinterpretation." *Journal of Economic History* 64, 4 (2004): 1108–1129.

Guide to U.S. Elections. 6th ed. Washington, DC: CQ Press, 2010.

Hackney, Sheldon. *Populism to Progressivism in Alabama.* Princeton, NJ: Princeton University Press, 1969.

Hahn, Steven. *The Roots of Southern Populism: Yeoman Farmers and the Transformation of the Georgia Upcountry, 1850–1890.* New York: Oxford University Press, 1983.

Harrington, Fred H. "The Anti-Imperialist Movement in the United States, 1898–1900." *Mississippi Valley Historical Review* 22, 2 (1935): 211–230.

Harvey, William H. *Coin on Money, Trusts, and Imperialism.* Chicago: Thomas Knapp, 1899.

———. *Coin's Financial School.* Chicago: Coin, 1894.

Hicks, John D. *The Populist Revolt: A History of the Farmers' Alliance and the People's Party.* 3rd ed. Lincoln: University of Nebraska Press, 1961.

Hilkey, Judy Arlene. *Character Is Capital: Success Manuals and Manhood in Gilded Age America.* Chapel Hill: University of North Carolina Press, 1997.

Hoar, George F. *Autobiography of Seventy Years.* Vol. 2. New York: Charles Scribner's Sons, 1903.

Hoelscher, David Wayne. "Genuine Populist: William V. Allen in the United States Senate, 1893–1901." M.A. thesis, University of Nebraska at Omaha, 2003.

Hofstadter, Richard. *The Age of Reform: From Bryan to F.D.R.* New York: Vintage Books, 1955.

———. *The Paranoid Style in American Politics, and Other Essays.* 1952. Reprint, Cambridge, MA: Harvard University Press, 1996.

Hoganson, Kristin L. *Fighting for American Manhood: How Gender Politics Provoked the Spanish-American and Philippine-American Wars.* New Haven, CT: Yale University Press, 1998.

Holbo, Paul S. "The Convergence of Moods and the Cuban-Bond 'Conspiracy' of 1898." *Journal of American History* 55, 1 (1968): 54–72.

Hollingsworth, J. Rogers. *The Whirligig of Politics: The Democracy of Cleveland and Bryan.* Chicago: University of Chicago Press, 1963.

Horsman, Reginald. *Race and Manifest Destiny: The Origins of American Racial Anglo-Saxonism.* Cambridge, MA: Harvard University Press, 1981.

Hunt, Geoffrey R. *Colorado's Volunteer Infantry in the Philippine Wars, 1898–1899.* Albuquerque: University of New Mexico Press, 2006.

Hunt, James L. *Marion Butler and American Populism.* Chapel Hill: University of North Carolina Press, 2003.

Hunt, Michael H. *Ideology and U.S. Foreign Policy.* Rev. ed. New Haven, CT: Yale University Press, 2009.

Ileto, Reynaldo. *Pasyon and Revolution: Popular Movements in the Philippines.* Quezon City, Philippines: Ateneo de Manila University Press, 1979.

Jacobson, Matthew Frye. *Barbarian Virtues: The United States Encounters Foreign Peoples at Home and Abroad, 1876–1917.* New York: Hill & Wang, 2000.

Jameson, Elizabeth. *All that Glitters: Class, Conflict, and Community in Cripple Creek.* Chicago: University of Illinois Press, 1998.

Jensen, Richard. *The Winning of the Midwest: Social and Political Conflict, 1888–1896.* Chicago: University of Chicago Press, 1971.

Johnson, Arthur C. *Official History of the Operation of the First Colorado Infantry, U.S.V., in the Campaign in the Philippine Islands.* San Francisco: Hicks-Judd, 1899.

Johnson, Claudius O. "George Turner, Part I: The Background of a Statesman." *Pacific Northwest Quarterly* 34, 3 (1943): 243–269.

Johnson, Robert David. *The Peace Progressives and American Foreign Relations.* Cambridge, MA: Harvard University Press, 1995.

Jones, Stanley L. *The Presidential Election of 1896.* Madison: University of Wisconsin Press, 1964.

Kaplan, Amy. *The Anarchy of Empire in the Making of U.S. Culture.* Cambridge, MA: Harvard University Press, 2002.

Kazin, Michael. *A Godly Hero: The Life of William Jennings Bryan.* New York: Anchor Books, 2006.

——. *The Populist Persuasion: An American History.* Rev. ed. Ithaca, NY: Cornell University Press, 1998.

Kent, Noel Jacob. *America in 1900.* New York: M. E. Sharpe, 2002.

Keyssar, Alexander. *The Right to Vote: The Contested History of Democracy in the United States.* New York: Basic Books, 2000.

Kleppner, Paul. *The Cross of Culture: A Social Analysis of Midwestern Politics, 1850–1900.* New York: Free Press, 1970.

Kloppenberg, James. *The Virtues of Liberalism.* New York: Oxford University Press, 1998.

Koenig, Louis W. *Bryan: A Political Biography of William Jennings Bryan.* New York: G. P. Putnam's Sons, 1971.

Kohl, Lawrence Frederick. *The Politics of Individualism: Parties and the American Character in the Jacksonian Era.* New York: Oxford University Press, 1989.

Kramer, Paul A. *The Blood of Government: Race, Empire, the United States, & the Philippines.* Chapel Hill: University of North Carolina Press, 2006.

LaFeber, Walter. *New Empire: An Interpretation of American Expansion, 1860–1898.* Ithaca, NY: Cornell University Press, 1963.

Lanzar, Maria C. "The Anti-Imperialist League." *Philippine Social Science Review* 3, 1 (1930): 7–41.

Larson, Robert W. *Populism in the Mountain West.* Albuquerque: University of New Mexico Press, 1986.

Lasch, Christopher. "The Anti-Imperialists, the Philippines, and the Inequality of Man." *Journal of Southern History* 24, 3 (1958): 319–331.

——. *The True and Only Heaven: Progress and Its Critics.* New York: W. W. Norton, 1991.

Laurie, Clayton D., and Ronald H. Cole. *The Role of Federal Military Forces in Domestic Disorders, 1877–1945*. Washington, DC: Government Printing Office, 1997.

Lee, R. Alton. *Principle over Party: The Farmers' Alliance and Populism in South Dakota.* Pierre: South Dakota State Historical Society Press, 2011.

Leger, Ann L. "Moorfield Storey: An Intellectual Biography." Ph.D. diss., University of Iowa, 1968.

Leonard, Gerald. *The Invention of Party Politics: Federalism, Popular Sovereignty, and Constitutional Development in Jacksonian Illinois.* Chapel Hill: University of North Carolina Press, 2002.

Leonard, Stephen J., and Thomas J. Noel. *Denver: Mining Camp to Metropolis.* Niwot: University Press of Colorado, 1990.

Lester, Connie L. *Up from the Mudsills of Hell: The Farmers' Alliance, Populism, and Progressive Agriculture in Tennessee, 1870–1915.* Athens: University of Georgia Press, 2006.

Linderman, Gerald F. *The Mirror of War: American Society and the Spanish-American War.* Ann Arbor: University of Michigan Press, 1974.

Linn, Brian McAllister. *The Philippine War, 1899–1902.* Lawrence: University Press of Kansas, 2000.

Livingston, James. *Origins of the Federal Reserve System: Money, Class, and Corporate Capitalism, 1890–1913.* Ithaca, NY: Cornell University Press, 1986.

Love, Eric. *Race over Empire: Racism and U.S. Imperialism, 1865–1900.* Chapel Hill: University of North Carolina Press, 2004.

Luebke, Frederick C. *Immigrants and Politics: The Germans of Nebraska, 1880–1900.* Lincoln: University of Nebraska Press, 1969.

Luhn, William L. *Official History of the Operations of the First Washington Infantry, U.S.V., in the Campaign in the Philippine Islands.* San Francisco: Hicks-Judd, 1899.

Lumry, Oscar F. *National Suicide and Its Prevention.* Chicago: George F. Cram, 1886.

May, Ernest R. *Imperial Democracy: The Emergence of America as a Great Power.* 1961. Reprint, New York: Harper & Row, 1973.

May, Glenn Anthony. *Battle for Batangas: A Philippine Province at War.* New Haven, CT: Yale University Press, 1991.

———. *Social Engineering in the Philippines: The Aims, Execution, and Impact of American Colonial Policy, 1900–1913.* Westport, CT: Greenwood Press, 1980.

McCartney, Paul T. *Power and Progress: American National Identity, the War of 1898, and the Rise of American Imperialism.* Baton Rouge: Louisiana State University Press, 2006.

McConnell, Stuart. *Glorious Contentment: The Grand Army of the Republic, 1865–1900.* Chapel Hill: University of North Carolina Press, 1992.

McCormick, Thomas J. *China Market: America's Quest for Informal Empire, 1893–1901.* Chicago: Quadrangle Books, 1967.

McCoy, Alfred W. *Policing America's Empire: The United States, the Philippines, and the Rise of the Surveillance State.* Madison: University of Wisconsin Press, 2009.

McCoy, Alfred W., and Francisco A. Scarano, eds. *Colonial Crucible: Empire in the Making of the Modern American State*. Madison: University of Wisconsin Press, 2009.

McGerr, Michael. *A Fierce Discontent: The Rise and Fall of the Progressive Movement*. New York: Free Press, 2003.

McMath, Robert C., Jr. *American Populism: A Social History, 1877–1898*. New York: Hill & Wang, 1992.

McSeveney, Samuel. *The Politics of Depression: Political Behavior in the Northeast, 1893–1896*. New York: Oxford University Press, 1972.

Mead, Rebecca J. *How the Vote Was Won: Woman Suffrage in the Western United States, 1868–1914*. New York: New York University Press, 2004.

Miller, Stuart Creighton. *"Benevolent Assimilation": The American Conquest of the Philippines, 1899–1903*. New Haven, CT: Yale University Press, 1982.

Miller, Worth Robert. *Oklahoma Populism: A History of the People's Party in the Oklahoma Territory*. Norman: University of Oklahoma Press, 1987.

——, ed. *Populist Cartoons: An Illustrated History of the Third Party Movement of the 1890s*. Kirksville, MO: Truman State University Press, 2011.

Mojares, Resil B. *The War against the Americans: Resistance and Collaboration in Cebu, 1899–1906*. Quezon City, Philippines: Ateneo de Manila University Press, 1999.

Morgan, H. Wayne. *William McKinley and His America*. Syracuse, NY: Syracuse University Press, 1963.

Morgan, William Michael. *Pacific Gibraltar: US-Japanese Rivalry over the Annexation of Hawaii, 1885–1898*. Annapolis, MD: Naval Institute Press, 2011.

Morgan, W. Scott. *History of the Wheel and Alliance and the Impending Revolution*. Fort Scott, KS: J. H. Rice & Sons, 1889.

Mowry, George E. *The California Progressives*. Chicago: Quadrangle Books, 1963.

——. *The Era of Theodore Roosevelt, 1900–1912*. New York: Harper & Brothers, 1958.

Mulanax, Richard. *The Boer War in American Politics and Diplomacy*. Lanham, MD: University Press of America, 1994.

Muncy, Robyn. "Trustbusting and White Manhood in America, 1898–1914." *American Studies* 38, 3 (1997): 21–42.

Murphy, Kevin P. *Political Manhood: Red Bloods, Mollycoddles, & the Politics of Progressive Era Reform*. New York: Columbia University Press, 2008.

Nasson, Bill. *The South African War, 1899–1902*. New York: Oxford University Press, 1999.

Neather, Andrew. "Popular Republicanism, Americanism, and the Roots of Anti-Communism, 1890–1925." Ph.D. diss., Duke University, 1993.

Nelsen, Jane Taylor, ed. *A Prairie Populist: The Memoirs of Luna Kellie*. Iowa City: University of Iowa Press, 1992.

Nugent, Walter T. K. *Money and American Society, 1865–1880*. New York: Free Press, 1968.

——. *The Tolerant Populists: Kansas Populism and Nativism*. Chicago: University of Chicago Press, 1963.

Offner, John. *An Unwanted War: The Diplomacy of the United States and Spain over Cuba, 1895–1898.* Chapel Hill: University of North Carolina Press, 1992.

Osborne, Thomas J. *"Empire Can Wait": American Opposition to Hawaiian Annexation, 1893–1898.* Kent, OH: Kent State University Press, 1981.

Ostler, Jeffrey. *Prairie Populism: The Fate of Agrarian Radicalism in Kansas, Nebraska, and Iowa, 1880–1896.* Lawrence: University Press of Kansas, 1993.

——. "The Rhetoric of Conspiracy and the Formation of Kansas Populism." *Agricultural History* 69, 1 (1995): 1–27.

Paine, S. C. M. *The Sino-Japanese War of 1894–1895: Perceptions, Power, and Primacy.* New York: Cambridge University Press, 2003.

Painter, Nell Irvin. *Standing at Armageddon: A Grassroots History of the Progressive Era.* 1987. Reprint, New York: W. W. Norton, 2008.

Palmer, Bruce. *"Man over Money": The Southern Populist Critique of American Capitalism.* Chapel Hill: University of North Carolina Press, 1980.

Pascoe, Peggy. *Relations of Rescue: The Search for Female Moral Authority in the American West, 1874–1939.* New York: Oxford University Press, 1990.

Peal, David. "The Politics of Populism: Germany and the American South in the 1890s." *Comparative Studies in Society and History* 31, 2 (1989): 340–362.

Pederson, James F., and Kenneth D. Wald. *Shall the People Rule: A History of the Democratic Party in Nebraska Politics.* Lincoln, NE: Jacob North, 1972.

Peffer, William A. *The Farmer's Side: His Trouble and Their Remedy.* New York: D. Appleton, 1891.

Pérez, Louis A., Jr. *Cuba between Empires, 1878–1902.* Pittsburgh: University of Pittsburgh Press, 1983.

Pettigrew, Richard F. *Triumphant Plutocracy: The Story of American Public Life from 1870s to 1920.* New York: Academy Press, 1921.

Pletcher, David M. *The Diplomacy of Involvement: American Economic Expansion across the Pacific, 1784–1900.* Columbia: University of Missouri Press, 2001.

Pollack, Norman. "Hofstadter on Populism: A Critique of 'The Age of Reform.'" *Journal of Southern History* 26, 4 (1960): 478–500.

——. *The Humane Economy: Populism, Capitalism, and Democracy.* New Brunswick, NJ: Rutgers University Press, 1990.

——. *The Just Polity: Populism, Law, and Human Welfare.* Chicago: University of Illinois Press, 1987.

——. *The Populist Response to Industrial America: Midwestern Populist Thought.* Cambridge, MA: Harvard University Press, 1962.

Postel, Charles. *The Populist Vision.* New York: Oxford University Press, 2007.

Putnam, John C. *Class and Gender Politics in Progressive-Era Seattle.* Reno: University of Nevada Press, 2008.

Rana, Aziz. *Two Faces of American Freedom.* Cambridge, MA: Harvard University Press, 2010.

Renda, Mary A. *Taking Haiti: Military Occupation and the Culture of U.S. Imperialism, 1915–1940*. Chapel Hill: University of North Carolina Press, 2001.

Report of the Industrial Commission on the Relations and Conditions of Capital and Labor Employed in the Mining Industry. Vol. 12. Washington, DC: Government Printing Office, 1901.

Report on the Census of Cuba, 1899. Washington, DC: Government Printing Office, 1900.

Richardson, Heather Cox. *West from Appomattox: The Reconstruction of America after the Civil War*. New Haven, CT: Yale University Press, 2007.

Richardson, James D., ed. *A Compilation of the Messages and Papers of the Presidents, 1789–1908*. Vol. 10. Washington, DC: Bureau of National Literature and Art, 1908.

Riddle, Thomas W. *The Old Radicalism: John R. Rogers and the Populist Movement in Washington*. New York: Garland, 1991.

——. "Populism in the Palouse: Old Ideals and New Realities." *Pacific Northwest Quarterly* 65, 3 (1974): 97–109.

Robbins, William G. *Colony and Empire: The Capitalist Transformation of the American West*. Lawrence: University Press of Kansas, 1994.

——. "The 'Plundered Province' Thesis and the Recent Historiography of the American West." *Pacific Historical Review* 55, 4 (1986): 577–597.

Robinson, Edgar Eugene. *The Presidential Vote, 1896–1932*. 1947. Reprint, New York: Octagon Books, 1970.

Rogers, John Rankin. *The Inalienable Rights of Man*. Olympia, WA, 1900.

——. *The Irrepressible Conflict, or an American System of Money: A Compilation of Facts Leading to a Knowledge of the Money Question*. Puyallup, WA: Rogers, 1892.

——. *Life*. San Francisco: Whitaker & Ray, 1899.

——. *Politics: An Argument in Favor of the Inalienable Rights of Man*. Seattle: Allen, 1894.

Rystad, Göran. *Ambiguous Imperialism: American Foreign Policy and Domestic Politics at the Turn of the Century*. Lund, Sweden: Esselte Studium, 1975.

Saldin, Robert. *War, the American State, and Politics since 1898*. New York: Cambridge University Press, 2011.

Saltvig, Robert D. "The Progressive Movement in Washington." Ph.D. diss., University of Washington, 1966.

Sanders, Elizabeth. *Roots of Reform: Farmers, Workers, and the American State, 1877–1917*. Chicago: University of Chicago Press, 1999.

Schirmer, Daniel B. *Republic or Empire: American Resistance to the Philippine War*. Cambridge, MA: Schenkman, 1972.

Schlesinger, Arthur M., Jr. *History of American Presidential Elections*. Vol. 3. New York: McGraw-Hill, 1971.

Schoonover, Thomas. *Uncle Sam's War of 1898 and the Origins of Globalization*. Lexington: University Press of Kentucky, 2003.

Schurz, Carl. *American Imperialism: The Convocation Address Delivered on the Occasion of the Twenty-Seventh Convocation of the University of Chicago.* Boston, 1899.

——. *Speeches, Correspondence and Political Papers of Carl Schurz,* edited by Frederic Bancroft. New York: G. P. Putnam's Sons, 1913.

Schwantes, Carlos. *Radical Heritage: Labor, Socialism, and Reform in Washington and British Columbia, 1885–1917.* Seattle: University of Washington Press, 1979.

Shaw, Barton C. *The Wool-Hat Boys: Georgia's Populist Party.* Baton Rouge: Louisiana State University Press, 1984.

Silber, Nina. *Romance of Reunion: Northerners and the South, 1865–1900.* Chapel Hill: University of North Carolina Press, 1993.

Silbey, David J. *The Boxer Rebellion and the Great Game in China.* New York: Hill & Wang, 2012.

Silva, Noenoe K. *Aloha Betrayed: Native Hawaiian Resistance to American Colonialism.* Durham, NC: Duke University Press, 2004.

Sinopoli, Richard C. *The Foundations of American Citizenship: Liberalism, the Constitution, and Civic Virtue.* New York: Oxford University Press, 1992.

Sklar, Martin J. *The Corporate Reconstruction of American Capitalism, 1890–1916: The Market, the Law, and Politics.* New York: Cambridge University Press, 1988.

Smith, Duane A. *Henry Teller: Colorado's Grand Old Man.* Boulder: University Press of Colorado, 2002.

——. *Rocky Mountain Boom Town: A History of Durango, Colorado.* Boulder: University Press of Colorado, 1992.

Smith, Edwin Burritt. *Essays and Addresses.* Chicago: A. C. McClurg, 1909.

Sparrow, Bartholomew H. *The Insular Cases and the Emergence of American Empire.* Lawrence: University Press of Kansas, 2006.

Speeches and Addresses of William McKinley: From March 1, 1897 to May 30, 1900. New York: Doubleday & McClure, 1900.

Sproat, John G. *The Best Men: Liberal Reformers in the Gilded Age.* New York: Oxford University Press, 1968.

Statement of Hon. Lyman J. Gage, Secretary of the Treasury, before the Committee on Banking and Currency, in Explanation of the Bill H.R. 5181. 55th Cong. Washington, DC: Government Printing Office, 1897.

Stock, Catharine McNicol, and Robert D. Johnston, eds. *The Countryside in the Age of the Modern State: Political Histories of Rural America.* Ithaca, NY: Cornell University Press, 2001.

Suggs, George G., Jr. *Colorado's War on Militant Unionism: James H. Peabody and the Western Federation of Miners.* 1972. Reprint, Norman: University of Oklahoma Press, 1991.

Summers, Mark Wahlgren. *Party Games: Getting, Keeping, and Using Power in Gilded Age Politics.* Chapel Hill: University of North Carolina Press, 2004.

Tate, Merze. *The United States and the Hawaiian Kingdom: A Political History.* New Haven, CT: Yale University Press, 1965.

Thomas, Sewell. *Silhouettes of Charles S. Thomas: Colorado Governor and United States Senator.* Caldwell, ID: Caxton Printers, 1959.

Thorson, Winston B. "Washington State Nominating Conventions." *Pacific Northwest Quarterly* 35, 2 (1944): 99–119.

Timberlake, Richard. *Monetary Policy in the United States: An Intellectual and Institutional History.* Chicago: University of Chicago Press, 1993.

Tompkins, E. Berkeley. *Anti-Imperialism in the United States: The Great Debate, 1890–1920.* Philadelphia: University of Pennsylvania Press, 1970.

Tone, John Lawrence. *War and Genocide in Cuba, 1895–1898.* Chapel Hill: University of North Carolina Press, 2006.

Trask, David F. *The War with Spain in 1898.* Lincoln: University of Nebraska Press, 1981.

Trefousse, Hans L. *Carl Schurz: A Biography.* Knoxville: University of Tennessee Press, 1982.

Tucker, David M. *Mugwumps: Public Moralists of the Gilded Age.* Columbia: University of Missouri Press, 1998.

Turner, James. "Understanding the Populists." *Journal of American History* 67, 2 (1980): 354–373.

US Department of the Interior. *Report on the Statistics of Agriculture in the United States at the Eleventh Census: 1890.* Washington, DC: Government Printing Office, 1895.

——. *Thirteenth Census of the United States, Taken in the Year 1910.* Vol. 7, *Agriculture 1909 and 1910, Reports by States with Statistics for Counties.* Washington, DC: Government Printing Office, 1913.

——. *Twelfth Census of the United States, Taken in the Year 1900.* Vol. 5, *Agriculture,* pt. 1, *Farms, Livestock, and Animal Products.* Washington, DC: Government Printing Office, 1902.

US Works Progress Administration. *Messages and Proclamations of the Governors of Nebraska, 1854–1941.* Vol. 2, *1887–1909.* Sponsored by the University of Nebraska, 1942.

——. *Nebraska Party Platforms, 1858–1940.* Lincoln, NE, 1940.

Wallerstein, Immanuel. *World-Systems Analysis: An Introduction.* Durham, NC: Duke University Press, 2004.

Watkins, Albert. *History of Nebraska, from the Earliest Explorations to the Present Time.* Vol. 3. Lincoln, NE: Western Publishing and Engraving, 1913.

Weaver, James B. *A Call to Action: The Great Uprising, Its Source and Causes.* Des Moines: Iowa Printing Company, 1892.

Weir, Robert E. *Beyond Labor's Veil: The Culture of the Knights of Labor.* University Park: Pennsylvania State University Press, 1996.

Welch, Richard E. *George Frisbie Hoar and the Half-Breed Republicans.* Cambridge, MA: Harvard University Press, 1971.

——. *The Presidencies of Grover Cleveland.* Lawrence: University Press of Kansas, 1988.

———. *Response to Imperialism: The United States and the Philippine-American War, 1899–1902*. Chapel Hill: University of North Carolina Press, 1979.

Weston, Rubin Francis. *Racism in U.S. Imperialism: The Influence of Racial Assumptions on American Foreign Policy, 1893–1946*. Columbia: University of South Carolina Press, 1972.

White, Richard. *"It's Your Misfortune and None of My Own": A New History of the American West*. Norman: University of Oklahoma Press, 1991.

———. *Railroaded: The Transcontinentals and the Making of Modern America*. New York: W. W. Norton, 2011.

Wiebe, Robert H. *The Search for Order, 1877–1920*. New York: Hill & Wang, 1967.

Will, Allen S. *World Crisis in China, 1900*. Baltimore: John Murphy, 1900.

Williams, R. Hal. *Realigning America: McKinley, Bryan, and the Remarkable Election of 1896*. Lawrence: University Press of Kansas, 2010.

Williams, William Appleman. *The Roots of Modern American Empire: A Study of the Growth and Shaping of Social Consciousness in a Marketplace Society*. New York: Random House, 1969.

———. *The Tragedy of American Diplomacy*. Rev. ed. New York: Dell, 1962.

Wills, Jocelyn. "Respectable Mediocrity: The Everyday Life of an Ordinary American Striver, 1876–1890." *Journal of Social History* 37, 2 (2003): 323–349.

Wilson, Kevin, ed. *The International Impact of the Boer War*. New York: Palgrave, 2001.

Wisan, Joseph E. *The Cuban Crisis as Reflected in the New York Press (1895–1898)*. New York: Columbia University Press, 1934.

Wooddy, Carroll H. "Populism in Washington: A Study of the Legislature of 1897." *Washington Historical Quarterly* 21, 2 (1930): 103–119.

Woodward, C. Vann. *Tom Watson: Agrarian Rebel*. 1938. Reprint, New York: Oxford University Press, 1963.

Wright, James Edward. *The Politics of Populism: Dissent in Colorado*. New Haven, CT: Yale University Press, 1974.

Young, Marilyn Blatt. *The Rhetoric of Empire: American China Policy, 1895–1901*. Cambridge, MA: Harvard University Press, 1968.

Zwick, Jim, ed. *Mark Twain's Weapons of Satire: Anti-Imperialist Writings on the Philippine-American War*. Syracuse, NY: Syracuse University Press, 1992.

INDEX